THE POLITICS OF MARKET REFORM
IN FRAGILE DEMOCRACIES

KURT WEYLAND

The Politics

of Market Reform

in Fragile Democracies

Argentina, Brazil, Peru, and Venezuela

PRINCETON UNIVERSITY PRESS • PRINCETON AND OXFORD

Published by Princeton University Press, 41 William Street, Princeton, New Jersey 08540

In the United Kingdom: Princeton University Press, 3 Market Place,
Woodstock, Oxfordshire OX20 1SY

Library of Congress Cataloging-in-Publication Data

Weyland, Kurt Gerhard.
    The politics of market reform in fragile democracies : Argentina, Brazil, Peru, and
Venezuela / Kurt Weyland.
        p. cm.
    Includes bibliographical references (p.) and index.
    ISBN 0-691-09643-0 (alk. paper)
    1. South America — Economic policy — Case studies.   2. South America — Economic
policy — Public opinion.   3. Public opinion — South America.   4. South America —
Economic conditions — 1918 — Political aspects.   5. Democracy — South America.
I. Title.

    HC165 .W46 2002
    338.98 — dc21   2002016903

British Library Cataloging-in-Publication Data is available

This book has been composed in Sabon

Printed on acid-free paper. ∞

www.pupress.princeton.edu

Printed in the United States of America

10 9 8 7 6 5 4 3 2 1

CONTENTS

FIGURES AND TABLES

AD	Acción Democrática (Venezuela)
AP	Acción Popular (Peru)
APRA	Alianza Popular Revolucionaria Americana (Peru)
CCD	Congreso Constituyente Democrático (Peru)
CEA	Consejo Empresario Argentino
CENDA	Centro de Documentación y Análisis para los Trabajadores (Venezuela)
CENDES	Centro de Estudios del Desarrollo, Universidad Central de Venezuela
CEPAL	Comisión Económica para América Latina y el Caribe, Naciones Unidas
CESOP	Centro de Estudos de Opinião Pública, Universidade Estadual de Campinas (Brazil)
CGT	Confederación General del Trabajo (Argentina)
CIUP	Centro de Investigación. Universidad del Pacífico (Peru)
CNI	Confederação Nacional da Indústria (Brazil)
COB	Central Obrera Boliviana
CONASSEPS	Consejo Nacional para Supervisión y Seguimiento de los Programas Sociales del Ejecutivo Nacional (Venezuela)
CONFIEP	Confederación Nacional de Instituciones Empresariales Privadas (Peru)
COPEI	Comité de Organización Política Electoral Independiente (Venezuela)
COPRE	Comisión Presidencial para la Reforma del Estado (Venezuela)
CORDIPLAN	Oficina Central de Coordinación y Planificación, Presidencia de la República (Venezuela)
CTV	Confederación de Trabajadores de Venezuela
CUT	Central Única dos Trabalhadores (Brazil)
FEDECAMARAS	Federación Venezolana de Cámaras y Asociaciones de Comercio y Producción
FIESP	Federação das Indústrias do Estado de São Paulo (Brazil)
FONCODES	Fondo Nacional de Compensación y Desarrollo Social (Peru)
FREPASO	Frente del País Solidario (Argentina)

IADB	Inter-American Development Bank
IBOPE	Instituto Brasileiro de Opinião Pública e Estatística
IDESP	Instituto de Estudos Econômicos, Sociais e Políticos de São Paulo (Brazil)
IESA	Instituto de Estudios Superiores de Administración (Venezuela)
IFI	international financial institution
IIDH	Instituto Interamericano de Derechos Humanos (Costa Rica)
IMF	International Monetary Fund
INFES	Instituto Nacional de Infraestructura Educativa y de Salud (Peru)
ISI	import-substitution industrialization
IU	Izquierda Unida (Peru)
LARS	*Latin American Regional Reports — Southern Cone*
LASA	Latin American Studies Association
LAWR	*Latin American Weekly Report*
MARE	Ministério da Administração Federal e Reforma do Estado (Brazil)
MAS	Movimiento al Socialismo (Venezuela)
MEFP	Ministério da Economia, Fazenda e Planejamento (Brazil)
MERCOSUR	Mercado Común del Sur
MF	Ministério da Fazenda (Brazil)
MODIN	Movimiento por la Dignidad y la Independencia (Argentina)
MTSS	Ministerio de Trabajo y Seguridad Social (Argentina)
MVR	Movimiento V República (Venezuela)
NACLA	North American Congress on Latin America
NATO	North Atlantic Treaty Organisation
NIC	newly industrialized country
OAEF	Oficina de Asesoría Económica y Financiera, Poder Legislativo Nacional (Venezuela)
OCI	Oficina Central de Información (Venezuela)
OPEC	Organisation of Petroleum Exporting Countries
PDVSA	Petróleos de Venezuela, S.A.
PFL	Partido da Frente Liberal (Brazil)
PJ	Partido Justicialista = Peronist Party (Argentina)
PMDB	Partido do Movimento Democrático Brasileiro
PNBE	Pensamento Nacional das Bases Empresariais (Brazil)
PPB	Partido Progressista Brasileiro

PPC	Partido Popular Cristiano (Peru)
PRI	Partido Revolucionario Institucional (Mexico)
PRONAA	Programa Nacional de Asistencia Alimentaria (Peru)
PSDB	Partido da Social Democracia Brasileira
PT	Partido dos Trabalhadores (Brazil)
RFE/RL	Radio Free Europe/Radio Liberty
SDS	Secretaría de Desarrollo Social (Argentina)
SENIAT	Servicio Nacional Integrado de Administración Tributaria (Venezuela)
SEPLAN	Secretaria de Planejamento da Presidência da República (Brazil)
SIEMPRO	Sistema de Información, Monitoreo y Evaluación de Programas Sociales, Secretaría de Desarrollo Social (Argentina)
SIP	Secretaría de Ingresos Públicos, Ministerio de Economía (Argentina)
SUNAT	Superintendencia Nacional de Administración Tributaria (Peru)
UCeDé	Unión del Centro Democrático (Argentina)
UCR	Unión Cívica Radical (Argentina)
UIA	Unión Industrial Argentina
UOM	Unión Obrera Metalúrgica (Argentina)
UPP	Unión por el Perú
URV	Unidade Real de Valores (Brazil)
USIA	United States Information Agency

ACKNOWLEDGMENTS

As a graduate student at Stanford in 1990, I participated in a dissertation writers' group that included Rose McDermott, who had studied with the late Amos Tversky and was using prospect theory in her thesis on U.S. foreign policy (published as McDermott 1998). At that time, influenced by institutionalism (cf. Weyland 1996a) and quite interested in rational choice, I was not drawn to the application of cognitive-psychological insights to political analysis (to put it mildly). Years later, I began to analyze the unexpected wave of neoliberal reform in Latin America, focusing on the populist political strategies that many chief executives used to enact these daring changes (Weyland 1996c). I now recognized the limitations of institutionalism, which downplays leadership and underpredicts change, and the deficiencies of conventional rational-choice approaches, which depict political leaders as cautious calculators scared of offending powerful constituents. Neither one of these frameworks accounts well for the bold initiation of market reforms, which carry tremendous economic and political risks. Risk, risk-taking . . . suddenly, I remembered Rose's analysis of risk-seeking in the domain of losses and recognized that it promised to explain systematically why political leaders would introduce daring changes. After using the core finding of prospect theory in some articles devoted to specific topics (Weyland 1996d, 1998b, 1998c), I came to believe that the real test for such a novel argument was whether it could account for the tortuous trajectory of adjustment politics in Latin America during the last twenty years. The present book tackles this task.

Given the study's serendipitous origin, my first debt of gratitude is to Rose McDermott, without whom I may never have been seriously confronted with prospect theory. Undisturbed by my initial skepticism, she has been tremendously helpful in guiding me through the cognitive-psychological literature and in checking my application of its central ideas to political analysis. Her excellent comments on different incarnations of this project have been invaluable. Two other scholars were crucial at the formative stage of this project, namely, Wendy Hunter (acknowledged below) and David Bartlett, who drew on his profound understanding of political economy, thorough knowledge of a wide range of countries, and penetrating comparative perspective to provide outstanding, tough, yet friendly feedback on a multitude of manuscripts during our joint assistant professor years at Vanderbilt. His keen insights and penetrating criticisms were crucial for sharpening my thinking on adjustment politics. Also, since our graduate student days at Stanford, Ken Roberts has been an important source of comments, suggestions, ideas, and support in an ongoing exchange about all aspects of our research, conducted in a variety of settings, from hotel lounges in the United States to "popular" restaurants off the Alameda in Santiago de Chile and the beautiful beach of Choroní in Venezuela.

Over the years, I ran my ideas by a large number of scholars, country observers, and decision-makers, who provided important insights and suggestions. For these exercises in brainstorming, I am grateful to Mauro Bogéa, Roberto and Lúcia Brügger da Costa, Celecino de Carvalho Filho, David Collier, Brian Crisp, Antonio Delfim Netto, Paco Durand, Antônio Kandir, Peter Kingstone, Celso Barroso Leite, Scott Mainwaring, Yemile Mizrahi, Marcelo Vianna Estevão de Moraes, Marcos Novaro, Tito Palermo, Aldo Panfichi, Cynthia Sanborn, Marcel Domingos Solimeo, Martín Tanaka, Nicolás Toledo, and Friedrich Welsch. In more formal settings, I presented arguments of this book at several conferences and greatly appreciate the insightful and thorough comments I received from an illustrious group of discussants, namely, Barry Ames, Valerie Bunce, Thomas Callaghy, Gretchen Casper, John Echeverri-Gent, Barbara Geddes, Kirk Hawkins, Robert Kaufman, Herbert Kitschelt, Jack Levy, María Victoria Murillo, Orlando Pérez, Tim Power, Karen Remmer, and Bill Smith. I also thank the participants of seminars at Universidad de Buenos Aires, Duke University, University of Illinois at Urbana-Champaign, Johns Hopkins' School for Advanced International Studies, the Woodrow Wilson Center, and Yale University for stimulating discussions. The thoughtful, penetrating comments on parts of this study that I received from Leslie Armijo, James Booth, Michael Coppedge, Carol Graham, Erwin Hargrove, Simon Hug, Fabrice Lehoucq, Cynthia McClintock, Marcos Novaro, Phil Oxhorn, Tony Pereira, Nancy Powers, Ben Schneider, Jay Smith, Rich Snyder, Susan Stokes, and Harrison Wagner were tremendously useful. I am particularly grateful to Wendy Hunter, Ken Roberts, Joe Tulchin, and two reviewers for Princeton University Press for carefully reading the whole manuscript and writing up many pages of thoughtful comments on theoretical, empirical, and presentational issues, which greatly improved the book. Last not least, I thank James Booth, Simon Collier, Marshall Eakin, Don Hancock, Erwin Hargrove, Jane Landers, and Rick Pride for providing a stimulating intellectual environment at Vanderbilt and for engaging in many interesting conversations about topics related to this project.

Numerous individuals offered generous assistance with my research. I thank especially the large number of decision-makers who agreed to formal interviews. They provided indispensable information and, often, valuable documents. Furthermore, I am indebted to the survey researchers who gave me ample access to their data, especially Carolina Barros and Julio Burdman (Centro de Estudios Unión para la Nueva Mayoría, Buenos Aires), Mema Montero Barré (Mora y Araujo, Noguera y Asoc., Buenos Aires), Paula Vanina Cencig and Rachel Meneguello (CESOP, Campinas), Silvia Cervellini (IBOPE, São Paulo), Eduardo Fidanza (Catterberg & Asoc., Buenos Aires), Ginebra González Cueva (IMASEN and Datum, Lima), Dámaso Huarcaya Terry (IMASEN, Lima), Guillermo Loli (Apoyo, Lima), Graciela Römer (Estudio Römer, Buenos Aires), Edmond Saade (Datos, Caracas), Martín Sánchez (IMASEN, Lima), Nicolás Toledo (Consultores 21, Caracas), Israel Valcárcel (Datanálisis, Caracas), and Nelson Villasmil (Mercanálisis, Caracas). Paula Vanina Cencig and Nicolás Toledo were especially generous with their help. I thank François Gélineau (University of New Mexico) and Robert Barr (University of Texas at Austin) for generously sharing some of the data that they had collected.

I would also like to acknowledge excellent research assistance by Jennifer Brauer, John Hahn, Fabián Vallas, Yu-Chun Wang, Sabrina Williams, and especially Erin Chlopak and Jeffrey Lehtman. I thank the Institute of Humane Studies at George Mason University and especially the University Research Council of Vanderbilt University for generous funding for my field research. I am grateful to the Woodrow Wilson Center for offering an extremely stimulating and congenial environment when I was finishing the manuscript. Joe Tulchin and his able crew, in particular, really know how to take good care of their fellows. Moreover, I thank Sarah Harrington, Anita O'Brien, Linny Schenck and especially Chuck Myers for their excellent work in shepherding this book through the review and production process at Princeton University Press. Finally, I appreciate the permission granted by Blackwell Publishers to reproduce parts of my article on "The Political Fate of Market Reform in Latin America, Africa, and Eastern Europe," which was originally published in *International Studies Quarterly* 42:4 (December 1998): 645–73.

Most importantly, it is a special pleasure to acknowledge my greatest supporter and toughest critic, Wendy Hunter. I am privileged to be married to such a special person, who is also an outstanding Latin America specialist—and who was willing for years to hear about prospect theory over breakfast, lunch, and dinner. Our research trips to South America—starting with our joint dissertation research in Brazil—are unforgettable. Without her excellent comments, suggestions, criticisms, and objections, the present study would be unimaginable. And she patiently waded through—and greatly improved—countless pages of turgid Teutonic prose. I will always be grateful for her generous offer to take care of our son Niko during my stay at the Wilson Center, when she was pregnant with our second boy, Andi. I apologize to Niko for abandoning him during that difficult semester, and to both boys for working on many beautiful weekend mornings, when they wanted to play with me. I promise, I will have more time after finishing my *next* book project!

THE POLITICS OF MARKET REFORM
IN FRAGILE DEMOCRACIES

CHAPTER ONE

THE PUZZLE OF RISKY REFORMS IN UNSTABLE DEMOCRACIES

W hat explains the surprising willingness of several Latin American democracies to enact harsh neoliberal reforms? What accounts for the high level of approval that these costly measures initially elicited in some countries, especially Argentina, Peru, and Brazil, whereas similar policies provoked rejection and protest in Venezuela? And why did structural reforms advance quickly in Argentina and Peru, but much more haltingly in Brazil and especially in Venezuela? My study explores these important and intriguing questions by analyzing the politics of economic policy-making in Argentina, Brazil, Peru, and Venezuela, the major Latin American democracies that enacted market reforms in the late 1980s and 1990s.

Many observers had assumed that democratic governments would avoid implementing painful adjustment measures for fear of massive popular disapproval. In this view, only dictatorships—such as the Pinochet regime in Chile (1973–90)—had the power to impose draconian neoliberal reforms (Foxley 1983: 16, 102; Pion-Berlin 1983; Sheahan 1987: 319–23). The refusal of new democracies in Argentina, Brazil, and Peru to enact orthodox adjustment policies in the second half of the 1980s seemed to confirm this argument.

Yet contrary to these expectations, several democratic governments initiated and successfully implemented neoliberal shock programs in Latin America during the last decade. After their predecessors had hesitated for years, the governments of Carlos Saúl Menem in Argentina (1989–99), Fernando Collor de Mello in Brazil (1990–92), Alberto Fujimori in Peru (1990–2000), and Carlos Andrés Pérez in Venezuela (1989–93) imposed drastic stabilization plans shortly after taking office. Unexpectedly, these painful policies aroused little protest and much support—or at least acquiescence—in Argentina, Brazil, and Peru, while triggering unprecedented riots in Venezuela. And despite the hardships that orthodox adjustment caused, presidents Menem and Fujimori managed to win convincing reelection victories in fairly open, democratic contests, whereas presidents Collor and Pérez faced widespread opposition and suffered impeachment on corruption charges.[1] The polit-

---

[1] The democratic credentials of the Fujimori government during most of its tenure are discussed in the section on "democracy" below.

ically successful adoption of market reform in some Latin American countries, but not in others, constitutes one of the most important puzzles currently facing the field of comparative politics (Remmer 1995: 114). What accounts for this surprising turn of events? And what explains the divergence in outcomes, especially the political triumph of market reformers Menem and Fujimori compared to the political failure of their counterparts Collor and Pérez?

To what extent democracy and capitalism—and the processes of instituting them—are compatible represents a crucial question for political science (Almond 1991; Offe 1991; Armijo, Biersteker and Lowenthal 1994; Oxhorn and Starr 1999). Some observers emphasize the commonalities between democracy and a capitalist market economy, which are both based on individual liberty and unfettered initiative. Theoretically, the main classes nurtured by modern capitalism—private business, industrial workers, and middle sectors—arguably have a stronger interest in democracy than the classes that predominated before, especially traditional landowners (Johnson 1958; Lipset 1981; Rueschemeyer, Stephens, and Stephens 1992). In fact, the two systems have successfully coexisted for decades in the advanced industrialized countries of the North Atlantic region.

Other theorists stress the tensions between democracy, which grants equal political rights to all citizens, and market capitalism, which allows for—and perhaps requires—considerable socioeconomic inequality.[2] This discrepancy may be particularly consequential in less developed countries that suffer from large-scale poverty and severe social inequality. In addition, democracy makes drastic change difficult because it institutes a separation of powers and thus deconcentrates political authority. Furthermore, by allowing for widespread political participation, it gives the sectors who lose from market reform political voice and potentially the capacity to hinder or block further change. In these ways, democracy may impede marketization, that is, the political process of instituting a capitalist market economy.

By examining how—and how successfully—fragile democracies in major Latin American countries instituted neoliberal programs, this book analyzes the preconditions for a convergence of democracy and free-market capitalism in a less developed region. What has allowed market reform to proceed under democracy in several Latin American nations at certain historical conjunctures, but not in other countries or at other points in time? Are the institutional powers of the government

---

[2] The market gives higher rewards to producers who control more capital, land, labor power, or knowledge; such differential rewards are also important for inducing producers to use these resources efficiently.

and its organizational mechanisms for garnering support, such as political parties, decisive (Haggard and Kaufman 1995)? Do deep economic crises paradoxically provide a golden opportunity for imposing painful adjustment measures (Drazen and Grilli 1993)? Or are the political skills of individual leaders more important (cf. Grindle and Thomas 1991)?

To answer these and other important questions, the book assesses a variety of theoretical arguments derived from economic-structural, political-institutional, ideational ("cultural"), rational-choice, and cognitive-psychological theories. Economic arguments emphasize that severe economic problems resulting from external dependency and strong pressures from international financial institutions forced Latin American governments to adopt orthodox adjustment (Stallings 1992). Political-institutional theories argue that the successful enactment of neoliberal reform depended on the institutional powers of chief executives and the support provided by strong political parties (Haggard and Kaufman 1995). Ideational accounts stress that political elites and citizens learned from the economic failure of state interventionism and therefore embraced neoliberal ideas (Kahler 1992: 123–31). Rational-choice arguments claim that, given severe economic crises, politicians rationally chose drastic shock programs over gradual market reform in order to minimize the political costs of structural adjustment and to reap political benefits by using neoliberal measures to weaken their adversaries (Przeworski 1991: 162–80; Geddes 1994a). Finally, cognitive-psychological findings suggest that severe economic crises induced political leaders to initiate — and common people to support — neoliberal shock programs despite their tremendous economic and political risks and despite the feasibility of more prudent, less painful adjustment policies (Weyland 1996d).

In examining these divergent theories, the study addresses some of the paradigmatic debates in political science, especially the discussion about the relative importance of structural and institutional constraints vs. political agency and choice, and the question of rationality in politics. As regards the debate about structure vs. choice, the current predominance of institutionalist approaches and the legacies of economic-structural theories leave little room for leadership. These constraint-oriented arguments account fairly well for normal politics, which tends to proceed in regular, consolidated patterns. But are they fully convincing in crises, when the existing parameters of politics are up for grabs? In such extreme situations, can leaders take advantage of severe challenges to evade, override, or even reshape the constraints they are facing? Can they create a new institutional framework that sets lasting parameters for normal politics in the future? If so, crises constitute critical junctures (Collier and Collier 1991) that have enduring legacies in institutional structures and policy patterns, giving rise to a historical pattern of "punctuated equilibrium" (Krasner 1984: 240–43).

As regards the issue of rationality, do leaders and their followers or opponents among the citizenry act in line with strict cost-benefit assessments and expected utility calculations in their decision-making? Or do they display some of the deviations from conventional rationality postulates that cognitive psychologists have consistently found? By exploring the extent to which rationality principles or psychological regularities are reflected in the politics of market reform, this study speaks to the emerging debate between adherents of rational choice and cognitive-psychological theorists of decision-making (Hogarth and Reder 1987; Cook and Levi 1990; Wittman 1991; Levy 1992: 296–99; Morrow 1995; Friedman 1996; Levy 1997; Kahneman and Tversky 2000). Whereas rational-choice approaches deliberately start from simplifying, ideal-typical assumptions about decision-making and strategic interaction, psychological theories are based on empirical findings about human cognition and action. Rational-choice approaches have been on the advance in political science during the last two decades, but they are facing new challenges from cognitive-psychological decision theories. Ironically, the latter theories have had a particularly strong impact on economics, the field from which political scientists borrowed the principles of rational choice. The rapid spread of this new "behavioral economics" in recent years (*Economist* 1999; McFadden 1999; Lowenstein 2001; Uchitelle 2001) may soon prompt the import of cognitive-psychological theories in political science, which has so far been infrequent. In fact, while those theories have attracted increasing attention in the field of international relations (Stein and Pauly 1993; Farnham 1994; Berejikian 1997; Levy 1997; McDermott 1998; Haas 2001), the present study is, to the best of my knowledge, the first book-length effort to apply some of these insights in the area of comparative politics.[3]

The Main Argument

My research suggests that economic-structural, political-institutional, ideational, and rational-choice theories alone cannot provide a satisfactory account of the puzzles under investigation, although they do offer many important insights. Structural, institutional, and ideational factors merely set the stage for leaders' choices and citizens' judgments. While guided to a considerable extent by self-interests, these choices and judg-

[3] For articles, see Berejikian (1992); Buendía (1995); Weyland (1996d, 1998b).

ments in turn reflect some of the deviations from strict rationality that cognitive psychologists have found. Thus, my research suggests the need to design a new explanation for adjustment politics by drawing from cognitive-psychological insights.

This new explanation rests on the robust psychological finding of risk-seeking in the domain of losses and risk aversion in the domain of gains (Kahneman and Tversky 1979, 2000; Tversky and Kahneman 1992; Payne, Bettman, and Johnson 1992: 96–97, 122): Whereas people who face the danger of losses prefer risky choices, people who can choose between different options of gains tend toward great—often excessive—caution. Accordingly, severe problems that pose grave threats of further deterioration tend to induce people to take particularly bold countermeasures. In politics, however, incumbents whose earlier policy choices contributed to the economic deterioration tend to persist in these courses of action even when they prove unpromising, thus "throwing good money after bad." With few exceptions, only new chief executives, who are untainted by past mistakes, escape from this "status quo bias" (Samuelson and Zeckhauser 1988; Arkes and Blumer 1985: 130–32; Thaler 1992: 63–78) and display unfettered risk-seeking in the domain of losses.

Thus, the intersection of two conditions—the assumption of power by a new leader and the eruption of severe problems that put this leader in the domain of losses—is crucial for the initiation of drastic adjustment. Since severe problems often trigger elite renovation, the crisis factor appears as the main cause for the adoption of drastic market reform. Cognitive-psychological results thus provide a microfoundation for crisis arguments, which scholars commonly advance in order to account for bold policy reform (Bates and Krueger 1993: 452–54, 457; Callaghy 1990: 263, 317; Grindle and Thomas 1991: chap. 4; Haggard and Kaufman 1995: 199–201; Waterbury 1993: 35, 67, 138, 157–58, 192, 265–66).[4]

Specifically, grave economic crises that threatened to cause rapid further deterioration motivated new political leaders to abandon the caution displayed by their predecessors and to enact tough, bold, and risky neoliberal programs of stabilization and restructuring. These drastic, daring adjustment plans held the uncertain promise of ending the crisis and turning the country around, but they also risked further disorganizing the economy, unleashing a full-scale collapse of production and consumption, and triggering social unrest and political turmoil, espe-

---

[4] They also offer an explanation for political leadership, which Merilee Grindle, in particular, has emphasized (Grindle and Thomas 1991; Grindle 1999, 2000: 204 and passim).

cially in politically unstable less developed countries. Where acute open crises prevailed, however, clear prospects of losses induced many citizens to endorse the painful, risky policies imposed by their new leaders. By contrast, where the predecessor government had hidden severe imminent problems from the citizenry and many people therefore did not see themselves in the domain of losses, preemptive adjustment measures elicited rejection and protest (Weyland 1996d).

The cognitive-psychological findings of risk-seeking in the domain of losses and risk aversion in the domain of gains also help account for the political fate of neoliberal reform in the medium run. Where drastic adjustment to a deep, open crisis eventually produced stabilization and recovery, political leaders entered the domain of gains, became more cautious and risk-averse, and therefore shied away from completing the program of drastic reforms recommended by their neoliberal advisers and the international financial institutions (IFIs). Similarly, more and more citizens turned risk-averse and accepted the new status quo, that is, the core of the market model instituted so far (but not additional neoliberal reforms). This widespread acquiescence prevailed despite persistent economic and social problems, which structural adjustment often exacerbated. This turn to risk aversion also induced a majority of people to vote for the experienced incumbent — e.g., presidents Menem and Fujimori — rather than making a risky electoral choice by supporting the untested opposition.

My research thus suggests that cognitive-psychological findings provide the core of a new explanation for the politics of neoliberal reform. As an account of political decision-making, however, this argument cannot stand alone. Indeed, the hypothesized shifts in leaders' and citizens' propensities toward risk depend on changes in the context of choice, which can put people from the domain of gains into the domain of losses, and vice versa. These contextual changes are conditioned by economic-structural, political-institutional, and ideational factors and developments. Thus, the cognitive-psychological arguments invoked in this study necessarily call for an integration of "choice" and "structure" (cf. Berejikian 1992: 652–55).

How did economic-structural, ideational, and political-institutional factors shape the context of leaders' and citizens' choices? As regards economic factors, the external debt problem and flawed domestic policies eventually caused deep economic crises, which culminated in hyperinflation in Argentina, Brazil, and Peru, but not in Venezuela. Depending on their severity, these economic crises put new political leaders and a larger or smaller fraction of common citizens in the domain of losses. As for ideational factors, learning from the failed heterodox adjustment efforts undertaken in Argentina, Brazil, and Peru — and pressures from

IFIs — foreclosed some potential responses to these crises and put a premium on neoliberal recipes. And as regards political factors, presidents' institutional powers conditioned the ways and means through which they sought to enact adjustment measures despite opposition. Furthermore, the structure of the party system, combined with the severity of the crisis, influenced the political support that leaders could muster. Finally, democratization strengthened the responsiveness of politicians to the large mass of voters, who were concerned about deep, open economic crises, and weakened the political stranglehold of vested interest groups with a strong stake in the established development model.

In these ways, economic-structural, ideational, and political-institutional factors set the stage for the choices of leaders and citizens and conditioned the impact of these choices. My project therefore embeds cognitive-psychological findings in elements of those approaches. It thus designs a complex yet systematically integrated explanation for the initiation and political fate of market reform in contemporary Latin America.

As is obvious, the central argument of this book stresses the role of grave, acute problems — crises — in triggering bold reforms. By demonstrating how these situational conditions affect individual choices, my prospect-theory interpretation provides a firm microfoundation for widely used crisis arguments (see citations above). While those accounts have great plausibility and ample empirical support, they do not systematically specify the mechanisms through which worsening problems prompt reform attempts; in particular, they are rarely grounded in theories of individual choice. Thus, it often remains unclear why, exactly, leading decision-makers responded to crises with bold countermeasures and why the citizenry sometimes — but not always — supported these rescue efforts. Crisis arguments have therefore been criticized as insufficiently specified and functionalist (Rodrik 1996; Corrales 1996: chap. 4). By invoking the cognitive-psychological finding of risk acceptance in the domain of losses, the present study fills this lacuna and explains systematically how individuals — both political leaders and common citizens — respond to crises. It thus puts crisis arguments on a strong footing. In fact, since my prospect-theory explanation rests on well-established empirical findings, not on unrealistic ideal-typical postulates, it provides a more solid microfoundation for crisis arguments than rational choice, which has turned the demand for such microfoundations into a powerful weapon against competing approaches. Most of those frameworks, especially economic structuralism, culturalism, and historical institutionalism, do not start from methodological individualism; therefore, they lack microfoundations and remain exposed to criticism from rational choice. By contrast, this book fulfills the demand advanced by advocates of rational choice: its central argument starts from a theory of individual choice. Yet by drawing on the amply corroborated insights of prospect theory, this new microfoundation offers a firmer basis for empirical analysis than conventional rational-choice models.

Research Design

To assess the cognitive-psychological arguments that the present study elaborates, scholars could examine countries that differ starkly in historical background, cultural traditions, development level, economic structure, and political-institutional framework.[5] Yet while an analysis that applies such a most different systems design promises to yield broadly generalizable results (Przeworski and Teune 1982: 34–39), it has some unavoidable limitations. Above all, such an investigation focuses on one set of variables only and necessarily neglects many other factors that influence the political success of neoliberal reform.

This book seeks to put flesh around these bare bones by embedding cognitive-psychological insights in a structural, institutional, and ideational context. Rather than pursuing a strictly analytical goal, the purpose of the present study is synthetic. The attention to causal complexity and to context factors, which differ widely across regions, requires a much narrower focus than a cross-regional comparison. By investigating countries that share many background factors and that actually initiated neoliberal reform, this study applies a most similar systems design. In this way, it seeks to elucidate the political conditions and repercussions of the specific market reforms enacted and implemented in four major Latin American countries. Thus, the current study is more case-oriented than variable-oriented (cf. Ragin 1987).

Argentina, Brazil, Peru, and Venezuela have many historical, cultural, economic, social, and political characteristics in common, such as Iberian colonization, predominance of Catholicism, significant import-substitution industrialization, advanced "social mobilization" (Deutsch 1961), serious problems of debt and dependency, similar constitutional structures (for instance, presidential systems), and exposure to common ideational trends (for instance, the temporary attraction and later rejection of heterodox recipes). These commonalities make it easier to assess the causal impact of the remaining differences — such as the severity of economic problems, or the strength of party systems — on the political processes and outcomes of market reform. It is also reasonable to assume causal homogeneity among the four countries: Causal factors are

[5] For a preliminary effort, see Weyland (1998b).

likely to have the same type of effect in these similar settings. Statistical analyses of large samples of different cases, by contrast, make this assumption of causal homogeneity with much less justification (Ragin 1987: chap. 4).

Small-N comparison among most similar cases is especially well-suited for the fine-tuned causal analysis required for investigating the reasons for the political success of market reforms in some countries and their (at least temporary) failure in others (see in general Ragin 1987: chap. 3; Collier 1998; Collier, Brady, and Seawright 2002). In particular, it is attentive to context factors from which statistical analysis tends to abstract. Yet the capacity of small-N comparison to isolate the causal impact of specific variables is hampered by potential interaction effects among the factors shaping the few cases under investigation. This high level of complexity makes analytical controls precarious (Ragin 1987: 42–44, 49–51; Lieberson 1991). As a result, causal inferences cannot be as rigorous and scientific as in statistical analysis — which, however, in its abstraction of variables from their context also suffers from serious problems (Ragin 1987: 61–67; McKeown 1999).

In compensation for this analytical problem, small-N analysis can directly analyze and reconstruct the process of political decision-making, which statistical studies infer by correlating "inputs" and "outputs." By contrast, in-depth qualitative research provides evidence for the operation of different causal factors. For instance, if government officials report that they watered down a draft bill because business leaders expressed their opposition in a meeting with the chief executive, interest group pressure most likely had substantial influence on policy-making. Or if decision-makers justify their abandonment of a policy by referring to its failure in another country, learning seems to play an important role. Thus, field researchers can ascertain causal mechanisms more directly than can scholars who apply the logic of statistical analysis (cf. King, Keohane, and Verba 1994).

The present study, by resorting to process tracing (George 1979; Collier, Brady, and Seawright 2002), therefore complements the combinatorial logic that underlies the scientific effort to isolate causal factors. Based on extensive field research that included interviews with key decision-makers, the book provides a longitudinal analysis of the unfolding of neoliberal reform efforts. By accounting for the twists and turns of reform politics, this approach focuses on the operation of specific causal factors at certain points in time and thus permits a tentative sequential isolation of these factors.[6] Also, process tracing is particularly

[6] This analytical strategy is masterfully employed in Skocpol (1979), as the recent explication in Katznelson (1997: 91–94) demonstrates again.

attuned to the path dependency that characterizes contextually embedded political processes: earlier decisions delimit later choice options, and prior experiences influence the content of later decisions through political learning. Statistical analysis, which assumes independence among cases and therefore has difficulty dealing with learning—which causes problematic autocorrelation—seeks to abstract from sequential causation. Case-oriented examination, by contrast, better captures factors such as learning, which result from conscious efforts at improving problem solving and which are among the most interesting features of politics. For all of these reasons, the present study relies primarily on small-N comparison.

Case Selection

What cases are most promising and useful for a small-N investigation of the politics of neoliberal reform under democracy? Most African countries are excluded because they moved to democracy only recently, if at all. Ghana, for instance, the showcase of neoliberal adjustment on the continent (Herbst 1993; Callaghy 1990: 271–86), initiated orthodox policy changes in 1983 but held its first reasonably free, honest, and fair presidential election only in 1992—and even this contest was rejected by the opposition as tainted (see Jeffries and Thomas 1993 vs. Oquaye 1995). Asian countries do not qualify because—despite their export-oriented development strategies—they have never enacted anything resembling neoliberal reform (see Wade 1990), at least until the financial crisis of late 1997. Only Latin America or Eastern Europe could therefore be the focus of the small-N investigation conducted in this book. The stark differences between these regions make it impossible to use a cross-regional sample for the similar systems design applied in this study (cf. Lijphart and Waisman 1996: 3–6; Offe 1991; Bartlett 1997: 5–13). Arguably, Latin American nations share more similarities than East European countries, which differ starkly in the salience of ethnic cleavages and the push and pull caused by international political and economic factors, as evident in their different relations with Russia,[7] NATO, and the European Union (Baer and Love 2000). By contrast, Latin America provides a better sample of cases for a most similar systems design.

Among Latin American countries, Argentina, Brazil, Peru, and Venezuela constitute the most similar cases for the purposes of this investigation. Mexico and Chile were not democratic at the time their governments initiated and enacted most neoliberal reforms. Colombia

[7] Compare, for instance, the very different postures of Poland and Belarus.

had since 1967 pursued a much more export-oriented development strategy than the rest of Latin America (Urrutia 1994; Juarez 1993). Therefore, the neoliberal reforms adopted since 1990 have had lower costs, triggered weaker opposition, and elicited stronger support. Consequently, they carried much less political risk and unleashed a different political dynamic than the more comprehensive, drastic, and painful adjustment measures decreed in the rest of the continent. Finally, Ecuador and especially Bolivia are at lower development levels and have less complex economies than the countries under investigation. Therefore, they do not form part of the group of most similar cases constituted by Argentina, Brazil, Peru, and Venezuela.

For the questions addressed in this study, those four countries are most similar inside Latin America. But they also differ along some important dimensions. It is precisely this combination of similarities and differences that facilitates causal inference. In addition to many common historical and cultural background characteristics, all four countries underwent considerable import-substitution industrialization between the 1930s and the 1970s; suffered severe economic problems in the 1980s; were democratic for at least five years before the time of reform initiation; had an institutionalized state apparatus, important nonpersonalistic parties, and a large number of interest organizations and social movements; and experienced broad mass participation in politics.

The differences among these countries concern factors that are often seen as crucial for explaining the initiation of determined policy reform, namely, the depth and severity of the economic crisis; the strength and configuration of the party system; and leadership strategies (see, e.g., Grindle and Thomas 1991; Haggard and Kaufman 1995). First, Argentina, Brazil, and Peru suffered from graver economic problems than Venezuela; above all, hyperinflation erupted in the former three countries, whereas Venezuela never experienced a price explosion, despite strong repressed inflation. Among the three hyperinflationary cases, Argentina and Peru experienced economic stagnation or decline during the 1980s, whereas Brazil achieved some net growth. Second, two strong parties long predominated in Argentina and Venezuela, whereas a host of mostly weak parties prevailed in Brazil and Peru.[8] Third, presidents Fujimori and Menem placated and allied with some crucial powers-that-be, especially big business groups and the military, whereas President Collor kept these actors at bay in a quest for complete personal autonomy. The following investigation assesses the extent

[8] Brazil's Partido dos Trabalhadores (PT) and Peru's Alianza Popular Revolucionaria Americana (APRA) constitute exceptions that are better organized.

to which these differences account for the dissimilar processes and outcomes of market reform in the four countries.

Central Concepts

Democracy

Following the literature on transitions from authoritarian rule, especially O'Donnell and Schmitter (1986: 7–14), Mainwaring (1992: 295–98), and Przeworski (1997), this study uses a minimalist, procedural concept of democracy. Specifically, I define democracy as "a set of institutions that, in the context of guarantees for political freedom, permits the entire adult population to choose their leading decision-makers in competitive, honest, regularly scheduled elections and to advance their interests and ideas through peaceful individual or collective action" (Weyland 1996a: 8).

According to this definition, Argentina has been democratic since 1983, Brazil since 1985,[9] and Venezuela since 1958. Democracy also prevailed in Peru from 1980 until President Fujimori's *autogolpe* of April 5, 1992. Scholars disagree on whether and when the country returned to democracy after this openly authoritarian measure (McClintock 1994b: 27–29; Tulchin and Bland 1994; LASA 1995; Palmer 1995; Conaghan 1996; Tuesta Soldevilla 1996; Cameron and Mauceri 1997). The Constituent Assembly election of November 1992 was fairly free and offered voters a wide range of choice. Certainly, several established parties refused to participate, but Peru's "political class" has been so discredited that their decision not to run may have helped, rather than hurt, the opposition, as the dismal showing of the traditional parties in the 1995 elections suggests. The 1992 election can thus be considered minimally democratic. President Fujimori's surprisingly narrow victory in the constitutional plebiscite of October 1993 provided further democratic legitimacy to the regime. Finally, the general elections of 1995 confirmed Peru's return to democracy. In this contest, voters had ample opportunities to cast their ballot for a variety of opposition parties and leaders, but a striking 64.3 percent chose the incumbent.

During the late 1990s, however, Peru suffered an involution that turned the regime ever less democratic. To prepare President Fujimori's second reelection, which the new constitution ruled out, the governmental majority in Congress trampled on institutional rules and democratic

[9] Since 1985, all political actors—even indirectly elected President José Sarney—have been subject to the re-electoral constraint that is decisive for democratic representation and accountability (Weyland 1996a: 8).

principles, especially with the destitution in mid-1997 of three Supreme Court judges who had upheld the 1993 charter (Cameron 1997b: 1–19). In addition, the congressional and presidential contests of 2000 were marred by many irregularities. Several authors therefore classified Peru at the end of the Fujimori government as semi-democratic or outright authoritarian (McClintock 1998; Levitsky 1999). While the freedom of speech, assembly, and press prevailing in Peru, the ample activities of the opposition, and the government's recognition of electoral defeat (as in the municipal contests of 1995 and 1998 in Lima) make the authoritarian label too harsh, the late 1990s certainly saw a political deterioration that threatened to drag Peru below the threshold of full democracy. The ample manipulation used to secure Fujimori's contested electoral victory in mid-2000 and the scandalous corruption discovered shortly thereafter jeopardized fundamental democratic principles. But the unexpected collapse of the Fujimori government interrupted this transition to authoritarian rule, and the clean elections held in mid-2001 restored full democracy.

In sum, the four countries analyzed in this study have been democracies for the period under investigation, with the exception of a nine-month hiatus in Peru in 1992 and a renewed involution at the end of the decade. For most of this time, however, the four democracies were not very stable. Besides the troubles and travails plaguing Peruvian democracy, Argentina's new civilian regime was rocked by several military rebellions in the late 1980s, by large-scale riots in 1989, and by presidential disrespect for institutional rules during the 1990s; Brazil's fledgling democracy suffered dangerous polarization in late 1989, a traumatic presidential impeachment in 1992, and a worrisome power vacuum caused by presidential incompetence in 1993–94; and even Venezuela's seemingly consolidated democracy was shaken by a massive popular uprising in early 1989 and two bloody coup attempts in 1992. Thus, by standard definitions (Linz and Stepan 1996: 5–6), the four countries' democracies were not consolidated during the late 1980s and early 1990s, when chief executives initiated neoliberal reforms. As political actors worried about the survival of competitive politics, democracy remained fragile in Argentina, Brazil, and Peru and became vulnerable again in Venezuela.

Neoliberalism and Market Reform

"Market reform" refers to measures that reduce state intervention in the economy, especially by eliminating or loosening different types of regulations and restrictions (such as import prohibitions and tariffs,

labor laws, and rules on foreign investment), by privatizing public enterprises, and by shrinking the public bureaucracy. Market reform thus
moves an economy closer to the ideal-type of capitalism, which is characterized by two main dimensions: private ownership of the means of
production and decentralized coordination of economic activities, that
is, free-market allocation of goods and services. The broad term "market reform," however, specifies only the direction of change, not the end
point. A government that enacts market reform does not necessarily
intend to install a full-scale free-market economy; it may merely seek to
strengthen substantially the market elements in a mixed economy while
preserving significant state intervention. By contrast, the narrower term
"neoliberal reform" does imply the radical goal of creating a free-
market economy.

According to this conceptual distinction, a Communist country that
moves toward a Swedish-style social democracy undergoes market reform, but not neoliberal reform. In Latin America, Argentina, Chile,
Mexico, and Peru enacted neoliberal reform, and President Collor attempted to do so in Brazil during the early 1990s. Brazil's current president Fernando Henrique Cardoso (1995–present), by contrast, is not
trying to establish a full-scale free-market system but is instituting pragmatic market reform that preserves substantial state intervention, including, for instance, governmental support for the automobile industry.

Even in countries that enact neoliberal reform, the state does not
abandon all of its earlier responsibilities in economy and society and
give the market completely free rein. For instance, in Chile and Mexico — two prototypical cases of Latin American neoliberalism — the state
has continued to own and run the enterprise producing the country's
most important export — copper and petroleum, respectively. Also, the
drastic reduction of state interventionism that neoliberal reform does
entail need not weaken the state's strength. Instead, the state may gain
political clout by retreating from excessive interventionism and by concentrating on its core attributions. Above all, budget austerity and tax
reforms may well strengthen the fiscal resources of the state and thus
allow it to reassert its authority, which had declined greatly during the
crisis preceding market reform. In sum, by becoming leaner, the state
may turn "meaner," that is, more powerful (Acuña and Smith 1994:
20–22; Mauceri 1995; Weyland 1996b: 16–17).

Market and neoliberal reforms have, in principle, different phases,
especially stabilization and structural reform. Stabilization measures are
efforts to rectify macroeconomic disequilibria, such as skyrocketing inflation, spiralling fiscal deficits, or exploding imbalances in a country's
external accounts. These measures combat immediate, acute problems
and seek to attain success in the short or medium run. Structural re-

forms, by contrast, seek to transform a country's development model by reshaping major economic, social, and political institutions. Important examples include the privatization of state firms; legal changes to make the central bank independent from governmental interference; the "flexibilization" of labor laws that used to guarantee ample social rights; reforms of tax laws and fiscal administration; and efforts to combat political corruption and guarantee the rule of law. Structural reforms are expected to have a long-term impact.

While stabilization and structural reform constitute logically distinct phases of market reform, they often overlap in practice. Indeed, governments commonly use structural reforms for purposes of stabilization. In Latin America, for instance, several governments intensified trade liberalization in order to allow for the influx of cheap imports and thus force domestic prices down. As another example, the Menem government justified its partially successful effort to reduce labor regulations with the need to stimulate job creation and thus reduce skyrocketing unemployment. Thus, in political reality, the distinction between stabilization and structural reform is much less clear than in the scholarly literature.

Authors have further differentiated structural reforms into two phases, namely, the dismantling of the old, nationalist, state-interventionist, inward-looking development model and the establishment of the necessary institutional framework for a market economy (see especially Naím 1995; Nelson 1997). Whereas the former task involved drastic acts of destruction, the latter requires patient efforts at reconstruction, especially at institution building. And whereas the first stage of structural reform centers on the economy, the second phase has a broader reach, affecting social and political-institutional spheres as well, for instance through pension privatization and the restructuring of the public administration. Thus, neoliberalism first resurrects the predominance of private property and the market in the economy and then seeks to extend these principles to other areas in order to create propitious social and political-institutional parameters for the new market-capitalist system.

While these two steps thus constitute a logical progression, the new emphasis on institution building that characterizes the second generation of market reforms also reflects some rethinking among academic experts and international financial institutions. Whereas initially the hope prevailed that the installation of a free-market economy would guarantee economic stability and renewed growth, a decade of experience has confirmed the earlier argument that in order to function properly, the market needs to be embedded in economic, social, and political institutions (see World Bank 1997; IADB 2000: 23–29, 163–95; cf. Po-

lanyi 1957). The unfettered pursuit of private self-interest and completely free initiative — coordinated only by market competition — are
not sufficient for creating outcomes that are acceptable to society. Instead, the market itself requires cultural, social, and institutional foundations and guidance, for instance guarantees of property rights, the
fair adjudication of conflicting claims, and — perhaps — a sense of trust.
Due to this rethinking, issues such as the rule of law, crime and violence, corruption, and "social capital" have attracted increasing attention in the development community (e.g., World Bank 1997; IADB 2000).
The discussion about the second stage of reforms embodies this renewed attention to the institutional, cultural, and social preconditions
of a market economy.

Organization of the Volume

Chapter 2 demonstrates that existing arguments do not provide a fully
convincing account of market reform under democracy. To complement
the extant economic-structural, political-institutional, ideational, and
rational-choice theories, chapter 3 designs a novel explanation based on
cognitive-psychological theories of decision-making, especially prospect
theory. The chapter embeds this new model of choice in an economic-
structural, political-institutional, and ideational context, thus acknowl-
edging the contributions made by the theories that chapter 2 criticized.

Chapters 4 through 8 use this new argument to elucidate the politics of economic policy in Argentina, Brazil, Peru, and Venezuela during
the 1980s and 1990s. Chapter 4 provides the necessary background for
the analysis of neoliberal reform by examining the emergence of severe
economic problems at the beginning of the 1980s; the failed adjustment
efforts — both of an orthodox and of a heterodox nature — that governments undertook in the early and middle parts of the decade; and the
notable postponement of determined stabilization measures despite the
significant economic deterioration at the end of the decade.

Chapter 5 focuses on the eventual enactment of neoliberal reform.
It first explains the rise of political outsiders who were willing to discard established policy patterns, embark on drastic stabilization, and
initiate radical market reform. An in-depth investigation of the perceptions, risk propensities, and decisions of the new chief executives follows. Finally, the chapter analyzes in a similar perspective the reactions
of common citizens to these painful, risky adjustment programs. Chapter 6 examines the next step in the reform sequence, namely, the efforts
to restructure the established development model, which were under-
girded by a populist political strategy. The discussion shows how mar-

ket reforms serve to weaken opponents of personalistic leaders and to strengthen their mass support, thus boosting their plebiscitarian leadership. The chapter also documents that structural reforms advanced much farther in Argentina and Peru than in Brazil and Venezuela; this uneven progress was due to the differential severity of the structural problems facing the four countries, not to institutional characteristics, as many authors claim.

Chapter 7 analyzes the reasons for the political sustainability of the new market model in the two cases of relative success, Argentina and Peru. It explains how presidents Menem and Fujimori engineered their own reelection; how the basic outline of the new development scheme attained relatively firm support, despite renewed economic difficulties; and how Menem's and Fujimori's populist leadership weakened and decayed in the second half of the 1990s. Chapter 8 examines the stop-and-go process of market reform among the two laggards, Brazil and Venezuela. After the initial push for neoliberalism failed politically in the early 1990s, Brazil experienced a slowdown and Venezuela a drastic reversal of efforts to restructure the old development model. But continued economic deterioration prompted the resumption of market reform in the middle of the decade. Determined stabilization measures were followed by only half-hearted structural reforms, however. The Brazilian and Venezuelan economies therefore remained vulnerable, and external shocks in the late 1990s caused a new round of serious economic difficulties. Especially in Venezuela, the future of the market model therefore remained unclear.

Chapter 9 draws theoretical conclusions from the extensive empirical investigation. The first part comments on the usefulness of prospect theory for political analysis; shows how this cognitive-psychological theory can strengthen crisis arguments and helps to reformulate the valid yet too rashly discarded insights of functionalism; and discusses under what conditions its arguments are analytically preferable to those of rational choice. An extensive second part demonstrates the applicability of my prospect-theory argument to a much wider range of cases, drawn from Latin America, Africa, and Eastern Europe. While economic-structural, political-institutional, and ideational context factors would obviously have to be considered for a comprehensive analysis of reform politics in those nations, the novel insights developed in this book seem to have more general validity far beyond the four cases studied in-depth below.

CHAPTER TWO

THE INSUFFICIENCY OF EXISTING ARGUMENTS

The scholarly literature has not yet resolved the puzzle posed by the enactment of painful, risky market reforms in fragile institutional settings. While making important contributions, established arguments cannot fully account for the daring decisions of political leaders to initiate drastic adjustment programs and for the surprisingly widespread popular support for these costly measures, despite their uncertain outcomes. These choices by leaders and citizens reflect a striking willingness to accept great risks, which extant writings underestimate or fail to explain.

Based on my field research, the following assessment shows the gaps left by the existing efforts to account for market reform under democracy. Specifically, economic structuralism overemphasizes the constraining force of external pressures and underestimates the margin left for political choice. Political institutionalism, which focuses on the regular patterns of normal politics, has difficulty elucidating the exceptional decisions made in crisis situations, when institutional parameters may crumble or collapse. Ideational theories depict decision-making too much as a matter of intellectual conviction, rather than political interest. Finally, rational-choice models correctly stress the importance of political interests, but in their effort to abstract from "real people" and start from simplifying assumptions, they cannot systematically account for actors' shifting propensities toward risk.

Economic Structuralism

Economic-structural arguments, which are often rooted in a dependency perspective (Stallings 1992: 41–48),[1] hold that the enactment of market

---

[1] Economic structuralism strictly defined stresses exogenous constraints that force actors' hands, as elucidated by dependency approaches. By contrast, arguments that emphasize the economic failure of the established development model and depict market reform as the adoption of a better alternative are more usefully classified as rational-choice models (see below). In those models, structural constraints guide actors' volition, whereas they overpower actors' volition in economic-structural accounts.

reform resulted mainly from the tight constraints imposed by global economic structures and the strong pressures exerted by international financial institutions, especially the International Monetary Fund (IMF) and the World Bank (Stallings 1992; Vacs 1994). In this view, Latin American governments had little choice but to initiate neoliberal programs of stabilization and restructuring. The severe problems caused by the debt crisis—such as deep recessions, worsening fiscal deficits, and skyrocketing inflation—called for determined adjustment measures. The IFIs, transnational corporations, and increasingly mobile domestic capitalists refused to support heterodox policies that employed incomes policies to stabilize inflation and stimulate growth at the same time. Governments therefore had to adopt orthodox stabilization and initiate structural reforms that dismantled the established nationalist, state-interventionist development model. Economic structures ("markets") and IFI influence ("leverage")[2] thus forced the hands of political leaders.

Economic structuralists expected this external imposition of severe adjustment programs to trigger frequent domestic rejection, if not protest (Walton and Ragin 1990; Walton and Seddon 1994: chap. 4). Some of these authors therefore downplay the support that neoliberal policies did in fact elicit in a number of instances. They suggest—and hope—that popular protest may still erupt once the social costs of market reforms become obvious and the neoliberal promises of renewed growth are revealed as illusions.[3] They therefore regard every incident of revolt—from the Zapatista uprising in Chiapas in January 1994 to the roadblocks in Argentina in mid-1997—as an indication that the popular sectors are finally throwing off the yoke of neoliberalism (Petras 1997).

Economic structuralists who seek to account for widespread acquiescence in drastic stabilization plans stress governmental repression and other obstacles to collective action, including the social atomization caused by the hardships of adjustment itself. They also point to the social compensation programs that IFIs have promoted and funded to cushion the costs of painful neoliberal reform. Though woefully inadequate in the eyes of those critics, these antipoverty programs give destitute people the illusion that governments care about their plight.

How convincing are these explanations? Economic-structural arguments make a number of important contributions, especially in elucidat-

---

[2] Stallings (1992); Vacs (1994). In general, see Strange (1996) and, for more nuanced views, Keohane and Milner (1996) and Gourevitch (1986).

[3] While economic structuralists blame these economic and social costs on neoliberal adjustment itself, advocates of market reform attribute them to earlier governmental mismanagement and the inherent flaws of the old development model, which they hold responsible for the severe crisis that necessitated drastic stabilization and restructuring.

ing some crucial reasons why Latin American governments shifted course and embraced neoliberal adjustment, and why several did so at roughly the same time. In fact, the wavelike character of market reform provides strong evidence for the importance of international factors, such as IFI pressure (Stallings 1992: 43, 82–83). In response to the persistent problems unleashed by the debt crisis, the IMF and the World Bank came to elaborate a comprehensive program of structural adjustment and exert great pressure on Latin American governments to adopt this "Washington consensus" (Williamson 1990). The debt crisis itself resulted to a considerable extent from international factors, especially the loan pushing by First World banks in the 1970s and early 1980s; the interest rate hike and recession in the United States in the early 1980s; and the chain reaction of banks, which deprived all Latin American countries of new funding once Mexico declared its illiquidity in August 1982. Thus, economic-structural arguments shed important light on the eruption of the crisis that triggered the adoption of neoliberal reform.

But economic-structural arguments alone cannot provide a complete explanation for the enactment of market reform. As Stallings (1992: 74, 85–88) herself stresses, "markets" and "leverage" did not determine governmental decisions; political leaders retained a margin of choice. After all, the debt crisis erupted in 1982–83, but governments postponed drastic adjustment until the end of the decade. The IFIs had long preached the benefits of neoliberalism, but their recommendations had for years fallen on deaf ears. Why did Latin American governments suddenly decide to listen? Structural constraints and outside pressures cannot fully account for this shift of course; political factors also played a crucial role (Acuña and Smith 1994: 18–24).

Investigations of the decision-making process show in fact that external influences had less impact than adherents of a dependency perspective — even Stallings with her measured version of this argument — claim. For instance, IFI involvement in the elaboration of adjustment programs was limited in the countries under investigation. While the stabilization plans imposed by President Pérez in February 1989 and by President Fujimori in August 1990 closely followed IFI recipes, President Collor's first adjustment program of March 1990 and Economy Minister Domingo Cavallo's convertibility plan of March 1991 were designed mainly by domestic economists (interview with Mello 1995; Cavallo 1997: 34, 137–39, 177–79; Llach 1997: 168–71, 191).

Indeed, the adjustment programs adopted in all four countries contained important measures that diverged from the "Washington consensus" or went much farther than the IFIs had recommended. Fearing strong opposition, if not violent protest, the IFIs recommended against overly drastic shock programs and advocated greater caution (interviews with Boloña 1996; Rodríguez 1996; Naím 1993a: 169–70; see also Durand and Thorp 1998: 149, n.16). But the Pérez, Collor, and Fujimori governments, in particular, were determined to pay the costs of adjustment at once. They therefore enacted stunning, even brutal measures, such as an unexpected austerity program in Venezuela, the unprecedented freezing of bank accounts in Brazil, and price rises of up to 3,000 percent for basic necessities in Peru. Presidents Menem and Collor also adopted important unorthodox policies that diverged from IFI recipes. Above all, they temporarily confiscated large amounts of financial assets, drastically reducing the real value of these investments. The IFIs were concerned about such gross violations of property rights, which threatened to undermine confidence in the banking system and hinder future savings and investments. In sum, Latin American governments had a considerable margin of autonomy from external pressures.

This autonomy persisted during the whole sequence of market reform. For instance, governments that achieved economic stabilization and recovery soon slowed down the enactment of further neoliberal measures. Presidents Menem, Fujimori, and Cardoso therefore failed to complete the full package of changes that the IFIs were promoting. Menem hesitated to impose profound labor reform; Fujimori decelerated privatization; and Cardoso pushed less hard for tax and social security reform. These "second-phase" reforms did not only face political and institutional obstacles (Naím 1995; Nelson 1997; Heredia and Schneider 1998: 5–8), but the reform impetus of governments diminished after they managed to overcome the most acute economic problems.[4] Once again, IFI exhortations fell on deaf ears. Governments' deviations from IFI recipes thus show that external pressures, while undeniably important, cannot fully account for the enactment of market reforms.

As regards the popular response to costly neoliberal adjustment, rejection and protest erupted much less frequently than economic structuralists had expected. This widespread acquiescence did not only result from collective-action problems and the threat of repression. Instead, a wealth of opinion polls shows that in Argentina, Brazil, and Peru, an often substantial majority of the population immediately endorsed draconian stabilization measures, even before their beneficial results appeared (Mora y Araujo 1990: 4; Datafolha 1990; IBOPE 1990a: 13; Apoyo, January 1991: 3, 16, 17). While persistent economic problems eroded this initial approval in all three countries, it often rose again with renewed adjustment efforts. Also, presidents Menem, Fujimori,

---

[4] Confidential author interviews with former leading economic policy-makers in Peru and Argentina.

and — for a while — Collor commanded high personal popularity; Menem and Fujimori even won immediate reelection. Thus, market reforms received surprisingly strong popular backing.

The social compensation measures advocated and funded by IFIs cannot account for this unexpected support. When initiating neoliberal shock programs, governments instituted meager (if any) social emergency measures (Weyland 1998c: 545–47). Few people believed that these palliatives would compensate for the costs of painful adjustment plans; few respondents therefore invoked them to justify their support for the government (Consultores 21 1989b: 29–30; Datum 1990d: 1A). In the three years following the initiation of market reform, the most extensive "safety nets" were established in Venezuela, but popular support for neoliberal restructuring and its initiator remained at the lowest level.[5] Thus, material compensation proposed and partly funded by IFIs cannot account for the surprising degree to which the population endorsed market reform.

In sum, economic-structural arguments help account for the context in which governments decided to enact structural adjustment but are less useful for explaining the popular response to these painful measures. Governmental decisions are not determined by structural economic problems and IFI pressures, as Stallings (1992: 74, 85–88) herself emphasizes. Since political leaders retain a good margin of autonomy, economic-structural arguments need to be complemented by political-institutional, ideational,[6] and/or choice-theoretical arguments.

Political Institutionalism

Political-institutional arguments maintain that a government's capacity for enacting drastic adjustment depends on its institutional strength and its control over organizational mechanisms that marshal support in society. In this vein, Haggard and Kaufman (1995: 163–82; similarly, Mainwaring 1999: 310–11) argue in their outstanding study that centralized executive authority and a cohesive, nonpolarized party system facilitate the adoption of neoliberal reforms and protect these measures from challenges by discontented social sectors and political opposition forces. Presidents who command great institutional clout manage to impose the unavoidable costs of economic restructuring and to coax different political actors and socioeconomic groupings into cooperating with

[5] Weyland (1998c: 546–47, 552–53); on Venezuela's extensive social compensation measures, see CONASSEPS (1994); Márquez (1995: 414–24).

[6] This includes Stallings' "linkage" (1992: 52–55), which does not constitute unidirectional influence but includes joint learning.

their adjustment policies. Institutionally powerful executives are thus able to overcome the problems of coordination and distribution that plague market reforms (Haggard and Kaufman 1995: 156–57, 163–65). In addition, strong parties that stand in centripetal competition contain radical opposition and moderate political conflict, thus facilitating the implementation of costly, potentially controversial reforms. And where disciplined parties have roots in society, they guarantee popular backing for tough adjustment programs. By contrast, where parties are fluid and disorganized, endorsement of stabilization measures is fleeting at best and easily undermined by the first signs of economic difficulties (cf. Packenham 1994: 8–9).

Furthermore, institutionalists see long-established, consolidated democracies as more likely to enact orthodox adjustment policies than fledgling civilian regimes that have only recently completed a transition from authoritarian rule (Kaufman and Stallings 1989; Haggard and Kaufman 1989: 59–65). A regime that commands solid legitimacy and does not face the danger of instability finds it easier to impose the costs of stabilization on powerful sectors than does a fragile, unconsolidated democracy. Immediately after a democratic transition, the new civilian government needs to provide benefits to a wide range of groups in order to buy support, prove its performance, and thus establish legitimacy gradually (see in general Easton 1979: chaps. 17–19; Valenzuela 1992: 80–81). A new democracy therefore rejects painful orthodox adjustment and prefers heterodox programs that promise to bring stability without major costs.

Despite the important contributions they make, however, these institutionalist arguments are not fully persuasive. Variations in presidents' institutional powers cannot explain the different political fate of neoliberal programs. Among the four countries under investigation, Shugart and Carey (1992: 155),[7] for instance, attribute by far the highest level of constitutionally defined legislative powers to Brazilian presidents.[8] But presidents Collor and Cardoso faced much greater difficulties in garnering congressional approval for their proposals than did

---

[7] Haggard and Kaufman (1995: 121) refer to Shugart and Carey's measurements of centralized executive authority. In a less exclusively institutionalist assessment, by contrast, Shugart and Mainwaring (1997: 51–52) stress that presidents' constitutional powers alone do not determine their actual political strength; "other factors like the relationship of presidents to their own parties and to the legislative majority" also matter.

[8] Based on Argentina's constitutional reform of 1994, which codified presidential decree authority, Shugart and Mainwaring (1997: 49) rank that country's chief executive as more powerful than Brazil's president. But the constitution that was valid at the initiation of neoliberal reform in 1989 did not give the president such extensive decree authority; Menem simply arrogated it to himself (Shugart and Mainwaring 1997: 45; Ferreira Rubio and Goretti 1998: 43, 51–56).

presidents Menem and Fujimori (1990–92), who enjoyed less extensive formal attributions. As regards nonlegislative powers, Peru's presidents ranked lower than their counterparts in Argentina, Brazil, and Venezuela because the Peruvian Congress had the right to censor government ministers. But President Fujimori simply disregarded this attribution by keeping a censored minister in the cabinet in late 1991. More importantly, he closed Congress in April 1992, revamped the constitution, and strengthened presidential powers.

As regards governments' capacity to marshal support, party strength, which was high in Venezuela and medium-high in Argentina, yet low in Brazil and Peru (Mainwaring and Scully 1995: 17), cannot account for the political success of market reforms in Argentina and Peru and their failure in Brazil under Collor and Venezuela under Pérez. For instance, a fairly disciplined governing party in a centripetal system with two predominant parties helped President Menem enact neoliberal policies (Packenham 1994: 8–9) but offered stubborn passive resistance to similar measures enacted by President Pérez.[9] Also, President Fujimori, who lacked backing from an organized party, managed to maintain high levels of popular support for years. By contrast, President Pérez became highly unpopular despite the long-standing societal roots of his Acción Democrática party.[10]

Formal institutions thus seem to have a limited impact on the initiation, implementation, and political success of neoliberal reform. In general, formal rules do not reliably guide and channel political activity in Latin America. Instead, they are often bent, broken, or changed (Chalmers 1977). As a result, divergences between constitutional provisions and actual practice are often stark in the region. For instance, in an audacious paraconstitutional move, President Menem vastly extended the use of decree powers that had been used only under exceptional conditions before (Ferreira Rubio and Goretti 1998: 33, 41–45). The application of formal-institutionalist reasoning to Latin America therefore rests on precarious foundations.

Most importantly, formal institutions are not "given" constraints on political action but are subject to change. While rules may impose restrictions on leaders, severe crises allow these leaders to overhaul the institutional framework, as the case of Fujimori reveals. It is therefore questionable to use formal rules as the central independent variable in political analysis.[11] In fact, formal institutionalism faces an important

---

[9] The social unrest and political conflict triggered by Pérez's drastic neoliberal reforms weakened party strength in Venezuela.

[10] Mainwaring (1999: 310–11) acknowledges Peru and Venezuela as exceptions.

[11] Haggard and Kaufman (1995: chap. 4) avoid this problem by explaining the character of the institutional framework in new democracies with an economic crisis argument.

endogeneity problem: The official "rules of the game" may not provide the *explanation* for political processes and outcomes but instead be the *product* of such processes. For instance, a two-party system may not be the outcome of an electoral system of single-member-district plurality, but be the cause of these rules, which two predominant parties may have enacted to perpetuate their predominance. The causal status of formal institutions is therefore unclear.

Institutionalist arguments that put less emphasis on formal rules are not fully persuasive either. The above-mentioned claim that long-established democracies are more willing and able to impose tough adjustment than recently inaugurated civilian regimes invokes a concept of institutionalization centered on habituation, valuation, and consolidation (cf. Huntington 1968: 12; Selznick 1957: 17–19). In line with this argument, Argentina, Brazil, and Peru did avoid drastic neoliberal stabilization immediately after their return to democracy in the early to mid-1980s.[12] Only at the end of the decade, when democracy had presumably become more consolidated, did these countries adopt shock programs.

But the consolidation argument cannot account for the decision of President Víctor Paz Estenssoro (1985–89) to decree full-scale market reform in Bolivia in 1985, only three years after an exceedingly precarious regime transition. Paz Estenssoro took this bold step despite the prevailing instability, which forced his predecessor to step down one year ahead of schedule. By contrast, market reforms faced great difficulties and suffered a clear reversal in Venezuela's longstanding, seemingly consolidated democracy. Indeed, the very notion of regime consolidation is questionable: Przeworski et al. (1996: 50) and Remmer (1996: 623) find that increasing age does not make a democracy less prone to breakdown. Thus, the consolidation argument seems questionable on both empirical and theoretical grounds.

In sum, institutional factors such as presidential powers, party system structure, and regime consolidation cannot account for the adoption and political fate of neoliberal reform. In general, institutional structures are by nature static and cannot explain the impetus of change, such as the move from heterodox to orthodox adjustment. What accounts for such a new departure?

Ideational Theories

Ideational theories claim to fill the gap left in institutionalist arguments by focusing on change over time. These theories emphasize the interna-

---

[12] In Peru, however, President Belaúnde's government (1980–85) adopted orthodox stabilization policies (Conaghan and Malloy 1994: chap. 6), though inconsistently and with limited zeal.

tional diffusion of ideas, policy learning by elites, and value shifts among the citizenry (Kahler 1992: 123–31; Edwards 1995: chap. 3; Teichman 2001; see in general P. Hall 1993; Goldstein and Keohane 1993). Accordingly, the promotion of neoliberal thinking by the IFIs and the Reagan government gradually took root in Latin America. For instance, more and more Latin American economists obtained graduate degrees from U.S. universities. This spread of neoliberal ideas rein-forced—and was reinforced by—the inferences that Latin American policy-makers drew from their own experiences with different economic policies and development models. Most importantly, the failures of the heterodox adjustment efforts in Argentina, Brazil, and Peru during the mid-1980s appeared as evidence that alternatives to neoliberalism were unpromising. In general, the collapse of communism seemed to prove that capitalism was the only viable system and that a "third way" of economic nationalism and heavy state intervention—as in Latin Amer-ica's import-substitution industrialization—was doomed to failure. The sustained growth achieved in Chile after 1985 and the tremendous suc-cess of the East Asian newly industrialized countries (NICs) seemed to show, by contrast, that market-oriented policies opened the path to prosperity. Thus, the economic policy experiences of the 1980s ap-peared to confirm the neoliberal ideas promoted by IFIs and the U.S. government.

Certainly, the validity of these inferences was questionable. For in-stance, alternatives to orthodoxy may well be feasible (Bresser Pereira, Maravall, and Przeworski 1993; Sheahan 1994; see also Waterbury 1989: 50–52). Also, the East Asian NICs did not apply free-market policies, but heavy state interventionism (Wade 1990; Gereffi and Wy-man 1990). Thus, policy-makers' learning was partly ideological, not purely rational.[13] Yet regardless of the truth value of their convictions, political leaders' conversion to neoliberalism induced them—according to ideational arguments—to adopt the orthodox recipes of the IFIs and revamp the established development model (Kahler 1992: 123–31; Ed-wards 1995: chap. 3).

Ideational theorists argue that a similar value shift occurred among the citizenry as nationalist, state-centered economic orientations receded and free-market ideas gained increasing support. This cultural change arose from people's daily frustration with the tremendous inefficiency, red tape, privileges for "special interests," and corruption associated

---

[13] Peter Hall (1993: 279–80, 284–92) likens the replacement of one economic ap-proach by an alternative to a "paradigm shift" (Kuhn 1970). Ideational arguments thus diverge from rational-choice accounts, which see learning as approximation of the truth. Ideational arguments, by contrast, maintain that policy-makers may well draw the wrong lessons from earlier experiences (e.g., Jervis 1976).

with extensive state interventionism. Revolted at these obstacles to free initiative, more and more people embraced economic liberalism. This conversion is said to explain widespread popular support for market reform, including the surprising acceptance of draconian adjustment (Mora y Araujo 1993: 311–21; review in Navarro 1995: 452–54).

These ideational arguments contribute to a comprehensive understanding of the neoliberal "revolution." In particular, learning from other countries' experiences and the international diffusion of ideas help explain the wavelike character of market reforms. But these explanations are not fully convincing. It is doubtful whether leading policymakers truly converted to orthodox economic ideas. For instance, Venezuela's Pérez roundly rejects the "neoliberal" label (Ovalles 1996: 127, 178; see also Naím 1993a: 82–83); in fact, while pursuing market reforms, he kept attacking the IMF with strong leftist slogans (Pérez 1989: 36, 49). Similarly, devoted neoliberals, such as Alvaro Alsogaray and Domingo Cavallo in Argentina and Carlos Boloña in Peru, question the ideological commitment of presidents Menem and Fujimori to the market credo (Alsogaray 1993: 171; Cavallo 1997: 273–74; Boloña 1993: ix, 28, 202). In their view, the two presidents enacted structural adjustment not out of deep conviction, but for pragmatic reasons, namely, in response to IFI pressures, acute economic crises, and the need to restore public authority. Thus, it seems that market reforms are triggered not only by learning and ideological conversion, but also by instrumental calculations and political decisions. In particular, chief executives use neoliberal policies to weaken established politicians and vested interest groups and to enhance their own political autonomy and power (cf. Weyland 1996c). Ideas thus do not determine policy shifts but are chosen in part for political reasons (cf. P. Hall 1993: 286, 289; see also J. Hall 1993: 43–47).

It is similarly questionable whether the 1980s saw a massive move from nationalist state-centrism to neoliberalism among the mass public that could account for the drastic policy changes initiated at the end of the decade. Even the data presented by the advocates of this argument show only a moderate change (Mora y Araujo 1993: 313–15).[14] Surveys conducted by other pollsters clearly do not find a dramatic value shift before the initiation of market reform (interview with Römer 1997; Stokes and Baughman 1998).[15] In fact, analyses of Latin American polit-

---

[14] In fact, frustration with red tape and corruption under the state-interventionist development model need not prompt people to embrace neoliberalism; they may instead reject the old elite that administered this development model and support an anti-neoliberal, such as Hugo Chávez in Venezuela.

[15] People's economic policy orientations changed more significantly *after* the enactment of neoliberalism (Carrión 1995; chapter 7 below).

ical culture during the last few decades suggest that people's economic policy orientations remained fairly stable through the 1980s. Already in the early 1960s, a majority of Latin Americans had rejected state ownership of enterprises and other aspects of the nationalist, state-interventionist development model. Thus, "in no way [was there] a mass conversion to free-market orientations" in the 1980s (Turner and Elordi 1995: 486).

Even to the extent that value shifts did occur, ideational arguments do not provide a full explanation for neoliberal reform because they point to intervening — not independent — variables. The very notions of learning and cultural change raise the question of what caused people's conversion to new ideas. Thus, arguments about cultural change cannot remain purely ideational but need to invoke other factors as root causes of this change.[16] For instance, the policy successes and failures from which decision-makers and citizens learned helped to induce these value shifts. And since chief executives embraced the new policy paradigm not only out of intellectual conviction, but also for instrumental reasons (see above), political interests shaped policy learning (cf. P. Hall 1993: 286–90). Ideational explanations for neoliberal reform therefore require integration with other accounts — both economic-structural accounts of the experiences that triggered learning, and theories of political choice that elucidate the purpose of adopting new policy models.

Rational-Choice Models

Whereas the preceding explanations stress context factors, rational-choice models focus directly on the decisions of leaders and citizens. These theories can be classified into two main categories, namely, distributional models designed by economists and decision models advanced by political scientists. Both of these currents seek to explain why, despite deepening economic problems, governments put off adjustment for many years — and why they eventually shifted course and adopted determined stabilization measures that they had avoided so long. For economists, who stress the long-term benefits of stabilization, the main challenge is to construct a rational explanation for the lengthy postponement of adjustment. For political scientists, who emphasize the social and political costs of stabilization, the tougher question is why governments finally mustered the courage to impose adjustment.

---

[16] Inglehart (1997) invokes increasing prosperity as the ultimate cause. Similarly, Eckstein (1988) focuses on the cultural effects of change, but treats this change itself as exogenous.

Economic-Distributional Models

Economists assume that despite their short-term costs, stabilization plans are beneficial for society in the long run by restoring economic equilibrium, the precondition for sustained growth and development. Why then do many governments refuse for years to combat worsening economic difficulties in a determined fashion? To account for this puzzle, economists point to distributional conflicts in society. Different classes or sectors fight over the allocation of the burden of adjustment. While these actors share a collective interest in economic stability, none of them wants to pay the price of stabilization. This incentive to "beggar-thy-neighbor" hinders adjustment, and further economic deterioration results. Distributional conflict thus produces a "war of attrition" (Alesina and Drazen 1991): Each group seeks to hold out while hoping that the increasing costs of the worsening economic crisis will force another group to capitulate and agree to bearing a disproportionate share of the adjustment burden. Once one of the warring groups throws in the towel or is defeated politically (for instance, in a realigning election or a military coup), adjustment proceeds smoothly. Thus, the deepening economic crisis finally outweighs distributional concerns and paves the way for stabilization policies that enhance collective welfare in the long run (Drazen and Grilli 1993).

In a similar vein, Rodrik (1994) stresses the distributional costs of trade reform, which are quite high, compared to the distributional gains and the welfare benefits that greater competitiveness and efficiency produce for society as a whole. As a result, the prospective losing sectors often manage to block trade reform. According to Rodrik, only a profound economic crisis, characterized especially by hyperinflation, transforms this constellation of interests. When drastic economic deterioration looms, the collective benefits of stabilization outweigh its distributional costs. Under these dire circumstances, it is possible to enact trade reform as part of a package of stabilization measures. Once again, deep crises provide the impetus for adjustment because they threaten to create massive losses that dwarf distributional concerns.

These models make an important contribution by systematically addressing the role of economic crises, which empirical analyses have found to be crucial triggers of drastic policy reform (Bates and Krueger 1993: 452–54; Bienen 1990; Haggard and Kaufman 1995: chap. 6). By designing deductive models to account for these inductive findings, economists help to clarify the logic of crisis arguments. Furthermore, these economic crisis models usefully diverge from the linear thinking that is predominant in the contemporary social sciences. Rather than assuming the perpetuation of problems and continuous decline, they advance the dialectical argument that problems can potentially stimulate efforts at improvement. This argument better accounts for the frequently observed cyclical patterns in economic and political development, which lead, for instance, to "the rise and decline of nations" (cf. Olson 1982; see also Kennedy 1987).

But these models — especially Drazen and Grilli (1993) — appear too functionalist in postulating that a deepening crisis will sooner or later lead to adjustment, and that adjustment will restore economic stability and growth. Based on their underlying rationality premise, economists assume that the initiators of adjustment will choose appropriate stabilization measures, which will have beneficial outcomes for society. But this optimistic view does not do justice to the tremendous uncertainty that surrounds drastic policy reform. Economic experts often disagree on the best stabilization measures; even in the era of neoliberal intellectual hegemony, there is a wide repertoire of policies to choose from, which ranges from tough austerity measures over pacted incomes policies to the temporary confiscation of financial assets. The technical soundness of certain adjustment policies — e.g., of Argentina's Bunge & Born plan of 1989 or of the second Collor Plan of early 1991 — is open to question, and the implementation of well-conceived programs may well be suboptimal.[17] Furthermore, economists pay little attention to the social and political repercussions of deep crises and draconian adjustment policies. While there may indeed be "benefit[s] of crisis for economic reforms" (Drazen and Grilli 1993), the fallout for politics may be disastrous if distributional conflict is "resolved" through a brutal military coup, for instance. Thus, the Panglossian view of market reform that underlies economic crisis models is problematic.

Economic-distributional models also overemphasize the role of societal sectors and classes and pay insufficient attention to politicians and the state, which may have considerable autonomy from societal groups. Empirical investigations of the politics of market reform show that opposition from business and labor, for instance, is much less crucial than these distributional arguments claim (Bates and Krueger 1993: 455–57; Geddes 1994a: 109–13). Political actors, such as politicians, parties, and state agencies, play a more central role in resisting neoliberal policies, and especially in initiating them.

Economic-distributional models are especially deficient in failing to elucidate the political motivations for governments to initiate market reform. Their assumption that sociopolitical forces are driven mostly by

[17] For instance, the first Collor Plan overshot in its liquidity freeze, but in response, the government opened many loopholes, releasing liquidity too rapidly (Andrei et al. 1995: 46–48).

the desire for economic gain is questionable. Politics—including the politics of market reform—raises not only issues of distribution, but also issues of domination and control (in general, Krasner 1984: 224–25). Governments and politicians, in particular, do not pursue first and foremost economic goals, but political goals, including both instrumental goals (such as maintaining themselves in power) and substantive goals (such as advancing their own ideology). Therefore, the economic argument that neoliberal policies bring long-run economic benefits by no means provides a sufficient motivation for politicians to adopt such reforms. Throughout history, governments have often adopted suboptimal economic policies to further their own political goals (e.g., North 1981, Bates 1981). It is therefore necessary to examine the political purposes that governments pursued by implementing market reforms.

In sum, economic-distributional models provide a one-dimensional perspective by underestimating the autonomy and importance of politics. It is precisely this gap that political decision models seek to fill.

Political Decision Models

In the 1980s, adherents of rational choice elaborated elegant and compelling explanations for the long postponement of adjustment. According to this line of reasoning, politicians used public policy to dole out patronage to a wide range of supporters (Bates 1981; Geddes 1994b). They therefore shied away from determined stabilization measures (Ames 1987: 214; Geddes 1994b: 104, 178–79), which would impose losses—not benefits—on important social sectors and political forces, thus carry heavy political costs, and endanger the political survival of the reform initiators. Viewed from this perspective, the sudden willingness of many governments to shoulder these risks and enact drastic stabilization measures came as a surprise (as stressed by Grindle 1991: 58–62; 1999: 15–20). What accounts for these unexpected decisions?

In a particularly interesting essay, Geddes (1994a) argues that the willingness to adopt tough stabilization measures depends on chief executives who rise to power as outsiders and who thus lacked the opportunity to provide patronage to their own followers. The substantial cost of adjustment policies therefore does not fall on the allies of the new chief executives, but instead burdens the cronies of their predecessors, that is, their political rivals. Cutbacks in public employment, for instance, hurt the patronage appointees of earlier governments. Thus, whereas leaders who have held office for many years or their hand-picked successors are reluctant to enact painful reforms and thus dismantle their own patronage networks, newcomers, who have not been able to pack the public administration with their own supporters, do not face this constraint. Indeed, they use neoliberal reforms as a welcome excuse to dismiss the cronies of their predecessors and thus increase their own margin of maneuver.

While Geddes focuses on the motives driving neoliberal reform, other authors elucidate the strategies that chief executives adopt. In his seminal study, Przeworski (1991: 162–80) argues that the initiators of market reform prefer drastic over gradual measures in order to pay the costs of adjustment quickly and to make neoliberal restructuring irreversible. Many voters support draconian policies despite the transitional costs if they have confidence in their capacity to restore economic stability and eventually reignite growth. In an excellent complementary discussion, Acuña and Smith (1994: 31–41) claim that during economic crises and the initial stages of adjustment, people have particularly low capacity for collective action and therefore refrain from protest. Stabilization and recovery, however, enable more and more citizens to engage in collective action and induce them to voice long-repressed demands, which may threaten the continuation of adjustment policies in the long run.

Political decision models make a crucial contribution by shedding light on the political motivations that underlie the enactment of drastic adjustment. As argued above in criticizing economic-structural perspectives, economic constraints and external pressures cannot fully account for the initiation of market reform; Latin American governments did retain a certain margin of choice. And as explained in the preceding section, economic crisis models cannot fill this gap because they consider only economic goals and disregard political aims. By clarifying the specifically political rationale of the initiation of market reform, political decision models help explain the politics of neoliberalism.

Political leaders can strategically distribute the massive costs and substantial benefits of these reforms in order to weaken their adversaries and reward their supporters.[18] For instance, they can use austerity measures to deprive their opponents of access to patronage; they can protect their own supporters from costly transformations, at least temporarily (cf. Gibson 1997: 359–70); and they can channel benefits — such as favorable privatization deals or proceeds from the sale of public enterprises — to their backers among entrepreneurs and politicians. Pressure from the IFIs provides a technical justification for these measures, which are often guided by thoroughly political goals. Thus, political decision models help explain why politicians, when facing considerable

---

[18] For an emphasis on the political purposes and payoffs of market reforms from a non-rational-choice perspective, see Weyland (1996c).

economic constraints and external pressures, choose to enact tough, painful reforms.

Specifically, Geddes's argument that political outsiders are the most willing to enact painful reforms fits the cases under investigation: Alberto Fujimori was a complete newcomer to politics; Fernando Collor was marginal to the national political elite; and even Carlos Menem and Carlos Andrés Pérez — while having played important roles in national politics before — were mavericks who had used populist political tactics to wrest the presidential candidacy away from the entrenched leadership of their own parties. By contrast, the predecessors of these new leaders — especially Raúl Alfonsín in Argentina (1983–89), José Sarney in Brazil (1985–90), and Jaime Lusinchi in Venezuela (1984–89) — had much closer ties to the political establishment. Thus, the presidents who adopted market reforms were in fact (relative) outsiders.

The outsider argument, however, constitutes a very proximate explanation. Above all, it does not explain why newcomers won office and thus had the opportunity to revamp economic policy. Institutionalist accounts help to fill this gap to some extent. The character of the party system, in particular, plays an important role.[19] Where the party system is fractionalized and inchoate, as in Brazil and Peru (Mainwaring and Scully 1995), newcomers to the national political elite can quickly rise to the top. In established two-party systems, by contrast, complete dark-horse candidates do not have a chance; the victorious outsiders emerge from the "out" faction of one of the predominant parties.[20] But institutionalist arguments yield only permissive causes and do not elucidate the impulse for the rise of outsiders. They therefore need to be combined with other theories. Given that these outsiders emerged under democracy, it is especially important to explain why citizens rejected established politicians and voted for notorious mavericks or complete newcomers. As the governmental performance of these outsiders was hard to predict, voters made risky choices. Why was a plurality or majority of citizens willing to incur such risks?

Przeworski's argument provides another piece of the adjustment puzzle. It helps explain why politicians who, for whatever reason, are committed to neoliberalism prefer drastic shock programs over more prudent, gradual adjustment measures. The desire to make reform irreversible constitutes an important motivation for such boldness. The ef-

---

[19] By contrast, specific electoral rules, which vary considerably across countries, cannot account for the rise of outsiders in several nations in 1989–90.

[20] Rafael Caldera, who won the Venezuelan presidency in 1993, had for decades been the leader of the Comité de Organización Política Electoral Independiente (COPEI), but he bolted when the entrenched party apparatus sought to block his bid for the candidacy.

fort to use the political capital that election victors have at the beginning of their term (Remmer 1993) and the need to signal to investors and creditors the government's firm commitment to neoliberalism (Rodrik 1989) provide additional reasons for this Machiavellian strategy of imposing unavoidable costs immediately (cf. Machiavelli 1947: 26). In fact, some governments deliberately overshoot stabilization targets in order to establish the credibility of their adjustment policies in the eyes of domestic and foreign investors and thus prevent these actors from forming self-fulfilling prophecies that the shock plan will fail (Rodrik 1989).

But despite their important contributions, these arguments are not fully convincing. Rodrik's signaling hypothesis fits only some of the cases under investigation. It is most persuasive where the new presidents enact drastic shock programs that they rejected as candidates. In these cases of stunning policy shifts (Stokes 2001a), new presidents use particularly brutal stabilization measures to "prove" their conversion to neoliberalism. But Rodrik's argument cannot explain why Fernando Collor, who ran on a platform of market reform, obtained an electoral mandate for these policies, and therefore did not face credibility problems, nevertheless imposed a much more draconian, audacious stabilization plan than expected. In fact, the most violent measure — the temporary asset freeze — antagonized the presumed audience of credibility signals, private business. The confiscation did not induce this crucial sector to cooperate with the government's adjustment policies but made it wary of the new president's unpredictability and impulsiveness (see debates in Bornhausen 1991). Thus, Rodrik's signaling argument cannot establish the rationality of Collor's boldness and therefore fails to account for this important case.

Similarly, Przeworski's argument cannot fully explain why leaders finally shouldered the high economic and political risks of adopting draconian policies that their predecessors had avoided for years. Przeworski's model of reform initiation presupposes a much higher propensity toward risk than the earlier rational-choice explanations for the postponement of reform had assumed (e.g., Bates 1981: chaps. 5–6; Ames 1987: 73, 214). But Przeworski does not justify this premise of risk acceptance nor account for the shift from longstanding risk aversion to eventual risk acceptance. Instead, rational-choice models commonly make ad hoc assumptions concerning leaders' propensities toward risk. Similarly, Przeworski does not explain why many citizens would have strong confidence in the eventual success of adjustment. People normally have "incredibly high" discount rates (Thaler 1992: 94), which prevent them from accepting short-term pain for long-term gain. Why did citizens deviate from this common tendency and accept great risks by endorsing neoliberal reform before its beneficial effects materialized? Przeworski's important model thus has a gap by leaving leaders' and citizens' shift from risk aversion to risk acceptance unexplained.

Moreover, presidents who had accepted great risks when facing crises turned to risk aversion after economic recovery began in cases of successful adjustment. Rather than persisting in their strong, daring push for market reform, they soon relaxed their politically risky efforts. Contrary to the demands of the international financial institutions and of domestic experts, they were reluctant to complete the process of restructuring and instead got stuck "in the middle of the path" toward transformation.[21] In sum, rational choice offers an insufficient explanation because it does not systematically account for these twists and turns in leaders' propensity toward risk.

Finally, Acuña and Smith (1994) make a crucial theoretical contribution by examining the opportunities for and constraints on collective action during economic crisis and reform. This focus on collective action is especially relevant to the analysis of market reform under democracy, which guarantees freedom of association. Specifically, Acuña and Smith's innovative argument helps account for the infrequency of protest against neoliberalism, which made it possible to implement painful measures without the "need" to resort to massive repression and, especially, authoritarian rule.

Opinion polls suggest, however, that Acuña and Smith may underestimate the strength of popular support for market reform in a number of countries, especially Argentina and Peru in the early to mid-1990s. Low capacity for collective action during times of economic hardship was not the only reason for citizens to refrain from protesting against drastic stabilization measures. Instead, many people actively supported their leaders' rescue efforts, at least as the lesser evil (Weyland 1998c: 550–52). Similarly, the prediction that many citizens would quickly escalate their demands once economic recovery set in did often not come true. Instead, many citizens were willing to keep their demands moderate in order not to endanger the recently restored economic stability. And where economic growth resumed, as in Argentina (1991–94) and Peru (1993–95), clear majorities voted for the incumbent in presidential elections. Thus, once the economy turns around, many citizens proceed with greater caution and less militancy than Acuña and Smith predict.

---

[21] Boloña (1993: ix, 179, 202); CEA (1997: 57–101). The latter study's main author was Juan Llach, a former top aide to Economy Minister Domingo Cavallo.

People appear reluctant to risk the benefits that restored economic equilibrium and renewed growth bring.[22] This risk aversion contrasts strikingly with the risk acceptance that underlay the willingness of many people to support the bold adjustment plans enacted at the nadir of the economic crisis. Once again, people's propensity toward risk plays an important role, which is left unexplained by rational choice models.

Conclusion

This chapter has shown that economic-structural, political-institutional, ideational, and rational-choice theories do not yield fully convincing explanations for the politics of economic adjustment. While these arguments make a number of valuable contributions, they also have important weaknesses or lacunae. Political leaders in fact face powerful pressures from external market forces and international financial institutions, but they have more latitude for choice than economic structuralists claim. Similarly, political institutions create crucial opportunities and constraints for political action, but leaders can often bend and, under certain conditions, reshape these strictures. Finally, ideas and the lessons of prior experiences can foreclose certain policy options and predispose decision-makers toward other solutions, but ideational theories downplay the political goals of politicians, which even shape their learning from earlier experiences.

Rational-choice models rectify these problems by stressing "choice" over "structure" and by emphasizing the political motivations and calculations underlying market reform. But these neat and parsimonious models do not include important factors and rely instead on ad hoc assumptions, for instance, on actors' shifting propensity toward risk. To overcome this deficit, the following chapter draws on theories that systematically account for crucial factors neglected by rational choice. In this way, it proposes an alternative microfoundation for a comprehensive theory of adjustment politics.

[22] In line with my prospect-theory interpretation, support for market reform and its initiators diminished substantially once the economy deteriorated again in the mid- and late 1990s, as chapter 7 analyzes. Furthermore, success in combating catastrophic threats such as hyperinflation boosts presidential popularity only for a limited time; this effect soon begins to fade as presidents' very success in restoring stability allows citizens to shift their attention to other pressing issues, such as economic growth and employment creation. Governmental performance in those areas therefore becomes decisive (Weyland 2000; chapter 7 below).

CHAPTER THREE

A NEW EXPLANATION
OF ADJUSTMENT POLITICS

Existing explanations of adjustment politics are not fully convincing, so this chapter proposes a more persuasive account by drawing on psychological theories of decision-making, especially prospect theory (Kahneman and Tversky 1979, 2000; Tversky and Kahneman 1992). These cognitive-psychological arguments are based on observed empirical regularities, not on ideal-typical postulates, like rational choice. And they provide a systematic account of crucial factors that rational choice treats ad hoc, especially changes in leaders' and citizens' propensities toward risk. For these reasons, cognitive-psychological theories constitute a more solid foundation for explaining adjustment politics than the paradigm that is currently on the advance in the field of comparative politics.

Psychological decision theories share with rational choice a focus on individual decision-making and choice, rather than structural determinants. Like rational-choice explanations (see recently Bates et al. 1998), these theories therefore cannot stand on their own but need to consider the context of opportunities and constraints, which the explanations discussed in chapter 2 elucidate. Specifically, economic-structural and political-institutional theories help account for the available decision options and the probabilities of attaining the intended outcomes, and ideational theories elucidate actors' preferences and the subjective payoffs they attach to different decision options. Thus, a comprehensive explanation—which is most appropriate for a case-oriented study—requires integrating elements of "choice" and "structure."

The present chapter discusses relevant cognitive-psychological findings, applies these insights to political analysis, and embeds them in an ideational, structural, and institutional context. In this way, it proposes a novel argument and synthesizes it with the valuable elements of established theories.

Psychological Decision Theories

In criticizing economic-structural and sociological-institutional arguments, advocates of rational choice have demanded that explanations have microfoundations (e.g., Przeworski 1985: 92–97; Tsebelis 1990: 19–24; Knight 1992: 4–18). In this methodologically individualist view, only individuals are actors; collectivities are aggregations of individuals, not actors in their own right; and institutional structures are products of the interplay of individual choices. Scholarly accounts therefore need to derive all political phenomena from individual choices. Holistic explanations that invoke supra-individual factors — such as economic structures, culture, or institutions — and depict them as shaping individuals are declared illegitimate and often denounced as functionalist.

My argument can pass this test: It rests on a clear microfoundation,[1] namely, cognitive-psychological findings on human choice. Arguably, these empirical insights, amply corroborated in experiments and field studies, provide a more solid microfoundation for explanations than the ideal-typical postulates of rational choice, which make unrealistic assumptions about human capacities for processing information. Any theory of choice that has an empirical purpose is well advised to start from empirical findings on human choice. Since the main psychological results I draw on have a situational character — risk-seeking *in the domain of losses* vs. risk aversion *in the domain of gains* — they also provide a more logical basis for incorporating macrofactors that fit less comfortably in methodologically individualist rational-choice accounts.[2]

Insights on Risk Propensity

Psychological theories of decision-making, especially prospect theory (Payne, Bettman, and Johnson 1992; Kahneman and Tversky 1979, 1984, 2000; Tversky and Kahneman 1992), provide the core of my explanation for the politics of neoliberal reform. Prospect theory's central empirical finding is that people tend toward risk-acceptant behavior when confronted with threats to their well-being but are cautious when facing more auspicious prospects.[3] Crises trigger bold actions, while bet-

---

[1] This does not imply an endorsement of rational choice's exclusive emphasis on microfoundations, which is problematic (Weyland 2002: 74–75).

[2] The following two sections draw heavily on Weyland (1998b: 648–57).

[3] For reasons of simplicity and clarity, this study draws only on the central finding of prospect theory and does not consider other interesting results concerning the way in which people frame decision options and subjectively weigh the probabilities of these scenarios' occurrence. Whereas books that focus on a limited number of decisions can analyze these different aspects (McDermott 1998), constraints of time and space force the present study, which examines policy-making in four nations over twenty years, to concentrate on prospect theory's most notable finding.

ter times induce risk aversion.[4] This finding systematically accounts for shifts in people's propensities toward risk, which extant rational-choice arguments leave unexplained.

Prospect theory's insights stand in clear contrast to conventional versions of expected utility theory, the rational-choice model of decision-making. The standard variant of expected utility theory postulates that among the available alternatives, people choose the option that offers the highest level of absolute value. Thus, "the standard utility function . . . is defined on wealth, or final asset position" (Quattrone and Tversky 1988: 720). In addition, conventional expected utility theories assume decreasing marginal utility: Subjective value diminishes with increasing wealth. A person who owns one dollar attributes greater value to gaining another dollar than a millionaire does. In technical terms, the standard utility function is concave. This postulate implies universal risk aversion as people prefer, for instance, a sure gain of $50 over a lottery in which they have a 50 percent chance of winning $100 and a 50 percent chance of winning nothing (see Kahneman and Tversky 1984: 342).

Prospect theory's findings diverge from these postulates. As innumerable experiments show, people make decisions based not on absolute levels of value, but in terms of relative gains and losses, using the status quo as their normal point of reference. Indeed, people act quite differently depending on whether they face gains or losses. Their subjective value function is concave only in the domain of gains, but convex in the domain of losses. When dealing with gains, they act on the principle of decreasing marginal utility and therefore adopt risk aversion. Yet when confronting prospects of losses, people also attribute greater importance to values that are less far removed from the reference point (decreasing marginal *dis*utility) and disproportionately shun small losses; they are therefore risk-acceptant in the hope of avoiding all losses. And since people display strong loss aversion, their subjective value function is "considerably steeper for losses than for gains" (Kahneman and Tversky 1984: 342). Accordingly, a loss causes subjective discomfort of greater magnitude than the pleasure created by an objectively equivalent gain. The resulting value function has the shape of an asymmetrical "S" (figure 3.1).

This value function has profound implications for decision-making.

---

[4] Due to the common tendency toward (unrealistic) optimism (Taylor and Brown 1988), only severe crises put a majority of people in the domain of losses. For the distortions that excessive optimism creates in people's economic assessments, see Haller and Norpoth (1994).

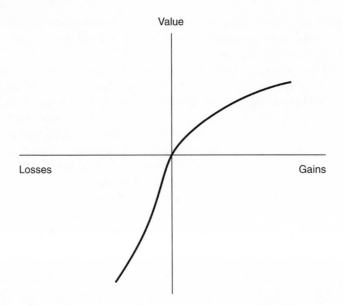

Figure 3.1. The Value Function of Prospect Theory. *Source:* Kahneman and Tversky (1984: 342).

Since people assess options in terms of gains vs. losses and display marked loss aversion, they imbue the status quo — their usual reference point — with a special legitimacy (Kahneman, Knetsch, and Thaler 1990): They defend it more fiercely against threats of losses than they seek further improvements. Decisions thus differ depending on whether a person faces prospects of gains or losses. When faced with the choice between different possibilities of gains, people tend to select risk-averse options (sure bets). They regularly prefer a certain gain of smaller magnitude to a less likely gain of much higher magnitude even if the expected value of the latter option (the product of its probability times its value) exceeds that of the former. In the domain of losses, however, many people opt for risk-seeking: They shun a certain loss of small magnitude and prefer instead a lottery that contains the promise of avoiding any loss, but also the risk of a big loss. The aversion to a certain, if moderate, loss induces them to choose this risky option even if — due to the low probability of avoiding all losses — its expected value is lower than the limited decline of the former option.

The following two choice situations provide examples of risk aversion in the domain of gains and risk acceptance in the domain of losses. In the first situation, people are asked to choose between a sure gain of $100 or a lottery that offers a 50 percent chance of winning $220 and a

50 percent chance of no gain. In this choice between different options of gains, two-thirds to three quarters of experimental subjects display risk aversion and select the safe option of $100.[5] Since the lottery has higher expected value — namely, $110 — these people make an excessively cautious choice, which diverges from strict cost-benefit calculations. Thus, they do not act in a conventionally rational fashion. In the second situation, people are asked to choose between a sure loss of $100 or a lottery that holds a 50 percent chance of losing $220 and a 50 percent chance of no loss. In this choice between different options of losses, two-thirds to three quarters of experimental subjects display risk acceptance and select the lottery, hoping to avoid any loss.[6] Since the lottery has lower expected value — namely, −$110 compared to the −$100 of the sure loss — all these people make an excessively daring choice, which again diverges from conventionally rational calculations (cf. Kahneman and Tversky 1979: 264–69; 1984: 341–43). The fact that depending on domain, experimental subjects shift between pronounced risk aversion and clear risk acceptance poses a particular challenge to expected utility arguments (Haas 2001: 252).

As these striking findings suggest, people tend toward prudence in their efforts to advance but are daring in their determination to avoid setbacks. When confronted with threats, they hedge their bets on the unlikely prospect of recouping the status quo, which risky choices offer, rather than accept a certain yet limited loss. In situations involving a single choice, risk aversion thus prevails in the domain of gains, whereas in the domain of losses, people tend toward risk acceptance.

Life is more complex, however, as choices arise sequentially. How do prior gains or losses affect future decisions? The outcomes of earlier decisions influence the reference point for assessing later gains and losses. Specifically, most people quickly assimilate gains by raising their reference point. This makes them see the reduction of a recent gain as a loss, a perception that tends to induce risk acceptance. By contrast to the quick assimilation of gains, people tend to retain the old status quo after suffering losses (Kahneman and Tversky 1979: 286–87). Clinging to the previous status quo as their reference point, many victims of privations see any option that falls short of restoring their prior position as involving a certain loss. To regain their "deserved" position, which they regard as their just endowment, they are willing to run consider-

---

[5] Thus, prospect theory is probabilistic, not deterministic.

[6] As the "lotteries" used in psychological experiments suggest, risk is a product of two factors: variance of outcomes (McDermott 1998), that is, width of the spread in the potential results of choice; and severity of the lowest-valued possible outcome, that is, its likelihood times value. Thus, risk is a product of unpredictability and potential cost (Weyland 1996d: 190).

able risks. This risk acceptance prevails especially when people who have suffered losses and who remain in the domain of losses face a decision option that offers the unlikely prospect of eliminating all earlier losses and recouping the old status quo, that is, of "breaking even" (Thaler and Johnson 1990: 657–59). In this situation, the uncertain hope to eliminate all losses triggers particular boldness. Thus, the endowment effect — people's tendency to regard the (old) status quo as their legitimate position — exacerbates risk-seeking in the domain of losses.

These experimental findings suggest a fairly conservative view of human decision-making. People tend to be cautious when pursuing improvements, and when trying to avoid losses, they are bold only in order to return to the status quo, their usual reference point. The endowment effect reinforces this concern with maintaining established positions. By prompting pronounced risk acceptance, however, threats to this conservative goal trigger the usage of bold means and may thus end up producing more profound change.

While prospect theory's findings were established through experiments, they are directly applicable to the "real world" outside the laboratory. Cognitive psychologists themselves have used prospect theory's insights to elucidate economic and political decision-making (e.g., Kahneman, Knetsch, and Thaler 1986; Quattrone and Tversky 1988). In fact, cognitive-psychological arguments have in recent years found a rapidly growing following among economists, challenging the long-standing predominance of conventional rationality assumptions (see especially Thaler 1992, 2000; Camerer 2000; McFadden 1999). This advance of "behavioral economics" has begun to transform the "dismal science" (*Economist* 1999; Lowenstein 2001; Uchitelle 2001). With less impact so far, a small but increasing number of political scientists has also drawn on prospect theory, especially in the field of international relations (Farnham 1994; Levy 1997; McDermott 1998; Stein and Pauly 1993; Haas 2001). This study uses the core result of prospect theory to shed light on the politics of economic stabilization and market reform.

One important caveat is in order, however, when applying cognitive-psychological findings outside the laboratory. Whereas experiments clearly define the payoffs and probabilities attached to different decision options, such precise information is unavailable in the "real world." Neither the numerical payoffs that policy-makers attach to different decision options nor their subjective probability estimates for the occurrence of these options can be ascertained with precision. As a result, the deviations from rational maximization predicted by psychological decision theories cannot be *proven* in any strict sense by analysts of politics. Yet for the same reason, the maximization postulates of rational choice cannot be proven either. Prospect theory thus faces exactly the same difficulties in empirical analysis as its main rival. In assessing the empirical value of prospect theory by comparison to rational choice, this study can therefore only achieve plausibility, not conduct a rigorous, "scientific" test (similar Haas 2001: 253).

In this spirit, I argue that risk-seeking in the domain of losses provides the central impetus for the adoption of draconian adjustment programs and their popular acceptance. It explains why heads of government take the risk to enact measures that neoliberal economists consider economically rational, but that political observers regard as politically irrational. Leaders who face severe crises tend to prefer daring countermeasures to more prudent adjustment policies, and many people endorse these bold efforts to save the country although they hold a substantial risk of failure and further deterioration.[7] Dramatic problems tend to put both leaders and citizens in the domain of losses and thus prompt a common tendency toward risk acceptance.

Economic or political crises put many people in the domain of losses. In crisis situations, further deterioration looms unless the government takes countermeasures — which is an unavoidable necessity because the status quo is utterly untenable. If these countermeasures are prudent and sequential, the ongoing deterioration is stopped only gradually, recovery will be slow in coming, and structural problems, which are not attacked head-on, may well persist. Thus, cautious policies entail a sure loss, but it has limited magnitude. If, by contrast, the government enacts comprehensive "packages" of drastic countermeasures, it takes a bold gamble: Given that the economic and political consequences of such shock plans are difficult to foresee, there is a substantial risk that a full-scale catastrophe — involving economic chaos and/or a breakdown of democracy — will erupt. But if the shock plan ends economic disequilibria and eliminates entrenched obstacles to prosperity, it can usher in a quick recovery and put the country back on a growth path. Determined shock plans thus hold the uncertain promise of rapidly stopping further losses and compensating for prior losses, but also the danger of a meltdown.

Crises thus pose a set of decision options that resemble the experimental design for the domain of losses. My prospect theory argument predicts that under these circumstances, political leaders and common citizens will display risk acceptance. Specifically, chief executives will prefer drastic countermeasures over more cautious policies,[8] and a clear majority of the population will endorse this risk-seeking choice.[9] Citizen

---

[7] While economists keep debating the economic wisdom of neoliberal shock treatment, it clearly holds grave political risks in the unstable Third World, as the introduction explained.

[8] Since presidents can impose many of these stabilization measures by decree, Congress's stance is of limited importance.

[9] Prospect theory thus provides a theoretical explanation for some of the cognitive

support helps the leader to stay the course on stabilization policies and to enact structural reforms as well.

By contrast, the enactment of market reform faces much greater political obstacles where a leader, who has access to confidential inside information, foresees an imminent, grave crisis, but many common citizens do not see the limited problems they are facing as foreshadowing a serious crisis. Where the government's and the people's economic assessments diverge in this fashion, the chief executive seeks to preempt the looming crisis with bold, drastic countermeasures, but many citizens do not share this risk acceptance and therefore reject the shock plan. Popular opposition weakens the reform-oriented government, threatens to undermine stabilization policies, and hinders structural reform.

In addition to accounting for variation across cases, prospect theory also helps explain change over time. In particular, it elucidates the subsequent political fate of shock programs that elicited initial popular support. If, despite their risks, these drastic plans overcome the acute, severe crisis, restore economic stability, and produce a recovery, political leaders enter the domain of gains and as a result turn to risk aversion. Chief executives therefore adopt more cautious policies and back away from the remaining part of the structural reform program that neoliberal experts and international financial institutions urge them to enact in its entirety. This move to risk aversion helps account for the frequently observed delay of the "second stage" of reforms. This delay arises not only from the technical difficulties of revamping economic and political institutions and from the need for broad political support, as Naím (1995), Nelson (1997), and Heredia and Schneider (1998) claim.[10] It also reflects the reluctance of chief executives who preside over an economic recovery to push as hard for further costly, risky changes as they did when combating the deep initial crisis.

---

schemes that people apply to assess economic policy (Stokes 2001b: 12–18). Specifically, risk-seeking in the domain of losses prompts an "intertemporal" stance: People accept short-term pain for the uncertain—i.e., risky—promise of long-term gain. By contrast, risk aversion in the domain of gains underlies "normal economic voting": People base their judgments on current costs and benefits, not uncertain future prospects.

[10] A factor that slowed down the completion of market reform in Eastern Europe—namely, the special benefits gained by early winners, who did not want to see these "rents" eroded by comprehensive liberalization (Hellman 1998)—had only a limited effect in Latin America. While some beneficiaries of early, ill-prepared privatization deals (especially in Argentina) resisted later regulation efforts, business offered strong support for most other second-stage reforms, especially the liberalization of labor laws, the privatization of social security and health care, the introduction of efficiency principles in the public administration, and many aspects of tax reform. Overall, the "rents" that Latin American market reforms provided to business groups served as an impulse for the advance of neoliberalism, not an obstacle (Schamis 1999).

If the end of the deep crisis and the return of growth begin to benefit broader sectors of the population or if people anticipate such "trickle down," an ever larger number of citizens also moves into the domain of gains. Therefore, they turn to risk aversion and prudently accept the new status quo. While becoming more reluctant to support additional neoliberal reforms, they embrace the basic outline of the newly instituted market model despite its flaws, rather than boldly pushing for drastic improvements. In a similar vein, a large number of people endorses the incumbent initiator of neoliberal reform at least as the lesser evil and refuses to support the opposition, which has not proven its capacity to administer the new development model and therefore constitutes a risky alternative. Due to this popular support, which is crucial in the age of opinion polls and media politics, the recently established market system achieves political sustainability.

This argument diverges from the claim based on rational-choice premises that the end of the initial crisis will lead people to demand compensation for their sacrifices and call for an immediate fulfillment of their needs. According to that line of reasoning, the first signs of recovery induce and enable people to advance the demands for rapid improvements that they had to postpone during the crisis. This outpouring of pent-up demands threatens to nip the recovery in the bud and to produce "an opposition majority that threatens the continuation of the reform process" (Acuña and Smith 1994: 40; see also 31–41). By contrast, my application of prospect theory expects that a country's emergence from the initial crisis enhances the political sustainability of the new market model.

In sum, prospect theory's insights about people's situationally defined propensity toward risk provide the core of a new explanation for the adoption and endorsement of drastic neoliberal measures, and a microfoundation for common insights on the role of crises in reform initiation (Bates and Krueger 1993: 452–54, 457; Bienen 1990: 729–30; Callaghy 1990: 263, 317; Grindle and Thomas 1991: chap. 4; Haggard and Kaufman 1995: 199–201; Waterbury 1993: 35, 67, 138, 157–58, 192, 265–66). But whereas several extant crisis arguments — especially Drazen and Grilli (1993) — assume positive, beneficial responses to problems,[11] my prospect-theory interpretation emphasizes the dangers inherent in risk-acceptant reactions to crises. In this way, it does justice to the economic problems caused by neoliberal shock treatment — as stressed by Bresser Pereira, Maravall, and Przeworski (1993) and Sheahan (1994) — and accounts better for the political failure of many initiators of adjustment, exemplified by the spectacular impeachment of

---

[11] Corrales (1996: chap. 4) therefore criticizes crisis arguments.

presidents Collor and Pérez. Thus, my cognitive-psychological interpretation captures the uncertainty and indeterminacy of crisis situations
(cf. Vierhaus 1978: 322) better than other crisis arguments, particularly
political economy models, as elaborated by Drazen and Grilli (1993)
and Rodrik (1994).[12]

The Prior-Option Bias

The shifts in risk propensity predicted by prospect theory are mediated
by people's strong "status-quo bias" or, more correctly, prior-option
bias.[13] Due to loss aversion, including a reluctance to admit failure, people tend to stick to an earlier choice and persist in an unpromising
course of action, hoping against all odds that it will finally bring success
and thus limit, or even erase, past losses. Taking into account sunk
costs — not only the prospects of future benefits, as strict rationality requires — they refuse to cut their losses and instead cling to established
strategies. This prior-option bias, which psychologists commonly find,
also reflects a deviation from rational value maximization (Samuelson
and Zeckhauser 1988; Arkes and Blumer 1985: 130–32; Thaler 1992:
63–78).

Translated into the terminology of prospect theory, the prior-option
bias skews people's assessment of different decision options. Given the
high cost of admitting the failure of earlier efforts and given the dangers
involved in drastically changing course, new departures appear to people who are clearly responsible for earlier choices as entailing unaccept-
ably high losses and risks. This makes the risk-averse option of staying
with the devil one knows more attractive. Thus, whereas people in the
domain of losses who are not subject to the prior-option bias choose to
take bold action, people who are trapped by the prior-option bias choose
the risk-averse option of continuing to pursue their earlier strategies. In
this way, they do not have to admit that the costs incurred so far are a
pure, unmitigated loss. Instead, desperately hoping that hitherto unsuccessful efforts will finally bring results, they can justify these costs as the
necessary effort ("investment") for eventually achieving success.

Applied to politics, this prior-option bias intensifies the "stickiness"
of earlier policy choices and prevents established political leaders, who
are clearly responsible for those decisions, from responding to new chal-

[12] On this advantage of prospect theory, see in general McDermott (1998: 184–86).

[13] The widely used term "status-quo bias" is misleading. This bias entails persistence
in a course of action chosen earlier — i.e., a prior option — not adherence to the status
quo — i.e., the currently existing situation that usually serves as reference point for assessing gains and losses.

lenges by drastically shifting course. Longstanding incumbents and their hand-picked successors cannot disregard the "sunk investment" that these prior choices constitute and freely adapt to new circumstances. Instead of running the risk of innovation, they merely tinker with established policies, keep applying similar recipes, and in this way "throw good money after bad." In sum, the prior-option bias induces political insiders to persist with unpromising policy approaches even when the economy deteriorates ever more clearly.

For longstanding incumbents and their designated successors, the prior-option bias thus reinforces and extends risk aversion in the domain of gains and checks risk acceptance in the domain of losses. It leads to excessive conservatism and greater persistence in policy-making than prospect theory alone would expect. In the terminology of punctuated equilibrium (Krasner 1984: 240–43), the prior-option bias causes protracted equilibria, which are punctuated only by turnover in office.

The prior-option bias differs from the rational calculation of chief executives to avoid the short-term costs of adjustment at the end of their term because only their successor would reap the long-term benefits. Instead, the fallacy of sunk costs traps incumbents with finite as well as indefinite tenures in office. Thus, it prevails not only under presidential systems of government that rule out immediate reelection, as in Brazil at the end of President José Sarney's term (cf. Weyland 1996a: 116). It also holds sway in parliamentary systems, which do not limit chief executives' tenure in office. A prime example was Margaret Thatcher's stubborn pursuit of orthodox neoliberal reform, which threatened the electoral prospects of the Conservative Party and eventually led to Thatcher's downfall in November 1990. Similarly, the prior-option bias operates with great intensity under authoritarian regimes of personal leaders—such as Zambia's Kenneth Kaunda in the 1980s or Indonesia's Suharto in 1997–98—who seek to extend their tenure as long as possible. Thus, this bias reflects excessive obstinacy, not rational cost-benefit calculations. It therefore fits in with the cognitive-psychological framework applied in this book.

Given the strength of the prior-option bias, neoliberal reform only gets under way when the chief executive is not associated with established policies and not tainted by earlier mistakes. Political outsiders do not feel bound by the policies of their predecessor but on the contrary find it attractive to disavow these policies in order to mark a new beginning. In fact, they can blame their predecessor's mistakes for the crisis and in this way shift responsibility for the pain of adjustment.[14] There-

---

[14] The escape from the prior-option bias thus allows for an "antidotal" and "exonerating" posture (Stokes 2001b: 15–16).

fore, political outsiders display unfettered risk acceptance in the domain of losses. Psychological decision theories thus suggest that the intersection of two conditions is decisive for drastic neoliberal reform, namely, the accession to power of a new leader, who is not subject to the prior-option bias, and the eruption of a severe crisis, which puts the new chief executive in the domain of losses and thus triggers risk acceptance.

Yet what leaders are new? Who counts as a political outsider? Since politicians strongly respond to competitive pressures,[15] the conditions of their most recent accession to power are decisive. Challengers of incumbents or their hand-picked candidates commonly attack the "insiders" and depict themselves as outsiders. Given the limited memory span of many people and the rapid renewal of the citizenry in Latin America's youthful societies, this self-stylization is often successful. Thus, politicians are outsiders if they rise to power by opposing the established leadership. Depending on the political bastion of this established leadership, there are three types of outsiders. Factional outsiders win office against the dominant faction of their own party or the core group of the established elite. Party/elite outsiders defeat the incumbent party or the established elite as a whole. Regime outsiders transform the existing regime in taking power.[16]

By allowing for the rise of political outsiders and thus creating an escape from the prior-option bias, alternation in power is a crucial precondition for the enactment of drastic market reform. Democracy, which permits regular alternation in power, therefore facilitates the initiation of drastic reform. Psychological decision theories thus provide additional support for the counterintuitive finding that democracy does not necessarily impede — and may even further — the adoption of tough adjustment (Nelson 1990: 22–23; Haggard and Kaufman 1995: 151–53).

Ideational Factors: Learning from Prior Experiences

Psychological decision theories explain whether chief executives tend toward risk-acceptant or risk-averse choices. But these theories cannot explain the *content* of the policies that decision-makers choose. For instance, will the economic shock plan adopted by a new leader in the

---

[15] Even under authoritarian rule, leaders face competition, especially the risk of coups (Ames 1987; see also North 1981: 27–28).

[16] Accordingly, Carlos Andrés Pérez, who won the presidential candidacy in 1988 against the leadership of his Acción Democrática, was a factional outsider. Carlos Menem, who accomplished a similar feat and then vanquished the incumbent Radical Party, was a factional and party/elite outsider. Chile's Augusto Pinochet, who took office by coup, and Zambia's Frederick Chiluba, whose election established democracy, were regime outsiders.

domain of losses be of an orthodox or a heterodox nature? Learning helps to fill this gap by elucidating the substance of chief executives' policy choices. In the terminology of prospect theory, learning shapes the framing of the options among which decision-makers choose, depending on their propensity toward risk.[17] Specifically, lessons drawn from prior experiences delimit the range of options that a decision-maker considers. Learning prompts leaders to disregard some available policy approaches and to favor others. With these insights, ideational arguments systematically complement the psychological decision theories applied in the present study.

Learning uses prior experiences to guide current decisions. Policy-makers evaluate programs enacted by their predecessors or by governments of other countries and use this assessment to inform their own policies. Most basically, perceived success provides positive feedback, inducing decision-makers to continue an established policy or emulate a foreign model. By contrast, perceived failure yields negative feedback and prompts efforts to try out another approach and experiment with innovative solutions. Both of these processes often interact, as domestic policies that are seen as flawed lead political leaders to adopt foreign models that appear promising.

Since complete innovation is rare, and since the available policy options are usually arrayed along a one-dimensional spectrum (e.g., free market vs. state interventionism), learning from costly failures often leads not to incremental adjustments in policy, but to a widening "swing of the pendulum" between alternative approaches. A failed effort to respond to a challenge by moving closer to one end of the policy spectrum is likely to trigger an attempt to resolve the deepening problem by shifting course and moving toward the other end of the spectrum. For instance, Argentina, Brazil, and Peru responded to the economic deterioration exacerbated by the debt crisis in this zig-zag fashion: They first adopted orthodox policies in the late 1970s and early 1980s, then embraced the heterodox alternative in the mid-1980s, and eventually returned to orthodoxy — though in the form of drastic shock treatment — during the late 1980s and early 1990s. Thus, learning can produce policy alternation in a pendular pattern of intensifying amplitude.[18]

In these ways, learning — especially learning from perceived mistakes — can counteract the inertia caused by the prior-option bias. Whereas the prior-option bias causes sequences of excessive continuity

---

[17] On other aspects of framing, see McDermott (1998: 20–27).

[18] For a "swing-of-the-pendulum" interpretation of Peru's economic development, see Gonzales de Olarte and Samamé (1994).

in policy-making, the lessons drawn from perceived failures can lead to significant change. Learning allows new decision-makers, who are not tied down by commitment to established policy approaches, to repudiate the unsuccessful policies of their predecessors and to embark on new, more promising courses of action. Learning thus opens up an opportunity for reassessment, correction, and improvement — that is, an escape from the fallacy of sunk costs. While in the metaphor of punctuated equilibrium (Krasner 1984: 240–43) the prior-option bias leads to temporary stability and equilibrium, learning produces occasional punctuation. In statistical terminology, the prior-option bias causes long stretches of positive autocorrelation, whereas learning from perceived failure brings about occasional instances of strong negative autocorrelation.

It is important to note that the lessons drawn from earlier experiences are not necessarily accurate. Disentangling the causal factors that shape outcomes in a single case is exceedingly difficult. Therefore, faulty inferences about the reasons of recent failures are always possible. Even if the assessment of past courses of action is correct, designing better recipes for the future constitutes a daunting task. In particular, correct lessons drawn from earlier experiences may no longer be applicable because important context factors may have changed. Decision-makers, however, have a systematic tendency to overestimate the similarities between a current challenge and an earlier precedent.[19] This analogical reasoning (Jervis 1976: chap. 6; McDermott 1998: 51–64) can lead to serious misjudgments.

For all of these reasons, the new policies enacted as a result of learning are not guaranteed greater success than the preceding ones, which are perceived as failures. In fact, the abandonment of old policies can make the situation worse. Thus, the concept of learning used in this book differs from rational-choice notions such as Bayesian updating, which postulate an approximation to the truth. While such improvement is certainly intended, it is by no means assured. Indeed, trying out new options can backfire and aggravate problems.

Policy experiments inspired by learning therefore carry considerable risk. Prospect theory is crucial for elucidating the conditions under which decision-makers take such risks — namely, when they see themselves in the domain of losses. Political learning thus fits in with the psychological decision framework applied in this book. Specifically, learning suggests the content of new policies, and risk-seeking in the domain of losses provides the impulse for adopting these new policies and thus accepting the danger inherent in any innovation.

---

[19] President Bush, for instance, "saw" Adolf Hitler when confronting Saddam Hussein in 1990–91.

Economic Structures

Economic Causes of Crises

Prospect theory advances a situational argument on people's risk propensity by predicting risk-seeking in the domain of losses and risk aversion in the domain of gains. But prospect theory does not explain under what conditions people see themselves in the domain of gains or the domain of losses. In principle, a variety of factors—including subjective predispositions, such as individual aspiration levels—can shape a decision-maker's perception of domain. For an analysis of economic policy, however, objective economic conditions—specifically, recent trends in a nation's well-being—are most important.[20] Structural economic factors are crucial, in turn, for explaining whether a country enjoys economic prosperity or suffers deterioration and crisis. Arguments about economic development are therefore a necessary complement to my prospect-theory interpretation.

As regards Latin America's development in recent decades, international factors have created considerable commonality in the economic experiences of various nations, whereas domestic factors have tended to lead to differences among countries. External shocks, especially the disruptions in world trade caused by the Great Depression and World War II, stimulated the pursuit of import-substitution industrialization (ISI) all over the region from the 1930s on. But specific country characteristics influenced when this process began in each nation, how far it proceeded, and when it ran into crisis. The balance of influence between urban industrial sectors, on the one hand, and agrarian elites and other primary exporters, on the other, accounts for the early start and impressive advance of ISI in Argentina and Brazil, compared to its delayed beginning and limited progress in Peru and Venezuela. Smaller market size contributed to Argentina's economic stagnation after the 1960s, compared to Brazil's dynamic growth through the mid-1980s. The rash pursuit of drastic ISI policies in Peru during the 1960s and 1970s helps explain the especially deep crisis that country suffered in the 1980s (Wise 1994). And the poor usage of Venezuela's abundant oil revenues aggravated the boom-and-bust cycle experienced by this "petro-state" (Karl 1997).

Despite these different development trajectories, First World banks reacted in uniform ways to the debt crisis of the early 1980s: They

---

[20] I emphasize objective economic conditions to make my prospect-theory argument more testable than if it focused mostly on subjective perceptions.

suddenly ended voluntary lending to most Latin American countries. This international contagion effect caused severe problems for the whole region, despite countries' different debt loads, international competitiveness, export success, and capacity to service their loans. The drastic reduction in capital inflows and the strong pressures to maintain debt service caused a huge financial drain and a deepening fiscal crisis because the state assumed the private sector's external obligations. Chronic fiscal deficits in turn fueled inflation, which hindered investment and growth, disorganized the economy, and unleashed distributional conflict. The indecisive and unsuccessful stabilization plans enacted in response to these problems often ended up making the situation worse by unpredictably and arbitrarily interfering in the market. As a result, economic agents acted on worst-case scenarios and adopted measures of anticipated self-protection, such as particularly high price increases. Economic problems therefore worsened further and soon "forced" the government to intervene, thus confirming the initial fears. Many countries seemed trapped in this vicious circle of self-fulfilling prophecies.

Despite similar general characteristics, however, the economic problems afflicting the four countries under investigation had different degrees of severity, at both the conjunctural and the structural level. As regards conjunctural difficulties, inflation—the most important problem for the majority of the population[21]—increased at strikingly divergent rates. Recent transitions to precarious, unconsolidated democratic regimes and the deep fiscal crises of the state unleashed hyperinflation in Argentina, Brazil, and Peru at the end of the 1980s. By contrast, Venezuela's (seemingly) consolidated democracy and stable two-party system and the control of the country's tremendous oil wealth by the state, which limited fiscal problems, kept inflation at much more manageable levels. In Argentina, Brazil, and Peru, hyperinflation—price rises above 50 percent per month—threatened to cause economic chaos, imposed heavy losses on most sectors, especially poorer people, and further undermined the fiscal sustenance and political authority of the state. Its impact was particularly devastating in Argentina and Peru, whereas the widespread indexation instituted in Brazil guaranteed partial protection from inflationary losses to people in the formal sector (but the poor in the informal economy remained unprotected).

Hyperinflation rapidly erodes the income and savings of large masses of people and threatens to destroy their livelihood. The speed of this

---

[21] On people's predominant concern about inflation, especially in times of hyperinflation, see Catterberg (1991: 26), Myers (1993: 53), Almeida (1996: 70–71), Apoyo (June 1990: 35), Consultores 21 (1989b: 6).

deterioration keeps people from gradually lowering their reference point for assessing gains and losses and from adjusting their aspiration levels downward. Therefore, skyrocketing price rises create a clear, unmitigated perception of severe losses. Hyperinflation thus puts a majority of common citizens in the domain of losses. Other economic problems, such as unemployment, do not erupt at the same speed or affect a large majority of people.[22] Hyperinflation is therefore the single most important condition for massive numbers of people to see themselves in the domain of losses. In turn, the more people have such negative economic prospects, the stronger mass support for the bold, drastic stabilization measures enacted by new chief executives is likely to be.

By contrast, the absence of hyperinflation and the gradual nature of Venezuela's economic deterioration during the 1980s prevented a similar perception of dramatic crisis from emerging. In fact, Venezuela's abundant oil reserves always kept the hope for a magic rescue from conjunctural problems alive. A rise in international petroleum prices, which a military incident in the conflict-ridden Middle East could trigger at any moment, would quickly turn the country's economic situation around. Thus, pessimistic perceptions of economic prospects were not as profound and widespread in Venezuela as in Brazil and especially in Argentina and Peru. Therefore, drastic neoliberal adjustment was much less likely to elicit strong mass support in Venezuela.

Compared to common citizens, political leaders and economic elites consider a greater variety of conjunctural economic variables in defining their perception of prospects of gains or losses. Furthermore, they have access to technical and inside information, which allows them to anticipate severe imminent problems that most people are not aware of. And they understand that the mechanisms an outgoing government can use temporarily to suppress signs of conjunctural difficulties — for instance, price controls — are likely to cause a graver crisis later on. Finally, political leaders and economic elites have ample knowledge of comparative experiences, which enables them to foresee the eventually disastrous results of policies that promise substantial short-term benefits, such as "economic populism" (Sachs 1989; Dornbusch and Edwards 1991).

The subjective perceptions of domain that political leaders and economic elites hold are therefore harder to predict on the basis of objective economic indicators. Severe open crises — especially hyperinflation, but also a collapse of fiscal revenues or exploding deficits in a country's external accounts — are sufficient for chief executives to see themselves in the domain of losses. But such manifest grave problems are not necessary for such a perception. Indications of imminent crises that have

---

[22] Also, a large "informal sector" provides alternative sources of sustenance.

not yet erupted into the open can also put chief executives in the domain of losses.

The capacity of political leaders to foresee severe conjunctural problems can cause a perceptual divergence between chief executives and a majority of the population. Whereas common citizens may enjoy the lingering benefits of an endangered prosperity or take advantage of the artificial measures employed by the outgoing government to cover up the approaching crisis, political leaders may well be aware of the imminent drastic deterioration. Paradoxically, if a new chief executive faces the looming problems immediately and tries to forestall great losses before the imminent crisis becomes manifest, he or she will probably not receive strong popular support. Instead, large parts of the surprised population reject the seemingly unnecessary stabilization plan and thus leave the foresighted (though overly bold) leader with particularly low backing.

While the severity of conjunctural problems shapes the willingness of political leaders to adopt daring stabilization plans and of common citizens to support these bold decisions, the depth of structural problems provides the impetus for leaders to enact and for citizens to accept profound market reforms designed to revamp the established development model. The graver, more acute, and more longstanding a country's structural difficulties are, the more willing are leaders and citizens to incur the costs and risks of a systemic transformation. By contrast, if a nation's development model has a long record of reasonably good performance despite current conjunctural problems, structural reform provokes much more skepticism and rejection.

The three countries whose chief executives attained initial support for their drastic stabilization plans and therefore had the political opportunity to enact comprehensive market reform differed clearly in the depth of their structural problems.[23] Whereas Argentina and Peru were in dire straits, Brazil faced better prospects. Basically, limited market size made ISI a much less promising development strategy in Argentina and Peru than in Brazil. Due to the early start of ISI, Argentina had therefore experienced decades of virtual stagnation. In Peru, the belated yet particularly rash effort to build industry quickly caused severe prob-

---

[23] By contrast, obvious, longstanding structural problems do not allow for costly structural reforms if a political leader anticipated a conjunctural crisis that citizens did not foresee, if the preemptive stabilization plan therefore elicited widespread rejection, and if the government lacks political clout, as it happened in Venezuela in 1989. Also, while Venezuela experienced substantial impoverishment during the 1980s, the exogenous trigger—the decline in international oil prices—created the hope that any tightening of the world petroleum market would improve the situation, making painful structural reforms unnecessary.

lems such as spiraling debt, which led to tremendous impoverishment in the 1980s. By contrast, Brazil followed up on its economic miracle of the late 1960s and 1970s by achieving substantial net growth in the turbulent 1980s, despite high, eventually skyrocketing inflation. Since the differential performance of their country's development model was obvious to important sectors of the population, reform-minded governments faced much greater opportunities to enact the market reform program in Argentina and Peru than in Brazil.

In sum, conjunctural and structural economic factors are crucial for explaining whether political leaders and common citizens see themselves in the domain of gains or the domain of losses. Specifically, international constraints and pressures—such as the debt crisis—caused serious economic difficulties in all four countries under investigation. But due to domestic factors, these difficulties had different levels of severity. Argentina and Peru were worst off as long-term economic stagnation or acute decline culminated in devastating hyperinflations. Brazil also suffered from hyperinflation, but widespread indexation limited its costs, and the country's impressive growth record in the 1970s and mid-1980s instilled higher hopes of an economic recovery. Venezuela, finally, experienced economic decline and rising inflation, but price increases remained far below the level of hyperinflation, and huge petroleum reserves created the possibility of a rapid recovery. By shaping the attitudes of political leaders and common citizens toward risk, the differential domain perceptions that these different levels of economic deterioration generated had an essential impact on the initiation, implementation, and political fate of neoliberal stabilization plans and market reform programs.

Economic Conditions of Recovery

While a severe, open economic crisis places political leaders and many common citizens in the domain of losses, economic recovery puts more and more people into the domain of gains and thus induces them to turn risk-averse and accept the new status quo, namely, the recently instituted market model and its initiator. A turnaround in a country's economic fate is therefore a necessary—though not sufficient—condition for the political sustainability of neoliberalism.

What then accounts for economic recovery? Certain economic factors, which this study treats as exogenous variables, condition a country's emergence from a deep crisis. The competitiveness and export potential of its enterprises, the availability of foreign capital for loans and investment, and the willingness of external lenders to accept a limited write-off of outstanding debt are among the most important of these conditions.

Factors that are endogenous to my explanation, especially the nature of the initial economic problems and the policies designed to overcome them, also play an important role. Where hyperinflation devastated an economy, drastic, painful adjustment can offer some quick benefits to many people and sectors, at least by averting a full-scale catastrophe.[24] Stabilization also constitutes a necessary—though not sufficient—condition for renewed growth. The end of hyperinflation and renewed growth help especially poorer sectors, who suffered disproportionate income losses from accelerating price increases (Ahumada et al. 1992) and whose employment opportunities were restricted by recession and adjustment. As a result, poverty tends to diminish from its high point during the peak of the hyperinflationary crisis (Morley 1995). By contrast, in countries that suffered from repressed inflation, neoliberal reforms unleash a torrent of price increases that hurt especially poorer sectors and discredit the new policies. This explosion of inflation undermines stabilization efforts, strengthens resistance to neoliberal reforms, and turns economic recovery precarious.

The type of stabilization measures that a country enacts also affects the chances for recovery. The orthodox programs recommended by the IMF use restrictions on demand to force down inflation. They therefore tend to bring about prolonged recessions, which entail considerable social cost. By contrast, programs that rely on exchange-rate anchors or currency boards, such as Argentina's convertibility plan of early 1991, can bring about quick stabilization and spur renewed growth. But by making it difficult for the government to protect the economy from external shocks and by requiring high interest rates to attract foreign capital, these programs can impose long-term limits on growth.[25]

Economic recovery is a necessary, but not sufficient, condition for large numbers of people to enter the domain of gains.[26] Given the deep

---

[24] Thus, bold stabilization plans may produce improvements although they are suboptimal. Specifically, they can end a full-scale crisis and avoid a complete meltdown, although due to their inherent risks, they have less expected value than more prudent alternatives.

[25] Furthermore, their enactment requires earlier stabilization efforts, which are often of an orthodox nature, as in Argentina in 1990 (Smith 1991: 53–62). A government is therefore best off if its predecessor(s) already imposed most adjustment costs so that the new economic team can reap the political benefits of economic stabilization without having to decree further drastic losses. In this vein, Brazil's Fernando Henrique Cardoso profited from the politically fatal yet economically significant adjustment efforts undertaken by Fernando Collor, especially his trade liberalization and fiscal measures.

[26] Since individual mobility is not determined by the national economy, some people may benefit from grave crises, whereas others suffer even during recovery. But the major-

social inequality prevailing in many Latin American countries, aggregate economic growth may benefit only a few narrow sectors, not the mass of the population. Due to the urgency of unfulfilled basic needs, the predominance of clientelism (the exchange of political support for particularistic benefits), and the social atomization caused by the deep crisis (O'Donnell 1993: 1363–66), voters are guided less by sociotropic considerations — i.e., concern for the well-being of the whole country — than by pocketbook concerns for their individual and family well-being.[27] It is therefore of great political importance that governments create mechanisms designed to spread some benefits from economic recovery to large numbers of voters.

For this purpose, governments need to institute social programs that demonstrate the administration's concern for the disadvantaged (Nelson 1992; Graham 1994; Waterbury 1993: 197–208). Ongoing electoral competition provides a strong political incentive for such initiatives. If these social programs are targeted at large numbers of poor people and manage to enhance their welfare — or at least create the hope of doing so — they put more and more citizens in the domain of gains and thus turn them risk-averse. In this way, social programs enhance the acceptance of the newly established market model, create support for its initiators and implementors, and prevent the less well-off from giving the opposition a try.

Where a deep, open crisis (especially hyperinflation) is followed by economic recovery, and where the government creates wide-ranging social programs, neoliberalism attains active approval or at least passive acquiescence (contra Acuña and Smith 1994: 31–41). As a result, no significant electoral contender advocates a drastic turnaround in economic policy. Even the opposition candidates — such as Javier Pérez de Cuéllar in Peru (1995) and José Octavio Bordón in Argentina (1995) — promise to maintain the new development model and propose only limited modifications. Especially in countries with fluid, fragmented party systems, where new challengers could easily rise, this absence of a fundamental attack on neoliberalism serves as a strong indicator for the continued political sustainability of the market system.

By contrast, where economic recovery is weak or social policies lag, many people remain in the domain of losses. Therefore, they soon reject the new market model and search for alternative solutions to their country's persistent crisis. Riding on a wave of resentment to market reform, old populist leaders or new personalistic politicians who advocate nation-

---

ity's domain perceptions tend to reflect trends in the national economy, which create benefits or costs for many people or induce them to anticipate such changes in their well-being.

[27] For an investigation with Venezuelan data, see Weyland (1998a).

alistic and interventionist economic policies—such as Rafael Caldera (1994–99) and Hugo Chávez (1999–present) in Venezuela—may win office. Political learning from the real or seeming failure of neoliberalism can thus cause a backlash and result in a drastic policy reversal.

Political Interests

This chapter has elaborated a new microfoundation for arguments that depict drastic neoliberal adjustment as a response to severe economic crises. But chief executives adopt market reforms not only to attain certain economic goals, but also to pursue their political interests. While these reforms certainly are efforts at economic problem-solving, they are also attempts by political leaders to maintain and increase their own influence and weaken their rivals, adversaries, and enemies. These political interests shape decisions on economic policy reform, as advocates of rational choice, in particular, point out correctly.

Market reforms serve to reduce the political clout of bureaucrats, interest groups, and opposition politicians and to expand the chief executive's power and latitude. Specifically, trade liberalization and the resulting increase in foreign competition weaken trade unions and a number of business sectors; the dismissal of civil servants puts the public bureaucracy on the defensive; and the general reduction of state interventionism limits patronage and thus hurts opposition politicians. In fact, chief executives can use the benefits of market reform—such as favorable privatization deals—to buy support while imposing the costs—such as cuts in patronage—on their rivals and adversaries. And they can justify their quest for increased power by invoking the need to promote policies that are beneficial to the country as a whole (i.e., the "common good") and to overcome resistance from selfish "special interests." Furthermore, market reforms can enhance the public standing of their initiators. Drastic, tough stabilization measures and profound structural reforms prove the courage and determination of political leaders who confront a deep crisis. By trying to save the country from impending doom, chief executives confirm their charismatic qualities. In all of these ways, neoliberal reforms can serve as powerful weapons in political struggles (cf. Geddes 1994a; Weyland 1996c).

Yet while this book agrees with rational-choice authors on the political motivations of economic policy reform, it incorporates this factor into a cognitive-psychological framework. Chief executives did adopt and use market reforms partly for their instrumental political interests— but not in a strictly rational way. Rather, the deviations from value maximization embodied in shifting, asymmetrical propensities toward risk and in the prior-option bias shape presidents' political calculations. The political aspects of neoliberal reform, especially the attack on established politicians, bureaucrats, and veto groups that it embodies, exacerbate its inherent risks. Since market reform involves a struggle over power, it can easily unleash strong conflict. Reform initiators face pervasive passive resistance, and any weakness they show is likely to trigger fierce active opposition. If they stumble, they may well fall. It thus takes a strong willingness to incur risk for a leader to adopt such reforms, especially in the precarious institutional settings of the countries under investigation.

Only new chief executives who see themselves in the domain of losses run such risks. These outsiders do not just muddle through and adjust to prevailing circumstances. Instead, they reject established political constraints. They boldly cut the Gordian Knot that threatened to strangle their predecessors, revamp the constellation of political forces, overhaul institutional structures, and thus exert clear "transforming leadership." By contrast, incumbents or their hand-picked successors tend to maintain established political alliances, use conventional strategies and tactics, and confine themselves to leadership by "transaction" (Burns 1978). Similarly, leaders who do not face severe challenges and who therefore see themselves in the domain of gains prefer this prudent, risk-averse course of action.

Thus, risk-seeking in the domain of losses and risk aversion in the domain of gains—as mediated by the prior-option bias—affect not only the choice of economic policies, but also the selection of the underlying political strategies. The political implications of market reform aggravate the risk that decision-makers incur in adopting such measures, which not only have uncertain economic success, but also can trigger severe political conflict. Thus, the political motivations and purposes of drastic market reforms make it even more difficult for rational-choice authors to explain their adoption, given that rational chief executives are generally thought to shy away from offending powerful sociopolitical forces (cf. Ames 1987; Geddes 1994b).

Institutional Factors

Psychological decision theories account for individual choices. Politics, however, is the realm of collective action and strategic interaction, which are mediated by the institutional context. To be useful for political analysis, cognitive-psychological insights therefore need to be integrated with the valid elements of institutionalist approaches. For instance, the institutional prerogatives of chief executives condition the extent to which their individual, situationally defined risk propensity affects policy-making. And the institutional structures of representational mechanisms, especially of political parties, shape the aggregation of the individual choices of common citizens into collective decisions.

The Regime Level: Democratization and Neopopulist Politics

How do institutional structures affect the politics of market reform? While political regime *type* does not have a significant impact on structural adjustment, as chapter 2 has shown, regime *transitions* do appear to make a difference. Democratization—like other types of regime change—opens up a "window of opportunity" for reform (cf. Keeler 1993) by undermining established sociopolitical forces and by allowing new or previously excluded actors, who are dissatisfied with the status quo, to enhance their influence. This fluidity in the constellation of power facilitates drastic economic and political change, including market reform.

Democratization reduces the political clout of some of the vested interests that benefited the most from the old development model, such as protectionist business sectors and the military. At the same time, it enhances the role of the electorate, including the large mass of poor people who received meager benefits under the old development model and who felt politically excluded as well. In these ways, a transition from authoritarian rule can help to pave the way for structural adjustment (cf. Bartlett 1997: 3–13).

Democratization weakens politically some prime beneficiaries of state interventionism. By causing turnover in political personnel, regime change disrupts longstanding particularistic connections to governmental decision-makers that protectionist business groups used to enjoy. And by boosting the role of Congress, it makes these direct connections less consequential and forces business groups to develop a new style of lobbying, which is a difficult task (Silva and Durand 1998). By fueling party-political divergences inside the private sector, democratization also creates new cleavages that diminish the political power of business associations, which were often dominated by protectionist sectors.[28]

By contrast, the biggest firms, which are more likely to be competitive and therefore support neoliberal trade liberalization, rely less on business organizations for advancing their demands. Also, their huge resources make it easy for them to establish new connections to policy-

---

[28] On the diminution of interest group influence resulting from democratization, see Schmitter (1992: 439–45).

makers in the executive and legislative branches. Thus, a transition from authoritarian rule tends to weaken entrepreneurs who are lukewarm or opposed to neoliberalism, while preserving the clout of the advocates of market reform.

Even more clearly, democratization reduces the political influence of the military. The formal abdication of power at the moment of transition is usually followed by a further diminution in political clout as civilian politicians reclaim resources and responsibilities that the armed forces monopolized under authoritarian rule (Hunter 1997a, 1997b). This shift in power facilitates neoliberal reform because the military was one of the mainstays of the nationalist, state-interventionist development model. Concerned about national security and independence from foreign influence, the armed forces played a leading role in pushing industrialization ahead and participated directly in a number of economic ventures, centered around, but by no means confined to, the arms industry. Earlier efforts to enact neoliberal reforms under military rule had therefore faced considerable opposition from inside the armed forces (Biglaiser 1999). The restoration of democracy made this resistance less and less effective.

At the same time, democratization boosts the importance of the mass electorate because democratic leaders need to attract and maintain voter support. Even if presidents can use their decree powers to initiate unpopular measures, they know that sooner or later, electoral success is decisive for continuing the push for neoliberal reform. To preclude a quick reversal, major policies need to be minimally acceptable to large numbers of voters. In order to implement market reform, chief executives therefore must appeal to the hopes and fears of "the people," including their resentment of the privileges guaranteed to "special interests" by the old development model.

Although most of the mass electorate lacks a firm commitment to neoliberalism, many people reject the established development scheme as unpromising and corrupt. Furthermore, severe crises induce the citizenry to put a strong premium on the restoration of stability and to support an alternative development model. Under such circumstances, many voters are therefore open to drastic policy change. In times of trouble, they also prefer bold, decisive leaders who promise to combat acute problems in a determined fashion. The popular attitudes prevailing under crisis conditions thus allow reform initiators to find acquiescence and support among wide sectors of the population and to survive electoral challenges. These leaders therefore appeal to the large, unorganized mass of common citizens and use its backing in elections and opinion polls to limit and outflank the opposition of vested interests in organized civil society. As a result, neoliberal reform is nowadays often accompanied and supported by a populist political strategy (Roberts 1995; Weyland 1996c, 1999; Oxhorn 1998; Demmers, Fernández Jilberto, and Hogenboom 2001).

Another corollary of transitions from authoritarian rule has contributed to neoliberal reformers' frequent reliance on political populism: the introduction of systematic opinion polling. Before the recent wave of democratization, surveys were rare and unsystematic. At that point in time, "public opinion" consisted of newspaper editorials, the views of party leaders and militants, and the demands of organized interest groups. Benefiting considerably from the established state-interventionist development model, these sectors generally had a stake in its preservation. The large sectors of the population who received few benefits from import-substitution industrialization and who were hurt by high prices and low quality had barely any voice in politics; if represented at all, their views were mediated by clientelist networks, corporatist interest associations, and largely elitist parties.

The spread of systematic opinion polling brought an important change. For the first time, politicians and government leaders gained direct access to the views of the common people. Many of these people had long held a critical view of the established development model, which did not provide them with any of the relative privileges that the middle class, special interest groups, and party leaders enjoyed. Politicians and government leaders thus "discovered" considerable discontent with the established system and a wider commitment to economic liberty than had been known before (Turner and Elordi 1995). Thus, regular, systematic polling may have transformed public opinion by finally giving the longstanding views and values of the unorganized "mass" of people an outlet. This transformation gave leaders additional opportunities to use populist political tactics to dislodge established interest groups and parties and to enact neoliberal reform (Weyland 2001).

By applying a populist political strategy, many contemporary market reformers thus use to their own advantage the growing political importance of elections and opinion polls relative to pressure politics.[29] They appeal especially to the largely unorganized mass of common people and attack established interest groups, politicians, and bureaucrats as selfish impediments to the pursuit of the "common good." These attacks play into the hands of neoliberal experts, who seek to bar political interference in the market, combat the lobbying influence of rent-seeking "special interests," and dislodge the sectors that benefited from

[29] The crucial political importance of elections and opinion polls, through which collective choices are made via the simple summation of individual choices, justifies the application of psychological insights on individual decision-making to the mass public.

the established, state-interventionist, protectionist development model. Thus, the new populist politics proves functional for the enactment of profound neoliberal reform.

The preceding arguments use a purely political definition of populism that discards the socioeconomic factors often associated with the concept, such as expansionary economic policies or generous social programs. Accordingly, populism is a political strategy through which a personalistic leader seeks or exercises government power based on direct, unmediated, uninstitutionalized support from large numbers of mostly unorganized followers (Weyland 2001). A populist leader appeals to a heterogeneous mass of followers who feel "left out" and are available for mobilization. The leader reaches the followers in a quasi-personal manner that relies heavily on the modern mass media, nowadays primarily television, and ascertains the "will of the people" via opinion polls (Conaghan 1995). This quasi-personal relationship bypasses established intermediary organizations, especially parties. If the leader builds new parties or revives old populist parties, they remain personal vehicles with low levels of institutionalization (Weyland 1999: 381).

Populism embodies a majoritarian notion of political rule. By appealing to largely unorganized masses of people and criticizing "special interests," populist leaders stress numbers—rather than intensity of preference or other forms of special weight—as the only legitimate criterion for considering citizens' interests. In fact, while hierarchical in its focus on a personal leader, populism has a strong egalitarian, democratic element as chief executives base their rule on appeals to the mass of the populace, distance themselves from organized civil society, and attack "selfish elites," nowadays especially the "political class." Furthermore, to limit the influence of established elites on the "little people," populists stress aggregative, nondeliberative mechanisms for the expression of popular preferences, especially voting and opinion polls.

My political definition encompasses both the classical populists of the 1930s through 1950s and the neopopulists of the 1980s and 1990s. Despite considerable differences in the sociopolitical setting and in their economic policies, Juan Perón, Getúlio Vargas, Lázaro Cárdenas, Alan García, Carlos Menem, Fernando Collor, and Alberto Fujimori all based their governments on a quasi-direct, personalistic relationship to largely unorganized masses of people.

But there also are some differences between classical populism and neopopulism, even in their specific political strategies. Above all, neopopulism is more anti-organizational and therefore more precarious than classical populism. Leaders like Perón and Vargas founded populist movements in societies with low to medium levels of organization. They attracted many followers who lacked an associational affiliation, but who, as formal-sector workers, had considerable capacity for collective organization. Effecting the "primary incorporation" of these organizable sectors (Collier and Collier 1991: chaps. 2, 5), classical populists built parties and trade union confederations that, while being too leader-centered to be firmly institutionalized, created lasting loyalties.

By contrast, Menem, Collor, and Fujimori rose in societies with much higher levels of organization and therefore — as outsiders — adopted a more anti-organizational stance. Although existing parties and trade unions were discredited, these organizations continued to have support among the industrial working class and the professional middle sectors that had a high capacity for collective organization. The primary targets of Collor and Fujimori's mass appeals were therefore the urban informal sector and rural poor, who are too heterogeneous to form strong national-level organizations. And precisely because established intermediary organizations were discredited, Collor and Fujimori refrained from forming their own mass party. Instead, they created narrow, personalistic vehicles and technocratic movements. Their mass following therefore remained unorganized and particularly precarious. Due to this lack of solid political sustenance, any serious difficulty that the leader seemed unable to resolve posed a political threat, as confirmed by Collor's eventual impeachment. Neopopulism therefore contains even greater risks of failure than classical populism.

This political concept of populism has two decisive implications for a prospect-theory interpretation of the politics of neoliberal reform. First, its uninstitutionalized, fluid nature and the adversarial relationship to intermediary organizations and established elites turn populism into a high-risk strategy. The political sustenance of populist leaders is always precarious; when they encounter difficulties, their followers may desert them quickly. Thus, while populism promises high rewards — namely, particularly great presidential power and autonomy — it also carries a substantial danger of failure, if not disaster. Risk acceptance in the domain of losses best explains why political leaders kept embracing this dangerous strategy after winning presidential elections and taking office.[30]

Second, the leader-mass relationship underlying populism makes insights on individual choice, like those offered by prospect theory, particularly relevant. Given the disproportionate power and autonomy of populist leaders, which reinforce the chief executive's predominance in Latin America's presidential systems, economic policy is decided ulti-

---

[30] This continued use of populist tactics contradicts Drake's (1991: 36) "bait-and-switch" interpretation.

mately by a single individual.[31] Therefore, this individual's situationally conditioned propensity toward risk is of great importance. As for the political role of the masses, populism gives the aggregated choices of individual citizens in elections and opinion polls crucial significance. Therefore, scholars need to elucidate people's propensity toward risk, which shapes their political choices (cf. Quattrone and Tversky 1988).[32] Thus, populist politics strengthens the plausibility of applying a psychological approach like prospect theory to political decision-making.

In sum, deep crises make possible the rise of charismatic, neopopulist leadership and the initiation of drastic adjustment and structural reform. Facing a domain of losses, new chief executives embrace both a high-risk political strategy and a daring program of economic change. Neopopulist politics facilitates the enactment of market reforms, and those reforms in turn boost the political power and autonomy of populist leaders. Thus, there is an interesting synergy between political populism and economic liberalism.

This synergy persists during the second stage of neoliberal reform, helping to make the new market system politically sustainable. If despite its economic and political risks, shock therapy succeeds in stabilizing the economy and stimulating renewed growth, neopopulist leaders enter the domain of gains and turn more risk-averse. Economic recovery also yields resources for new spending programs. Without endangering the hard-won stability, neopopulist leaders can therefore shift their policies from the imposition of costs to the provision of benefits. Indeed, leaders eagerly resort to more traditional means of buying support in order to strengthen their base of political sustenance. Because they have to face electoral challenges, they institute social programs designed to spread the benefits of growth and to demonstrate their concern for "the people."

The targeting of these social programs may, in principle, favor either the groups who suffered the highest relative losses from neoliberal reform — usually, sectors of the middle and organized working class — or the sectors who are absolutely worst-off, namely, the urban and rural poor (Nelson 1992; Graham 1994: 6–12). Several reasons suggest that neoliberal populists will prefer the latter option. Democracy in general and populist politics in particular turn votes decisive and thus provide a justification for targeting social programs at the large number of absolutely poor people. Also, limited social spending, which does not

---

[31] Bueno de Mesquita (1981: 17–18) advances a similar argument to justify the application of expected utility theory to foreign policy decision-making.

[32] While stressing the significance of the mass of "the people," populism seeks to weaken and marginalize organizations for collective action, which prospect theory has not yet managed to model (Levy 1997: 102–5).

threaten budget equilibrium, buys more support among the very poor than among somewhat better-off sectors. Finally, the common psychological tendency to overvalue losses makes it difficult to compensate people for the costs resulting from market reform (Weyland 1998c). Rather than seeking to buy off the losers, governments find it politically more promising to create new winners by extending benefits to the poorest sectors, who had received only minimal payoffs from the old development model (Graham 1994: 9–10 and passim). For these reasons, neopopulist leaders tend to direct new social spending toward the largely unorganized mass of destitute people — the principal targets of their political appeals.

Since the new social programs provide benefits to people who had long been neglected and since they symbolically integrate these "excluded" sectors into national development, they strengthen the incumbent's political support, especially in electoral contests. The implementation of these programs thus enhances the chances for maintaining the course of structural reforms and for turning the new market model politically sustainable.

In sum, democratization facilitates market reform in a number of ways. It weakens the power of vested interests that have a stake in the old development model, especially protectionist business sectors and the military. It increases the clout of the large mass of voters, who received few benefits from ISI and who had to bear much of the cost of its decline. Most importantly, the growing importance of elections and opinion polls has allowed for the rise of neopopulist leaders, who can use neoliberal measures for their own political purposes. Neopopulism, however, carries a substantial risk of failure. Prospect theory makes a crucial contribution to explaining both chief executives' willingness to embrace this daring political strategy and citizens' support for these populist leaders.

Institutions Below the Regime Level: Presidential Powers and Party Systems

As shown in chapter 2, specific institutional rules and structures do not determine the political success or failure of market reform. In interaction with crisis conditions, however, they have a strong impact on the political fate of neoliberal policies. Specifically, the severity of a country's economic problems shapes the operation of institutional opportunities and constraints, which in turn affect the ways and means that governments use to enact market reform.

Institutional factors do condition the difficulties that political leaders face in trying to effect change. *Ceteris paribus*, the more extensive presidential powers are, the easier it is for political leaders to enact profound, costly reform. A president's legislative attributions, particularly his decree powers, are especially important in this respect. By contrast, if a broad range of substantive policy decisions is protected from change, especially through constitutional provisions,[33] it is difficult to transform a country's development model. Complicated amendment procedures and the need for qualified majorities hinder or impede reform.

But institutional structures — especially formal rules and attributions — are subject to change. Indeed, political leaders can invoke procedural constraints that hinder their efforts to combat severe problems as a justification for demanding institutional reform; under crisis conditions, other "veto players" may readily accede. Many chief executives who faced acute challenges have sought — and often managed — to extend their powers in this way (Weyland 1999: 391–92). When confronting a deep crisis, a chief executive may also usurp additional institutional powers without any formal authorization. In this vein, President Menem greatly extended the use of presidential decrees, disregarding all constitutional precedent. Finally, if the crisis is exceptionally severe, a president may simply overthrow the established constitutional order and impose a new framework of rules and procedures. Invoking the need to combat a tremendous economic crisis as well as a dangerous guerrilla challenge, President Fujimori took this drastic step, and Russia's Boris Yeltsin proceeded in similar ways. By contrast, President Pérez of Venezuela — a country that was in far less dire straits — did not act on suggestions to follow the same route.

Thus, formal institutions shape presidential powers, but only as long as presidents respect the official procedural framework. Severe crises allow presidents to override these constraints, extend their attributions and powers, and thus enhance their capacity to enact drastic, risky reforms, such as neoliberal adjustment. By giving presidents a good pretext for reshaping the constitution, a particularly constraining procedural framework may dialectically create the opportunity for such an institutional revamping. In a country facing an acute, severe crisis, such an institutional straightjacket may thus, in a long-term perspective, favor neoliberal reform.

How do chief executives muster solid, lasting support for their reform initiatives? In principle, a strong party system could provide such backing and thus facilitate market reform (Haggard and Kaufman 1995).

---

[33] Brazil's 1988 constitution, for instance, contains specific entitlements — such as generous public pensions — that create firm spending commitments and thus make austerity difficult.

In fact, however, party strength is a double-edged sword, as chapter 2 has shown. Rather than supporting a president's move to neoliberalism, as the Peronist Party did in Argentina under Menem, a well-organized, programmatically oriented party may offer passive or active resistance, as Acción Democrática (AD) did in Venezuela under President Pérez. Conversely, fluid, fragmented parties may make it difficult for a president to garner reliable support, as in Brazil under President Collor. But weak parties may also allow a president to overthrow the established constitutional order and boost his or her own attributions, as in Peru under President Fujimori.

Once again, there is an interaction between institutional characteristics and crisis conditions: The impact of party strength vs. party weakness depends on the severity of the economic and political problems facing a country and, especially, on a president's success in overcoming these problems. Where hyperinflation devastated an economy and where a government's adjustment measures succeed in stopping this price explosion, a strong party tends to provide solid support for the president, even if this endorsement of neoliberalism diverges from the established party ideology. By contrast, where economic difficulties (particularly price rises) are less severe and where a government's stabilization plan does not bring substantial improvement (especially in reducing inflation), a strong party is likely to worry about voters' response to the seemingly unjustifiable costs of reform. As a result, it may oppose a president's adoption of neoliberalism ever more clearly — and with much greater force than a weak party could muster.

The effect of party weakness also depends on crisis conditions. Where a leader faces exceptionally profound economic and political challenges that can serve as an excuse for overthrowing the constitutional order, party weakness lowers opposition to this extra-constitutional effort to concentrate power in the presidency. As a result, party weakness may in the end make it easier to combat the crisis with costly, risky neoliberal measures. By contrast, where a leader confronts less acute problems and therefore cannot take such a drastic step, party weakness greatly hinders presidential efforts to gather solid support for reform initiatives. Thus, party strength and party weakness can cut both ways, depending on the depth of the crisis confronting a country.

Given these interaction effects, institutional factors cannot stand on their own.[34] The propensities toward risk stressed by prospect theory — as mediated by the prior-option bias — explain why some political leaders

---

[34] Haggard and Kaufman's institutionalist explanation of market reform takes economic crisis into account, but in a sequential fashion: Crisis shapes the creation of institutions (1995: chaps. 1–4), which in turn affect the fate of reform (chaps. 5–10). This book, by contrast, assumes a continuous interaction of crisis conditions and institutions.

cautiously stay inside the established institutional framework ("transactional leadership," Burns 1978), whereas other chief executives boldly try to reshape these institutions ("transforming leadership," Burns 1978). Since under certain conditions leaders can bend, change, or eliminate institutional constraints, the crisis argument drawn from prospect theory is more fundamental than institutional arguments for explaining the ultimate political outcome of neoliberal reform efforts.

The opportunities and constraints posed by institutional factors are, however, important in helping to explain the ways and means through which leaders pursue policy reform. For instance, in a country with a strong party system, a leader facing a deep crisis can marshal solid support and thus enact costly change inside the established democratic framework. By contrast, in a weak party system, a leader confronting severe challenges may well resort to extra-constitutional means in order to impose reform in the absence of firm, reliable political support (cf. Haggard and Kaufman 1995: 204–9). Thus, institutional structures — as mediated by crisis conditions — do have a crucial impact on the politics of neoliberalism.

Conclusion

This chapter has elaborated a new explanation for the adoption of neoliberal reform in precarious democracies by drawing on psychological decision theories, especially prospect theory. The initiation of drastic, painful change in unstable institutional settings involves tremendous economic and political risk. Cognitive psychologists have shed new light on the conditions under which people tend to take such risk. My explanation borrows the most robust and striking finding, namely, risk-seeking in the domain of losses vs. risk aversion in the domain of gains. By applying this insight to politics, this chapter constructs a novel microfoundation for explanations of policy change.

Since the behavioral regularities found by cognitive psychologists deviate from calculations of expected value, this new approach diverges from conventional rational-choice approaches. With their solid empirical basis, arguments derived from prospect theory promise to provide greater explanatory power for political analysis than the ideal-typical assumptions of rational choice, which lead to predictions that are often empirically inaccurate (as criticized by Thaler 1992; Green and Shapiro 1994). While psychological decision theories are more complicated and less well-elaborated than the neat, elegant models of rational choice, their realistic foundation in empirical regularities may make them more useful for political analysis (McDermott 1998: 33, 36, 177).

In addition to borrowing important insights from cognitive psychology, the present chapter has integrated these findings in an economic-structural, political-institutional, and ideational context. Prospect theory itself suggests such a synthesis because it advances situational arguments: Propensities toward risk depend on the domain a decision-maker is in. And to explain which domain prevails, other theories need to be invoked, especially structural arguments about a country's economic development. Thus, prospect theory itself calls for an integration of "structure" and "choice" (Berejikian 1992). Furthermore, while prospect theory explains which one of the available options is chosen, it does not account for the range of options that a decision-maker considers. It therefore needs to be combined with ideational arguments, which emphasize learning from prior experiences. Moreover, prospect theory elucidates individual choices, not collective decisions and outcomes.[35] To be useful for political analysis, it needs to be integrated with institutional arguments, which shed light on the translation of individual choices into collective decisions.

The present effort to embed cognitive-psychological insights in a structural, institutional, and ideational context follows Lichbach's (1997: 260–74) recent proposal to integrate the major theoretical schools in comparative politics, which, in Lichbach's classification, emphasize economic and political structures, culture, or rationality.[36] As Lichbach stresses, each school has theoretical lacunae that create the need for synthesis. Therefore, it is most fruitful to elaborate complex explanations that draw on different approaches.

This chapter diverges from Lichbach's synthesis in one crucial aspect, however. Rather than assuming rationality, my synthesis rests on an empirical model of choice. This cognitive-psychological theory admits the importance of self-interest and focuses on individual choice (Levy 1997: 100–102) but diverges from the assumption that actors maximize expected value. Rather, people's complex assessments of probability and value, especially their asymmetrical valuation of gains vs. losses, lead to deviations from strict maximization postulates. By not starting from conventional rational-choice premises, my explanation rests on a microfoundation different from Lichbach's synthesis.

How successful is this new argument in accounting for adjustment politics in Argentina, Brazil, Peru, and Venezuela? The following chapters present a systematic empirical assessment.

---

[35] Levy (1997: 102–5). For initial steps toward filling this gap, see Kameda and Davis (1990) and Bottom and Miller (1997).

[36] Lichbach's "structure" comprises both economic structures and political institutions, that is, the first two explanations considered in chapter 2.

CHAPTER FOUR

ECONOMIC DETERIORATION AND POSTPONED ADJUSTMENT IN THE 1980s

For Latin America, the 1980s constituted a lost decade. Economic development, which had advanced greatly in earlier decades, screeched to a halt, and per capita income stagnated or diminished in most countries. Bouts of hyperinflation devastated the economies of Argentina, Bolivia, Nicaragua, and Peru and inflicted considerable damage in Brazil as well. Mexico's and Venezuela's dreams of turning their petroleum resources into easy prosperity also faltered, due only in part to drastically falling oil prices.

What accounts for these severe economic problems? And, above all, why did the four countries under investigation fail to combat these difficulties in a timely and determined fashion? Why did the orthodox measures adopted initially in all four countries fail to restore economic stability? And why did the governments of Argentina, Brazil, and Peru, which eventually adopted heterodox stabilization plans, refuse to shift course for years after the failure of these policies had become obvious? Similarly, why did Venezuela artificially maintain its oil rentier model, rather than taking determined steps to diminish its dependence on petroleum?

Applying arguments developed in chapter 3, the present chapter explains economic deterioration and delayed adjustment in the four countries during the 1980s. Structural economic factors and problematic policy design and implementation were responsible for the worsening economic difficulties. The import-substitution industrialization pursued in Latin America since the 1930s had inherent limitations (such as the difficulties of using economies of scale), which led to considerable inefficiency. Although these flaws became ever more evident, the prior-option bias induced incumbent governments to persist with the established development strategy and throw good money after bad. In fact, early signs of economic problems prompted more intense efforts to complete national industrialization, sustained by the abundant bank loans that were available in the 1970s. But the debt crisis foreclosed these attempts to give ISI a new lease on life.

The military governments of Jorge Videla in Argentina (1976–81), João Figueiredo in Brazil (1979–85), and Francisco Morales Bermúdez in Peru (1975–80) and the democratic administration of Fernando Belaúnde in Peru (1980–85) responded to these worsening problems with orthodox adjustment measures, which remained half-hearted and incomplete, however. The Christian Democratic administration of Luis Herrera Campíns in Venezuela (1979–84) initially pursued similar policies, though in an even more watered-down version. Inconsistently implemented and coinciding with the eruption of the debt crisis, these recessionary policies had minimal success and even exacerbated the difficulties, especially run-away inflation.

Learning from these perceived failures inspired the heterodox experiments undertaken in the mid-1980s under presidents Raúl Alfonsín in Argentina (1983–89), José Sarney in Brazil (1985–90), and Alan García in Peru (1985–90) as well as the effort of the Jaime Lusinchi government in Venezuela (1984–89) to cover up the problems of the decaying petroleum rentier model through intensified government interventionism. In addition to learning, political interests inspired this repudiation of economic orthodoxy. Chief executives in new democracies were reluctant to impose open losses on important sectors. They were therefore tempted to believe the promise of heterodox experts that fairly cost-free stabilization was feasible. Political expediency — not only intellectual arguments — thus made the theories of inertial inflation attractive in Argentina and Brazil and induced the García government to embrace the claim that renewed development would lower inflation by eliminating economic bottlenecks.

These heterodox policies failed, however, due especially to the state's fiscal crisis and the resource drain caused by continuing debt service. But the incumbent governments refused to embark on a drastic shift of course, falling prey to the prior-option bias. Chief executives were reluctant to admit the failure of their initial policy approach and to adopt neoliberal programs that they had rejected before — sometimes vocally, as in the case of Alan García. To avoid a loss of face, they desperately sought to shore up their heterodox policies and made concessions to orthodoxy only under utter duress. President Sarney, for instance, enacted two stabilization programs that were similar to the failed Cruzado Plan of 1986, and they failed even more quickly — a striking example of the temptation to throw good money after bad.

Thus, learning from the perceived failure of the initial orthodox measures and, later, the prior-option bias that locked incumbents into a heterodox policy approach account for the delays in countries' adjustment to steadily worsening economic problems.

The Exhaustion of Import-Substitution Industrialization

Adopted from the 1930s onward, import-substitution industrialization brought tremendous economic development to Latin America. Countries with largely rural economies established impressive urban industrial sectors. Some of these nations, especially Argentina, Brazil, and Mexico, even came to produce sophisticated consumer and capital goods, such as computers and airplanes. Seeking to follow the example of First World countries, the most advanced nations hoped to complete national industrialization quickly and thus leave Third World status behind.

ISI also had some inherent flaws, however, which caused ever graver constraints as industrialization advanced. Oligopolistic ownership, protected from foreign competition by a host of trade barriers, led to considerable inefficiency, which—contrary to the implications of infant-industry arguments—did not seem to diminish over time. The resulting lack of international competitiveness in sectors where Latin America's low labor costs did not yield a decisive comparative advantage limited industrial exports. Since ISI depended on continued imports of machinery and semifinished goods, however, it was always plagued by foreign-exchange bottlenecks. The establishment of ever more sophisticated industries, which required particularly expensive imports of machinery and which found particularly limited demand inside Latin American countries, aggravated these difficulties. The inward-looking, heavily protectionist development strategy embodied in ISI was thus headed toward a cul-de-sac as further progress bred intensifying problems.

In fact, since short-term solutions aggravated long-term problems, policy-makers pursuing ISI were particularly susceptible to the prior-option bias. When a country suffered from an acute foreign exchange constraint, the logical recipe seemed to be to substitute for more imports with new local production, that is, to drive ISI forward. As this new push towards import substitution ended up tightening foreign-exchange constraints, policy-makers were tempted to try the same recipe with another sector of imports. As each advance of import substitution soon appeared to call for an ever larger dosage of the same medicine, policy-makers were hooked on the ISI strategy and sorely tempted to throw good money after bad.

Compared to these efforts to shore up the established development model, any attempt to shift course by lowering trade barriers, turning industry more competitive, and adopting an export-oriented strategy appeared much more risky. Such a move to economic liberalism threatened to cause high immediate losses because many coddled sectors of industry would have to take costly adjustment measures, and some were unlikely to survive the onslaught of foreign competition. At the same time, potential benefits were uncertain because it was impossible to predict which domestic sectors could be successful in competitive world markets.

Since the "neoliberal" alternative was therefore widely rejected, decision-makers considered only whether the effort to complete ISI should be pursued more or less aggressively. In line with the core prediction of prospect theory, the governments of the 1960s and 1970s tended to adopt risk-acceptant policies when they hit stumbling blocks that placed them in the domain of losses. The Brazilian military regime, for instance, adopted an ambitious program to establish basic and capital goods industries and develop new raw material exports when faced with the sudden quadruplication of the oil price in 1973–74, which caused a tremendous trade deficit and thus threatened to strangle ISI. Instead of slowing down economic development, as his fiscally conservative advisers recommended, President Ernesto Geisel (1974–79) sought to push ISI ahead with full speed. Specifically, the fear that Brazil would otherwise miss "the last train to Paris" (Velloso 1986) — that is, clear prospects of losses — triggered this *fuite en avant* (Sola 1994: 163; Barros de Castro 1994).

The Debt Crisis

These intensified efforts at industrialization in Brazil, Peru, and Venezuela were facilitated by the easy availability of cheap foreign loans in the 1970s, which was boosted further by the abundance of petrodollars deposited in First World banks after the 1973 OPEC oil price hike. Rapidly rising debt thus allowed for the further "deepening" of ISI and for a while covered up its problems (Fishlow 1986: 65–78). In fact, the reliance on external debt led to an even more drastic departure from market principles. Since a large proportion of foreign bank loans was channeled through the state, the public sector's share in the economy grew further. This expansion of state interventionism triggered concern among private entrepreneurs, as expressed especially in the "antistatization" campaign of the mid-1970s in Brazil (Velasco e Cruz 1984).

The rapidly rising debt brought short-term relief from fiscal and external constraints but created growing financial commitments for the future. Given Latin America's limited export performance, payments of interest and principal were likely to outstrip the influx of new credits sooner or later. This net fiscal drain appeared earlier than expected because of the dramatic rise in U.S. interest rates in 1980 and 1981. Since Latin America's debt with private banks had adjustable interest rates, debt service suddenly skyrocketed. When Mexico declared its incapacity to pay in August 1982, First World banks immediately lowered their voluntary lending to other Latin American countries as well. This chain reaction plunged the whole region into a serious debt crisis.

In order not to lose access to international capital markets, the governments of Argentina, Brazil, Peru, and Venezuela could not afford to repudiate the debt. They therefore had to ask for debt rescheduling to stretch out their payments of interest and principal. In the resulting negotiations, First World banks were in a stronger bargaining position because they closely coordinated their position, whereas the debtor countries were unable to form a debtors' cartel to extract substantial concessions (O'Donnell 1985).

In the absence of voluntary bank lending, continued debt service — even at the lower levels resulting from debt rescheduling — created a tremendous net outflow of fiscal resources. Since the public sector, which had contracted a good part of the debt in the first place, also agreed to assume the private sector's obligations, the debt crisis pushed the state into a fiscal crisis. Unable or unwilling to raise taxation, many states resorted to the printing press to cover growing public deficits. The debt problem thus aggravated inflationary pressures, contributing to the eruption of hyperinflation in several countries.

The structural problems inherent in ISI; the prior-option bias, which prevented governments from resolutely addressing these problems; and the acute pressures caused by the debt crisis thus account for the enormous economic difficulties that most Latin American countries suffered during the 1980s. The commonalities in the fate of different countries show the importance of both policy learning, which initially made the ISI model attractive, and international economic constraints, such as the rise in interest rates and the abrupt end of voluntary bank lending. Despite these commonalities, however, country experiences also differed in some important respects.

Differences in Country Experiences

While proceeding along broadly similar lines, ISI had different specific characteristics in the countries under investigation. These differences in economic development affected the nature and severity of the economic problems afflicting these nations during the 1980s.

First of all, ISI advanced much farther in Argentina and Brazil than in Peru and Venezuela. In Brazil and especially in Argentina, industrialization started early, namely, in the late nineteenth century, when development was driven mainly by primary exports. Adopting nationalist, protectionist economic policies in the 1930s and 1940s, both countries made great strides toward building durable consumer, basic, and capital goods industries in subsequent decades. Thus, by the 1970s, both countries had an extensive and sophisticated industrial base. Yet in Argentina, growth decelerated after 1950, and per capita income increased relatively slowly thereafter. Indeed, efforts by the military government of the late 1970s to revitalize development through market-oriented policies actually caused considerable deindustrialization as cheaper foreign imports outcompeted local production. Brazil, by contrast, experienced a tremendous growth spurt in the late 1960s and 1970s. Despite recessions at the beginning and end of the decade, even the 1980s saw considerable economic development. Thus, Brazil was the most successful case of ISI in the region, due in part to its enormous market size and its ample natural resources, which allowed for substantial exports.

Compared to Argentina and Brazil, industrialization started much later in Peru and Venezuela. Seeking to overcome this backwardness quickly, the Peruvian military regime of Juan Velasco Alvarado (1968–75) embarked on a crash course of ISI by greatly expanding public investment, financed to a considerable extent by foreign debt (Wise 1994). Yet the country soon found it difficult to service its debt and had to undergo severe adjustment in the late 1970s, which put an end to rapid industrialization. In Venezuela, efforts to "sow the petroleum" by establishing industry began in the mid-1940s (Karl 1997: 84) and received a strong impulse from the OPEC oil price hike of 1973. As the distributor of oil rents, the state assumed primary responsibility for economic development, focusing on heavy industry in order to exploit the country's wealth of mineral and energy resources. This resource abundance, however, limited any pressure for efficiency and created a particularly high temptation to misuse public enterprises for purposes of political patronage. In addition, the country's coddled private sector was far from attaining international competitiveness (Bitar 1989).

Due to these differences in economic development, the debt crisis of the 1980s had distinct characteristics and consequences in the four countries under investigation. In Argentina, Brazil, and Peru, fiscal problems exacerbated by the debt crisis fueled drastic price rises, which eventually erupted in hyperinflation, namely, price increases above 50 percent per month. In Venezuela, by contrast, the government's direct control over oil wealth mitigated the state's fiscal crisis, and inflation remained at comparatively moderate levels of up to 30 percent per year (Zambrano Sequín and Riutort Merino 1990). In fact, price rises never acquired the strong inertial component that kept inflation high and pushed it to progressively higher levels in Argentina, Brazil, and Peru. Thus, inflation — the problem of economic instability that most severely affects the largest number of people — was much less grave in Venezuela than in the other three countries under investigation.

The four nations' economic growth record also differed markedly. Argentina's longstanding lack of economic dynamism, Peru's failed effort at rapid industrialization, and the collapse in the price of Venezuela's main export — petroleum — led to considerable per capita income losses in those countries during the 1980s. By contrast, Brazil's more vigorous economy, which was reaping the benefits of the ambitious development projects initiated by the Geisel government, yielded a net increase in per capita income during the decade, despite considerable short-term fluctuations in economic fortunes.

In sum, Argentina and Peru were worst off in facing tremendous challenges in both price stability and economic growth. Brazil, by contrast, combined run-away inflation with continued economic development, whereas Venezuela maintained relative price stability, yet suffered from a considerable, albeit gradual, economic downturn. The hope, however, that any increase in international oil prices would immediately renew growth — as happened with the Iraq/Kuwait crisis of 1990–91 — limited Venezuelans' perception of serious economic decline (see Karl 1997: 161; similarly, Keller 1996: 67–68), which had taken hold in Peru and especially in Argentina. In the countries under investigation, governments thus had to confront economic problems of a different type and severity during the 1980s.

The First Attempt at Orthodox Adjustment

After their predecessors used external loans to bolster and push forward ISI in the 1970s, the governments of João Figueiredo in Brazil, Francisco Morales Bermúdez and Fernando Belaúnde in Peru, and Luis Herrera Campíns in Venezuela changed course: They responded to signs of economic deterioration with efforts at orthodox adjustment and some liberalizing reforms. In a much more determined fashion, the military government of Jorge Videla in Argentina sought to overcome the country's longstanding economic stagnation by enacting a comprehensive program of neoliberal reform in the late 1970s. While governments in the other three countries embarked mainly on short-term stabilization and moderate trade and financial liberalization, the team led by José Alfredo Martínez de Hoz sought to revamp Argentina's development model and shift the emphasis from protectionist industrialization to export promotion, taking advantage of Argentina's agricultural wealth.

These efforts attained some short-term achievements, such as temporary reductions in inflation and increases in exports. But none of these programs had much lasting success. In fact, inflation ended up increasing considerably in Argentina, Brazil, and Peru, and all four countries racked up a large amount of additional debt, which was bound to exacerbate economic problems in the future. Why did this first round of orthodox adjustment efforts fail? This question is particularly puzzling given that a few years later, orthodox, neoliberal programs succeeded in restoring economic stability in Argentina, Peru, and — eventually — Brazil.

International conjunctures, especially changes in the availability of foreign capital, played an important role. The first round of orthodox adjustment plans coincided with a particularly intense manic-depressive cycle of international lending. In the late 1970s and early 1980s, foreign bankers pushed loans on Latin American governments, which used this influx of foreign capital as an easy way to mitigate serious economic problems. The time bomb created by this mutual irresponsibility detonated in August 1982 when Mexico declared its inability to maintain its debt service on schedule. Panicked, foreign banks quickly stopped their voluntary lending to the whole region, which suddenly had to cope with a huge outflow of capital. Due in part to the neoliberal dogmatism espoused by the Reagan administration, international financial institutions confined themselves to keeping the debtor countries afloat while refusing to support a lasting economic recovery. These dramatic, unpredictable shifts in international capital availability hindered the elaboration and implementation of consistent, responsible adjustment plans.[1]

Yet while important, this external factor alone cannot account for the failure of the orthodox stabilization programs. These efforts faced serious problems before the eruption of the debt crisis, especially in Argentina. What caused these difficulties?

First of all, important policy-makers and other influential political forces did not recognize the true severity of the problems facing their countries. While all four nations confronted unprecedented difficulties, many actors hoped that limited adjustment measures would be sufficient for restoring stability and growth. For instance, committed to stimulating development, Planning Minister Antonio Delfim Netto —

---

[1] By contrast, the neoliberal shock programs of the late 1980s and early 1990s coincided with the resumption of voluntary lending, which — due to learning from the debt crisis — was more cautious than in the late 1970s and early 1980s. And where externally financed boom-and-bust cycles did occur, as in Mexico and Argentina, domestic and international policy-makers now had more experience in coping with these problems, and newly liberalized economies had a greater capacity for adjustment, for example, through increases in exports.

Brazil's economic czar — first tried out expansionary, unorthodox policies, which greatly exacerbated economic disequilibria, and shifted course only belatedly and half-heartedly (Fishlow 1989: 101–9; Lamounier and Moura 1986: 175–79). Peruvian President Belaúnde consented to orthodox stabilization measures merely to curry favor with international financial institutions and thus maintain the influx of foreign capital required for financing his ambitious infrastructure projects (Webb 1999: 124–25). Venezuelan President Herrera remained torn between his economic advisers, who advocated austerity, and important sectors of his party COPEI, which sought higher social spending to advance their electoral fortunes (*LAWR* 1980, 1981). Finally, powerful sectors of the Argentine military rejected severe austerity measures that could usher in a deep recession and large-scale unemployment. They also defended state ownership in broadly defined strategic sectors of the economy and blocked privatization efforts (Lewis 1990: 453–56, 460–61, 477–78).

This lack of commitment by crucial actors, which reflected a limited sense of crisis, posed enormous obstacles to stabilization plans, especially in Argentina, Peru, and Venezuela. Whereas many economic experts had a fairly good grasp of the problems afflicting their country, other, "political" actors had different perceptions, and different interests. Important sectors of the Argentine military, for instance, simply ranked national security above economic stability and prosperity. And as the mainstay of the dictatorial regime, the armed forces obviously had tremendous veto power.

Even economic experts were tempted to underestimate the difficulty of overcoming their countries' problems. Above all, they tended to extrapolate temporary positive trends into the future, rather than seeing them as a cyclical upswing, which would soon be followed by a downswing. For instance, the dramatic recovery in Peru's export prices during 1979–80 and the resulting improvement in external accounts diminished the sense of urgency prevailing among Belaúnde's economic team (Webb 1999: 124–26, 156). Similarly, the tremendous influx of foreign capital during the late 1970s induced Martínez de Hoz to postpone the painful but necessary decision to adjust Argentina's increasingly overvalued exchange rate (Ramos 1986: 88). And in Venezuela, the drastic rise of international petroleum prices in 1979–80 made decision-makers feel less of a pressing need to adjust to economic disequilibria and, particularly, to reorient the country's development model (Martz 1984: 74–75; Quenan 1990: 110).

This limited perception of crisis hobbled adjustment efforts from the very beginning. In line with prospect theory, it induced actors who did not clearly see themselves in the domain of losses to proceed with relative caution. They therefore rejected the economic and especially political risks entailed in determined, radical stabilization and reform efforts. For this reason, painful austerity measures were postponed and remained limited (Karl 1997: 175–76; Fishlow 1989: 101–9; Pastor and Wise 1992: 87, 90–92; Ramos 1986: 40–41, 52, 86; Schvarzer 1986: 237–53; Webb 1999: 100–102, 124–25, 158–59). Fiscal problems therefore persisted, helping to keep inflation high. Structural reform efforts — such as privatization in Argentina — were scaled down greatly and implemented in an incomplete fashion. As a result, the gradual trade liberalizations enacted in Argentina, Peru, and Venezuela did little to combat inflation by pressuring domestic producers through the influx of cheap imports (Ramos 1986: 80, 88–91, 119; Webb 1999: 107–10). Brazil never even initiated such structural reforms.

Limited progress on one front exacerbated the goal tradeoffs plaguing the adjustment programs. For instance, since domestic producers continued to face low competition, devaluations ended up boosting inflation. And due to persistently high price rises, the preannounced schedule of devaluations at diminishing rates led to a growing appreciation of the currency in Argentina and Brazil. This overvaluation in turn hindered exports, whose promotion was one of the reformers' main goals (Ramos 1986: 42, 51, 86–91).

Facing these difficulties, decision-makers also made important policy mistakes. These flawed decisions were due in part to ideological dogmatism. For instance, rigid adherence to economic orthodoxy led Martínez de Hoz to embark on a premature, excessively radical liberalization of financial markets, which typically triggered unsound lending practices that eventually caused many banks to collapse (Schvarzer 1986: 60–101). Similar ideological blinders made Brazil's Delfim Netto underestimate the importance of inertial mechanisms, especially widespread indexation, which prevented his orthodox medicine from bringing down inflation (see Branco and David 1989: 169–70; see also Schydlowsky 1986: 235–36, on Peru).

Additional policy mistakes resulted from the prior-option bias. For instance, Argentina's economic team stubbornly kept preannounced devaluations in place even after their deleterious impact on the real exchange rate, the country's external accounts, and its indebtedness had long become obvious. Despite occasional doubts (Schvarzer 1986: 92–95), Martínez de Hoz decided to throw good money after bad, thus getting deeper and deeper into a cul-de-sac. When a devaluation eventually became unavoidable, it had to attain such a magnitude that inflation skyrocketed and the whole adjustment effort collapsed (Smith 1989: 239–42). Similarly, the Herrera Campíns government maintained Venezuela's fixed exchange rate for much too long, despite tremendous and growing capital flight (Alvarez de Stella 1988: 215–20; LAWR 1982).

Typically, the short-sighted postponement of a necessary correction—the trademark of the prior-option bias—magnified the deleterious repercussions of the adjustment.

In sum, the initial efforts to combat the serious economic problems caused by the decay of ISI and the enormous debt burden failed for a number of reasons.[2] Drastic shifts in the availability of foreign capital made the design and implementation of adjustment plans difficult. Furthermore, important political actors did not grasp the full depth of the crisis and therefore—in line with prospect theory—proceeded with excessive caution and refused to accept determined, risky adjustment plans. They provided at best lukewarm support for the painful measures proposed by economic experts or offered active resistance, as sectors of the Argentine military did. Finally, policy mistakes—caused by ideological rigidity and the prior-option bias—exacerbated these problems.

Heterodox Programs

In a typical swing of the pendulum (Pastor and Wise 1992: 83), learning from the failure of orthodox adjustment paved the way for heterodox stabilization plans in inflation-ridden Argentina, Brazil, and Peru and—eventually—for expansionary economic policies in Venezuela, which suffered from income losses caused by declining oil prices. Compared to the recessionary effects of orthodox stabilization plans, heterodox programs—the Plan Austral in Argentina, the Plano Cruzado in Brazil, and the Plan Inti in Peru—had the political advantage of promising to bring about economic stability in a distributionally neutral and therefore politically cost-free fashion. This prospect was especially attractive to the leaders of fragile new democracies, namely, Raúl Alfonsín in Argentina, José Sarney in Brazil, and Alan García in Peru.

But in economic terms, heterodox programs rested on unconventional, untested ideas and were therefore quite risky. The theories that inspired these stabilization plans were new and unconsolidated. The short- and long-term results of these adjustment programs were unforeseeable. In Brazil, for instance, a number of economic experts and politicians who participated in the design of the Plano Cruzado feared

[2] Specifically political problems contributed to the failure of orthodox programs in some cases, but not others. In Argentina and Brazil, orthodox economic policies had low political acceptability due to their association with military regimes of diminishing legitimacy. But the liberalizing program of the Belaúnde government in Peru's restored democracy and the initial austerity measures enacted by the Herrera Campíns government in Venezuela's longstanding democracy provoked similar rejection. Thus, regime type cannot account for the failure of orthodox policies.

that it would cause a recession and therefore elicit popular rejection (Solnik 1987: 154–56; Sardenberg 1987: 251, 291–94) — precisely the opposite of the actual outcomes. Also, it was unclear how economic agents would respond to the enactment and especially the eventual lifting of price freezes, which constituted an important element of heterodox plans. The secretive elaboration and surprising imposition of these shock programs exacerbated these dangers. In the absence of ample consultations with economic and political actors, it was difficult to calibrate these comprehensive "packages" of drastic measures and to correct potential mistakes through subsequent modifications. Thus, heterodox programs held considerable economic and political risks (Smith 1990: 9; Solnik 1987: 27–28, 86–87; Torre 1993: 75).

In line with prospect theory, decision-makers were willing to incur these risks because they saw themselves in the domain of losses. Inflation had demonstrated a stubborn capacity to persist at very high levels, and it was on a clear upward trajectory at the beginning of the Alfonsín, Sarney, and García governments. The danger of hyperinflation threatened to undermine economic predictability and thus stifle investment and growth. By imposing particularly high costs on the large numbers of poorer people, skyrocketing price rises also aggravated social tensions and jeopardized the popularity of the government. For these reasons, decision-makers saw themselves ever more clearly in the domain of losses (Giussani 1987: 193–96; Sardenberg 1987: chap. 9). As prospect theory would predict, this perception triggered risk acceptance. Thus, the worsening crisis induced decision-makers to implement bold new ideas that promised a magical turnaround but could also produce economic and political failure.

What, exactly, were the unconventional ideas inspiring these stabilization plans? Heterodox experts saw as a root cause of the accelerating price rises the widespread formal and informal indexation mechanisms that gave inflation a strong inertial component. Since many prices, wages, taxes, interest rates, and other values were automatically readjusted for past price increases, it was impossible ever to lower inflation. Moreover, in a heavily indexed economy, any exogenous shock — such as a rise in import prices or a failed harvest — had the effect of pushing inflation permanently to a higher level. Heterodox experts argued that these inertial mechanisms were responsible for the failure of the preceding orthodox stabilization programs to diminish inflation effectively (Smith 1990: 10).

This novel diagnosis suggested unconventional recipes for economic stabilization, which diverged from the categorical market orientation of the initial adjustment efforts. Heterodox experts enlisted the state as the main agent for breaking inflationary inertia. They recommended a temporary price freeze to interrupt widespread expectations of ever increasing inflation, which drove the demand for indexation mechanisms (Solnik 1987: 162). This government intervention, which was designed to break abruptly the self-reinforcing dynamic of inflation, drastically interfered in the market and thus diverged from the principles of economic orthodoxy. To avoid anticipatory price raises, the freeze had to be imposed by surprise, that is, as part of a secretively designed shock program.

This temporary interruption of inertial mechanisms was accompanied by the abolition of indexation procedures for taxes, bank accounts, and short-term contracts. Furthermore, to suppress inflationary memories and mark a clean break with the past, heterodox plans created a new currency and pegged it to the dollar as a stabilizing anchor. The designers of heterodox plans hoped that the link to a stable foreign currency would help to break the prevailing inflationary mentality. The monetary reform thus sought to accustom people to living under stability, rather than expecting constant price rises. The resulting sense of stability would prevent economic actors from resorting to anticipatory defense mechanisms, such as price or wage increases designed to compensate for expected future inflation. Thus, these programs not only enlisted actors' economic self-interests (as orthodox adjustment programs do), but also sought to reshape their expectations, which had triggered individually rational but collectively suboptimal behavior.

While departing from economic orthodoxy in crucial ways, several of the Argentine and Brazilian authors of heterodox stabilization plans agreed with neoliberal economists on the urgent need to reduce the public deficit, especially by slashing state spending (Smith 1990: 9–10; Solnik 1987: 84, 164). Like their orthodox counterparts, they saw excessive demand as a serious risk for efforts to control inflation. By contrast, other, more politically motivated experts, such as the economists aligned with the former opposition party Partido do Movimento Democrático Brasileiro (PMDB) in Brazil, downplayed the need for austerity and emphasized instead the importance of stimulating development and attaining greater social equity. The Brazilian Plano Cruzado therefore contained significant redistributive and expansionary elements, especially an initial increase in wages.

The desire to transcend mere stabilization by promoting development and redistribution was especially pronounced in impoverished Peru. Going far beyond the heterodox emphasis on inertial mechanisms, President García's leading economic advisers attributed persistent inflation to structural bottlenecks, which caused scarcities of supply (Pastor and Wise 1992: 96–98; Thorp 1987: 163–67). In their view, stabilization therefore required increases in production and investment. Besides expansionary policies to stimulate growth and benefit the poor, they therefore enacted supplyside measures to promote investment, such as tax and interest rate cuts. They hoped that the resulting economic reactivation would increase public revenues, despite the reduction in tax rates. They also sought to reduce the fiscal drain on the state by limiting external debt service to 10 percent of export revenues. This radical move, which defied international financial institutions, was intended to leave the government with ample resources for stimulating domestic development.

Politically speaking, this structuralist approach had the advantage of offering socioeconomic benefits to a wide range of domestic groups, who had suffered considerable losses from Belaúnde's orthodox adjustment efforts. Economically speaking, however, the Peruvian plan disregarded orthodox concerns that the public deficit and excessive private demand fuel inflation (Pastor and Wise 1992: 100–102). In addition, the decision to limit external debt service threatened to cut Peru off from the international financial community and thus stifle development in the medium run.

The Failure of Heterodox Programs

Initially, these heterodox programs were highly successful in bringing down inflation while simultaneously promoting economic growth. This reactivation resulted from the dramatic reduction of the inflation tax, which permitted especially poorer sectors to engage in much higher consumption. Ample unused capacity, particularly in Peru, also permitted considerable growth without reigniting inflation. The wage increases decreed by presidents Sarney and García and the cuts in taxes and interest rates enacted in Peru further boosted consumption and production. Heterodox programs thus seemed to "square the circle" by bringing stability while fueling development—a miracle that had eluded the unsuccessful, recessionary orthodox programs.

This easy success itself, however, had problematic repercussions by easing the prevailing sense of crisis. As prospect theory would predict, the turnaround put many decision-makers into the domain of gains. Politicians, in particular, who lacked a thorough grasp of the underlying economic problems facing their country, considered the painful task of adjustment as completed already. This shift in perception induced the Argentine and Brazilian governments, in particular, to adopt a much more cautious posture and to shy away from following up on the initial stabilization measures with profound structural reforms that economic experts were urging them to adopt. Since top governmental leaders thought the battle was won, they did not want to open up new fronts. They refused to take tough measures that would impose considerable costs on important sectors and thus threaten their own base of support. Therefore, they missed the opportunity to consolidate the hard-won economic stability (de Pablo 1987: 230–33; Sardenberg 1987: 312; Smith 1990: 13–14; Solnik 1987: 166–72; Torre 1993: 80).

The prior-option bias also kept top political leaders from making further adjustments that many economic experts considered indispensable. In particular, price freezes and fixed exchange rates had beneficial effects only for a short while, especially in a setting of rapidly increasing demand and strong economic expansion. Kept in place for too long, these controls created economic distortions that undermined successful stabilization. But political leaders, especially Brazil's President Sarney, who suffered from a legitimacy deficit,[3] were reluctant to incur the short-term risks of loosening price controls and devaluing the currency; instead, they sought to postpone the day of reckoning (Solnik 1987: 91, 97, 104, 166–69). Unfortunately, the eventual negative repercussions of this overly cautious posture were disproportionally high.

As a result of these problems, the initial success of heterodox stabilization plans was short-lived. In the absence of timely corrections, the economy in all three countries soon became overheated, external accounts deteriorated, and inflationary pressures resurfaced. It therefore proved impossible to loosen price controls without triggering a new round of price increases. To stem resurgent inflation, the Argentine economic team reimposed controls on several occasions, yet with ever diminishing success as producers resorted to anticipatory price raises (Machinea 1993: 128; Smith 1990: 14, 17, 23). In Brazil, fear of inflation induced the Sarney government to postpone the lifting of controls until after crucial legislative and gubernatorial elections (Baer and Beckerman 1989: 45–46, 56; Sardenberg 1987: chaps. 11–12; Sola 1988: 49–52). By that time, however, the economic disequilibria caused by excessive demand — such as scarcities, informal price increases (ágio), falling exports, and growing imports — were so severe that the eventual flexibilization of the price freeze quickly unleashed strong inflation.

In Peru, the expansionary, redistributive policies of the García ad-

---

[3] An accidental president, Sarney took office only because President-elect Tancredo Neves fell ill and died. Whereas Neves represented the main government party PMDB, which had opposed the preceding dictatorship, Sarney had served the military regime as head of the government party until one year before the transition, when he joined a number of his colleagues and made an opportunistic move to ally with his former opponents, who had much better political prospects under the incoming civilian regime. Sarney therefore had a much weaker political position than Raúl Alfonsín, for instance, who had defeated the powerful Peronist Party in Argentina's transition election of 1983.

ministration also put strong pressure on the price level, the exchange rate, and the country's external accounts, especially from 1986 onward. Facing growing difficulties, the president sought to shore up his heterodox program with a bold new step, namely, the nationalization of the private banking system in July 1987. This surprising, radical move was designed to force higher investment and stem capital flight and thus counteract the increasing hesitancy of the private sector, which had come to regard the heterodox program as unsustainable and therefore refused to invest at the levels sought by the government. Rather than beating a more or less orderly retreat, as heterodox policy-makers did in Argentina and Brazil, the Peruvian president thus went on the attack.

But the unexpected nationalization decision backfired by undermining business confidence and by revitalizing right-wing political forces (Durand 1990: 245–87), which the failure of the second Belaúnde administration had silenced. Facing strong economic and political opposition and important legal challenges, President García eventually had to back away from the bank nationalization. Nevertheless, his heterodox program suffered severe damage from heightened business distrust and the further postponement of necessary adjustments, due to the government's preoccupation with the nationalization issue. As a result, Peru slid into an ever more severe economic crisis from late 1987 on.

Tragically, the failure of heterodox stabilization plans hurt especially poorer sectors, who had benefited the most from their temporary success (Camargo and Ramos 1988: chap. 3; Crabtree 1992: 45–58; Lago 1991: 292, 311–13; Morley and Alvarez 1992: 18, 24; Smith 1990: 30–31). Renewed inflation and governmental austerity measures, such as budget cuts and increases in public sector prices, eliminated the significant income gains that the less well-to-do had made initially. By the late 1980s, these disadvantaged sectors were worse off than before the adoption of heterodox programs, especially in Peru (Crabtree 1992: 138–47).

In Venezuela, a country that was suffering from moderate inflation, the government of Jaime Lusinchi embarked on much more conventional economic policies than the innovative stabilization programs enacted in Argentina, Brazil, and Peru. In fact, the Lusinchi administration followed the typical "political business cycle," starting with restrictive policies but promoting economic expansion during the second half of its term in preparation for the 1988 elections. The initial austerity policies were made possible by the political strength of the president, who had won the 1983 contest with an unprecedented vote differential and was presiding over a (seemingly) consolidated democracy. Therefore, Lusinchi had the clout to stabilize the economy, whereas Alfonsín, Sarney, and García—the leaders of fragile democracies—saw themselves compelled to buy support by promoting economic expansion and avoiding the imposition of costs on important groups.

Lusinchi initially continued the restrictive policies begun by his predecessor because he faced a further drop in the price of petroleum, which provided most of Venezuela's export revenues and a large share of the state's fiscal resources. Further budget cuts and devaluations and the resulting drop in imports restored internal and external equilibrium and allowed Venezuela to service its rescheduled debt while avoiding an agreement with the IMF (Quenan 1990: 112–14).

Soon, however, the Lusinchi administration shifted course and — despite a drastic drop in petroleum prices during 1986 — began to reactivate the economy, which had suffered from years of recession. Expansionary budget and monetary policies restored growth but fueled inflation and created a substantial deficit in Venezuela's external accounts, which the government financed with its dwindling currency reserves. Despite a recovery of the oil price in 1987, these irresponsible economic policies were clearly unsustainable. Once again, the prior-option bias helped prevent a timely correction. In addition, loose economic policies brought short-term political benefits. Lusinchi's Acción Democrática handily won the elections of December 1988, and the president left office in February 1989 with unprecedented approval ratings. But he bequeathed to his successor an explosive economic situation, characterized by grave inflationary pressures and negative foreign reserves (LAWR 1988, 1989).

The Reluctance to Shift Course

As the heterodox programs adopted in Argentina, Brazil, and Peru proved to be failures and Venezuela's expansionist policies had negative side effects, the economies of the four countries underwent considerable deterioration. Argentina and Brazil experienced virtual stagnation from 1987 to 1989, and Peru suffered a severe contraction of 8.8 percent in 1988 and another 10.4 percent in 1989 — the deepest recession on record. Annual inflation shot up to 174 percent (1987) and 387 percent (1988) in Argentina; 1,037 percent (1988) and 1,782 percent (1989) in Brazil; and 1,722 percent (1988) and 2,775 percent (1989) in Peru. When prices exploded by 114 percent in September 1988, Peru entered hyperinflation. While Venezuela was much better off, average GDP growth of 4.6 percent from 1986 through 1988 came at the cost of increasing inflation (from 11.6 percent in 1986 to 29.5 percent in 1988), plummeting public finances (from +6.3 percent of GDP in 1985 to −9.3 percent in 1989), and a rapidly deteriorating balance of payments (from +5.6 percent of GDP in 1985 to −9.6 percent in 1988). Thus, the country's reactivation clearly was unsustainable.

These worsening problems threatened the political survival of the incumbent government in Argentina, Brazil, and Peru. President Sarney, who had come to power following President-elect Tancredo Neves's death, faced constant demands to shorten his tenure in office, even after the Constituent Assembly of 1987–88 fixed his term. President García, who in addition to an economic collapse confronted an increasingly powerful guerrilla challenge, was threatened by coup preparations (Tanaka 1998: 163). And President Alfonsín, who was weakened by military rebellions, had to step down five months ahead of schedule to prevent an economic and political meltdown.

As a result of these difficulties, all three governments clearly entered the domain of losses. In the economic sphere, they faced exclusively negative prospects as none of the feasible courses of action promised positive outcomes. First, letting the economy continue to deteriorate posed serious political dangers and was therefore unacceptable. Second, limited adjustment measures would prevent a full-fledged catastrophe but achieve stability slowly at best and require a long series of painful measures. Third, shifting course by abandoning heterodoxy and adopting the neoliberal programs "recommended" by international financial institutions held the uncertain promise to turn the economy around; but such an about-face was highly risky by imposing intense transitional costs on important sectors and by offending the governments' current backers without reliably attracting a new support base. Thus, while the status quo was clearly unsustainable, determined reform programs held greater promise, but also graver risks than limited adjustment measures.

In principle, prospect theory predicts that presidents who see themselves in the domain of losses choose bold, risky policies. But the prior-option bias skews presidents' propensity toward risk by increasing the cost of a dramatic shift of course.[4] The adoption of orthodox shock programs would have required presidents Alfonsín, Sarney, and García, who had boldly rejected "neoliberalism," to admit that their heterodox experiments had been a mistake. Such a mea culpa would have under-

---

[4] This reluctance to learn from the failure of heterodoxy and embark on determined orthodox stabilization plans resulted not only from the rational calculation of presidents to avoid the high short-term costs of orthodox adjustment at the end of their terms because most of the benefits would accrue only to their successors. Longstanding incumbents who did not face fixed terms of office and who therefore had an indefinite "shadow of the future," such as Kenneth Kaunda in Zambia (1964–81) and Suharto in Indonesia (1965–98), responded to economic crises in exactly the same way: After pursuing nonorthodox policies, they refused to convert to orthodoxy and sought instead to muddle through.

mined their reputation, credibility, and leadership.[5] The earlier embrace of heterodoxy induced these presidents to persist with their basic policy approach and keep concessions to orthodoxy at the necessary minimum.

As a result, the last two to three years of Alfonsín's, Sarney's and García's tenure saw constant vacillation between unavoidable yet half-hearted orthodox adjustment measures and renewed efforts at heterodox or expansionist policies. Only under utter duress did these presidents adopt tough stabilization plans, but they loosened these painful policies as soon as they regained minimal breathing space. Moreover, they did not embark on determined structural reforms. As the indecisive orthodox programs attained little success, the three presidents returned to more heterodox policies.

President Sarney, in particular, fell prey to the prior-option bias. After the Plano Cruzado's collapse, he decreed two similar adjustment programs, which also relied on heterodox price controls. But these programs — the Bresser Plan of June 1987 (Bresser 1994) and the Summer Plan of January 1989 — were even less successful. Therefore, the Sarney government experimented with moderate orthodox policies — Finance Minister Maílson da Nóbrega's *feijão com arroz* of 1988 — and made a lukewarm effort to establish a social pact with major unions and business associations (Moura 1993: 8–13, 22–23). All of these variegated stabilization efforts sought to lower inflation inside the confines of the established development model. Only at the end of his term did Sarney take modest steps toward liberalization by initiating a "new industrial policy" that stipulated slow tariff reductions.

Confronting much graver deterioration, including the exhaustion of Peru's foreign currency reserves and eventually hyperinflation, President García reluctantly adopted five fairly orthodox stabilization packages between December 1987 and November 1988. But in every instance he watered down the more ambitious proposals of his economic experts (Crabtree 1992: 131–38) and retained heterodox elements, such as temporary price freezes. These more or less half-hearted orthodox efforts failed to bring down inflation but produced a severe recession and deepening poverty. Eventually, García returned to more heterodox policies in order to engineer an economic reactivation before the municipal elections of November 1989 and the presidential contest of mid-1990 (Crabtree 1992: 147–51). Furthermore, García never enacted structural reforms, such as trade liberalization or privatization. Thus, while Peru's

---

[5] Their adoption of bold, risky stabilization programs in the early phases of their presidency suggests that their reluctance to shift course did not arise from basic personality traits, but from situational factors, namely, the "stickiness" created by earlier policy commitments.

dramatic economic problems forced García to adopt tougher orthodox stabilization measures than Sarney, he remained even more committed to the established development model.[6]

President Alfonsín also vacillated between orthodox and heterodox adjustment (Paz 1989: 91–103; Smith 1990: 17–29). When the Plan Austral faced increasing problems, he decreed austerity measures in 1986, but another heterodox shock in early 1987. Thereafter, the government adopted ever more orthodox policies but occasionally resorted to heterodox instruments, such as price freezes. These inconsistent policies had meager results, and the economic situation kept worsening. Eventually, in August 1988, the administration imposed the Spring Plan, a fairly tough orthodox program with some heterodox components. But temporary success in reducing inflation came at the price of an increasingly overvalued exchange rate, which triggered a speculative attack on the currency in early 1989. The resulting turbulence destroyed any remaining trust in the government's capacity to manage the economy and pushed the country into hyperinflation.

Compared to these vacillations in macroeconomic policy, Alfonsín responded to Argentina's longstanding stagnation by making greater efforts than Sarney and García to revamp the country's development model through the privatization of public enterprises, trade liberalization, and fiscal reform. But the government elaborated these proposals only in 1987, when the failure of the Plan Austral and the Radical Party's defeat in legislative elections had already weakened it severely. As the Peronist Party and trade unions offered opposition, Alfonsín, who did not want to convert to "neoliberalism," was reluctant to provoke an all-out battle. Thus, vacillation and hesitancy doomed the belated orthodox adjustment efforts of the Alfonsín government.

Thus, the prior-option bias kept the three presidents from giving up their heterodox policy approach, despite its lack of success. In addition, political caution posed an important obstacle to determined stabilization and structural reform. Presidents Sarney, García, and Alfonsín feared the social costs of neoliberal programs, which threatened to undermine the government's political support and possibly endanger democracy itself. While economic experts recommended determined adjustment, presidents shied away from such a bold approach. Thus, as the crisis deepened, economic and political exigencies came to diverge ever more starkly. At the end of the 1980s, Argentina, Brazil, and Peru, which were in much more dire straits than Venezuela, seemed to face a

---

[6] García's refusal to shift to "neoliberalism" even in the face of hyperinflation shows that skyrocketing price rises do not force the adoption of drastic stabilization and structural reform.

cruel dilemma: either to preserve democracy and perpetuate economic vacillation and crisis, or to impose economic adjustment and jeopardize democracy. Was there any way out of this dilemma?

Political Repercussions of the Deepening Economic Crisis

Surprisingly, the very crisis that seemed to make it difficult to maintain democracy and at the same time stabilize the economy also paved the way for overcoming this dilemma. As the next chapter will show, deep, open crises provided the impulse for new presidents to adopt drastic adjustment programs and for large numbers of citizens to support these painful measures. And as the present section argues, the crisis undermined the established "political class" and allowed for the rise of political outsiders, who were willing to enact such bold changes.

Democratization had initially enhanced the image of politicians and political parties, which had been at the forefront of opposition to discredited military regimes. The high hopes pinned on the new democracies were quickly disappointed, however. This *desencanto*, common at the end of transition processes, was greatly aggravated by the severe problems of the 1980s, which in the eyes of many citizens revealed the incompetence and irresponsibility of many politicians. As countries suffered from worsening difficulties, partisan competition and factional disputes appeared as unnecessary bickering that hindered the resolution of the crisis. And as politicians used their institutional positions to secure their own economic well-being, even by extracting bribes, they came to be seen as self-serving, frivolous, and corrupt. Many citizens developed a deepening aversion to the professional political class as a detached, unrepresentative, and purely self-interested group that comfortably lived off of politics while the majority of the population had to struggle ever harder to make ends meet. As a result, trust in and appreciation of politicians and political parties fell significantly in the course of the decade (on Argentina, Catterberg 1989: 88–89; Mora y Araujo 1991: 133–34, 138–40, 148; on Brazil, Mainwaring 1999: 114; Moisés 1993: 164, 170; on Peru, Degregori and Grompone 1991: 23–34; Parodi and Twanama 1993: 68–89; on Venezuela, Alvarez 1996: 134–49; Salamanca 1997: 228–51).

The crisis also reduced the political clout of sociopolitical forces that opposed neoliberalism. Trade unions, for instance, suffered from similar image problems as parties. Peruvian unions, the Brazilian Central Única dos Trabalhadores (CUT), and the Ubaldini wing of the Argentine Confederación General del Trabajo (CGT) appeared as overly radicalized, and many Argentine and Venezuelan unions looked corrupt and—in the former case—close to organized crime. In general, unions' defense of their members against skyrocketing inflation required frequent strikes and protests, whose direct costs often fell on the general public. Sectors of the middle class and especially the poor, who did not have powerful unions to advance their interests, became particularly resentful of these constant disruptions of their daily routines, such as unexpected strikes of transportation workers. As a result, public endorsement of and trust in trade unions diminished during the 1980s, especially in Argentina and Peru (Catterberg 1989: 88; Mora y Araujo 1991: 77–81, 99–101; Balbi 1993; Alvarez 1996: 149–52). By contrast, the extreme levels of social inequality prevailing in Brazil, which seemed to justify demand-making by workers, and the association of the more radical wings of the labor movement with the long struggle for democracy guaranteed unions greater legitimacy (De Souza 1992; Moisés 1993: 164, 170).

Important business organizations also suffered criticism. This questioning prevailed in spite of—and in some ways because of—the gradual advance of neoliberal ideas, which depicted business people as innovative, modern entrepreneurs and the mainstay of a new, more dynamic development model. Compared to these lofty ideas, established business associations, especially corporatist organizations, appeared as bastions of distinctly unentrepreneurial "rent-seekers" who hid from competition behind high protectionist barriers and lived off of subsidies doled out by the state.[7] As businesspeople used constant price hikes to defend themselves against and profit from inflation, wide sectors of the population saw them as taking advantage of the crisis. Therefore, there was considerable popular resentment against big business organizations and their leaders (Catterberg 1989: 89; Lima Figueiredo 1992: 89–93; Alvarez 1996: 150).

Democratization reinforced these image problems. Leading business associations, such as Argentina's Consejo Económico Argentino (CEA) and Brazil's Federação das Indústrias do Estado de São Paulo (FIESP), had very cozy relationships with the outgoing military regimes, which discredited them in the eyes of ascendant democratic forces (on Argentina, Birle 1995: 209). Furthermore, businesspeople found it difficult to justify their demands in public because they seek political influence by using their economic clout, which contrasts with the democratic principle of political equality.[8] Democratization also stimulated tensions in-

---

[7] For a theoretical presentation of this image, see De Soto (1989).

[8] Fernando Collor reflected the resulting popular aversion when he scornfully rejected FIESP's endorsement of his candidacy for the second round of the 1989 presidential election.

side business associations because the owners of small or medium-sized firms invoked their large numbers to combat the traditional predominance of big business. For instance, a vocal opposition movement arose inside FIESP, challenging the entrenched leadership and giving labor and especially the government the opportunity to use divide-and-rule tactics. In sum, the regime transition turned business politically more vulnerable.

Above all, democratization diminished the political power of the military. After the transfer of government responsibility, which obviously had a tremendous effect, democratic competition induced politicians to keep chipping away at military prerogatives and resources (Hunter 1997a, 1997b). They were especially successful where the preceding military regime was discredited by economic failure, brutal human rights violations, and — as in Argentina — defeat in war. Since the armed forces were one of the mainstays of the old development model, which subordinated efficiency and competitiveness to national security concerns, the diminishing influence of the military was an important precondition for the advance of market reform. For instance, whereas the Argentine military had successfully opposed the large-scale privatization plans of Economy Minister Martínez de Hoz, its veto power dropped drastically under the new democracy.

In sum, the established political class, many parties, and other intermediary organizations faced growing popular aversion and distrust. This rejection by public opinion weakened the political clout of forces that had long opposed market reform. In addition, it loosened their hold over their own members and over previously sympathetic citizens. In this way, the decay of intermediary organizations boosted the number of political independents and increased the unorganized mass of the population that was available for mobilization by political outsiders who were willing to enact drastic change. In all of these ways, the severe crisis, which to many initial observers seemed difficult to resolve under democracy, in fact ended up paving the way for the initiation of determined adjustment.

CHAPTER FIVE

THE INITIATION
OF NEOLIBERAL ADJUSTMENT

The very crisis that seemed to pose the cruel dilemma of economic adjustment vs. democracy surprisingly paved the way for the enactment of drastic orthodox stabilization measures under democracy, which in turn initiated a turnaround in the economic and political fate of Argentina, Peru, and, eventually, Brazil. To account for this unexpected reversal of fortune, the present chapter shows that the particularly severe problems afflicting these three countries put a majority of the population into the domain of losses and thus induced them to reject the established political class and opt instead for daring, untested — i.e., risky — outsiders in upcoming presidential elections. Facing a rapidly deteriorating economy, the new chief executives also saw themselves in the domain of losses and therefore turned highly risk acceptant. Furthermore, as newcomers, they were not tied down by the prior-option bias, and they had learned from the failure of heterodox stabilization programs. For all these reasons, presidents Fernando Collor, Alberto Fujimori, and Carlos Menem decreed draconian adjustment plans. These bold measures imposed high short-term costs on important sectors, initiated a profound transformation of the established development model, and led their countries into uncharted territory. Therefore, these neoliberal shock plans embodied significantly greater economic and political risks than feasible, more prudent alternatives, as will be shown below.

One of the main dangers inherent in neoliberal adjustment was the uncertain response of common people and major interest groups. In fact, several reform initiators were quite apprehensive, fearing protests and riots, which in Latin America's unstable institutional settings could endanger presidents' political survival. But a large majority of the suffering population initially approved of risky and costly shock programs, even before they yielded beneficial outcomes. Risk acceptance in the domain of losses accounts for the surprisingly massive support that neoliberal policy packages immediately elicited. While this initial approval eroded quickly if stabilization efforts failed or produced improvements only slowly, it had a crucial political impact by demonstrating the political payoff of economic stability and by enabling presidents to win congressional approval for the initiation of crucial structural reforms.

While the politics of neoliberalism in Argentina, Brazil, and Peru had many similarities at this stage of reform initiation, the Venezuelan case differed due to the lower intensity of the country's economic problems and the Lusinchi government's efforts to hide them. A majority of Venezuelans therefore did not see themselves in the domain of losses and made a risk-averse choice in the 1988 presidential election by reelecting Carlos Andrés Pérez, who had presided over an unprecedented oil boom during his first term (1974–79). Pérez, however, was a maverick who had wrested the presidential candidacy away from the established leadership of his own party. Aware of the grave economic difficulties facing Venezuela and deterred by the dramatic failure of Alan García's heterodoxy, he faced clear prospects of losses and therefore enacted a drastic adjustment plan upon taking office. Unprepared and not seeing itself in the domain of losses, a majority of the population rejected this shock plan. Since the stabilization program itself imposed substantial and seemingly unjustified losses, large-scale riots erupted, shaking Venezuela's longstanding political stability. The resulting drop in presidential popularity weakened the Pérez government and encouraged established sociopolitical forces—including growing sectors of his own party—to oppose his neoliberal policies.

Thus, the differential severity of the crises facing their countries dialectically affected the initial political success of Menem's, Collor's, Fujimori's, and Pérez's rescue efforts. In line with my application of prospect theory, the graver the open problems that a country confronted, the stronger was electoral support for bold outsiders and the more massive was the popular endorsement of the new presidents' drastic adjustment measures. By contrast, where problems did not look that severe, a new president's efforts to preempt a crisis and thus avert high losses were politically unsuccessful.

The Rise of Political Outsiders

The severe economic crisis of the late 1980s and the disrepute into which the established political class, parties, and other intermediary organizations had fallen—their *desgaste*—allowed political outsiders to rise. Institutional erosion thus constituted a permissive cause for drastic elite renovation. The impulse for the emergence of newcomers stemmed, however, from risk-seeking in the domain of losses. Since a majority of Argentines, Brazilians, and Peruvians suffered from hyperinflation, experienced recent losses, and faced a serious threat of additional, poten-

tially catastrophic losses, they took considerable political risks by supporting outsiders with weak track records and vague, unclear campaign
programs. Since these candidates, particularly Collor and Fujimori,
were untested in national politics and since their future behavior was
impossible to predict, they constituted a risky vote option. My application of prospect theory makes a crucial contribution to explaining why
a majority of the population, which was particularly large in Brazil's
and Peru's inchoate party systems, opted for such outsiders and rejected
both the incumbent parties and the established moderate opposition (cf.
Quattrone and Tversky 1988: 723–24). In Venezuela, by contrast, the
outgoing government concealed burgeoning economic problems from
the population. A majority therefore did not see itself in the domain of
losses, and ex-president Pérez, who was an insider — although he sought
to act like an outsider — won the December 1988 contest.

In the four countries, voters faced three types of options in these
presidential elections and the open primaries preceding them: the candidate of the incumbent party; the moderate opposition, which had substantial political experience and a long track record; and unpredictable
outsiders or political radicals. Which option emerged victorious depended on the electorate's propensity toward risk. This attitude reflected whether a majority of the citizenry saw itself in the domain of
gains or the domain of losses. These perceptions in turn arose from the
nature and depth of the economic problems facing the country.

The economic shock that quickly pushes a large proportion of citizens into the domain of losses is incipient or full-scale hyperinflation —
that is, price rises above 50 percent per month. Hyperinflation threatens
to disorganize a country's economy completely. By destroying the main
measure of value, hyperinflation makes calculation and planning exceedingly difficult and creates a pervasive sense of uncertainty. Furthermore, it threatens most people with losses of enormous magnitude.
Since these costs appear quickly, people cannot gradually lower their
reference point for assessing gains and losses. The sudden costs caused
by hyperinflation therefore induce large numbers of people to see themselves in the domain of losses. By contrast, gradual income losses allow
for a lowering of people's aspiration level and may thus be absorbed
over time, and sudden losses that affect people at different times — such
as unemployment — do not hit a majority of citizens at once. Thus, hyperinflation is the most important economic problem that throws a
large majority into the domain of losses. In times of incipient hyperinflation, this issue therefore becomes citizens' primary concern (Mora y
Araujo 1989b: 8; Catterberg 1991: 26; IBOPE 1989: question 8;
Apoyo, June 1990: 35; see even Consultores 21 1988: 2).

How can scholars ascertain whether citizens see themselves in the domain of gains or losses? Opinion polls that ask for people's retrospective assessments of recent changes in their economic well-being provide the best indicator.[1] In pre-electoral periods, expectations for the future, which at first sight appear as the more valid indicator, tend to be overly optimistic (Haller and Norpoth 1994) because people hope that their favorite candidate will "turn the country around." Prospective assessments do not yield good evidence for people's perception of their current situation, but of the situation they *hope* will prevail — assuming their preferred candidate wins. Thus, during election campaigns, prospective assessments encompass both the hypothesized cause and the hypothesized effect, namely, perception of domain and vote choice. Therefore, they are not good indicators of domain perceptions alone. Since retrospective assessments are not affected by these distortions, they are more useful.

In the four countries, the diverse economic problems of the late 1980s led to different perceptions of domain and, therefore, to divergent vote choices in presidential elections. In Venezuela, the gradual nature of economic decline during the 1980s seems to have induced many people to lower their reference point for assessing gains and losses. In fact, the Lusinchi government pursued expansionary policies from 1986 onward, repressed inflation through price controls, and hid growing external disequilibria from the public. Price rises, while high by Venezuelan standards, were far from spinning out of control. They stood at 28.1 percent for the whole year of 1987 and 29.5 percent for 1988 — compared to *monthly* rates of up to 114.5 percent, 81.3 percent, and 63.2 percent in Argentina, Brazil, and Peru, respectively. And per capita GDP grew from 1986 to 1988, while falling in Argentina (1988–89) and especially in Peru (1988–90).

In the absence of an open crisis, Venezuelans were divided in their domain perceptions. While 39 percent of the population complained in 1988 surveys about a recent decline in their economic well-being, 24 percent reported a gain and 37 percent no change; expectations for the future were equally varied (Templeton 1995: 81–82, 107–8; similar Consultores 21 1988: 4). Thus, a majority of Venezuelans did not see themselves in a domain of losses. Since loss aversion makes people with neutral perceptions cautious (Quattrone and Tversky 1988: 726), psychological decision theory would expect a majority of Venezuelans to be risk-averse.

[1] In Latin America, pocketbook assessments of people's own well-being seem more important than sociotropic assessments of the country's situation (e.g., Weyland 1998a), which are often more influential in developed countries (Kinder and Kiewiet 1981; Lewis-Beck 1988). This "individualistic" focus may result from the atomization caused by severe economic problems (O'Donnell 1993).

As a result, the moderate opposition party COPEI lost the presidential election of December 1988, and radical outsiders such as the leftist Causa R obtained negligible vote shares; for the first time since 1963, the winner hailed from the incumbent party. As an ex-president, Pérez was widely seen as part of the political establishment, although, as usual, he came from the "out" faction of Acción Democrática (cf. Coppedge 1994: 123–28) and depicted himself as an outsider opposed to the party apparatus. Thus, given the absence of a deep, open crisis, risk aversion prevailed among Venezuelans, who chose relative political continuity (Marta Sosa 1989: 199–202). In fact, since Pérez was associated with the oil boom of the mid-1970s, his supporters hoped for a return to the prosperity of the past.[2]

In Argentina, Brazil, and Peru, by contrast, incipient hyperinflation exacted considerable immediate losses, threatened to cause a dramatic further deterioration, and thus put clear majorities into the domain of losses. The collapse of Argentina's Spring Plan and a severe speculative attack on the currency in February 1989 made the government lose control of the economy. As a result, prices exploded, rising by 33.4 percent in April 1989 and 78.5 percent in May (Birle 1991: 4). The failure of Brazil's Summer Plan caused an irresistible increase of inflation during 1989, which reached 44.3 percent in November. The Peruvian government temporarily managed to contain price rises during 1989, but they resumed a clear upward trajectory in 1990, attaining 37.3 percent in April (Toledo Segura 1993: 168).

Due to the costs caused by such staggering price increases and the clear and present danger of full-scale hyperinflation, majorities of the population saw themselves in the domain of losses. In Argentina, 57 percent of survey respondents reported in April 1989 a deterioration in their own economic situation over the last year (Catterberg 1991: 92); in 1988, 60 percent had felt the same way (Catterberg poll reported in Muszynski and Mendes 1990: 74; see also Mora y Araujo 1989a: 8, 17). In Brazil, a retrospective assessment conducted in the city of Niterói in 1989 showed that 51.6 percent regarded their own economic situation as worse than a year before; only 17.9 percent reported an improvement. In fact, asked how "things" (as coisas) in Brazil had changed over the last three to four years, a whopping 84.5 percent checked "worse"; 69.4 percent, "much worse" (IDESP 1989: variables 21, 45; similarly, a 1988 IDESP poll reported in Muszynski and Mendes 1990: 74). Peru, of course, was in the most dire straits. As a result, 77

---

[2] The largest proportion of Pérez voters—a combined 33 percent—justified their choice with his "good earlier government" and "experience" (Consultores 21 1989a: question 15).

percent of respondents rated their family's economic situation in May 1989 as worse than a year earlier,[3] and 59–61 percent did so in February and April 1990 (Apoyo, February 1990: 26–29; Apoyo, April 1990: 41–42). Furthermore, 88.1 percent reported in July 1990 that "the economic situation" had deteriorated during the preceding six months (Datum 1990b). In sum, large numbers of Argentines, Brazilians, and Peruvians were facing starkly negative prospects in the late 1980s.

In line with the core finding of prospect theory, this perception of a domain of losses led a majority of citizens to make risk-acceptant vote choices. As a result, the candidates of the incumbent governments and parties, who represented political continuity, clearly lost presidential elections (cf. Quattrone and Tversky 1988: 723–24). In Brazil, the standard bearers of the two main government parties, PMDB and Partido da Frente Liberal (PFL), suffered stinging defeats by receiving a mere 4.4% and 0.8% of the vote. In Peru, the Alianza Popular Revolucionaria Americana (APRA) candidate was eliminated in the first round, although stronger party loyalty secured him 22.6 percent of the valid vote. In Argentina, Eduardo Angeloz of the Unión Cívica Radical (UCR) also lost clearly, but the consolidated two-party system and many citizens' lingering aversion to Peronism gave him a surprisingly high 37 percent of the vote. Thus, risk-seeking in the domain of losses induced voters to reject decisively the candidates of the incumbent government, which had been discredited by worsening problems (*desgaste*).

The moderate opposition, however, constituted a realistic alternative that offered change at much lower risk than outsiders like Collor, Fujimori, and Menem. Brazil's new Partido da Social Democracia Brasileira (PSDB), for instance, assembled well-qualified technical cadres and experienced political operators, such as Fernando Henrique Cardoso and José Serra. Alfonso Barrantes, leader of Peru's nonradical left, had a good track record in local politics and public administration.[4] And the Renovación wing of Argentina's Peronist Party, headed by presidential precandidate Antonio Cafiero, had made great strides toward turning the party into a modern organization and ridding it of its corrupt, undemocratic elements (Cavarozzi and Grossi 1992: 190–95). These moderate opposition forces promised to combat the economic and social crisis while deepening democracy. Given their experience, organizational capacity, and technical capabilities, they arguably offered a

[3] Poll by Michelsen Consultores reported in "Habría Vuelto la Confianza," *Caretas* 24 February 1992: 14.

[4] While the "United Left" coalition was divided by ideological conflicts and political infighting, Barrantes himself was a promising candidate, ranking second in vote intentions until February 1990, two months before the election's first round (Schmidt 1996: 329, 335–36, 341).

more promising alternative to the discredited incumbents than the eventual winners.

But a majority of the people rejected this reasonable, safe option for change because the moderate opposition appeared too much as part of the political establishment. Risk-seeking in the domain of losses induced the citizenry to vote against the political class as a whole. Thus, all political old-timers in Brazil—including the PSDB's Mario Covas, conservative Paulo Maluf, and veteran populist Leonel Brizola—were eliminated in the first round of the 1989 presidential contest. Only newcomers Fernando Collor and Luis Inácio Lula da Silva, a former worker who led the upstart socialist Partido dos Trabalhadores (PT)—the clear outsider in Brazil's party system—advanced to the second round. Similarly, the representatives of Peru's political class were defeated by two newcomers, Alberto Fujimori, a complete dark-horse candidate, and Mario Vargas Llosa, an antipolitician, liberal ideologue, and cosmopolitan intellectual (see the fascinating account in Vargas Llosa 1994; Rospigliosi 1992: 352–55). In Argentina's two-party system, the internal primary held by the opposition Peronist Party, which was open to nonparty members, served as the functional equivalent to the first round of the presidential election. In this contest, the modern, democratic Renovación leader Cafiero lost to provincial *caudillo* and maverick Carlos Menem.

The eventual winners of these presidential elections were self-proclaimed outsiders whose vague campaign rhetoric and obscure track record provided little indication of their future course of action, but who promised to "save" their countries (cf. O'Donnell 1994: 65). Fernando Collor was marginal to Brazil's national elite and not affiliated with a major party (Weyland 1993, 6–9). After an unremarkable career start in the small, backward state of Alagoas, he had won fleeting national attention by deriding highly paid public employees as "maharajas." Given his inexperience and complete lack of organized support, he did not seem to have the slightest chance of winning when he entered the presidential race in early 1989 (interview with Assis 1995). Alberto Fujimori was a complete novice to national politics without links to established political forces or social groups (Degregori and Grompone 1991: 34–36, 125–28; Rospigliosi 1992: 353–55; see also Fujimori 1991: 97). He became a presidential candidate only to enhance his visibility for the Senate race on which he planned to concentrate (Schmidt 1996: 330–31). Thus, both Collor and Fujimori were virtually unknown to the voters.

The predominance of two stable parties in Argentina impeded the successful rise of complete outsiders. Protest candidates such as extreme-right Aldo Rico remained confined to the fringes as longstanding party loyalties, which assume a quasi-religious character among many Peronists, persisted. In fact, a respectable 26.4 percent of Argentines were affiliated with the Partido Justicialista (PJ) or UCR in 1991 (Centro de Estudios Unión para la Nueva Mayoría 1993: 2–4). As a result, it was impossible in Argentina for a newcomer to rise out of nowhere, as Fujimori did in Peru.

Carlos Menem, however, was a relative outsider among the viable aspirants and precandidates for the 1989 contest. During his stints as governor of small, backward La Rioja, he had demonstrated abysmal administrative competence and pursued an unclear zig-zag course in his political strategy.[5] For instance, he added innumerable patronage employees to the public payroll, undermining fiscal equilibrium. To persuade the national government to bail him out, he cozied up to President Alfonsín, whose administration the Peronist movement was obstructing with all means and whom Menem himself later attacked. And after helping to found the Renovación current inside the Peronist Party, Menem ran against its leader Cafiero in the internal primary, drawing support from the traditional, undemocratic, and corrupt sectors of the party and its affiliated trade union movement (Cavarozzi and Grossi 1992: 194–96). His long sideburns, which evoked the memory of Facundo Quiroga, a brutal nineteenth-century *caudillo*, best symbolized his appeal to the "low" elements of the Peronist movement and of Argentine society (cf. Ostiguy 1997). Thus, Menem certainly was an unconventional character — an outsider among Argentine politicians.

In all three countries, the president-elect was the clearest outsider among the viable candidates, who as a leader personified a particularly high level of risk. The winners' capacity to fulfill their main campaign promise, namely, end the crisis and turn the economy around, was highly doubtful. In Argentina, sober Eduardo Angeloz, who had performed quite well as governor of the important province of Córdoba and who offered a reasonable, balanced program (Angeloz 1989), lost to flashy buffoon Menem.[6] Given his personal unpredictability and his lack of an administrative team and a strong track record, Menem clearly was the more risky choice.

In Brazil, both Collor and "Lula" were outside the political mainstream and embodied high risks, yet in different ways. Lula's program was more radical in calling for a profound transformation of Brazilian society. A Lula presidency therefore could have caused considerable

---

[5] One of Menem's own ministers called him "an *awful* provincial administrator" (confidential author interview, Buenos Aires, June 1997).

[6] On the importance of economic factors in Menem's vote, see "Más de la mitad de los Argentinos votó pensando en la crisis económica," *Clarín* 28 May 1989: 22–23.

conflict. But Collor was less predictable because of his impulsive and headstrong personality, which worried even his own supporters. In fact, although Collor had closer connections to Brazil's socioeconomic elite, Lula was the more familiar face in national politics. Thus, whereas Lula's program was more confrontational, Collor was more unpredictable as a candidate.[7] Interestingly, Lula attracted disproportionate support from better-off, educated sectors, who tend to pay attention to political programs, while Collor won stronger backing among poor, less educated sectors, who focus more on the leader's personality. Thus, risk-seeking in the domain of losses shaped the electoral behavior of much of the citizenry. Yet the final outcome in this surprisingly close contest was determined by the strategic voting of better-off, risk-averse sectors who were scared of Lula's ideological radicalism and who preferred Collor as the lesser evil. Thus, the runoff format prompted a temporary coalition of risk-averse and risk-acceptant sectors that gave a narrow victory of 53 percent vs. 47 percent to the slightly less risky one of two risky candidates.

In Peru, the complete newcomer Fujimori was much more unpredictable and therefore riskier than well-known, aristocratic Vargas Llosa, who was allied with the conservative Acción Popular and Partido Popular Cristiano, two mainstays of the political establishment. In fact, Vargas Llosa's coalition with these parties, which had a long track record in Peruvian politics, made many voters question his status as an outsider and therefore prefer Fujimori "because he hadn't done anything yet," as a street vendor expressed the prevailing popular sentiment (quoted in Guillermoprieto 1990: 124; see Boggio, Romero, and Ansión 1991: 19–20, 34, 51, 99–102; Vargas Llosa 1994: 505–6; Rospigliosi 1992: 352–55). Similarly, Fujimori's simplistic slogan "honesty, technology, and work," his failure to present a campaign program until right before the second round (Loayza Galván 1998: 24–26, 69–73), and the vague generalities that his movement finally published (Cambio 90 1990) embodied much greater uncertainty than Vargas Llosa's clearly defined proposals. Certainly, the content of Vargas Llosa's program was more radical as he advocated painful shock treatment for Peru's economic crisis. But polls suggest that Fujimori's rejection of this bold proposal (see Vargas Llosa and Fujimori 1990: 31, 38, 46, 57, 60, 65, 71, 75, 81, 85, 91) had much less influence on vote choices than did his political independence and outsider status.[8] Given the common betrayal

[7] On the crucial importance of candidate personality in the 1989 election, see Olsen (2000: 76–77).

[8] Most respondents in surveys conducted in Lima justified their second-route vote for Fujimori with arguments such as "he represented change," "was the best option," "is

of campaign promises, voters seem to have paid limited attention to candidates' platforms. Since the character, background, and political alignment of the candidates counted more than their programs (Degregori and Grompone 1991; Rospigliosi 1992), Fujimori constituted the riskier option.

Menem, Collor, and Fujimori reinforced their outsider status through their populist campaign rhetoric, which attacked established political elites as inept and corrupt and appealed to common people as the source of national regeneration. Collor, for instance, depicted himself as the most fervent opponent of incumbent Sarney, whom he called a thief (Nêumanne 1989: 54–55, 62, 66; Rosa e Silva 1993: 220–52). Collor, Fujimori, and — to a lesser extent — Menem used anticorruption slogans to mark their distance from the "political class." They thus tapped into widespread popular resentment against those held responsible for causing — or not effectively combating — the grave problems of the 1980s (Diretrizes 1989: ii, 1; Fujimori's call for "honesty" in Cambio 90 1990; Menem and Duhalde 1989: 15).

In sum, the deep crises afflicting Argentina, Brazil, and Peru put a majority of citizens into the domain of losses and thus triggered risk-acceptant vote choices, which led outsiders to victory.

The Initiation of Drastic Adjustment

The Depth of the Crisis

The four new presidents faced a drastic aggravation of economic problems during and after the election campaign. In fact, this further deterioration resulted in good part from the political and economic uncertainty produced by the election of outsiders. Also, many economic actors anticipated some kind of stabilization plan and therefore sought to raise prices and wages as a cushion against likely austerity policies. Structured like a classical "prisoners' dilemma," these uncoordinated efforts at self-protection aggravated the economic crisis. In particular, inflation exploded, rising from 33.4 percent during April 1989 to 114.5 percent in June in Argentina; from 44.3 percent in November 1989 to

---

independent" and "honest"; they also stressed their dislike for Vargas Llosa's alliance with AP and PPC. By contrast, rejection of shock treatment ranked among "other factors," named by less than 5 percent as reason for supporting Fujimori (Datum 1990b). Similarly, only 17.5 percent of respondents after the first round stressed the shock proposal as the reason for rejecting Vargas Llosa; the rest mentioned his political orientation, ideology, character, and partisan alignments (Datum 1990a; similarly Degregori and Grompone 1991; Rospigliosi 1992: 352–54, 365–66; Dietz 1998: 218–19, 280).

81.3 percent in February 1990 in Brazil; and from 32.8 percent in April 1990 to 63.2 percent during July in Peru. In Venezuela, where price controls repressed inflation, shortages of goods kept worsening. Furthermore, some of the outgoing presidents, especially García and Sarney, wanted to leave office on a good note and therefore awarded last-minute favors to important groups, for instance by raising public-sector salaries. These irresponsible "gifts" further exacerbated fiscal crises and fueled inflation.

In preparing to assume office, the presidents-elect also gained full access to inside information guarded by the public bureaucracy. In this way, they became aware of the full depth of the crisis, which their predecessors sought to hide. For all of these reasons, the new presidents took over the reins of the state under much worse economic conditions than when they had entered the race, and they had much more accurate information about the severity of the problems facing their country.[9]

Yet while all four presidents-elect confronted grave economic trouble, the depth of the crisis differed considerably across countries. Hyperinflation clearly set Argentina, Brazil, and Peru apart from Venezuela, where price rises remained moderate in comparative terms. Among the former three countries, Peru was in the most dire straits because hyperinflation had erupted in September 1988 already and because the 1980s had brought tremendous impoverishment. Furthermore, the government was confronting two powerful, brutal guerrilla movements, which pushed the nation to the brink of civil war. While not facing such desperate circumstances, Argentina was clearly worse off than Brazil because it had suffered from economic stagnation for decades, whereas the Brazilian economy had achieved considerable growth even during the turbulent 1980s. Thus, although Argentina, Brazil, and Peru shared the same acute problem — hyperinflation — the underlying economic difficulties differed in severity.

Even hyperinflation had a different impact, depending on the extent of indexation. The Brazilian economy was almost completely indexed. The automatic readjustment of prices, wages, and taxes shielded business, organized labor, and the state from a good part of the losses caused by hyperinflation (Garcia 1996: 139–43, 156–57), whose burden fell most heavily on the unprotected informal sector. By contrast, in Argentina and especially in Peru, indexation was much less developed. Furthermore, Peru's organized working class, which directly benefits from salary readjustments, was quite small, whereas the unprotected

[9] On Fujimori, see "Resultará difícil aplicar propuestas de su campaña," *Expreso* 9 July 1990.

informal sector had swelled to 50–60 percent of the urban population. The costs of hyperinflation therefore diverged across the three countries.

The Impact of External Constraints and Pressures

Despite these differences, all four countries clearly faced economic problems of great severity. How would the new leaders respond to these worsening difficulties? Two context factors nudged all four presidents toward some kind of market-oriented stabilization. First, international financial institutions forcefully recommended orthodox structural adjustment. Second, learning from prior experiences — especially the disastrous heterodox experiments of the mid-1980s — inspired the new leaders to shift course and act in line with IFI exhortations. But while these two context factors help explain the general nature of the policies adopted, they cannot account for the drastic nature of the shock programs imposed. The impetus for taking such courageous steps emerged from risk-seeking in the domain of losses.

Pointing to the grave problems plaguing the countries under investigation, the IFIs, especially the IMF and the World Bank, strongly recommended a turn to economic liberalism (e.g., World Bank 1989, 1990). To ease the short-term pain of orthodox adjustment, the IFIs offered substantial loans and held out the prospect of debt relief through the Brady Plan. By using tangible material incentives to push for their recipes, they commanded important levers of power.

In none of the four countries, however, did IFI pressure come close to determining the outcome. The extent of IFI influence varied considerably, depending on the institutional capacity of the state and the technical expertise of the economics profession. In Peru and Venezuela, where both of these assets were more limited,[10] the IMF, in particular, had substantial — though not decisive — influence on the design of the adjustment plans (interviews with Pennano 1996 and Iturbe de Blanco 1996; Hurtado Miller 1992: 62; on limits of IFI influence in Peru, see Iguíñiz 1991: 420–21; interview with Amat y León 1996); above all, Fujimori's abandonment of his "no shock" campaign promise and his embrace of a drastic stabilization plan were triggered in good part by direct IFI pressure (interviews with De Soto 1996, Figueroa 1996, Pennano 1996). By contrast, the stabilization programs imposed by Menem in Argentina and Collor in Brazil, while following the broad outlines of the vague "Washington Consensus," were mostly designed by domestic

---

[10] Conaghan (1997) stresses the weakness of Peru's economics profession.

economists. Domestic experts and (former) state officials elaborated the Bunge & Born Plan of mid-1989, the Convertibility Plan of early 1991, and the Collor Plan of early 1990 with little direct input from the IFIs (interviews with Ferreres 1995, Kohan 1995, and Mello 1995).

In fact, the adjustment plans enacted in all four countries diverged in important ways from IFI recommendations. Above all, they were uniformly bolder and riskier than the IFIs advocated. As regards Peru and Venezuela, the IFIs worried that the drastic, tough stabilization plans elaborated by the aides of presidents Fujimori and Pérez would unleash fierce domestic opposition and trigger protest and turmoil. They therefore recommended greater caution, warning that neoliberal programs should not be enacted at such breakneck speed.[11] As regards Argentina and Brazil, the IFIs disliked the internal debt moratoria and temporary financial confiscations decreed in early 1990, which violated property rights, threatened to undermine trust in the banking system, and set a dangerous precedent for an external debt moratorium.[12] In addition, the IMF was very skeptical about Argentina's convertibility plan, advocating a fiscal approach to stabilization instead of an exchange-rate–based approach (Cavallo 1997: 34, 137–39, 177–79; Llach 1997: 171). Even President Fujimori antagonized powerful international actors with some of his decisions, especially his *autogolpe* of April 1992.

As these divergences on the speed and substance of adjustment programs show, the IFIs did not determine economic policy-making in Argentina, Brazil, Peru, and Venezuela; rather, Fujimori, Pérez, and especially Menem and Collor retained a substantial degree of autonomy in decision-making. In fact, as mentioned in chapters 2 and 4, earlier governments had often resisted strong IFI pressures and refused to enact neoliberal adjustment out of fear of political turmoil. Why were the new governments willing to go ahead and accept this political risk? IFI influence alone cannot explain why these countries finally adopted neoliberal recipes.

Learning from Prior Experiences

Learning from prior experiences also helps account for the general direction of the economic policies pursued by the new presidents. The

[11] Interviews with Boloña 1996, DuBois 1999, Martínez Móttola 1996; Naím 1993a: 169–70; Ashoff 1993: 32. Velarde (interview 1996) reported that, fearing a social rebellion as in Caracas in 1989, the IMF advocated a "timid" devaluation to 200,000 *intis* per dollar, but the Fujimori government drastically devalued to 450,000 *intis*.

[12] Welch 1991; "EUA vêem plano com reserva," *Estado de São Paulo, Economia* 18 March 1990: 11.

eventual failure of the Argentine Plan Austral, the Brazilian Plano Cruzado, and the Peruvian Plan Inti was widely seen as proof that heterodox adjustment alone would not work. In all three countries, heterodox shocks had lost appeal; experts critical of "neoliberalism" recommended at most eclectic programs that combined orthodox and heterodox elements. Even President Pérez in Venezuela, a country that had not conducted a heterodox experiment, learned from the disaster left behind by his center-left friend Alan García, with whom he had ample contact through the Socialist International (interviews with Pérez 1996, Naím 2000). As an additional inspiration for enacting neoliberal policies, Pérez and his advisers mentioned the success of market reforms in Chile, Mexico, and Spain (interviews with Pérez 1996, Iturbe de Blanco 1996, Martínez Móttola 1996, Rodríguez 1996, Rosas 1996; Naím 1993b: 46).

Thus, in addition to IFI pressure, learning from prior experiences induced the new presidents to move in the direction of market reform. But this learning did not provide any lessons on the specific stabilization plans to adopt. In fact, the heterodox shocks of the mid-1980s revealed the tremendous risks inherent in drastic policy packages, whose concrete measures were difficult to calibrate and whose overall outcomes were therefore impossible to foresee. The lessons suggested by the "Chilean model" were not sanguine either: The dogmatic neoliberal policies adopted via shock plan in the mid-1970s caused a tremendous crisis in the early 1980s; only the more pragmatic neoliberal measures enacted in a more gradual fashion thereafter ensured economic stability and sustained growth. Thus, while prior experiences provided guidance on the general direction to take, they did not make tough shock programs look particularly attractive.

In fact, the popular response to the earliest experience of drastic neoliberal adjustment enacted in the four cases under investigation should have cautioned the other three presidents. As discussed below, the first step in the implementation of President Pérez's stabilization plan triggered unprecedented large-scale rioting that caused at least three hundred deaths.[13] All over Latin America, this outburst of turmoil in a longstanding, seemingly consolidated democracy was interpreted as a sign of widespread popular rejection of neoliberalism. Given the unconsolidated nature of democracy in Argentina, Brazil, and Peru, the new presidents would have been well advised to proceed with caution. Thus, while economists argue that hyperinflation can only be defeated via shock treatment (e.g., Llach 1990), political instability turned this

---

[13] *Cuadernos del CENDES* 10 (January–April 1989) and *Politeia* 13 (1989) analyze these tragic events.

recommendation into a potential recipe for disaster. Leading decision-makers in the four countries were aware of these risks (e.g., interviews with Curia 1995, González 1995).

The Importance of Risk-Seeking in the Domain of Losses

Why, then, did the new presidents systematically use the latitude left by economic and ideational context factors to enact shock plans? The core finding of prospect theory — risk-seeking in the domain of losses — is essential for explaining the drastic nature of the four presidents' adjustment plans and the breakneck speed of their enactment. Contrary to their predecessors, who resisted pressures for orthodox stabilization at all cost, the four presidents engaged in systematic overshooting of the targets set by IFIs and clearly "owned" the adjustment programs they implemented. While this determination was undoubtedly meant to build credibility (Rodrik 1989) and win the confidence of IFIs and private investors, it emerged from a striking willingness to take enormous political and economic risks. Even more tellingly, this boldness contrasts with the notable caution displayed later by those of the four leaders who ended up presiding over an economic recovery (as discussed in chapter 6 below). As soon as the acute crisis passed and growth resumed, presidents Menem and Fujimori — and later Brazil's Cardoso — moved to risk aversion in their economic policy-making. Prospect theory can best account for these situationally conditioned shifts in propensity toward risk.

Risk-seeking in the domain of losses came to the fore because as real newcomers or self-proclaimed outsiders, the new presidents were not tied down by the prior-option bias. Unfettered by clear policy commitments assumed in the recent past, the four leaders were free to chart a new course — even when they had given the impression to reject neoliberalism in their vague campaign rhetoric. In fact, the deepening crisis afflicting their countries and the access to intragovernmental information that they gained after their election victory allowed them to disavow their earlier promises. Claiming to have realized the true severity of the crisis only upon preparing to take office, they proceeded to chart a new course.

To substantiate the argument derived from prospect theory, the following analysis establishes three crucial points: First, in the arena of economic policy-making, the four new presidents in fact saw themselves in the domain of losses. Second, in response to the economic challenges they were facing, they systematically chose the boldest options among the alternatives considered as viable. Finally, and most importantly, due to their inherent risk, the options chosen were arguably less promising than some of the more prudent alternatives considered.

Leaders' Perceptions of a Domain of Losses

In the sphere of economic policy, the new chief executives clearly saw themselves in the domain of losses. Given the eruption of hyperinflation in Argentina and the resulting social disturbances, President Menem's economic and political aides were facing starkly negative prospects (interviews with Kohan 1995 and Rapanelli 1997; Curia 1991: 18, 34–36, 68–69; Llach 1997: 59–82, 125–26; Programa 1989: 4, 21, 25). Minister Rapanelli (interview 1997), for instance, stressed that the country was virtually "destroyed" by raging hyperinflation, a huge public deficit, and negative foreign currency reserves. Similarly, President Collor and his aides knew that they quickly had to get inflation under control in order to make the administration politically viable, given its weak base in Congress and the fickle nature of its mass support (interviews with Gonçalves 1995 and Collor 1995; *Diretrizes* 1989: 1–5, 24, 118–21). Collor himself stressed that he had a "single bullet to kill the tiger of inflation."[14] Finally, President Fujimori's advisers saw their country "on the verge of collapse" (Hurtado Miller 1990: 3), facing "the gravest crisis of its recent history" (Hurtado Miller 1992: 103) due to renewed hyperinflation and strong guerrilla challenges (similarly Boloña 1993: 24; interviews with Figueroa 1996 and Torres y Torres Lara 1996).

Pérez and his team also were aware of the imminent crisis that Venezuela was facing. Since Venezuela's fiscal deficit had ballooned to 9.4 percent of GDP in 1988; since inflation had been artificially repressed through price controls; and since severe external disequilibria were looming, the incoming government thought that the country was "[t]eetering on the brink of collapse" (Naím 1993b: 31; Hausmann 1995: 252–53, 261–66; similarly interviews with Pérez 1996 and Rosas 1996). President Pérez's early speeches and government documents from 1989 dwell on the grave problems that the new economic team had identified (Pérez 1989: 13–14, 21–23, 35; CORDIPLAN 1989b, 1989c). Specifically, the new chief executive saw the need to "stop Venezuela's free fall into the abyss of the crisis that other countries in Latin America suffer today" (Pérez 1989: 118; similarly interview with Pérez 1996).

The new presidents and their aides also realized that there was no easy, cost-free solution to the serious problems plaguing their countries.

---

[14] See "Aperto de liquidez ajudará a controlar a inflação," *Gazeta Mercantil* 14 March 1990; Crabtree (1991: 119).

All options for tackling the crisis involved transitional losses. Drastic countermeasures, which promised to produce a faster recovery, would cause particularly high adjustment costs in the short run, which is politically crucial in fragile institutional settings. More gradual programs would limit these immediate costs yet stretch out the pain and bring stabilization and recovery much later. Thus, all of the available alternatives included the visible, politically costly imposition of further losses, for which the desired economic turnaround could compensate only in the medium run.

The Choice of Particularly Risky Options

Facing a domain of losses — and realizing the complete unsustainability of the rapidly deteriorating status quo — the four leaders discarded more prudent alternatives and chose the most risky proposals for confronting the crisis that they and their aides were considering as feasible. While sometimes disregarding the most daring recommendations as absolutely unviable, the presidents clearly made risk-acceptant rather than risk-averse choices.

VENEZUELA

This systematic preference for boldness over caution is especially noteworthy in the case of President Pérez, who was not facing hyperinflation. While economists commonly argue that skyrocketing price rises can only be stopped through shock treatment, the less severe problems afflicting Venezuela did not require such a risky approach.[15] In fact, the incoming economic team stressed that "despite the critical macroeconomic situation prevailing at present [and the need for 'effective and relatively severe adjustment policies'], Venezuela currently has an ample margin of maneuver in its economic policy."[16] Therefore, some of Pérez's ministers opposed the initiation of the shock plan (Naím 1993a: 93), and even some members of the economic team, such as the finance minister, initially advocated a more gradual approach (interviews with Iturbe de Blanco 1996, Naím 2000, Rosas 1996). Also, political observers, including sectors of his own party, warned the new president

[15] A comparison of the proposals left behind by the outgoing Lusinchi administration (CORDIPLAN 1989a) and the Pérez administration's economic strategy (CORDIPLAN 1989b, 1989c) shows what a new departure Pérez's shock plan was.

[16] CORDIPLAN 1989b: 16. Naím (interview 2000; similarly Naím 1993b: 54–57) argued that there was "no choice" but to use a shock approach, but he also stressed that decision-making in such crisis situations proceeds not by rational cost-benefit calculation, but according to the psychological mechanisms explicated in the present study.

about the social costs and the resulting political risks of shock treatment (Kornblith 1989: 24), and the military intelligence service had for months alerted the government to the danger of a spontaneous social rebellion (Müller Rojas 1989: 142–43). Nevertheless, Pérez had his aides design a drastic stabilization plan, which he depicted as part of a "great turnaround" (*el gran viraje*) in the country's development (COR-DIPLAN 1989b: 16–30; Naím 1993b: 45–46). The president was aware of the risks inherent in this course of action: "With profound anxiety, but with firmness, we assumed the responsibility of proposing and applying the measures [of the shock plan] in order to keep the country from entering a dead-end street, confronting the risks of defining the new direction of Venezuela."[17]

This program raised public sector prices, eliminated numerous subsidies, lifted price, interest rate, and exchange controls, and drastically devalued the currency (Naím 1993b: 49–54; Ashoff 1993: 29–33). Its enactment initiated a comprehensive restructuring of the economy, designed to cut public spending, reduce state interventionism, and open the country to foreign trade and investment (CORDIPLAN 1989c, 1990). Interestingly, the government clearly erred on the side of boldness and risk-taking by enacting unnecessarily drastic adjustment measures. Its tough austerity plan led to considerable overshooting of the initial fiscal targets, worsening the deep recession that Venezuelans suffered in 1989 (interview with Rodríguez 1996; Hausmann 1990: 230; compare actual results with projections in CORDIPLAN 1989b: 4, 10, 32, 44).

Furthermore, Pérez executed this structural adjustment package at breakneck speed, even after the first measure provoked large-scale rioting (see below). Although his political advisers and many economic experts urged him to respond to this unexpected expression of widespread opposition with caution and scale down the stabilization program (interviews with Martínez Móttola 1996 and Naím 2000), Pérez refused to compromise and insisted on sticking to the original plan. The protests actually strengthened his determination. Reluctant to appear as weak — and thus incur a sure loss of limited magnitude — he decided to push ahead at full speed, hoping to attain his initial goals even at the danger of provoking more opposition and protest — "*cueste lo que cueste*," that is, "whatever the cost may be" (interviews with Pérez 1996, Rosas 1996; Pérez 1989: 63, 78; Rodríguez 1994: 379). Displaying clear risk acceptance in the domain of losses, Pérez decided to play the lottery that promised to avert any loss in his economic program and political standing, but at the risk of a severe loss of great magnitude (Pérez 1989: 17,

[17] Pérez (1990: 3). Rodríguez (interview 1996) also mentioned the "great political courage" required for enacting such a drastic adjustment plan.

23, 33; Ovalles 1996: 136; Hausmann 1995: 262–63). In this way, he braved great political risks and overrode important sectors of his own party, which advocated greater prudence in order to boost AD's electoral chances in the upcoming gubernatorial and municipal elections of December 1989.[18]

Pérez chose this risky course of action although the IFIs allowed him to ease his adjustment plan and proceed at a slower pace. Thus, the measures that Pérez selected and the persistence and speed with which he implemented them disregarded the demands of prudence and reflected risk-seeking in the domain of losses.

Interestingly, however, the temporary oil bonanza of 1990–91 made the Pérez administration slack off in its austerity program. As Venezuela emerged from the deep recession of 1989 and as the Persian Gulf crisis raised international oil prices and thus swelled Venezuela's fiscal revenues, the government increased its expenditures in order to stimulate growth and placate opponents of structural adjustment, including important sectors of AD (Ashoff 1993: 37; Naím 1993b: 74–76, 162–63; Corrales 1996: 242–44). Thus, as soon as the economy seemed to turn around, the Pérez government became more risk-averse and relaxed its adjustment efforts, as prospect theory would predict.

ARGENTINA

President Menem also discarded caution and proceeded with great boldness as he faced hyperinflation and a disintegrating economy and society in mid-1989. The new president took a big economic and especially political gamble by initiating a stunning reversal of decades of Peronist economic policies. Diverging from his vague campaign rhetoric, he decided to dismantle the state-interventionist import-substitution model that his party's founder, Juan Domingo Perón, had built and to embark instead on radical economic liberalization (Programa 1989: 1, 4, 18; Smith 1991: 52–55). To signal this change of direction credibly and win business support, Menem forged a surprising alliance with traditional enemies of Peronism, especially the Bunge & Born conglomerate,[19] and with doctrinaire advocates of economic liberalism, particularly Alvaro Alsogaray (interviews with Alsogaray 1995 and Kohan 1995; Alsogaray 1993: 161–71).

[18] Corrales (1996: 198, n. 22). In fact, combining economic adjustment with political reforms, such as the direct election of governors and proposals for democratizing the ossified government party, further "increased the danger" (interview with Pérez 1996; similarly interviews with Martínez Móttola 1996 and Rosas 1996).

[19] Ferreres (interview 1995) stressed the ostentatious way in which Menem established his alliance with Bunge & Born.

These decisions were much more drastic than the more limited adjustment measures that most economic specialists in the Peronist Party — with the exception of recent import Domingo Cavallo and his group (Santoro 1994: 236–37) — were advocating.[20] They were politically risky because the reaction of the Peronist Party, the trade union movement, and the electorate was difficult to foresee.[21] For instance, some cabinet members condemned in internal debates the drastic price raises of the Bunge & Born Plan as *una barbaridad* (interview with Curia 1995). In fact, the recent popular rebellion against tough adjustment measures in Caracas (see below) created particular concern.[22] Whether Menem's new allies among business and economic liberals would trust his sudden "conversion" and provide solid support was also unclear.[23] Thus, Menem took a big gamble when he initiated this striking realignment of sociopolitical forces and the fundamental revamping of Argentina's development model (Baizán 1993: 28; Curia 1991: 19).

Yet while laying down the basic guidelines of his government with great boldness and determination, Menem initially handed over responsibility for economic policy-making to some of his new business allies. The leading members of his first economic teams came from the Bunge & Born conglomerate. Representing private interests that would suffer from the shock program of stabilization and restructuring advocated by Domingo Cavallo and his aides, economy ministers Miguel Roig and — after his untimely death — Néstor Rapanelli preferred a more gradual approach.[24] As a result, fiscal adjustment and trade liberalization proceeded cautiously during the first few months. Thus, Menem's delegation of decision-making authority — a crucial part of his bold realignment — initially limited the concrete changes his government effected (excellent analysis in Carrera 1994).

---

[20] "Anunciaron un paquete económico de inusual dureza," *Clarín* 10 July 1989: 2–3.

[21] "Miguel se opone al congelamiento salarial," *Clarín* 12 July 1989: 2; interviews with Miguel (1995) and Ubaldini (1995). Ferreres (interview 1995) stressed the great tension, acrimony, and revulsion that his presentation of the adjustment plan caused among the Peronist congressional delegation on 5 July 1989. Rapanelli (interview 1997) reported a similar episode. Kohan (interview 1995), by contrast, described Peronist and union opposition as limited.

[22] Interview with Curia (1995). Ferreres (interview 1995) also reported Menem's concern about a social explosion (*estallido social*).

[23] For instance, Crotto (interview 1995) reported initial doubts and hesitation; similarly Martínez (interview 1997).

[24] Compare Programa de Gobierno (1989) with *Proyecto de Ley* (1989), Sachs (1989), and Llach (1990). On this debate, see Curia (1991: 33–64); Graziano (1990: 77–92); interviews with Alsogaray (1995), Curia (1995), Ferreres (1995), Kohan (1995), Llach (1995), Rapanelli (1997). Santoro (1994: 227–39, 299–300) provides an excellent journalistic account.

The first stabilization plan failed within a few months, however, and prices exploded again at the end of 1989. Confronted with a second bout of hyperinflation, that is, facing a domain of losses, Menem — in his own words — "ended up convincing himself that the best way to get out of this impasse was to reinforce the bet" (Menem in Baizán 1993: 41). He therefore took the bold decision to forcibly retain a large amount of financial assets by transforming weekly renewable investments, especially internal debt papers, into bonds with ten years' maturity. This arbitrary, confiscatory measure (Plan Bonex) was highly risky by antagonizing powerful investors and by threatening to undermine trust in the banking system;[25] according to some observers, it contributed to the renewed outbreak of hyperinflation from January through March 1990 (interview with Ferreres 1995). Yet this measure neutralized a dangerous time bomb, namely, the rapidly accumulating internal debt, which had pushed up the public deficit (interviews with González 1995 and Alsogaray 1995). In the following months, the new economy minister, Antonio Erman González, also took draconian steps to attain fiscal equilibrium by cutting spending and raising revenues (interview with González 1995; Smith 1991: 59–62). A deep recession was the price.

During the second bout of hyperinflation in late 1989 and early 1990, Menem, González, and their economic advisers rejected as completely infeasible the proposals to establish full currency convertibility. Given Argentina's low foreign reserves and the impossibility to obtain a large external loan, the introduction of convertibility at this moment would have required a tremendous devaluation and an immediate fiscal shock that would have drastically lowered real wages and impoverished large sectors of the population. Fearing a grave risk to sociopolitical stability, the president temporarily shelved this proposal as absolutely unrealistic.[26] But the controversial Plan Bonex, the painful fiscal measures enacted by Minister González during 1990, and the accumulation of foreign reserves paved the way for the adoption of Cavallo's convertibility plan in early 1991 (interview with Llach 1995; Carrera 1994: 349; Starr 1997: 91) when, after some initial success, Economy Minister González faced increasing difficulties and inflation again threatened to spiral out of control.

[25] Interviews with Curia (1995); Graziano (1990: 186–94); Santoro (1994: 269–70); "Los aliados del Lázaro," *Clarín* 5 January 1990: 12–13. The press judged: "The exchange of internal debt for external debt appears like an extremely risky wager (*una jugada sumamente riesgosa*)": "Salió el cero, pierden todos," *Clarín Económico* 7 January 1990: 1. See also Echegaray and Elordi (2001: 194–96).

[26] Interviews with González (1995), Kohan (1995), Rapanelli (1997); see also Graziano (1990: 167–69, 186–87); "El día después," *Clarín* 4 January 1990: 12–13.

Still stuck in the domain of losses, Menem again opted to gamble and substituted for González the main advocate of the convertibility plan, Foreign Minister Domingo Cavallo. González's achievements in reducing the fiscal deficit and augmenting Argentina's international reserves had turned this highly risky project feasible, and Menem, facing another deterioration of the economic crisis, decided to make this desperate move (Cavallo 1997: 174–81; interviews with Alsogaray 1995, Vasconcelos 1997; Santoro 1994: 291–96, 302–4). Minister Cavallo pushed for a particularly tight self-limitation of economic policy by having the exchange rate for the freely convertible currency fixed by law (interview with Llach 1995). This firm symbolic and legal commitment forced the government to maintain economic equilibrium, even at high social and political cost. Cavallo indeed had to enact additional adjustment measures, including budget cuts, dismissals of public employees, and tax reforms (Smith 1991: 63–65; Llach 1997: 135–39).

By tying the government's hands, the convertibility plan constituted the type of highly risky decision that actors typically adopt in the domain of losses. If this desperate, last-ditch effort failed to stop inflation immediately, the real exchange rate would appreciate significantly, thus putting economic policy-makers before a terrible dilemma. Having relinquished any room for maneuver, they would be unable to combat capital flight or trade deficits effectively; but touching the exchange rate would undermine governmental credibility, trigger full-scale hyperinflation, and plunge Argentina into economic chaos (Carrera 1994: 360–61; Smith 1991: 63, 65; interview with Curia 1995).

BRAZIL

Acting with particular recklessness (interview with Assis 1995), President Collor chose the most radical measures that his aides were considering. Immediately upon taking office, he imposed the most audacious stabilization package in Brazilian history.[27] On March 16, 1990, he decreed spending cuts, numerous tax hikes, dismissals of public officials, and the extinction of state agencies, and he initiated structural reforms, such as the reduction of trade barriers and the privatization of public enterprises. Most remarkably, he went far beyond conventional monetary and fiscal measures by confiscating 70–80 percent of Brazil's total liquidity for eighteen months. This unprecedented decision, which was

[27] See, e.g., "Plano revoluciona economia," Estado de São Paulo, Economia 17 March 1990: 1; "Os sacrifícios dos mais ricos," Gazeta Mercantil 19 March 1990; Bank of Boston (1990); comments by numerous economic experts in Faro (1990: 49, 52, 55–58, 84, 97–104, 140, 186, 209, 235, 268–69); Panizza (2000: 184–86).

controversial inside Collor's own economic team,[28] sought to reduce the value of the government's internal debt, slash debt service, cut domestic demand, and in these ways force prices down. Without hesitation, Collor froze even regular savings accounts, a measure that his economic aides considered highly controversial and that his political advisers accepted only reluctantly (interview with Collor 1995; Sabino 1991: 111–12). As Collor gave unconditional support to the bold proposals elaborated by his economic advisers (interviews with Assis 1995, Collor 1995, Gonçalves 1995, Kandir 1995), his political supporters were appalled at the brutal nature of the stabilization plan and warned the president-elect about its tremendous political risks (interview with Collor 1995; Sabino 1991: 111–12, 126, 131–32). But Collor would not flinch.

Thus, Collor's first stabilization plan was highly daring in economic and political terms (Bresser Pereira 1991: 17–19, 26–30; Crabtree 1991: 119). Given the need for secrecy in the elaboration phase, his economic team was unable to gain access to reliable governmental information and therefore faced difficulties in calibrating different measures, especially the threshold above which financial assets would be frozen (interviews with Assis 1995, Eris 1992, Gonçalves 1995). Typically opting for boldness, they overshot by setting this limit too low (interviews with Assis 1995, Gonçalves 1995). On the political front, the reaction of societal groups to Collor's tough decisions and the response of Congress, whose majority was not aligned with the government, were hard to predict.[29] Politicians and experts supporting Collor were shocked at the drastic nature of his projects, which needed parliamentary approval to become law (Sabino 1991: 111–12, 131–32; interviews with Kandir 1995, Pojo de Rego 1995). Given Collor's weak party backing, he took a big gamble in decreeing his shock program.

PERU

President Fujimori had the courage to enact a stunningly tough adjustment program that raised prices of basic necessities by up to 3,000 percent from one day to the next, abruptly devalued the currency, and greatly increased taxes.[30] The impact on the popular sectors was "catastrophic" (Iguíñiz 1991: 405). This stabilization plan was more drastic

[28] Ibrahim Eris, the most prominent economist among the stabilization plan's designers, initially opposed this drastic infringement on existing contractual rights (interview with Mello 1995).

[29] For business reservations, see Bornhausen (1991); interviews with Amato (1992), Temporal (1992).

[30] Hurtado Miller (1990: 12). De Soto (interview 1996) stressed that it was very difficult for Fujimori to find an economy minister who would enact such a tough shock. Torres y Torres Lara (1992: 104) calls the first cabinet a "fuse," due to its inherently low chance of success.

than the "shock" that his main opponent in the presidential campaign, avowed neoliberal Vargas Llosa, had considered. And it clearly was much tougher than the proposal to stabilize the economy through a monetary reform and dollarization that Fujimori's first group of economic aides had elaborated and that was similar to the core idea of the Argentine convertibility plan and the Brazilian Plano Real enacted successfully in 1991 and 1994, respectively (Dancourt et al. 1990; interviews with Figueroa 1996, Roca 1996). In enacting his painful stabilization plan, Fujimori thus chose the most draconian and politically risky option under consideration.[31] Given the impoverishment that many Peruvians had suffered during the 1980s, Fujimori's cabinet feared that the resulting further depression of this low standard of living could trigger severe social unrest and political protest. To quell any turmoil, the government therefore prepared a state-of-siege decree, which it could enact at a moment's notice (interviews with De Soto 1996, Hurtado Miller 1996, Pennano 1996; see also Hurtado Miller 1990: 12). Thus, the Fujimori government imposed a particularly brutal and risky stabilization plan.[32] It also initiated an ambitious program of structural reforms (Hurtado Miller 1992: 57–79).

When this bitter medicine proved insufficient for curing inflation, Fujimori intensified the dosage. Stuck in the domain of losses, he made additional risky decisions. In February 1991, he appointed as his economy minister free-market enthusiast Carlos Boloña, who accelerated the pace of profound structural reforms designed to liberalize the economy (Boloña 1993: 54–56; Velarde and Rodríguez 1994: 18–21).[33] Rather than applying another macroeconomic policy shock, the new minister used these drastic changes, which dismantled the state-interventionist development model and radically freed market forces, to achieve eco-

[31] Interview with Hurtado Miller (1996). Velarde (interview 1996) reported that among two options, the economic team chose the more drastic increase in public sector prices and an "intermediate, or medium-high" level for currency devaluation, overriding Fujimori's own preference for a lower level (on the devaluation debate, see also Velarde and Rodríguez 1992b: 13–19). Velarde and Rodríguez (1992a: 16–20) argue powerfully that the Fuji-shock was less risky than available alternatives but confine their analysis exclusively to economic issues and completely disregard the shock's social and political repercussions, which actually weighed on the minds of leading political decision-makers (interview with Hurtado Miller 1996).

[32] On the tremendous uncertainty and tension that the government faced in the initial stages of the adjustment plan, see the fascinating insider account by Torres y Torres Lara (1992).

[33] Before taking office in July 1990, Fujimori had already faced strong pressures to nominate Boloña as his economy minister. But to preserve his own power, Fujimori initially refused. Boloña demanded complete control over economic policy, including the appointment of the Central Bank president (Boloña 1993: 25–26; interviews with De Soto 1996, Pennano 1996). In finally appointing Boloña, Fujimori had to compromise his political goals.

nomic stabilization.[34] In his view, import liberalization would force prices down, and the gamut of neoliberal measures would boost exports and attract foreign capital. The quick adoption of structural reforms for short-term purposes paid little attention to their long-term effects. Since different measures — such as the early resumption of debt service and the effort to overcome the fiscal crisis of the state — obstructed each other, this drastic plan held great risks (Paredes 1991; on business complaints, see interview with Majluf 1996).

In sum, the new presidents in the four countries under investigation picked the most daring adjustment measures among the options that their advisers considered. While neoliberal experts were happy about receiving presidential support for their determined programs of radical transformation, the political supporters and advisers of the new chief executives warned against the tremendous political risks inherent in these plans, but to no avail.

The Comparatively Low Expected Value of Risk-Seeking in the Domain of Losses

Due to the enormous risks they embodied, the options chosen by the four presidents arguably had lower expected value than some of the more prudent alternatives. But whereas a more cautious posture would only have limited the damage, bold measures held the uncertain promise of quickly turning the country around, decisively overcoming the crisis, and thus "breaking even" (cf. Thaler and Johnson 1990: 657–59). Only these drastic shock programs opened up the possibility of recuperating the old status quo in the foreseeable future — but they also held the risk of causing a complete economic and political meltdown. By making such risky choices, the four presidents therefore seem to have deviated from conventional rationality postulates.

Of course, clear *proof* of the deviations from expected utility calculations postulated by prospect theory is infeasible because it is impossible to ascertain the exact pay-offs and subjective probability estimates that decision-makers attach to different options — especially in unique crisis situations characterized by profound uncertainty (similar Haas 2001: 253). In fact, the possibility to resort to a "revealed preferences" approach could allow expected utility theorists — and actors — to rationalize any decision retrospectively. Since it is virtually impossible to dis-

---

[34] Boloña (interview 1996) stressed the social and political costs of his tight fiscal policies, mentioning, for instance, that 300,000 teachers struck and protested in the streets for three months.

prove an expected utility argument, the following discussion claims only plausibility.

VENEZUELA

President Pérez's decisions to persist with his tough adjustment plan even after the severe riots it provoked and to seek a complete revamping of Venezuela's development model were arguably less promising than a more cautious, gradual course of action. The widespread protests weakened Pérez politically and encouraged economic and political forces that were lukewarm or opposed to his adoption of neoliberalism (interview with Hospedales 1996). From the beginning, the government had done little to garner support for its adjustment policies (Hauser 1990: 172). In this context, the government's insistence on its tough adjustment program was most probably counterproductive. For instance, Pérez's opponents inside his AD charged that the severe recession of 1989 contributed to the party's meager electoral results in the important gubernatorial contests of December 1989 (Celli 1993: 9–29; interview with Celli 1996). The resulting disaffection made it much more difficult for the president to win legislative support for his structural reform proposals (interview with Celli 1996; Corrales 1996: chaps. 6–7). In turn, the failure to pass tax reforms and other measures hindered a lasting stabilization. Worsening economic prospects, finally, eroded the president's popularity (Weyland 1998a), intensifying the vicious circle that led to his impeachment on trumped-up charges of malfeasance. In sum, Pérez's boldness had negative political repercussions that helped to undermine his adjustment plan as well as his hold on power.

The president's ambitious effort to restructure Venezuela's development model also had lower prospects of success than a more gradual approach. It was unclear whether the coddled private sector, which had for decades lived off the state, could quickly turn competitive and withstand stiff foreign competition.[35] It was even more questionable whether Venezuela's obese yet weak state apparatus (cf. Karl 1997) had the institutional capacity to regulate newly unleashed market forces effectively. Large-scale privatization, liberalization, and deregulation therefore held grave risks, as evidenced by the collapse of Venezuela's too radically liberalized banking system in early 1994. In sum, President Pérez's tough stabilization plan and bold program of structural reform held lower expected value than a more prudent, gradual approach, which was feasible in Venezuela due to the absence of hyperinflation.

[35] Jongkind (1993: 81–86). Business expressed many concerns about the drastic adjustment program (FEDECAMARAS 1993).

ARGENTINA

President Menem's stunning adoption of neoliberalism and ostentatious alliance with long-time enemies of Peronism also held tremendous political and economic risks that arguably kept the expected value of his policies lower than that of more prudent alternatives. Certainly, the desire to signal the seriousness of this turnaround and thus win the trust of domestic and foreign investors provided a rationale for these unexpected decisions. But especially after President Pérez had just provoked severe unrest with a similar about-face, Menem's betrayal of his vague campaign rhetoric and of his supporters' expectations held grave danger. His control over the Peronist movement, especially the trade unions, was not sufficiently consolidated to preclude internal opposition,[36] as it indeed erupted with the split inside the union confederation CGT. Also, Menem's gamble that the power hunger of the Peronist Party and its tradition of personalistic leadership would override its longstanding substantive policy commitments had uncertain odds. At the same time, it was unclear whether the new allies whom Menem courted would overcome their traditional distrust of Peronism and their limited respect for buffoon Menem.[37] By antagonizing firm supporters in order to win allies who were probably fickle, Menem charted a course that seemed to deviate from the commands of political rationality.

Even in economic terms, Menem's adjustment plans had limited expected value. The unprecedented initial decision to hand over economic policy-making to a business conglomerate rather than a "neutral" expert failed to consider that market competition would make it exceedingly difficult for the Bunge & Born managers in the Economy Ministry to win cooperation from other capitalists for their negotiated stabilization efforts (interview with Rapanelli 1997); also, the new economic authorities might be reluctant to take indispensable tough measures that would hurt their own firm and their business friends' enterprises (Carrera 1994: 347; interview with González 1995; see also Damill and Frenkel 1991: 28; Smith 1991: 55). Ministers Roig and Rapanelli indeed had very limited success in persuading business to accept sacrifices, for instance by retracting their preemptive price increases. Even the owner of Bunge & Born himself opposed some parts of the stabilization program, such as the tax reform effort (interview with Ferreres 1995; Curia 1991: 57; Llach 1997: 190), undermining Minister Rapanelli's

[36] Corrales (1996: 206–10); "¿Dónde encaja Ubaldini?" Clarín 3 July 1989: 8–9.
[37] For instance, Alsogaray's Unión del Centro Democrático (UCeDé) split over whether to join the Menem government. Alsogaray himself doubted Menem's commitment to neoliberalism (Alsogaray 1993: 171). See also interview with Crotto (1995).

standing. As a result of these difficulties, the first stabilization plan failed quickly.

The drastic measure taken in response to the second bout of hyper-inflation, the temporary confiscation and effective devaluation of financial investments, also held tremendous possibilities of failure. By jeopardizing trust in the banking system, it threatened to undermine financial intermediation in Argentina and disorganize the economy (De la Balze 1995: 73; Curia 1991: 98). The final desperate move, the convertibility law, also was suboptimal. While Minister Cavallo's plan was strikingly successful in the short run,[38] it had problematic consequences in the medium and long run by tying the government's hands and impeding future corrections, especially adjustments of the quickly overvalued exchange rate (Curia 1991: 126, 136–40). In particular, this tight self-constraint left the Menem administration few policy instruments for making Argentina's exports competitive and for defending the country against external shocks, such as the Mexican tequila crisis of 1994–95 (Starr 1997; Pastor and Wise 1999). The short-term focus of the convertibility law differs from the logic that — according to economists and rational-choice theorists — drives structural adjustment decisions, namely, "short-term pain for long-term gain." If this logic is rational, then the convertibility law deviated from conventional rationality calculations, as prospect theory would expect.

President Menem's decision to plunge immediately into structural reform and privatize important public enterprises without adequate preparation also caused considerable economic opportunity costs and tainted the Menem administration with the smell of corruption (Verbitsky 1991), which hobbled it for years. And the radical nature of economic liberalization arguably limited Argentina's export development by precluding active governmental policies to upgrade the country's comparative advantages,[39] as neighboring Chile, for instance, has pursued them successfully. In sum, President Menem's stabilization and adjustment policies had lower expected value than feasible alternatives.

BRAZIL

President Collor's first stabilization plan also held such enormous economic and political risks as to be less promising and rational than more conventional fiscal and monetary policies. The boldest and most costly measure, the freezing of financial assets, constituted a blatant violation

---

[38] But Llach (1997: 129) mentions that many economists at the time thought convertibility could be maintained only for a short while.

[39] For the categorical rejection of active industrial policies, see interview with Rodríguez (1997).

of existing contracts and infringement of property rights. This arbitrary intervention threatened to undermine trust in the banking system and obstruct savings and investment, the basis of economic development (Werneck 1994: 132–33). A complete meltdown of the Brazilian economy could have resulted, especially if Congress, in whose lower chamber Collor's party held a mere 4.4 percent of the seats, had not approved the decree imposing the asset freeze (interview with Kandir 1995). Even if this immediate risk was avoided, the violation of contractual rights required much higher interest rates in the future, hindering private investment as well as governmental efforts to incur internal and, perhaps, external debt.

The first Collor Plan also suffered from a striking internal contradiction that undermined its effectiveness. Whereas the asset freeze drastically boosted state control over the economy, the structural reforms announced by the new president sought to unleash market forces and enhance the role of private business as a crucial engine of development. These opposing moves created confusion and offended many entrepreneurs,[40] whose cooperation the president needed to make structural adjustment work. Collor's rhetorical attacks on business and refusal to consult with its organizations, especially the powerful São Paulo industrialists' association FIESP, further antagonized capitalists (interview with Macedo 1995).

Collor took these economic risks and affronted powerful sociopolitical forces without having a firm base of political sustenance. In a typical strategy of burning the bridges, he and his aides gambled that Congress would not dare to lift his asset freeze in order to avoid an economic catastrophe (interviews with Assis 1995, Collor 1995, Mello 1995). While successful in the short run, this brinkmanship bred disaffection among Brazil's political class, which resented the hardball tactics used by the imperious upstart president (interviews with Assis 1995 and Delfim 1995). Thus, Collor's bold stabilization plan quickly exhausted the political capital he had acquired by beating the socialist left in the presidential election. Lacking organized support, the president remained vulnerable to economic setbacks and political obstruction,[41] as revealed by his eventual impeachment on corruption charges (see chapter 6).

[40] Bornhausen (1991); interviews with Amato (1992) and Temporal (1992). This confusion also prevailed among researchers, who had difficulty classifying Collor's economic policies along conventional categories (discussion in Schneider 1991).

[41] Even members of Collor's own team saw this as a grave risk (interview with Gonçalves 1995). How political and social opposition hindered economic stabilization even during Collor's honeymoon is stressed in Andrei, Sampaio, and Portugal (1995: 17–19, 48–49, 87).

In general, the autocratic style with which Collor made, announced, and implemented his decisions was suboptimal and further increased the dangers inherent in his stabilization measures. Rather than trying to win supporters, Collor deliberately picked fights.[42] And rather than disassociating his presidency from any specific stabilization plan, he heightened the cost of failure by emphasizing that "he had only one shot to kill the tiger of inflation" (interview with Kandir 1995). In fact, other presidents used their economy ministers as "fuses" that could be exchanged at limited political cost, thus protecting the president himself from an early burnout (interview with Hurtado Miller 1996; Torres y Torres Lara 1992: 104–5). By contrast, Collor insisted on sticking out his neck by claiming that he would personally guide economic policy (Sabino 1991: 114, 161). As he concentrated responsibility in himself, he became unable to shift the blame for failure (interview with Kandir 1995; see also interview with Gonçalves 1995). In sum, Collor's drastic adjustment program contained enormous economic and political risks.[43] Therefore, it arguably had lower expected value than available alternatives.

PERU

The same argument applies to Fujimori's draconian stabilization plan. The extreme nature of some measures, such as the exorbitant price increases for basic consumption items, could well have unleashed social unrest, as the government itself feared (interview with Hurtado Miller 1996) and as it had happened in Venezuela the year before. Given Fujimori's complete lack of organized political backing, the blatant betrayal of his campaign promise to avoid a shock program could also have caused a massive desertion of his followers, including his supporters in Parliament.[44] Weakened in this way, the president's political sur-

[42] On Collor's distaste for traditional politicking, see Rosa e Silva (1993: 157, 249, 386) and interviews with Collor (1995) and Moreira (1995).

[43] Collor's willingness to run risk was partly a personality trait, but it was reinforced by the situational factors elucidated by prospect theory, as the similar behavior of Pérez, Menem, and Fujimori suggests. Also, risk-acceptant Collor was elected president only because of the risk acceptance prevailing among citizens afflicted by incipient hyperinflation.

[44] In fact, a number of his initial supporters and aides resigned when Fujimori adopted the shock approach ("Parlamentarios de Cambio 90 rechazan 'shock' de Fujimori," Hoy 18 July 1990). Also, Fujimori's first cabinet was quite heterogeneous; a lengthy conflict between the ministers of economy and of industry paralyzed economic policy-making for months and undermined the government's credibility (Velarde and Rodríguez 1992b: 28–29, 33, 40; cf. Pennano 1990: 410–17).

vival could have been in danger.[45] Furthermore, by pushing large numbers of poor people deeper into poverty, the Fuji-shock played into the hands of the two ferocious guerrilla movements that were attacking the Peruvian state. The years 1990 to 1992 saw the high point of the virtual civil war that caused many casualties and enormous material damage, hindering economic recovery. Thus, the Fujimori government could well have fallen into a vicious circle of mutually reinforcing economic and political problems, especially if the Peruvian police had not been lucky to decapitate the Shining Path guerrilla movement in late 1992.

What made the Fuji-shock particularly risky and suboptimal was the government's neglect of a social emergency program that could have cushioned the tremendous costs of adjustment. Despite international credit offers, the president failed to enact a significant antipoverty scheme because he could not guarantee monopolistic control over these resources (Graham 1993: 45, 51–55). The absence of a minimal social safety net imprudently aggravated the social and political risks of the stabilization program.

The speed with which the Fujimori government—especially under Economy Minister Boloña (early 1991 to early 1993)—enacted structural reforms in a still unstabilized economy was also counterproductive (Paredes 1991: 312–17). A number of its drastic measures obstructed each other. For instance, the early resumption of external debt service prolonged the fiscal crisis of the state (Velarde and Rodríguez 1992b: 30). And quickly opening up the economy to foreign competition during a profound recession threatened even viable enterprises with bankruptcy (González Izquierdo 1991: 32).

In sum, the painful, politically risky shock programs and rash structural reforms enacted by the four presidents most probably had lower expected value than feasible less drastic alternatives.

The Popular Response to Drastic Adjustment Plans

The preceding section has established that all four presidents faced severe economic problems, saw themselves in the domain of losses, and therefore adopted bold, risky adjustment plans that were suboptimal in economic and political terms. But the differential severity of the open problems facing the citizenry led to a great divergence in the immediate popular response to these drastic stabilization plans. Where hyperinflation rapidly imposed tremendous costs on large sectors of the popula-

[45] There was considerable concern among Fujimori's aides that his government would fail and the president would not manage to complete his term (interview with Hurtado Miller 1996).

tion and thus put most citizens in the domain of losses, as in Argentina, Brazil, and Peru, a strong majority endorsed the risky rescue efforts undertaken by their new leaders.[46] By contrast, where people were unaware of the imminent grave crisis that the new president foresaw, as in Venezuela, many rejected the adjustment plan decreed by their president. Ironically, then, President Pérez, who acted with foresight in seeking to preempt an economic collapse, encountered much less support than Menem, Collor, and Fujimori.

How would the people react to the neoliberal shock plans, which brought severe, immediate hardship for important sectors? The four presidents and their aides were quite concerned about the popular response to their tough programs. They feared rejection and perhaps protest; Fujimori even sent the military into the streets of Lima (interviews with Ferreres 1995 and Hurtado Miller 1996; Sabino 1991: 111–12, 131–32; Naím 1993b: 59; Hausmann 1995: 262–64). These concerns are of crucial importance for my prospect-theory interpretation. If Menem, Collor, and Fujimori had foreseen the widespread endorsement of shock programs, their adoption could be fully rational in political terms: Leaders adjusted opportunistically to citizens' risk acceptance in the domain of losses. While citizens deviated from calculations of expected value, leaders did not; they rationally executed what most people preferred. The fact, however, that the new presidents did not anticipate popular approval of their shock programs shows that they did not act as simple agents of the citizenry.[47] On the contrary, they were willing to brave the dangers of popular rejection. Thus, both leaders and citizens displayed risk-seeking in the domain of losses.

To substantiate my argument, I need to demonstrate three points. First, a majority of Argentines, Brazilians, and Peruvians saw themselves in a domain of losses, whereas a majority of Venezuelans had positive or neutral assessments of the economic situation, as the first section of this chapter has shown. Second, a majority of Argentines, Brazilians, and Peruvians approved of drastic shock programs, whereas a majority of Venezuelans rejected Pérez's tough stabilization plan. Third, given the highly uncertain success of structural adjustment plans

[46] Risk-seeking in the domain of losses thus induced many people to adopt an "intertemporal" posture (Stokes 2001b: 13–15).

[47] In interviews with this author, Assis (1995), Collor (1995), Ferreres (1995), Hurtado Miller (1996), Kandir (1995), Mello (1995), Pennano (1996), Torres y Torres Lara (1996), and Velarde (1996) all stressed their governments' surprise at the strong popular support that painful adjustment plans elicited. Torres y Torres Lara (interview 1996) reported the same for Fujimori's self-coup of April 1992. In mid-1990, however, Fujimori allegedly claimed: "My political intuition (*mi olfato político*) tells me that the people will accept a shock to end this chaos" (interview with Figueroa 1996).

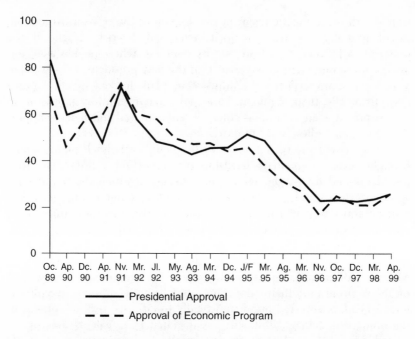

Figure 5.1. Popular Approval of Menem and His Economic Plan, 1989–99.
Source: Mora y Araujo & Asociados, as reported in Gelineau (2000: 21).

in Argentina, Brazil, and Peru, the popular approval they elicited diverged from rational calculations of expected value.

Initial Popular Approval vs. Rejection of Neoliberal Shock Programs

Large numbers of Argentines supported President Menem's costly and risky efforts at economic adjustment and restructuring. The stabilization plan of July 1989 was endorsed by 77 percent and 72 percent of Greater Buenos Aires residents in August and October 1989, respectively, and the president himself received positive evaluations from 89 percent and 85 percent (Mora y Araujo 1990: 4). After subsequent economic problems depressed Menem's popularity during parts of 1990 and 1991, the stabilization measures enacted by Economy Minister González in 1990 and the Convertibility Plan of 1991 raised it again to 45–70 percent of positive endorsements (see fig. 5.1).[48] The congressio-

[48] The lines in figure 5.1 refer to evaluations of Menem and the stabilization plan as "very good" and "good" — exclusive of "fair" (*regular*) — and are therefore lower than

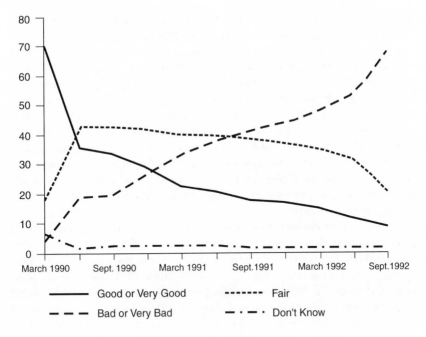

Figure 5.2. Popular Evaluation of the Collor Government's Performance, 1990–92. *Source:* Datafolha no. 1180 (September 1992).

nal and gubernatorial elections of late 1991 yielded a Peronist victory, commonly interpreted as a clear endorsement of the government's move toward economic liberalism. Thus, through survey responses and votes, many people expressed their support for Menem's daring adjustment policies.[49]

Despite the enormous hardships caused by the Collor Plan, a large majority of Brazilians supported the new president's bold attack on inflation (fig. 5.2). Reaching 58 percent immediately after its announcement, popular approval of the stabilization package rose to 71–81 percent during the following weeks (Datafolha 1990; IBOPE 1990a: 13); in August 1990, 59.7 percent assessed the plan as successful and only 35.2 percent as unsuccessful (IBOPE 1990b: question 17). The Collor government was rated as good or very good by 63 percent of respondents

---

those that binary question wording ("do you approve or disapprove?") would most likely yield (as reported for the Venezuelan case below). Argentine polling is of surprisingly poor quality (Kennamer 1995); surveys often have small samples and are confined to Greater Buenos Aires.

[49] I am very grateful to François Gélineau of the University of New Mexico for giving me access to his data.

from ten major cities in April (Datafolha 1990). While the resurgence of inflation diminished support for the president and his stabilization policies from mid-1990 onward, the enactment of a second adjustment plan in January 1991 received initial approval from 49 percent of respondents vs. 35 percent rejection in one poll; another survey, however, showed only 28 percent approval, but 42 percent rejection.[50] Thus, facing a domain of losses, a majority of Brazilians took a risk-acceptant stance and endorsed President Collor's daring stabilization efforts, at least initially. The failure of Collor's plan to reach its proclaimed goal of zero inflation eroded this support, however, while the more limited cost of high inflation in Brazil—a result of widespread indexation—made many sectors less enthusiastic about renewed stabilization efforts than in Argentina and Peru.

President Fujimori's draconian stabilization plan of August 1990 also encountered surprisingly high levels of acceptance (fig. 5.3). Despite its brutal impact on the already low living standard of many Peruvians,[51] the Fuji-shock won—after three days of initial confusion—approval from 52–59 percent of poll respondents during the remainder of 1990, while rejection reached only 25–30 percent. This substantial support prevailed although 87 percent classified the stabilization plan as a shock treatment (Apoyo, August 1990: 10); thus, the public was aware that the president had deviated from one of his few campaign promises. Despite this turnaround, Fujimori achieved approval ratings of 51–61 percent, against 25–33 percent disapproval.[52] While a resurgence of inflation in late 1990 and a persistent recession in 1991 depressed presidential popularity, Fujimori's boldest step—the self-coup of 1992—boosted it to unprecedented levels.

In sum, incipient hyperinflation induced large numbers of Argentines, Brazilians, and Peruvians to become risk-acceptant and endorse the drastic stabilization efforts undertaken by their new presidents. While in several instances the tremendous costs of adjustment and failure to control inflation soon eroded this approval, the initial outpouring of support had tremendous political significance. First, by demonstrat-

---

[50] IBOPE poll reported in "Plano Collor 2 tem apoio da maioria," *Estado de São Paulo, Economia* 23 February 1991: 1; Datafolha 1991: question 1. The different results reported by IBOPE and Datafolha throughout the Collor government led observers to suspect political motivations on both sides.

[51] In September 1990, 51 percent of respondents rated their "current family situation" as "bad" (Apoyo, December 1991: 30), an unusually negative assessment.

[52] Apoyo, January 1991: 3, 16, 17; similarly Datum (1990c: fig. no. 2). IMASEN (1990: 14-E) reports a similarly positive "image" of Fujimori in October 1990, but IMASEN (1991: 1-A) finds approval of presidential performance (*gestión*) diminishing strongly in late 1990 already.

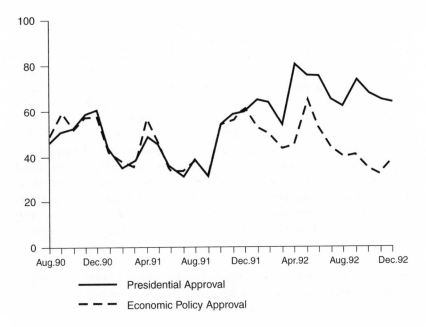

Figure 5.3. Popular Approval of Fujimori and His Economic Policy, 1990–92.
Source: Apoyo, *Informe de Opinión* (December 1991: 23; June 1999: 6, 15).

ing that bold stabilization plans boost presidential popularity, it encouraged renewed adjustment efforts in cases of temporary failure. Second, strong initial support in public opinion allowed presidents to push through Congress decisive neoliberal reforms, such as Menem's "law on state reform" and Collor's privatization plan.[53] Thus, it opened up a window of opportunity for creating the political and legal bases of far-reaching structural transformations.

In contrast to the strong immediate support for drastic stabilization plans in Argentina, Brazil, and Peru, a majority of Venezuelans, who did not face hyperinflation and therefore did not see themselves in a domain of losses (Myers 1993: 45–46), disapproved of Pérez's similarly costly and risky measures. In the weeks after the president enacted his reform package, only 25.6 percent of Venezuelans endorsed this decision; 52 percent regarded the austerity measures as unnecessary.[54] The shock program lowered the new president's popularity from 70 percent in January 1989 to 46 percent positive (vs. 42 percent negative) ratings

[53] In addition, deep crises created support for market reforms among interest groups (Torre 1998: 69–72).

[54] *Foreign Broadcast Information Service-Latin America* 16 June 1989: 67; similarly Consultores 21 (1989b: 31–32).

in April (Consultores 21 1989b: 11). In fact, 34 percent of respondents declared that the new administration had "already failed due to the [economic] measures it had taken and that it could not recover"; even during the president's presumed "honeymoon," only 41 percent believed that "the government . . . would be a success at the end of its term" (Consultores 21 1989b: 31). Even worse, large-scale riots erupted as the real and anticipated costs of the "unnecessary" stabilization plan pushed many people into the domain of losses (Consultores 21 1994c: 70–71), turning them risk-acceptant—but against Pérez. This unprecedented popular rebellion, which left at least three hundred people dead, had a traumatic impact (Kornblith 1989), shattering the tranquil image of Venezuela's seemingly consolidated democracy. It further undermined trust in Pérez and his administration, even inside the government party (interview with Hospedales 1996). Pérez never managed to overcome these negative judgments and recuperate his aura of success (Consultores 21 1994c: 76). In subsequent years, the government faced a continuing wave of strikes and protests (López Maya 1999), and support for the president and his shock program remained limited in polls (fig. 5.4).[55]

Deviations from Calculations of Expected Value

The high level of initial approval for draconian adjustment measures in Argentina, Brazil, and Peru diverged from calculations of expected value. The shock programs imposed considerable short-term losses on many sectors, yet the promises of future benefits were quite uncertain. In fact, brutal, arbitrary interventions such as Menem's and Collor's financial confiscations carried the danger of destroying the economy. Furthermore, many prior stabilization plans had failed and often made the situation worse; any prudent assessment would therefore have doubted the promises accompanying this new round of draconian adjustment programs. Considering this dismal track record, citizens' faith in the new rescue efforts was not fully rational. In fact, people generally discount future benefits heavily (Thaler 1992: 94). Many Argentines',

---

[55] A comparison of the skillful TV announcement of Fujimori's first shock program (Graham 1994: 87) and Pérez's blunder in surprising the population with price increases decreed over a weekend might suggest that governments' communication efforts shaped the popular response to drastic stabilization plans. But the announcement of the first Collor Plan was an unmitigated communications disaster ("Collor se irrita com má divulgação do Plano," *Jornal do Brasil* 18 March 1990: 2), yet popular support nevertheless rose sky-high.

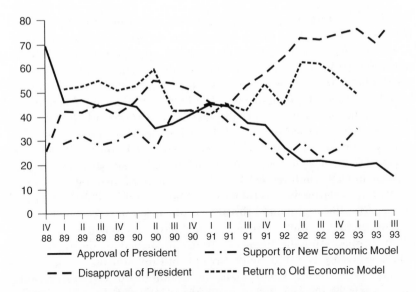

Figure 5.4. Popular Evaluation of Pérez and His New Economic Model.
Source: Consultores 21 (1994c: 60, 75).

Brazilians', and Peruvians' divergence from this tendency, especially in a situation of tremendous uncertainty that could well justify a high discount rate, provides strong evidence of risk acceptance in the domain of losses. People did accept "short-term pain for long-term gain," but contrary to the claims of economists and rational-choice theorists (cf. Przeworski 1991: 162–80), the hope for future benefits was not conventionally rational; instead, it deviated from strict cost-benefit calculations.

Fujimori's stabilization plan was the most brutal by raising the price of basic necessities by up to 3,000 percent, pushing many Peruvians more deeply into poverty. Immediately after the adjustment program, inflation shot up by a whopping 397 percent. Thus, the Fuji-shock did not bring an immediate end to hyperinflation that could have justified popular approval (contra Rodrik 1996). In fact, prospects for the future were highly uncertain; the failure of all the adjustment efforts undertaken during the 1980s should have instilled healthy skepticism in the population. Thus, the initial support for Fujimori and his economic policy was due not to rational cost-benefit calculations, but to risk-seeking in the domain of losses.

Menem's first adjustment plan also brought substantial increases in public sector charges, and its announcement was preceded and followed by a considerable rise in private sector prices. The new government failed in its efforts to achieve a negotiated reduction of these anticipatory price raises. Thus, in the beginning costs were much more in evidence than benefits. Indeed, the medium-term prospects of Menem's stabilization effort were highly uncertain, dependent on the precarious rapprochement between old enemies, namely, Peronism and a transnational agro-export conglomerate. Therefore, in endorsing Menem's efforts, a majority of Argentines displayed considerable risk acceptance.

The direct burden of Collor's first shock plan — especially the temporary confiscation of financial assets — fell mostly on the middle and upper classes, not the poor. In Brazil's inegalitarian society, this progressive impact (Crabtree 1991: 124–27) enhanced the program's popularity. But by virtually paralyzing the economy, the Collor Plan created tremendous uncertainty and threatened to cause a severe recession. The specter of falling wages and mass unemployment posed a danger for many people. And the financial freeze threatened to disorganize the whole economy and undermine savings and investment. Thus, the immediate benefit of the Collor Plan — an instantaneous end of hyperinflation — came at the expense of grave risks. It is therefore questionable that the widespread initial endorsement conformed to calculations of expected value.

Certainly, after the initial uncertainty diminished and the success or failure of stabilization plans became clearer, many people responded to governmental incapacity to control inflation or to particularly grave adjustment costs by becoming more critical. As a result, the high approval for shock plans dropped in several instances (figs. 5.1–5.3). Thus, as better information about current gains and losses and especially about future prospects became available, many people changed their assessments accordingly. But in the initial phase of overwhelming uncertainty, risk-seeking in the domain of losses induced them to give presidents who boldly combated severe crises an important credit of trust, which was much more generous than rational cost-benefit calculation justified. And as mentioned above, widespread support at this critical juncture was politically decisive by guaranteeing presidents approval from Congress and interest groups for crucial adjustment measures with long-term effects.

Conclusion

This chapter has demonstrated that the core findings of prospect theory can best account for the initiation of drastic structural adjustment and the initial popular response. Where incipient hyperinflation put large numbers of people in the domain of losses, as in Argentina, Brazil, and

Peru, a majority of voters made particularly risky electoral choices. Therefore, untested outsiders won presidential elections, defeating the established political class. As the resulting uncertainty aggravated the economic crisis, the new presidents clearly faced a domain of losses. Upon taking office, they therefore imposed stunningly painful stabilization measures and/or began a striking restructuring of their country's development model. In this way, they chose risky over more cautious decision options. Due to their tremendous social cost and ensuing political risk, these audacious choices arguably had lower expected value than available alternatives. Nevertheless, stuck in the domain of losses, a large majority of the population endorsed these costly choices, setting their hopes in the uncertain prospect of an end to the deepening crisis.

In Venezuela, by contrast, the outgoing government covered up worsening economic difficulties. Since a majority of the population did not see itself in a domain of losses, a former president and member of the governing party won the election. The new chief executive did, however, confront grave problems and — seeing himself in the domain of losses — made the risk-acceptant decision of imposing a shock program. Given the absence of hyperinflation, this drastic choice was arguably suboptimal. In fact, a majority of the population rejected the painful adjustment measures, and large-scale riots erupted, which weakened the government politically.

In sum, the wealth of official documents, opinion poll data, and interviews with leading decision-makers mentioned in this chapter suggest that risk-seeking in the domain of losses best explains the adoption of draconian stabilization plans and the initiation of profound structural reform.

CHAPTER SIX

POPULIST POLITICS AND ECONOMIC RESTRUCTURING

The strong initial support for drastic adjustment in Argentina, Brazil, and Peru had two important ramifications for the politics of market reform. First, it boosted the personal leadership of presidents Menem, Collor, and Fujimori and strengthened their unmediated, quasi-direct relationship to large numbers of unorganized citizens. As true or self-proclaimed outsiders, the three leaders had used support from such a heterogeneous following to win presidential elections. Thus, they had applied a typically populist strategy to attain office, and they maintained populism as presidents.

Second, initial popular support and the use of populist tactics facilitated the launching of profound structural reforms that dismantled the inward-looking, state-interventionist development model and gave market forces free rein. Mass backing permitted Menem, Collor, and Fujimori to limit opposition from organized interests with a stake in the established system. In a systematic "mobilization of bias" (Schattschneider 1975: 30), they invoked "the will of the people" against "special interests" that defended their own "privileges" at the expense of the "common good." And as populist tactics furthered structural reform, those reforms in turn strengthened populist leaders by weakening organized interest groups and parties that sought to hem in leaders' latitude. Thus, neoliberal economics and populist politics went hand in hand in Argentina, Brazil, and Peru.

Conversely, the high level of popular disapproval for President Pérez's stabilization plan hindered his efforts to apply populist tactics and advance structural economic change. The president's weak standing in public opinion encouraged interest groups and especially sectors of his own party to offer passive resistance and, eventually, active opposition to market reform. The fact that Pérez was much less of an outsider than Menem, Collor, and Fujimori further complicated his task. Those presidents gained support for their populist leadership and neoliberal reforms by attacking the preceding government. Pérez, by contrast, could not criticize the AD administration of Jaime Lusinchi too openly without antagonizing important sectors of his own party. Populist efforts to gain mass support threatened Pérez's congressional backing, whereas for Menem, Collor, and Fujimori, these two requirements largely coincided.

As chapter 5 argued, both of these factors—popular rejection of tough stabilization measures and Pérez's hailing from the incumbent party—reflect the absence of an acute open crisis, such as hyperinflation. Thus, the main variable emphasized by my prospect-theory interpretation—the depth of the crisis—played a crucial role in the political difficulties that hobbled Pérez's government from the beginning. While a temporary economic recovery, fueled by the increase in petroleum prices stemming from the Persian Gulf conflict of 1990–91, allowed his administration to recover the appearance of normality, the subsequent economic downswing reignited popular discontent and fueled growing protest. When junior officers made an almost successful coup attempt and many citizens sympathized with this violent move, the Pérez government entered a terminal crisis that led to the president's impeachment in May 1993. Aversion to "neoliberalism" led a majority of voters in the 1993 presidential elections to choose candidates who promised to reverse market reforms. Victorious Rafael Caldera in fact reimposed a host of economic controls. Thus, Pérez's "great turnaround" ended in political and economic failure.

While initial popular support for drastic stabilization measures put presidents Menem, Collor, and Fujimori on a different trajectory, it did not guarantee political and economic success. In fact, whereas Menem and Fujimori managed to win democratic reelection, Collor suffered the same political fate as Pérez. Weakened by tenacious passive resistance and growing active opposition, he was impeached on corruption charges. Interestingly, however, his successor Itamar Franco did not reverse his market reforms, and Fernando Henrique Cardoso—as finance minister and president—advanced many structural changes that were moderate versions of Collor's plans. Thus, while failing politically, Collor did help to reshape Brazil's economic agenda irreversibly.

Why did the three governments that started out with massive popular support suffer such different political fates? Why did Collor fail to translate his initial political capital into a successful government performance? A comparison with Fujimori is particularly revealing. Contrary to Menem, both Collor and Fujimori lacked organized support. Furthermore, they faced institutional obstacles as the Brazilian constitution enshrined economic provisions that hindered neoliberal reform and the Peruvian charter allowed Congress to censor ministers, thus weakening the government. Yet whereas Collor remained tied down by these obstacles, the tremendous depth of Peru's economic and security crisis allowed Fujimori to cut the Gordian Knot by closing Congress and revamping the constitution. The less severe problems confronting Brazil did not permit Collor to take a similarly bold step.

Once again, the differential depth of the crisis appears as the crucial factor that accounts for the divergent political and economic fate of the countries under investigation. In line with my prospect-theory argument, particularly grave crises in Argentina and especially Peru allowed Menem and Fujimori to win widespread support, preempt, obstruct, or break opposition, and thus advance market reforms successfully. The absence of an acute open crisis undermined Pérez's effort to proceed along a similar course. And in an intermediate trajectory, hyperinflation helped Collor win broad support for orthodox stabilization, but the better performance of Brazil's established development model in the 1980s—compared to Argentina and Peru—limited the perception of decline and therefore made support for neoliberalism less strong and firm, rendering Collor vulnerable to political problems, such as corruption charges.

Neopopulist Politics

During their terms in office, Menem, Collor, and Fujimori maintained the neopopulist strategy that proved so useful in their electoral campaigns (Roberts 1995; Oxhorn 1998; Weyland 1996c; Panizza 2000; Demmers, Fernández Jilberto, and Hogenboom 2001). Several reasons account for the perpetuation of this bold political approach. First of all, the three leaders faced a domain of losses, tended toward risk acceptance, and therefore embraced a strategy that promised substantial payoffs, though at high risk of failure. Chapter 5 showed that in the economic sphere, Menem, Collor, and Fujimori faced clearly negative prospects. Incipient hyperinflation also created serious political threats, as recent experiences suggested: President Alfonsín had been forced to step down ahead of schedule, and Peru was rife with coup rumors at the end of President García's term. Thus, the grave economic problems afflicting their countries gave the new presidents good reason to fear for their own political survival.[1] Typically, these dangers induced the new chief executives to choose boldness by maintaining populism.

This daring strategy promised to reverse political losses that the predecessors had incurred and that the new presidents were inheriting. The economic deterioration of the 1980s had weakened effective presidential powers. For instance, pressure groups such as Saúl Ubaldini's

---

[1] Interviewed by this author, Assis (1995), Boloña (1996), Gonçalves (1995), and Hurtado Miller (1996) reported such fears.

CGT in Argentina had limited the government's latitude more and more. Political parties had defied presidential leadership, especially in Brazil. And sectors of the military had engaged in rebellions in Argentina, prepared coup plans in Peru, and claimed tutelage over civilian authorities in Brazil. By bypassing and weakening these organizations and by concentrating power in a personalistic leader, a populist strategy held the prospect of recuperating presidential authority — though at considerable risk.

These risks arose from the fickle foundation and adversarial style of neopopulist leadership. The largely unorganized mass support on which the new presidents based their governments was likely tq evaporate quickly if economic problems or political challenges were to arise. By contrast, the political class and the interest groups that neopopulists attacked commanded great and often durable political influence. Neopopulist leaders thus ran the risk of confronting powerful enemies without commanding strong, lasting support. And in the precarious institutional setting of Latin America's "politicized states" (Chalmers 1977), a collapse of support can threaten the chief executive's political survival, as attested by the successful pressure on presidents Alfonsín and Hernán Siles Suazo of Bolivia (1982–85) to abandon office ahead of schedule; by the constant coup rumors against President García in 1988–89; and by the later impeachment of Collor and Pérez. To avoid these dangers, it would have been prudent for the new presidents to abandon their neopopulist campaign strategy and find an accommodation with the powers-that-be, especially the political class, which held the key to their continuation in office.[2] But discarding such rational caution and displaying risk-seeking in the domain of losses, the four new presidents rejected such a bait-and-switch approach (Drake 1991: 36) and persisted instead with their bold neopopulist strategy.

While risk-seeking in the domain of losses provided the impulse for the maintenance of neopopulism, the outsider status of Menem, Collor, and Fujimori made this political strategy feasible and credible. Their distance from the preceding government allowed them to garner mass support by leveling accusations of incompetence, malfeasance, and corruption against their predecessors without offending their own support-

---

[2] Drake (1991: 36), Martins (1990: 31–32), and Bresser Pereira (1991: 13) predicted or recommended such an accommodation. The powers-that-be were interested in avoiding the threat posed by unpredictable neopopulists. In fact, the limited sectors with whom Menem and Fujimori sought good relations, such as leading business groups, uniformly showed receptivity. While a full-scale switch would have undermined neopopulists' mass appeal, it would therefore have substituted a firm for a fickle base of support. Prudence thus recommended the abandonment of neopopulism, but deep crises made these leaders risk-acceptant.

ers. And since these leaders had no direct responsibility for the grave crisis afflicting their countries, they were untainted by failure and able to depict themselves as saviors who could turn the nation around. The new presidents were able to justify their tough plans of stabilization and restructuring as indispensable for cleaning up the mess left behind by the outgoing administration. With this argument, they managed to shift responsibility for the pain caused by their own adjustment measures, thus protecting their popularity. Finally, since Collor and Fujimori, in particular, did not have many visible connections to established interests, they could claim the mantle of impartiality and objectivity (see Fujimori 1991). In this way, they were able to invoke the "common good" while painting their opponents as selfish "special interests."

Furthermore, hyperinflation was the type of problem that provided a golden opportunity for the rise of charismatic leadership. Tough countermeasures can quickly bring exploding price increases under control and thus provide a dramatic, visible benefit to the suffering population, at least by averting imminent further losses. By ending hyperinflation, personal leaders can thus turn their country around in a matter of weeks. As Menem came to realize, it is much easier to "pulverize" hyperinflation than unemployment (as he promised in the 1995 campaign). Attacking the crisis head-on proves leaders' courage and determination, especially compared to the hesitation and perplexity that their predecessors had displayed at the end of their term. By boldly cutting the Gordian Knot that had tied down the country, personalistic leaders seemingly perform magic and demonstrate their "supernatural" capacities.

Presidents Menem, Collor, and Fujimori thus encountered favorable conditions for retaining a neopopulist strategy. In some ways, Menem was in a particularly advantageous position because he had two bases of support: both the Peronist movement with its longstanding loyalties and the unorganized mass of followers that he attracted with his personal appeals. The populist origins of Peronism made this double-sided strategy possible. Inside the movement, personalistic leadership had always taken precedence over firm institutionalization (McGuire 1997; Levitsky 1998). Menem therefore managed to reshape important parts of the movement according to his own priorities. In the end, only small sectors, namely, the "group of eight" leftist congressmen and the Ubaldini wing of the trade unions, insisted on Peronism's traditional policy orientations and openly opposed Menem's conversion to neoliberalism (Novaro and Palermo 1998: 81–92; Murillo 2001: 149–52; interview with Ubaldini 1995). Most Peronists' willingness to follow the leader — a typical characteristic of populism — allowed Menem to marshal widespread acceptance of his drastic policy change inside the movement. Thus, established organizational loyalties gave Menem a firmer support base than other neopopulists have. Menem therefore confronted lower political risks than his counterparts Collor and Fujimori.[3]

By contrast to Menem, Collor, and Fujimori, Venezuela's Pérez faced greater hindrances to adopting a neopopulist strategy. Above all, his status as a political outsider was ambiguous, and his first stabilization plan provoked large-scale rejection. Since Pérez saw himself in the domain of losses when taking office in February 1989, he was tempted to adopt a neopopulist strategy, including efforts to bypass his own AD. In fact, he had long had tense relations with the established party apparatus, which he had antagonized further by endorsing the proposals of a constitutional reform commission for direct gubernatorial elections and internal party democracy. These tensions gave Pérez additional impetus for employing neopopulist tactics, appealing directly to the people, and bypassing or weakening the party.

But Pérez enjoyed much less favorable conditions for using a neopopulist strategy than Menem, Collor, and Fujimori. To begin with, his credentials as an outsider were questionable. Certainly, Pérez hailed from the "out" faction of AD and defeated his predecessor's handpicked candidate for the presidency. Also, Pérez made great efforts to depict himself as an outsider, stressing his personal leadership and criticizing the entrenched party oligarchy. His electoral campaign was highly candidate-centered and did little to help his own party in the simultaneous legislative contest. AD in fact won a much lower vote share for its congressional delegation than Pérez garnered for himself (43.76 percent vs. 54.56 percent: Stambouli 1989: 232, 234).

But while Pérez claimed the mantle of an outsider, his party clearly was the prototypical insider organization. By early 1989, AD had occupied the presidency for twenty out of the thirty years of the post-1958 democracy, including the immediately preceding term. Pérez himself had been president from 1974 to 1979, and he had many friends and followers inside the party and the state apparatus. Indeed, the bonanza caused by the OPEC oil price increase of 1973 had induced Pérez to spearhead a huge new spurt of state-led, debt-financed heavy industrialization, which soon exacerbated Venezuela's economic problems and thus helped precipitate the decline of the 1980s. Thus, Pérez's first presidency held considerable responsibility for the problems that he sought to resolve during his second term.[4] His earlier period in office was also notorious for exorbitant corruption (Karl 1997: 146–51), which many

---

[3] But as chapter 7 shows, the party and its affiliated trade unions constrained Menem's latitude somewhat, hindering both the advance of market reforms (especially labor market deregulation) and Menem's efforts to prolong his political predominance.

[4] In fact, Naím (interview 2000) reported that one of Pérez's main motivations for the *gran viraje* was to undo the mistakes he himself had made during his first presidency.

citizens saw as the main reason for the country's economic difficulties (Keller 1996: 67–68, 79).

Since the new president and his party were seen as sharing responsibility for Venezuela's decline, Pérez found it more difficult to depict himself as the providential savior who would turn the country around. His charisma — while still quite strong in early 1989 — was tainted by earlier policy failures and lingering suspicion of malfeasance. Since Pérez came from the incumbent party and needed its support in Congress, he also faced a trade-off in treating the preceding administration. Accusing the predecessor and his aides of incompetence, favoritism, and corruption is a typical neopopulist tactic for whipping up mass support; it is especially useful for reformers — such as neoliberals — who seek to delegitimate the status quo. But Pérez's use of such accusations drove powerful sectors of his own party into opposition (interviews with Celli 1996, Hospedales 1996, Martínez Móttola 1996); in addition, his own earlier involvement in shady deals left him vulnerable to similar attacks. Pérez's questionable track record also made criticism of the predecessor less credible with educated sectors of the public. For the new president, typical populist tactics thus carried much greater cost and risk than for Menem, Collor, and Fujimori.

An even more important source of political weakness was the large-scale rejection that Pérez's shock program provoked. From the traumatic riots of February 1989 onward, 33–48 percent of poll respondents consistently felt that the administration was decisively weakened and would not be able to recover.[5] Throughout Pérez's second term, presidential popularity remained at modest levels. Only in 1989 did approval outnumber disapproval, and by very low margins; in 1990 and 1991, his net ratings averaged −11 percent, before plummeting to very low levels in 1992 and 1993 (see fig. 5.4). Weak popular support made Pérez's claim to charismatic leadership appear questionable. In fact, the substantial disapproval encouraged his opponents among interest groups, politicians, and — most consequentially — the military.

For these reasons, the neopopulist strategy adopted by Pérez was much more costly and rested on weaker foundations than the similar efforts of Menem, Collor, and Fujimori. While Pérez clearly aspired to neopopulist leadership, he faced greater constraints and obstacles than his counterparts in Argentina, Brazil, and Peru. Right from the beginning, his chances for political success were limited.

---

[5] Consultores 21 (1994: 76). From late 1991 onward, this percentage increased above 50 percent, reaching a high of 74 percent in the second quarter of 1992.

Neopopulist Politics and Market Reform

Neopopulist politics facilitated market reform in a number of ways, and market reform in turn played into the hands of neopopulist leaders. First, the massive support that presidents Menem, Collor, and Fujimori elicited with their direct appeals to large numbers of people increased their influence against politicians and interest groups that sought to defend important aspects of the established development model. Second, the efforts of neopopulist leaders to extend their personal latitude by weakening and dividing interest associations, political parties, and bureaucratic structures facilitated the assault on the innumerable regulations, subsidies, and protections that shielded these sectors from the rigors of the market. Finally, neopopulist rhetoric legitimated neoliberal reforms. Appeals to the "will of the people" and the "common good" (cf. Novaro 1994: 80, 82, 86) and attacks on "special interests" helped to justify structural changes that entailed diffuse, uncertain benefits and clear, concentrated costs (cf. Haggard and Kaufman 1995: 9, 157).

Conversely, market reforms boosted neopopulist leadership because they gave personalistic leaders a technocratic mantle of legitimation and external support for eroding the clout of intermediary associations and political rivals that sought to constrain their autonomy. For instance, the deregulation of the labor market lowered trade union influence, and the downsizing of the public sector weakened traditional patronage politicians. Also, despite the prevailing free-market rhetoric, important neoliberal reforms strengthened the apex of the state and thus augmented the institutional capacities and financial resources at the disposal of neopopulist presidents. For instance, economic stabilization and tax reforms increased fiscal revenues, which allowed personalistic leaders to engage in new forms of discretionary spending and thus bolster their mass support. In sum, neopopulist politics and neoliberal reform reinforced each other. What specific mechanisms created this synergistic relationship?

First, strong popular support helped neopopulist leaders silence opponents of market reform. For instance, Menem's popularity made it difficult for trade unions to resist measures such as deregulation and privatization. Since many of their own constituents endorsed the president's adjustment efforts, union leaders could not claim to represent "the working people" if they resisted governmental initiatives.[6] Sim-

---

[6] McGuire (1997: 234–37). Also, union officials realized that low popular trust in their organizations made it difficult for them to oppose market reforms (interview with Jara 1997).

ilarly, the "group of eight" dissident Peronists, who threatened to attract wider sectors of the movement during the difficult year 1990, suffered a stinging defeat in the parliamentary elections of late 1991 and had minimal influence in the following two years (Novaro and Palermo 1998: 81–92). Thus, mass backing revealed by opinion polls and elections — the favorite instruments of neopopulist leaders — greatly helped Menem contain resistance to structural reform.

In a similar vein, Fujimori put unions and social movements on the defensive by winning surprisingly strong mass support for his brutal stabilization efforts (Balbi 1993: 103). And business firms were reluctant to challenge the stricter enforcement of tax rules, which received widespread endorsement in public opinion (Durand and Thorp 1998: 142). Most importantly, the massive acclamation of his self-coup of April 1992 made it much easier for Fujimori to push ahead with economic liberalization. Although the Peruvian Congress had approved many of Fujimori's market reforms in 1991 (interview with Pease 1996), opposition seemed to coalesce and intensify in early 1992 (Boloña 1993: 98; Torres y Torres Lara 1992: 73–100). The unconstitutional dissolution of Congress was followed by a spate of new structural reforms (Boloña 1993: 55). Fujimori took advantage of the institutional hiatus to decree some particularly controversial measures, such as the partial privatization of Peru's social security system. The outpouring of popular approval for closing Congress was crucial for giving Fujimori the clout to push ahead his ambitious reform program so quickly.

Collor also used his initially strong mass support to face down potential resistance. The thirty-five million votes he won in the presidential election and the high approval ratings for his first stabilization plan were among the main arguments that the president and his aides used to coax a reluctant Congress into passing his controversial adjustment program.[7]

Second, personalistic leaders resent the fetters on their latitude that pressure groups and established politicians try to impose; they therefore seek to weaken and divide these "veto players." These neopopulist attacks on intermediary associations and the political class put many potential opponents of market reform on the defensive and thus help to pave the way for structural change. In this vein, Menem encouraged a split inside the powerful Peronist trade union confederation CGT. This division undermined the CGT's clout and limited the resistance to the government's neoliberal program that incumbent CGT president Saúl Ubaldini could exert (interviews with Miguel 1995 and Ubaldini 1995).

Similarly, Collor's economic team built up as one of its main inter-

---

[7] Interviews with Kandir (1995) and Pojo de Rego (1995); "Collor usa pesquisa para obter apoio do Congresso às reformas," *O Globo* 23 March 1990.

locutors a new movement of young businesspeople that offered internal opposition to the established leadership of the powerful FIESP (interview with Butori 1992; Kingstone 1999: 136–37), which encompassed many import-substituting industries that were afraid of—if not resistant to—economic liberalization. Collor also courted a moderate trade union confederation in order to counterbalance the mighty socialist CUT, which opposed many of his market reforms, especially the privatization of state enterprises. Since Peru's civil society was already fragmented and weak, Fujimori directed most of his fire at the political class. In particular, he relentlessly attacked parties as coteries of elites that lacked connections to the people. His self-coup, which he justified in those terms (Fujimori 1992: 43–47), decisively undercut the resistance that politicians could pose to his market reforms.

Third, the rhetoric of neopopulist leaders, especially their attacks on "special interests," helped to legitimate their neoliberal programs. Several types of structural reforms—such as trade liberalization, the "flexibilization" of labor laws, and the dismissal of public officials—impose immediate, visible costs on concentrated, organized constituencies and therefore run the risk of provoking fierce resistance. Delegitimating these opponents as selfish defenders of special privileges can "mobilize bias" against them (cf. Schattschneider 1975: 30–35) and thus facilitate the enactment and implementation of reform. Conversely, since the potential beneficiaries of many market reforms—for instance, consumers—are unorganized and have difficulty foreseeing the positive effects of economic liberalization, appeals to their self-interests alone cannot attract widespread, strong backing. The neopopulist invocation of the "common good" helps to fill this support gap.

In this vein, Menem stressed upon taking office that it was one of the main purposes of the imminent "tough adjustment, costly adjustment, severe adjustment" to "abolish, from today on, the privileges of whatever type" and "to re-found a state at the service of the people, not at the service of the bureaucracies" (Menem 1990: 16–17). Collor went even further by publicly snubbing FIESP on several occasions, disqualifying it as a "den of the retrograde," and engaging in angry exchanges with FIESP president Mário Amato. And although the automobile industry was widely seen as one of Brazil's leading sectors, the president branded cars produced in Brazil as outdated *caroças* in order to justify his trade liberalization, which sought to improve productivity, efficiency, and competitiveness (interview with Macedo 1995; see also Kingstone 1999: 153, 171–72). In similar terms, Fujimori denounced "privileged groups" and "cliques of party leaders" (Fujimori 1992: 43–45), concentrating his attack mainly on the political class, especially electoral politicians and public officials.

Market reforms in turn strengthened the personalistic leadership of presidents Menem, Collor, and Fujimori. First of all, some adjustment measures deliberately fortified the apex of the state, giving neopopulist presidents more institutional prerogatives and economic resources for bolstering their power. While paradoxical in light of neoliberalism's antistate rhetoric, these efforts emerged from the recognition that a functioning market economy depended on public goods provided by the state and that the very enactment of economic liberalization required a strong state capable of overcoming sectoral resistance.

To enable the state to fulfill its basic tasks — such as the maintenance of order and the administration of justice — neoliberal experts (advised by international financial institutions) designed wide-ranging tax reforms that sought to strengthen the public sector's fiscal base. Together with macroeconomic stabilization, which ended the erosion of public revenues by high inflation via the "Olivera-Tanzi effect,"[8] these fiscal measures raised the effective tax burden, especially in Argentina and Peru (SIP 1995: 11; SUNAT 1996).

Alleviating the fiscal crisis was a crucial precondition for Menem and Fujimori to reassert state authority and restore order — one of the central tasks of neopopulist leaders. The revenue increase also allowed them to initiate new spending programs, including targeted antipoverty measures. The international financial institutions recommended such social emergency measures to compensate some of the losers from tough adjustment plans, create new winners, and thus protect economic liberalization against political challenges. Neopopulist leaders, in turn, used these social programs to strengthen their mass support by handing out visible benefits to large numbers of people (Graham and Kane 1998: 85–99; Roberts and Arce 1998: 231–37; Weyland 1998c: 556–62).

To push through market reforms and fortify their institutional capacities, Menem, Fujimori, and — less successfully — Collor also sought to concentrate power and attributions in the presidency, for instance, through drastic administrative reform. Fujimori created a new Ministry of the Presidency and boosted its attributions and budget. Collor tied several portfolios directly to the presidency. And Menem packed Argentina's Supreme Court to preempt any challenges to his decisions. The three presidents also usurped more extensive decree authority. Facing severe crises, Congress often acceded, at least through a temporary delegation of legislative powers. Collor, Fujimori, and Menem indeed enacted crucial parts of their neoliberal agenda, especially stabilization

---

[8] Since there usually is a time lag between a taxable event and the actual tax payment, inflation erodes the real value of fiscal revenues. Olivera and Tanzi designed the formula for calculating this fiscal loss.

measures, via decree (Ferreira Rubio and Goretti 1998; Power 1998b; Schmidt 1998).

In addition, Menem and Fujimori skewed the balance of power between the presidency and legislature through constitutional reform. Most drastically, Fujimori disbanded an opposition-controlled parliament and engineered a new constitution that strengthened presidential powers, though less than initially expected (Schmidt 1998: 113–14). To extend their personal leadership, Fujimori and Menem managed to eliminate constitutional rules that prohibited their immediate reelection. All of these measures, which neoliberal experts supported to advance market reforms against opposition, served the goal of neopopulist leaders to boost their own autonomy and preeminence.

Furthermore, neoliberalism provided a modern, technocratic rationale and support from international financial institutions for some of the neopopulist tactics employed by personalistic leaders, especially their attacks on intermediary associations and the political class and their concentration of power at the top of the state. Through their demand-making and pressure tactics, trade unions, for instance, hem in personalistic leaders. Orthodox stabilization plans weakened unions by increasing unemployment, which made workers reluctant to rock the boat. Labor market deregulation, which gave employers more discretion over their work force, had a similar moderating effect on union activism. The reduction of legal protection for workers, which governments justified with the need for greater productivity and competitiveness, increased the cost of strikes and other pressure tactics. In Peru, where the liberalization of labor laws has gone particularly far (Gonzales de Olarte 1998: 54, 117), trade unions therefore suffered a drastic reduction in their political clout (Balbi 1993).

Market reforms — especially the revamping of the state apparatus — are also useful for weakening the political rivals of neopopulist leaders (see in general Geddes 1994a: 113–17). During the long years that the political class controlled the government, it made innumerable patronage appointments, packing the state apparatus with its cronies and followers. Through the dismissal of public officials and the privatization of parastate enterprises, neopopulist leaders manage to restrict their adversaries' access to patronage. By restructuring public bureaucracies and boosting their discretionary authority over state officials, they also strengthen their preeminence inside the state. Neoliberal reforms thus allow neopopulist leaders to augment their autonomy and power.

Yet while neopopulist tactics facilitated market reform, it was dangerous carrying them to the extreme. In particular, attacks on established interest groups and the political class worked most effectively when combined with efforts to make some strategic allies. In this vein,

Menem and Fujimori applied systematic carrot-and-stick tactics, combating some powerful groupings while cooperating with others. This divide-and-rule strategy allowed the two presidents to establish alliances mostly on their own terms.

In their relations with businesspeople, for instance, Menem and Fujimori kept domestically oriented, protectionist sectors and associations at bay (interviews with Cassullo 1995 and Majluf 1996). But Menem and, to a lesser extent, Fujimori cooperated with internationally oriented conglomerates, whose compliance Menem guaranteed through favorable privatization deals.[9] And while Menem and especially Fujimori criticized the established political class, Menem cooperated with important sectors of the Peronist movement and Fujimori attracted some longstanding political leaders, such as his first prime minister, Juan Carlos Hurtado Miller, an AP politician. Finally, both Menem and Fujimori used selective appointments, promotions, and dismissals to establish an unprecedented degree of civilian—though personalistic—control over the military (Hunter 1997a: 463–67; Obando 1998: 198–207).

By contrast, Collor carried neopopulism to the extreme by refusing to make allies and by antagonizing all important sociopolitical forces.[10] Fearing that alliances with Brazil's powerful business sector and political class would stifle his reform goals, the new president refused to accommodate most pressure groups and invoked instead the thirty-five million votes he received in the 1989 election, that is, his neopopulist mass base (Martins 1990; Bresser Pereira 1991: 12–14; also interview with Assis 1995). Collor's unwillingness to consult and acrimonious disputes with business leaders—especially FIESP's Mário Amato—confirmed entrepreneurs' initial impression of his capricious and unpredictable temperament. And by stepping on the toes of the military—for instance, through the ostentatious disbanding of the old secret service—Collor exposed himself to retaliation.[11] Collor treated even his political allies in such a distant manner that they remained fair-weather friends and displayed little lasting loyalty (Rosa e Silva 1993: 85–86, 109–10,

[9] Interviews with Benavides (1999) and Martínez (1997); Birle (1995: 336–51); Corrales (1998: 39–41); Cotler (1998: 21–34); Durand (1998: 25–35); Manzetti (1999: 95, 135–36, 302, 315, 325); Mauceri (1995: 18–20). However, early in his term, Fujimori did not consult much with Peru's business peak association (interview with Aguirre Roca 1995).

[10] Interviews with Collor (1995) and Gonçalves (1995); see also Bornhausen (1991). For scholarly analyses, see Schneider (1991), Weyland (1993), and Kingstone (1999: chap. 5).

[11] For instance, a leading Collor aide told me in 1995 that in mid-1992, when the president was facing serious corruption charges, a top military official sought to persuade his colleagues jointly to pressure Collor to step down.

385–90). Thus, by pushing neopopulist tactics particularly far, Collor incurred especially grave political risks.

The Common Push for Market Reform and Its Differential Outcomes

In addition to the political motivations arising from neopopulist strategies, there were of course powerful economic reasons for following up on neoliberal stabilization plans with efforts to restructure the established development model. First, all four presidents and their expert advisers regarded structural reforms as decisive for achieving or maintaining economic equilibria. Risk-seeking in the domain of losses, which responded to acute economic problems and which prompted the adoption of drastic stabilization plans, thus provided a strong impulse for profound, socially costly, and politically risky structural reforms as well. Second, the international financial institutions urged the four presidents to adopt market reforms. These admonitions gained special force because restructuring became a precondition for favorable debt rescheduling deals under the Brady Plan, which would bring a permanent reduction in external obligations.

Contrary to the recommendations of economists to sequence stabilization and structural reform, the four presidents systematically used structural reforms as instruments for stabilization. For instance, in Argentina, Brazil, and Peru, where the first adjustment plans failed to keep inflation under control, governments accelerated trade liberalization in order to force prices down. Similarly, financial liberalization was designed to attract capital inflows and thus tap current account deficits. Even the privatization of public enterprises — that is, the sale of permanent state assets — served to resolve short-term fiscal problems (Álvarez Rodrich 1997: 10; Manzetti 1999: 80–81, 164, 167–68, 247–48). Furthermore, governments used determined structural reforms to signal to foreign investors their serious intention to conduct "responsible" economic policies. In this way, they hoped to attract new investment, which would bolster economic stability and boost growth.

Moreover, the Brady Plan of 1989 and, in general, the increased coordination between the IMF and World Bank had turned economic liberalization into a precondition for debt relief. Stressing the profound roots of the problems afflicting debtor countries, the IFIs conditioned their assistance on market reforms. The Brady Plan stipulated that only nations that "modernized" their economies qualified for the alleviation of the debt burden (Edwards 1995: 79–81). This provision constituted an important incentive for market reform because a reduction of the heavy debt service could contribute much to stabilization. IFI conditionality thus strengthened the connection between structural reform and stabilization. Political leaders who had decided to pursue drastic stabilization thus saw themselves pushed forward on the path toward full-scale market reform.

Yet while there were important reasons for the four presidents to follow up on drastic stabilization plans with bold structural reforms, these dramatic changes also held tremendous risk as their economic and political repercussions were difficult to foresee. For instance, would Latin America's pampered business sectors withstand the onslaught of foreign imports and manage to develop profitable export activities in a fiercely competitive world market? And would the highly uncertain promise of long-term gain lead social and political groupings to accept the stinging short-term pain of these reforms? Seeing themselves in the domain of losses in economic policy-making, the four presidents typically braved these risks. In fact, they chose a particularly bold — and arguably suboptimal — course of action by imposing restructuring at breakneck speed. Rather than sequencing changes, they tried to dismantle the old development model completely, radically freeing market forces without building new institutional structures, such as capable regulatory agencies. Risk-seeking in the domain of losses, which chapter 5 has documented in detail, provided the crucial impulse for this daring choice of strategy.

In Argentina, Menem initiated structural reforms immediately upon taking office — at the high point of the hyperinflationary crisis — in order to signal to domestic and foreign investors that his abandonment of Peronism's protectionist, state-interventionist economic policies and his conversion to neoliberalism were irreversible. The most prominent measures — the hasty, ill-prepared sales of the national airline and phone company — also served to buy support for this policy shift among businesspeople and politicians, who benefited from favorable privatization deals and outright corruption (Corrales 1998: 39–42; Palermo and Novaro 1996: 354–56; Schamis 1999: 263–65). After the first adjustment effort — the Bunge & Born plan — failed, new economy minister Erman González followed the advice of Alvaro Alsogaray, a longstanding advocate of economic liberalism, and used structural reforms for stabilization purposes. The economic team designed painful fiscal measures, especially tax raises and budget cuts, to improve public finances, and it accelerated trade liberalization to force prices down through more intense foreign competition (Smith 1991: 59–62). Minister Cavallo's convertibility plan of early 1991 necessitated a new round of structural reforms (Llach 1997: 132–40). Convertibility also tied the government's hand by turning any backtracking into an immediate threat to economic equilibrium. Thus, the perceived requirements of stabilization and the convertibility scheme, designed to guarantee stability, provided crucial impulses for restructuring Argentina's development model.

Risk-seeking in the domain of losses induced Menem to impose such painful reforms, which created high costs for important sectors in the short run, but whose consequences for Argentina's economic development — beyond their alleged contribution to stabilization — would be evident only in the long run. For instance, it was unclear whether trade and financial liberalization would usher in a successful export performance or overwhelm domestic industry with a flood of cheap imports. And even if the aggregate economic result were beneficial, the political response of losing sectors was unpredictable. Yet continuing to face negative prospects, Menem was willing to shoulder these risks. In fact, however, he received considerable support for his radical program of restructuring, even from some of the eventual losers. For instance, battered by two bouts of hyperinflation and decades of economic stagnation, large parts of the Peronist Party and union movement endorsed or acquiesced to draconian market reforms (interviews with Kohan 1995 and Jara 1997; McGuire 1997: 226–38; Ranis 1995: xx–xxiv; Murillo 2001: chap. 6). Thus, risk-seeking in the domain of losses gave Menem sufficient backing for his bold neoliberal project.

Furthermore, in a context of severe crisis, established party loyalties among Peronist politicians and unionists helped Menem in moments of failure, as during the second bout of hyperinflation in early 1990. But rather than basing his government on organizational connections, Menem applied a neopopulist strategy to keep his party subordinate, diminishing its institutionalization. For instance, he put party stalwarts on the defensive by endorsing the popular aversion to professional politicians (for instance, after the campaign over constitutional reform in Buenos Aires province in 1990) and by recruiting a new type of candidate who lacked a political background, such as former race car driver Carlos Reutemann and singer Ramón "Palito" Ortega (Novaro 1994: 76–77, 134–43; McGuire 1997: 241–51). The president also used divide-and-rule tactics to neutralize potential opponents to structural reform and provided special benefits to some groups, for instance by setting low sales prices for public enterprises, offering generous severance packages to some laid-off workers, and allowing for considerable corruption (Etchemendy 2001; Viguera 2000). In all of these ways, Menem guaranteed support for his market reform program and limited opposition.

Menem thus managed to execute a comprehensive, radical program of structural reforms. His government quickly lowered barriers to foreign trade and capital, thoroughly deregulated the economy, and privatized almost all of Argentina's public enterprises in the course of five years (good overviews in De la Balze 1995: 88–122; Llach 1997: 195–229; Manzetti 1999: chap. 3). In addition, it substantially improved the fiscal position of the state through budget cuts, profound tax reforms, and tougher rule enforcement, especially a determined campaign against evasion (interview with Tacchi 1997; Durán and Sabaini 1994: chap. 2). As a result, tax revenues increased from 12.52 percent of GDP in 1988 to 16.36 percent in 1993 (SIP 1995: 11). In sum, neoliberal reforms retrenched but also strengthened the state.

In Peru, Fujimori's second economic team used structural reforms even more directly for stabilization purposes. Despite the brutal adjustment measures of August 1990, inflation soon threatened to spiral out of control again, reaching 24 percent in December and 18 percent in January 1991. Stuck in the domain of losses, the president replaced his pragmatic economy minister Hurtado Miller with free-market enthusiast Carlos Boloña. Boloña decided to combat the threat of exploding inflation with determined, comprehensive structural reforms that thoroughly reshaped the economy.[12] Some measures — such as faster import liberalization — sought to lower domestic price increases quickly. With other measures, such as privatization and financial liberalization, Boloña signaled to investors that Peru had made an irreversible choice for a free-market economy; in this way, he hoped to attract new capital and thus reignite growth and expand exports (Boloña 1993: 109–20, 123–26). The new economy minister also expected that the whole package of market reforms would restore the trust of foreign creditors, which Alan García's combative stance had undermined, and meet IFI conditions for debt rescheduling along the beneficial lines of the Brady Plan.

Since the resurgence of inflation kept Fujimori in the domain of losses, he firmly supported Boloña's effort to push this reform agenda full speed ahead. The persistent economic crisis and the Shining Path's assault on the Peruvian state also limited resistance in Congress because many politicians feared complete chaos if Fujimori failed. Given these profound problems, the president's denunciation of politicians as selfish and unconcerned with the good of the country induced parliamentarians not to obstruct the government's rescue efforts.[13] Only in early 1992 did ex-president García try to unify the opposition in Congress. Fujimori, however, overrode any obstacle to Boloña's market reforms by boldly closing Congress on 5 April 1992. Shortly after this uncon-

[12] Boloña did not need another shock plan because public sector prices, which Hurtado Miller had readjusted dramatically, were not lagging behind inflation (interviews with Boloña 1996 and Velarde 1996).

[13] Pease (interview 1996) stressed that Congress approved virtually all of Fujimori's economic policy proposals from 1990 to 1992. Boloña (interview 1996) agreed but emphasized increasing resistance from late 1991 onward.

stitutional — but tremendously popular — act, the economy minister had the president decree another round of liberalization measures.[14]

Boloña's reforms rapidly opened the Peruvian economy to foreign imports and capital inflows (Seminario 1995: 119–45). After a slower start than in Argentina, privatization also advanced decisively, and due to better preparation, the process was less tainted by corruption (Manzetti 1999: chap. 5; Wise 1997: 86–89). Moreover, the government deregulated the labor market, removed restrictions on foreign investment, and privatized social security. After years of negotiations and the temporary setback caused by Fujimori's self-coup, Peru also managed to normalize relations with its foreign creditors and reschedule its debt in 1993. Thus, with Fujimori's firm support, Boloña profoundly restructured Peru's development model (Boloña 1993: 109–30; Gonzales de Olarte 1998: 49–67).

The Fujimori administration achieved particular success in the important area of taxation. Ambitious legal changes simplified the fiscal system, especially by replacing distortionary tax handles with an efficient value-added tax. Drastic administrative modernization allowed for stricter rule enforcement and an all-out attack on tax evasion. These measures, combined with the end of hyperinflation, boosted tax revenues from a woeful 4.9 percent of GDP in early 1991 to 14.1 percent in 1996 (Durand and Thorp 1998: 137, 144, 146; similarly SUNAT 1996). Thus, the Peruvian state regained a more solid fiscal base.

In Brazil, Collor also sought to employ structural reforms for purposes of stabilization. Yet after an initial push, he accomplished much less because he encountered serious political obstacles. The temporary success of the Collor Plan, which quickly reduced inflation, allowed the president to initiate a series of market reforms. Some measures, such as trade liberalization, had a lasting impact, forcing business to raise productivity (Fernandes et al. 1994: 188–89, 194; Moreira and Correa 1998: 1862, 1869). Yet other projects, such as the privatization drive, quickly ran into opposition. The government faced resistance from trade unions and some powerful business sectors (interviews with Moreira 1992 and Collor 1995; Andrei et al. 1995: 106–23) and never gained stable majority support in Congress.

The eventual failure of the first Collor Plan and of a stop-gap stabilization program enacted in January 1991 (see Faro 1991; interview with Kandir 1995) induced the administration to attempt more ambitious structural reforms. The economic team focused on fiscal adjustment, as a requirement for getting inflation under control. The 1988

---

[14] Boloña (1993: 55); confidential author interview with leading Boloña aide, Lima, August 1996; see also Durand and Thorp (1998: 143).

constitution enshrined many provisions — such as a far-reaching decentralization of financial revenues and generous increases in social spending — that greatly hindered governmental efforts to balance the budget. Collor's aides therefore elaborated an ambitious blueprint for thoroughgoing changes. But this "Project of National Reconstruction" (Collor 1991a) aroused widespread resistance among interest groups, state governors, and — most importantly — congressional politicians. The substantial decline of presidential popularity after mid-1990 prevented Collor from putting these opponents on the defensive and from imposing his program through neopopulist tactics. Although the government watered down its initial goals (Collor 1991b), Congress stubbornly refused to pass structural reforms, especially constitutional amendments. The government's claim that these changes were essential for economic stability fell on deaf ears. Thus, Collor was unsuccessful in pursuing the same strategy as Menem and Fujimori, namely, to use — and legitimate — market reform as a crucial instrument for macroeconomic stabilization. In particular, the fiscal situation of the Brazilian state remained precarious as the total tax burden fell from its temporary rise to 28.78 percent of GDP in 1990 — produced by the one-time tax measures of the first Collor Plan — to 25.24 percent in 1991 and 25.01 percent in 1992, little higher than under the preceding administration (Varsano et al. 1998: 39).

Venezuela's Pérez faced similar opposition to crucial structural reforms, especially privatization and tax reform. As in Collor's case, the failure to control inflation weakened the president politically. In fact, Pérez's shock program itself fueled inflation by lifting price controls and drastically devaluing the currency. Prices therefore rose by an unprecedented 84.3 percent in 1989. In subsequent years, inflation consistently surpassed 30 percent, its level before Pérez's costly stabilization plan, which therefore seemed unsuccessful to many people. As a result, disapproval of the president remained high; in fact, it outnumbered approval from early 1990 onward (see fig. 5.4). As mentioned above, Pérez's weak popularity obstructed his efforts to use neopopulist tactics and hindered his market reform program (Naím 1993a: 136).

Paradoxically, yet in line with prospect theory, an unexpected, fleeting success posed additional obstacles. Iraq's invasion of Kuwait suddenly raised petroleum prices in mid-1990, boosted Venezuela's export earnings and fiscal revenues, and intensified the recovery from the deep recession of 1989. As many politicians and government officials entered the domain of gains, risk aversion spread and the willingness to adopt painful structural reforms diminished. Since economic problems magically eased, a costly overhaul of Venezuela's development model appeared unnecessary. In particular, the plan to enact a comprehensive tax reform and thus lower the state's dependence on oil revenues seemed to have low urgency when the treasury was flush with petrodollars. The proposed value-added tax—a cornerstone of neoliberal fiscal reform—therefore did not find congressional approval, and the creation of numerous loopholes watered down the income tax reform (interviews with Palacios 1996 and Naím 2000; Naím 1993b: 74–76; González 1995: 10, n.1).

Interestingly, the strongest resistance to the government's reform agenda emerged from inside Pérez's own party, which dragged its feet and refused to pass presidential bills in Congress, except in strongly watered-down or distorted versions (interview with Celli 1996). In particular, tax reform proposals languished in Congress for years (González 1995). Also, the party helped to pass a labor law that increased regulations and protection for workers, thus contradicting the president's liberalization efforts. Privatization elicited similarly widespread opposition and proceeded only haltingly; for instance, the partial sale of the national telephone company, one of the few successful privatization deals under Pérez, required lengthy bargaining and concessions to opponents (interview with Martínez Móttola 1996). By contrast to this powerful resistance from electoral politicians, societal groups turned out to be "paper tigers" (Naím 1993b: 14, 91–92, 136). Many business sectors were dependent on the state and had limited capacity to obstruct governmental initiatives, and trade unions were weakened by the economic problems of the 1980s and discredited by corruption in their ranks.[15]

As a result, only reforms that did not require congressional approval went ahead on schedule. For instance, trade liberalization quickly exposed Venezuela's coddled business sector to stiff foreign competition (Jongkind 1993: 77–83). But privatization advanced at a glacial pace, social security reform stalled, and protectionist labor legislation became tighter, not more flexible. Most importantly, Pérez had minimal success with his tax reform proposals, which intended to give the Venezuelan state a more solid fiscal base than dramatically fluctuating petroleum revenues provided.

In sum, comprehensive structural reforms advanced rapidly in Argentina and Peru but proceeded haltingly and unevenly in Brazil and Venezuela, especially in the fiscal area.

Causes of the Differential Advance of Market Reforms

What are the root causes for the much greater speed and ease with which structural reform proceeded in Argentina and Peru than in Brazil and especially Venezuela? The initial outburst of approval for drastic stabilization plans in Argentina, Brazil, and Peru cannot account for

---

[15] On union opposition, see Murillo (2001: chap. 4).

successful restructuring; despite this — temporary — asset, Collor failed to revamp Brazil's development model. In fact, this initial popular support declined soon in all three cases; why did it recover promptly in Argentina and Peru, whereas it remained at low levels in Brazil and Venezuela? As chapter 2 showed, institutional factors alone — specifically, a strong presidency and an institutionalized, centripetal party system (Haggard and Kaufman 1995: 9–11, 163–74) — cannot explain the differential advance of market reform either.

Instead, the different severity of the crises plaguing the four countries was decisive by conditioning presidents' capacity to reshape the established institutional framework. In line with my prospect-theory interpretation, the more acute and profound the structural economic problems were that a country confronted, the more widespread was risk-seeking in the domain of losses among the population, its political representatives, and major interest groups; as a result, the more political support did neoliberal restructuring elicit and the more successfully did it advance. Thus, my prospect-theory interpretation — documented extensively in chapter 5 — provides a solid microfoundation for a crisis argument, which offers the best explanation for the divergent progress of determined market reform. Specifically, the crisis variable encompasses not only conjunctural problems such as hyperinflation, but also the exhaustion of the established development model and the resulting economic stagnation and decline. On these dimensions, Peru and Argentina clearly fared worse than Brazil, whereas Venezuela was in the best position. Market reforms therefore advanced much more rapidly in Argentina and Peru than in Brazil and particularly in Venezuela.

Among the four countries, Peru confronted the gravest economic and political challenges. Hyperinflation erupted in September 1988, two years before Fujimori assumed power. During these two years, large sectors of the population suffered dramatic losses and the Peruvian state virtually collapsed. This disaster capped fifteen years of economic decline, which was interrupted only briefly by the artificial boom resulting from García's heterodox experiment. Peru also faced enormous political problems. Powerful guerrilla movements — especially the brutal Shining Path — launched a full-scale attack on the state, causing tremendous economic damage and profound insecurity among the population.

Argentina also confronted grave difficulties. While erupting only in April 1989, hyperinflation had a much more explosive trajectory than in Peru and Brazil and quickly triggered widespread social unrest and military coup rumors. Furthermore, Argentina had suffered from relative economic stagnation since the 1960s, and the failed orthodox reform effort of the last dictatorship had ushered in a decade of decline and growing poverty (Morley and Alvarez 1992).

By contrast, Brazil's economic difficulties were less profound. The cost of hyperinflation was mitigated by comprehensive indexation, which protected business and formal-sector workers from dramatic losses. And despite recessions at the beginning and end of the decade, the Brazilian economy achieved considerable net growth during the 1980s, proving the continuing dynamism of import-substitution industrialization and of the country's longstanding export efforts.

Finally, Venezuela stands out among the four countries because it never approached hyperinflation. Also, its fabulous oil wealth seemed to offer a magic solution to the problems of the 1980s. If this abundance were administered well — so the widespread popular perception — the country could easily achieve growth and prosperity. Thus, the blame seemed to fall on corrupt politicians and inefficient administrators, not on the oil-dependent development model (Keller 1996).

As a result of particularly deep economic and political crises, Menem's and Fujimori's structural reforms elicited much more support than the similar initiatives undertaken by Collor and especially Pérez.[16] Also, when Menem and Fujimori faced institutional and political obstacles, they encountered much more backing for — or at least acquiescence in — their efforts to bend or break these constraints, especially by packing the Supreme Court (Menem) and by closing Congress and purging the judiciary (Fujimori).[17] Confronting less grave problems, Collor (at least after his short honeymoon) and Pérez were not able to engage in similarly drastic efforts to reshape institutional constraints and break political resistance to their liberalization efforts.

The stronger support for market reform in Argentina and Peru than in Brazil and Venezuela is evident in surveys. Unfortunately, comparable data exists only from 1995 onward, when Latinobarómetro began to ask the same questions in eight Latin American countries.[18] In the sur-

---

[16] This difficulty of finding support for market reform induced Collor to remain distant from interest groups and the political class; an accommodation threatened to hinder his bold reform initiatives. Therefore, Collor's determined pursuit of autonomy and power not only reflected his headstrong personality; it was also a reaction to the particularly tight constraints he was facing.

[17] For an excellent analysis of the *autogolpe*, see Cameron (1997a: 50–69).

[18] Using these data actually biases the results against my crisis argument because by 1995 Argentina's and Peru's worst problems had already passed, whereas Brazil had just brought inflation under control and Venezuela was sinking into ever deeper problems. Also, the initiation of market reform, which usually coincides with the high point of popular support for neoliberalism (Carrión 1995: 11–13; Graham and Pettinato 1999: 20), lay several years in the past in Argentina and Peru, whereas Brazil's new president Cardoso was just launching his restructuring efforts. Thus, the observable cross-country differences in the data, which corroborate my crisis argument, are particularly noteworthy.

vey conducted in May and June 1995, a private enterprise system with or without state intervention found support among 33.9 percent of Argentines, but only 18.7 percent of Brazilians and 29.3 percent of Venezuelans; by contrast, 21.9 percent of Argentines but 37.2 percent of Brazilians and 35.3 percent of Venezuelans preferred a private enterprise system with worker participation in important decisions.[19] And a majority of Argentines (54.2%) and Peruvians (60.8%) but a minority of Brazilians (34.9%) and Venezuelans (41%) listed economic growth — the main promise of the market model besides stabilization — as the primary goal among several options (question 67). Furthermore, a significantly larger proportion of Argentines (71%) and Peruvians (83.2%) than Brazilians (60.5%) and Venezuelans (59.8%) regarded foreign investment — a crucial neoliberal growth engine — as "beneficial for the economic development of the country" (question 56). Finally, material rewards for greater performance and efficiency appeared as "just" to significantly more Argentines (69.9%) and Peruvians (66%) than Brazilians (53.8%) and Venezuelans (49.1%, question 75). Thus, important underlying principles of the market reform effort found more popular support in the two countries that had suffered from the most profound, urgent economic problems.

More importantly for actual policy outcomes, the greater depth of the crisis induced electoral politicians and party delegations in Congress to offer much stronger support for liberalization efforts in Argentina and Peru than in Brazil and Venezuela. For instance, government parties of similar ideological background and comparatively firm organizational structure backed market reforms in Argentina but opposed them in Venezuela (Corrales 1996).[20] And presidents with similarly weak parties found considerable congressional backing for their reform proposals in Peru, even before 1992 (interview with Pease 1996; McClintock 1994a: 8–10), but not in Brazil (Kingstone 1999: chap. 5).

Certainly, the longer, deeper crises in Argentina and Peru also weakened societal groups that had a stake in the established development model and therefore disliked economic liberalization. At the same time, the problems of the 1980s strengthened groups such as the financial sector that preferred drastic restructuring. In Brazil, by contrast, import-substituting sectors continued to expand during the 1980s and thus commanded greater economic weight. But these cross-country dif-

---

[19] Support for a mixed economy and the predominance of public enterprises ran at similar levels of 20.4 percent to 23.1 percent in all three countries (Latinobarómetro 1995: question 59). Data on Peru is missing.

[20] While the Peronist Party had weaker formal institutions than AD (Levitsky 1998), both parties had much stronger organizations than most Brazilian and Peruvian parties (Mainwaring and Scully 1995: 17–20).

ferences in the balance of socioeconomic forces had limited political repercussions. Trade liberalization—the neoliberal reform most costly for protectionist sectors—advanced at a rapid pace in all four countries. Thus, the constellation of socioeconomic forces did not significantly affect the progress of restructuring (see in general Geddes 1994a: 109–13).

In sum, the differential severity of the conjunctural and structural economic problems facing a country largely accounts for a leader's political success or failure in advancing market reform. As for the initiation of neoliberal stabilization, the crisis variable again appears as crucial for the progress of restructuring. And while crisis arguments are often criticized as functionalist, my prospect-theory interpretation avoids this problem by specifying a novel, empirically based microfoundation for the tendency of political leaders to respond to grave problems with daring countermeasures and for the willingness of many citizens, politicians, and interest groups to accept these costly, risky changes. Given the importance of the crisis variable, institutional factors did not determine outcomes. But they influenced the means a leader used to attain his goals. In particular, Menem took advantage of Peronist loyalties to proceed inside the confines of democratic institutions, which he bent but did not break. By contrast, Fujimori, who lacked solid, organized support, eventually found it feasible and beneficial to overthrow the constitution. Thus, institutional factors influenced the political process of market reform, but only in interaction with the crisis variable.

Immediate Outcomes of Structural Adjustment Efforts

The divergent advance of economic restructuring, especially of fiscal adjustment and tax reform, put Argentina and Peru on a different economic and political trajectory than Brazil and especially Venezuela. Argentina and Peru achieved stabilization and renewed growth—indeed, a temporary boom. This economic turnaround put Menem and Fujimori in the domain of gains. The two presidents therefore shifted from risk acceptance to risk aversion and became much more cautious than at the beginning of their terms. As a result, the second stage of market reforms advanced much more haltingly than the initial round of restructuring. This deceleration resulted not only from increasing political and institutional obstacles, which Naím (1995), Nelson (1997), and Heredia and Schneider (1998) stress, but also from the diminishing reformist zeal of successful neoliberal neopopulists.

By contrast, Collor's and Pérez's incapacity to enact lasting fiscal adjustment and the political weakness that this failure revealed hindered

economic recovery in Brazil and dragged down the Venezuelan economy after the short-lived boom of 1990–91. This lack of economic success kept Collor in the domain of losses and pushed Pérez, whose economic team had misinterpreted the temporary recovery as a definite
victory, back into it. My prospect-theory interpretation expects that the
two presidents would *want to* take bold steps to combat these challenges. Collor and especially Pérez indeed considered very drastic measures, the latter especially in response to the coup attempt of February
1992. But the two leaders were greatly weakened and lacked the necessary standing in public opinion and the support of powerful sociopolitical forces (especially the military) to pull off any daring move. Unable
to stop further economic deterioration and suffering increasing political
isolation, the two presidents lacked the clout to suppress charges of
malfeasance, which resulted in their impeachments.

The Slowdown of Structural Reform in Argentina and Peru

After two years in which Menem's and Fujimori's stabilization efforts
achieved only limited, precarious success, Argentina and Peru finally
achieved economic recovery. Despite its inherent risks, the Argentine
convertibility plan managed to control inflation, which fell from 1,344
percent per year in 1990 to 17.5 percent in 1992 and 3.9 percent in
1994. Indeed, economic stabilization produced a boom from mid-1991
on. Average annual growth reached 7.5 percent between 1991 and 1994.
Employment grew. Poverty in Greater Buenos Aires diminished drastically from 47.4 percent of all residents in October 1989 to 21.6 percent in October 1991 and 16.1 percent in May 1994 (Ministerio de
Economía 1994: 53). The only blemish on this impressive record was
unemployment, which increased from 8.1 percent in May 1989 to 12.2
percent in October 1994.

In Peru, Minister Boloña's conservative macroeconomic policies and
determined structural reforms eventually paid off as well. Inflation diminished from 139 percent per year in 1991 to 39.5 percent in 1993. As
soon as stabilization seemed assured, the government eased its restrictive economic policies. Growth therefore rose to 7 percent in 1993 and
a spectacular 14 percent in 1994. Poverty fell from 54 percent in 1991
to 47 percent in 1994 (FONCODES 1995a: 21; similarly Medina Ayala
1996: 77). In addition, the guerrilla threat eased with the capture of the
Shining Path leadership. The restoration of minimal security and order
brought tremendous relief to the terrified population.

Argentina's and Peru's economic turnaround moved many people
from the domain of losses into the domain of gains. A growing number

of citizens saw their own economic situation and their country's fate improve in retrospective assessments, and an even larger proportion came to hold optimistic expectations for the future. In Argentina, 72–80 percent of respondents from late 1992 through mid-1995 thought their country's economic situation had improved or remained the same since the enactment of the convertibility plan; only 16–24 percent saw a deterioration (Estudio Graciela Römer 1999b: 5). During the same time period, 30–47 percent were optimistic about the country's future and another 33–43 percent had neutral expectations; only 20–30 percent remained pessimistic (Mora y Araujo 1995, 12). In Peru, 53.5 percent of respondents thought in January 1995 that the country's economic situation had improved during 1994, another 35.2 percent rated it as unchanged, and only 10.5 percent saw a decline. Similarly, 33.6 percent reported an improvement in their family's economic circumstances, 49.4 percent no change, and only 16.2 percent a deterioration.[21] Also, the percentage of Lima residents who expected an improvement in their family's and their country's economic situation rose from 29 percent in June 1992 to 48–51 percent in December 1994 (Apoyo December 1994: 36).

Economic stabilization and recovery—and the strategic defeat of the guerrilla challenge in Peru—also moved Menem and Fujimori from the domain of losses into the domain of gains. Menem, for instance, stressed in 1993 that his government had overcome a number of serious economic problems and restored growth (Baizán 1993: 46–48). These accomplishments bolstered the two presidents' political standing, as demonstrated in the election victories achieved by Menem's Peronist Party in late 1991 and late 1993 and by Fujimori's Cambio 90/Nueva Mayoría movement in late 1992. Rather than having to fear for their political survival, the two leaders could now focus on positive goals; above all, they sought to extend their reign by engineering their immediate reelection.

Entry into the domain of gains induced Menem and Fujimori to give up their initial boldness and adopt much greater caution. While the Argentine president had imposed exceedingly tough adjustment measures from 1989 to 1991, this reformist zeal waned with the success of the convertibility plan. Projects that were crucial for neoliberal restructuring, such as labor market deregulation and social security reform, languished in Congress, and additional privatization required ever more concessions (interview with Austerlitz 1995; Cavallo 1995: 1–2; Etchemendy and Palermo 1998; Ghio 1999; Hagopian 1998: 71–81; Llanos

---

[21] *IMASEN Confidencial* January 1995: 13. Similar—though somewhat less positive—results in *IMASEN Confidencial* January 1994: 17–18.

1998; Graham et al. 1999: 12–15). Certainly, some of these measures were of special symbolic and electoral importance to the Peronist Party and therefore aroused strong opposition. Yet they do not appear more costly than initial unpopular stabilization measures, such as the large-scale dismissal of civil servants, the hasty privatization of public enterprises, and the restrictions on the right to strike decreed in 1990. Thus, resistance was not stronger because of the particularly painful nature of the government's proposals. Rather, the economic recovery made the Peronist movement turn to risk aversion; it therefore refused to gamble by making further immediate sacrifices for the sake of uncertain long-term benefits, such as the reduction in unemployment predicted by the government.

Furthermore, the government's pressure on Congress to approve these bills was significantly weaker.[22] As a presidential adviser and a leading economic aide affirmed confidentially in 1995, the government's determination to push through these projects had diminished considerably in the preceding three years, due to the economic recovery. Menem's turn to caution frustrated the efforts of his economic team to complete the neoliberal reform program (Llach 1997: 92, 131, 237, 255, 267, 316, 386). As my prospect-theory interpretation predicts, the shift to risk aversion was arguably suboptimal for Menem's political interests. In particular, the reluctance to push hard for labor reform created tremendous social and political costs by helping to maintain high unemployment (Llach 1997: 251, 255–56), which became the central preoccupation of Argentines in subsequent years and their most important complaint against the Menem government (Estudio Graciela Römer 1999b: 3–4, 13). Thus, Menem's turn to risk aversion in the domain of gains prompted decisions that deviated from calculations of expected value.

Only the fallout of Mexico's crisis of December 1994 motivated the Menem administration to give market reform a renewed push. The *tequila* effect undermined investor confidence, interrupted Argentina's easy boom, and threatened the convertibility plan (Cavallo 1997: 214–22; Llach 1997: 232–33, 239). In this situation, a devaluation could have been catastrophic because exchange-rate parity remained decisive for controlling inflation and for enabling enterprises to service their high dollar-denominated debts. Thus, economic prospects suddenly worsened, putting the government back into the domain of losses.

---

[22] Uncharacteristically, the government sought a consensus on labor reform through tripartite negotiations with trade unions and business associations (MTSS 1994). Similarly, privatization now proceeded by negotiation, not imposition, as between 1989 and 1991 (Llanos 1998: 754–59).

This new threat induced the Menem administration to resort again to tough adjustment measures, such as budget cuts and tax raises.[23] Also, after years of hesitation, it finally pushed through Congress some stalled structural reforms, such as the partial flexibilization of labor laws (Cavallo 1997: 226). These painful steps carried considerable political risk. In fact, the government's political wing was highly concerned about the fallout in the upcoming elections of May 1995.[24] The economic team, by contrast, called the crisis an "opportunity" for completing its comprehensive reform project.[25] Thus, thrown back into the domain of losses, Menem again enacted bold changes.

Yet as soon as the new crisis eased and the convertibility plan emerged unscathed, the government resumed a cautious posture and diminished anew its push for further restructuring. For instance, the "second reform of the state," which sought to rebuild public institutions and turn them more productive and efficient (interview with Abad 1997; Jefatura de Gabinete de Ministros 1997), made little headway (Repetto 2001: 18–20). The comprehensive revamping of labor market institutions and of medical service delivery that neoliberal experts had pursued for years remained bogged down in debates between the economic and political wings of the government, which drew support from business and from Peronist politicians and trade unions, respectively. In 1998, Menem eventually settled for a compromise that satisfied unions yet disappointed market-oriented experts and business — a clear divergence from the bold steps he took during the deep crisis at the beginning of his first term.[26]

Menem's shifts between risk acceptance and risk aversion are of particular significance for my prospect-theory interpretation. By stressing that people's propensity toward risk depends on their perceived domain, prospect theory advances a situational — not a personality-based — argument. The fact that the wild fluctuations in Argentina's economic conjuncture during the 1990s induced the same person to move back and forth from boldness to caution corroborates this situational argument.

Fujimori also shifted his propensity toward risk in line with Peru's

---

[23] These measures are summarized in the government's memorandum to the IMF, reprinted in "El compromiso argentino ante el FMI," *El Cronista* 27 March 1995: 22–23.

[24] Confidential author interview with a presidential adviser, Buenos Aires, March 1995.

[25] "Cavallo acelera las privatizaciones," *Clarín* 22 March 1995: 27; Cavallo and Cottani (1997: 18); interview with Vasconcelos (1997); confidential author interview with a leading economic aide, Buenos Aires, March 1995.

[26] "Argentine Labour: Limited Reform," *Economist Intelligence Unit Country Monitor* 6:37 (16 September 1998): 2; Cook (2000: 17–20).

changing economic fortunes. After the economy achieved some level of stability in 1992, he revealed even more clearly than Menem his reluctance to impose additional profound market reforms at a breakneck speed. In late 1992, he removed doctrinaire neoliberal Carlos Boloña and appointed as his new economy minister traditional conservative Jorge Camet, a business leader. The outgoing architect of Peru's recovery warned that his departure threatened the further advance of the ambitious liberalization program, which had been enacted only halfway (Boloña 1993: ix, 178–80, 202). He saw his dismissal as evidence for the president's diminishing reform impulse—a drastic shift from Fujimori's earlier boldness.

Boloña was correct: Fujimori did turn more cautious in his economic policy from early 1993 onward. While Minister Camet maintained basic continuity with his predecessor, restructuring began to advance more slowly. The president either greatly delayed or did not enact a number of important proposals prepared by Boloña and already approved by the cabinet.[27] For instance, after the drastic measures taken from 1990 to 1992, labor reform did not progress much further. And the courageous efforts to reform the fiscal system and combat tax evasion grew significantly weaker after 1993 (Durand and Thorp 1998: 144–49). Furthermore, the "second reform of the state" announced in 1996 never got off the ground; the government, which had decreed brutal adjustment measures in its early years, now shied away from incurring the political costs involved in dismissing public officials.[28] Even privatization, which continued after Boloña's ouster due to the state's fiscal needs and the president's electorally motivated spending goals, slowed down considerably after 1996 (interview with Paredes 1999).

In addition to the deceleration of structural reform, Fujimori decided to soften tight austerity and use more resources for social projects, which have a high electoral payoff. As Peru's fiscal crisis eased, he expanded several expenditure programs, depicted as efforts to combat widespread poverty. For instance, the president embarked on a school-building spree that benefited many destitute communities in a highly visible way and allowed him to garner support by attending hundreds of festive inauguration ceremonies. Thus, as soon as the Peruvian economy turned the corner, Fujimori became less bold and adopted traditional means for perpetuating his influence and consolidating his leadership.

[27] Boloña (1993: 202, 239–45); "Boloña: El Ortodoxo," *Caretas* 30 September 1999: 5 <www.caretas.com.pe/1999/1587/bolona/bolona.htm>; confidential author interview with one of Minister Camet's leading advisers, Lima, July 1999.

[28] Interviews with Abugattás (1999) and Torres y Torres Lara (1999). Torres admitted this diminished push for structural reform: "Nos falta un poco la gasolina."

In sum, economic recovery in Argentina and Peru put the president and many citizens in the domain of gains and induced them to become more risk-averse. In both countries structural adjustment therefore lost its initial dynamism.

The Political Failure of Neoliberal Reform in Brazil

By contrast to Menem and Fujimori, Collor never achieved economic stabilization, not to speak of a recovery. After two shock plans had failed, inflation was again inching upward in early 1991. Collor's incapacity to stem price increases diminished his standing in public opinion (Datafolha 1991: variable 8; fig. 5.2), the government's main base of sustenance. Greatly weakened, the president finally realized that he and his brash economy minister, Zélia Cardoso de Mello, were moving ever deeper into a cul-de-sac with their confrontational style. In May 1991, he beat a retreat and appointed as economy minister Marcílio Marques Moreira, a cautious diplomat with close links to domestic and international financial circles. In this way, he sought to restore business confidence and ensure entrepreneurs that he would not impose new shock programs.

Thus, his political isolation and weakness forced Collor to assume a more cautious stance although Brazil's crisis had eased little and both the president and many common citizens still saw themselves in the domain of losses. Collor lacked the clout to follow Menem's and Fujimori's path and combat persistent problems with ever more daring stabilization measures, such as Cavallo's convertibility plan. Thus, Collor was unable to fulfill many citizens' expectation of a determined attack on the lingering crisis.[29]

At the same time, Minister Moreira faced considerable problems in pursuing his cautious, orthodox economic policy. He found it very difficult to restore the confidence of business and the broader public, which Collor's initial decrees and his impulsive, unpredictable style had undermined. The president's sporadic rhetorical attacks on entrepreneurs and international financial institutions did not help.[30] The conservative parties that increasingly "occupied" the government never lost their distrust of the president, and the center-left PSDB rejected Collor's calls for an alliance. Therefore, the administration continued to lack sufficient

[29] "Pesquisa mostra que País aceita sacrifício," *Estado de São Paulo* 5 May 1991: 4.

[30] See speech reprinted in "As tarefas produtivas não cabem mais ao Estado," *Jornal do Brasil* 26 October 1991: 4; see also "Collor cobra mais decisões de Marcílio," *Correio Braziliense* 10 August 1991: 11; interview with Macedo (1995). Moreira (interview 1995), however, downplayed this problem.

support for its structural reform program, which the economic team tried to sell as necessary for achieving economic stability. A package of constitutional amendments, submitted to Congress in October 1991, died in the committees, and an ample project of fiscal reform, elaborated in mid-1992, suffered a similar fate (Collor 1991b; MEFP 1992; interviews with Macedo 1995 and Moreira 1995). Thus, although Collor still tried to combat the persistent crisis with bold proposals, he lacked the clout to push them through Congress.

In particular, Collor would have been unable to break opposition to his structural reform proposals as Fujimori did in April 1992. Lack of support among ever larger sectors of the population, business, and the military ruled out any effort to reshape the institutional framework and concentrate power through extraconstitutional means. Collor did not have the political force to override institutional obstacles, which Fujimori gained by successfully combating Peru's particularly severe crisis. In fact, the failure of Collor's stabilization efforts and his weak base of support, which reflected the fickle nature of neopopulism, made him vulnerable to the corruption charges advanced by his own brother. Short of firm backers and besieged by numerous enemies, the president was unable to ride out the wave of public protest against his misdeeds. As a result, he suffered impeachment (Weyland 1993) — ironically at the hands of a Congress full of corrupt politicians, as revealed by the congressional budget scandal of late 1993. Thus, whereas in Argentina and Peru neopopulist leaders managed to outmaneuver or forcefully dislodge the political class, Brazil's political class defeated the neopopulist leader.

Yet while Collor failed politically, his government did change the direction of Brazilian development. He set in motion processes that facilitated the adjustment efforts undertaken under the successor governments of Itamar Franco (1992–94) and Fernando Henrique Cardoso (1995–present). For instance, his trade liberalization prompted domestic industry to increase its productivity and competitiveness (Fernandes et al. 1994: 188–89; Moreira and Correa 1998). More importantly even, Collor irreversibly changed the agenda of Brazilian politics. His high initial popularity demonstrated the political importance and payoff of painful measures to control inflation, and his apt rhetoric of modernization further discredited state interventionism and boosted support for principles like competitiveness and fiscal responsibility (Nóbrega 1992: 32–45; Kingstone 1999: chap. 5). In fact, Collor's structural reform plan (Collor 1991a) reads like an outline of Cardoso's projects. Thus, despite his spectacular political failure, Collor managed to put Brazil on the path toward market reform.

The Collapse of Neoliberal Reform in Venezuela

Pérez had less success than Collor in laying a foundation for economic liberalization. Throughout his second term, he suffered from low popularity ratings and faced stubborn resistance to his structural reform agenda; these difficulties in turn reflected the absence of a profound open crisis. Facing widespread popular discontent and opposition from his own party, Pérez sought to enhance his standing by using ambiguous rhetoric. For instance, while seeking support from the IMF, he attacked its "obscene conditions" and denounced its as an instrument of the First World "to maintain its exploitation of the developing countries" (OCI 1989: 24). Obviously, this self-contradictory discourse did not strengthen support for market reform.

Pérez's weak standing encouraged neoliberalism's enemies. The resulting lack of congressional support for presidential proposals and the ceaseless demonstrations and protests in the streets created a widespread sense of political vacuum and ungovernability. Even forces who had initially supported good parts of the president's economic and political reform agenda, such as a new "group of notables," turned increasingly critical. The only actors who seemed unaware of the government's fragile position were the president and his economic aides. Overly impressed by the short-lived boom of 1990–91 and confident in Pérez's charisma, leading ministers thought in late 1991 that they had managed to guarantee the sustainability of a free-market system in Venezuela (interviews with Rodríguez 1996 and Rosas 1996).

These illusions were rudely destroyed on 4 February 1992, when junior officers tried to overthrow and possibly assassinate Pérez. Shockingly, many citizens expressed support for the coup attempt (Norden 1998: 155), revealing their intense discontent with the president and his market reforms. Pérez was unable and unwilling to combat this dangerous challenge with the drastic means that Fujimori used in April 1992. Some businesspeople, in particular, suggested autocratic measures, but he refused.[31] Besides being committed to democratic norms, Pérez could not risk such a forceful response to the coup attempt. He had little support among politicians, his popularity was low, and loyalties within the military were unclear. Pérez therefore decided not to go on the offensive (interview with Blanco 1996).

The president sought instead to save his government through ac-

---

[31] Confidential author interviews with several leading Pérez aides, Caracas, June 1996.

commodation, especially an alliance with the main opposition party, COPEI. But given Pérez's low standing, only one sector of this divided party agreed to join the government, and merely for a few weeks. The president also appointed a consultative commission with ample representation, but it called for a reversal of economic liberalization, which Pérez rejected (Recomendaciones del Consejo Consultivo 1992: 462–71). All other proposals for overcoming the stalemate, for instance through a constitutional convention, were blocked by the government, AD, or the opposition parties.[32]

The growing political paralysis was punctuated by a second coup attempt in November 1992. Seeing democracy endangered and taking inspiration from the ouster of Collor in neighboring Brazil,[33] Venezuela's political class decided to impeach Pérez. Compared with his predecessor's reported misdeeds, the alleged infractions were minor, consisting of an illegal transfer of funds between different budget categories. Discovery of this formal misappropriation turned fatal for Pérez because his political support had virtually evaporated.

Thus, contrary to Collor, Pérez never managed to garner strong backing for market reform and demonstrate that such painful measures can bring substantial political payoffs. His stubbornly low popularity and the fiasco with which his government ended further discredited neoliberalism in Venezuela.

Conclusion

This chapter has shown that the successful enactment of market reform in Argentina and Peru, the difficulties in Brazil, and the failure in Venezuela reflect the differential depth of the economic crises facing those countries. Specifically, drastic restructuring went forward only in countries that were plagued both by dramatic disequilibria, especially hyperinflation, and by serious economic decline that discredited the established development model. By contrast, where hyperinflation erupted in an economy with considerable growth potential, massive approval for initial stabilization measures did not translate into support for structural reform. And where the absence of hyperinflation made the turn to neoliberalism appear unnecessary (chapter 5) and a bonanza resource inspired hope in an easy escape from economic decline, market reform confronted insurmountable obstacles.

[32] For analyses of and documents from the turbulent year 1992, see *Politeia* 15 (1992).

[33] " 'Collorgate' casts a long shadow," *Latin American Regional Reports-Andean Group* RA-92-09, 12 November 1992: 4.

In line with my application of prospect theory, acute disequilibria and severe stagnation and decline induced neopopulists Menem and Fujimori to push particularly hard for painful structural reforms designed to shore up their precarious adjustment efforts. In this way, they hoped to recuperate the broad support that their initial stabilization plans had elicited from a population that largely saw itself in the domain of losses. Acute open crises also facilitated determined reform efforts by weakening interest groups and politicians with a stake in the old development model. Crises eroded the power resources and organizational capacity of these "veto groups" and made their resistance look like the pursuit of narrow self-interests at the expense of the country's well-being.

By contrast, after Collor's shock plan stopped hyperinflation, but did not keep price increases under control, he lacked the political force to push through crucial market reforms, especially definitive fiscal adjustment. Support for a bold overhaul of Brazil's development model, which had produced substantial growth in the 1980s, was quite limited. The opponents of market reform therefore commanded substantial political resources and legitimacy and managed to obstruct the reform efforts of an increasingly isolated president. Finally, Pérez's liberalization efforts were always hobbled by the widespread rejection of his initial shock plan. Moreover, the temporary increase in petroleum prices and in Venezuela's OPEC quota from 1990 to 1992 reinforced the impression that the decline of the 1980s could be reversed in a painless way.

In sum, the political success or failure of market reform and its initiators depended on the perceived depth and obduracy of the developmental crisis plaguing a country. The four countries therefore entered two divergent economic and political trajectories. The rapid advance of neoliberal reform in Argentina and Peru raises the question whether the market model has become politically sustainable in those countries — the topic of chapter 7.

CHAPTER SEVEN

THE POLITICAL SUSTAINABILITY OF NEOLIBERALISM AND NEOPOPULISM IN ARGENTINA AND PERU

By 1993, presidents Menem and Fujimori had achieved considerable success with their neoliberal economic policies and their neopopulist political strategies. They had restored stability and brought back substantial growth; the prospects for future development seemed bright. At the same time, the two leaders had attained political predominance as their mass support remained strong while the opposition was fragmented and confused. Based on these tremendous assets, did Menem and Fujimori manage to perpetuate their neopopulist rule and make the new market model politically sustainable?

The present chapter first analyzes the two leaders' capacity to maintain their power for years—a considerable accomplishment, given the fragile nature of neopopulism. Most importantly, the economic recovery instilled risk aversion in the population, making a majority support Menem's and Fujimori's bid for immediate reelection, rather than experimenting with the untested opposition. This widespread risk aversion also prompted considerable, though not overwhelming, popular acceptance of the new development scheme in its basic outline. Paradoxically, yet in line with my cognitive-psychological arguments, the very cost of neoliberal reform functioned like a sunk investment, inducing many people to give the market model a chance, rather than demanding a new round of costly, risky changes.

As the grave crisis of the late 1980s receded into the past, however, daring neopopulist leaders became ever more dispensable to many citizens and interest groups. Whereas their willingness to concentrate power and bend or break institutional constraints had been crucial for combating grave pressing problems, it now became an obstacle to the institutionalization of the new market model and the flourishing of a high-quality democracy. Thus, as the salience of different issues shifted, in the eyes of many people neopopulism turned from a solution to problems into the problem itself. As a result, political support for Menem and Fujimori diminished considerably from the mid-1990s onward. Therefore, Argentina's relatively vibrant civil and political society imposed ever greater restrictions on Menem's latitude in the late 1990s, finally persuading him to give up his quest for a second immediate reelection. By contrast, Peru's atomized civil and political society had little clout, allowing Fujimori to engineer his continuation in office. But soon after he began his third term, a severe internal conflict — one of the great risks facing personalistic leaders — led to his ignominious downfall. The virtual absence of organized political forces in Peru, however, threatens to foreclose alternatives to neopopulist leadership in the foreseeable future. Thus, by the end of the decade, the political fate of the two countries began to diverge. Whereas democratic institutions reasserted themselves over neopopulism in Argentina, their tremendous weakness leaves the door wide open for resurgent neopopulism in Peru.

The Reelection of Neoliberal Neopopulists

The Engineering of Constitutional Reform

After they had successfully combated the initial crisis, the most important goal of presidents Menem and Fujimori was to perpetuate their own power by winning reelection. Personalistic leaders typically have a strong interest in extending their tenure. For Menem, the precedent of Juan Perón, who had his followers adopt a new constitution with a reelection clause in 1949 and who won a second term in 1951, provided additional inspiration. In the Peruvian case, the decay of intermediary organizations and the resulting personalization of rule allowed Fujimori to depict himself as indispensable for guaranteeing the recently won economic stability and political order, which continued to face threats.

To achieve their goal, Menem and Fujimori needed to change the constitution, which forbade immediate reelection. The precarious nature of economic stability — and of the restoration of political order in Peru — provided the successful initiators of neoliberal reform with an excellent argument to justify the need for another term: The country's "savior" had to stay on to forestall any relapse into economic chaos and political turmoil. Thus, the depth of the preceding crises, coupled with their proven capacity to cope with such severe challenges, helped Menem and Fujimori to reach their main political goal.

More importantly even, recovery from deep economic and political crises provided the two presidents with substantial support for extending their rule. As more and more people entered the domain of gains, they prudently preferred political continuity over change and experimentation. As a result, they endorsed the incumbent, rather than the opposition — contrary to the rational-choice argument advanced by

Acuña and Smith (1994: 31–41; see chapter 2 above). Many people therefore approved of constitutional reforms that lifted the prohibition of reelection. In sum, as psychological decision theories would expect, successful recoveries, combined with the memory of recent crises, paved the way for Menem and Fujimori to reach their principal political goal.

In line with institutionalist arguments, however, the two leaders used different means to pursue this goal, in accordance with the level of organization of their support base. As in the enactment of structural reforms, Menem could draw on firm backing from the Peronist movement and therefore managed to proceed in democratic ways. Fujimori, by contrast, lacked strong organized support and therefore could not hope to achieve a reelection amendment by constitutional means. But the particularly grave problems confronting Peru gave him the pretext and support for violating the existing constitution and engineering a new charter that allowed for his immediate reelection.

In his effort to push for a reform of Argentina's constitution that would make him eligible for a consecutive second term, Menem took advantage of the immediate success of the convertibility plan, which finally brought inflation under control and reignited growth. The Peronist Party, which hoped to prolong its control of the government with all its licit and illicit advantages, strongly backed this initiative. Given his relative youth and the limitations of his national-level support network, Menem's internal rival Eduardo Duhalde, the powerful governor of Buenos Aires province, saw no need and no chance to challenge the incumbent at this point.

The Radical Party, however, rejected institutional manipulation designed to benefit a neopopulist leader. In particular, Peronism's long-standing hegemonic aspirations made the UCR worry about the stability of Argentina's new democracy. In addition to principles, political interests dictated opposition to Menem's push for reelection because the popular incumbent would be difficult to beat. But battered by electoral defeat and riven by internal tensions between the national party leadership and Radical provincial governors, the UCR was on the defensive. By contrast, Peronism's victory in the legislative elections of October 1993 strengthened Menem's neopopulist leadership. The president used his clout to threaten the UCR with a plebiscite on the issue of constitutional reform and to put pressure on Radical governors, who depended on resource transfers from the federal government (Palermo and Novaro 1996: 413–15).

To prevent a split inside the UCR, party leader Raúl Alfonsín finally cut a deal with Menem, the controversial Pacto de Olivos. The UCR pledged support for a reelection clause, while the incumbent accepted some institutional constraints on presidential prerogatives, for instance, limitations on decree powers (Ferreira Rubio and Goretti 1998: 56–57). This agreement of the two titans of Argentina's new democracy paved the way for convoking a constituent assembly. The elections for this forum, held in April 1994, yielded a clear plurality for the Peronist Party. Together with the Radicals, it controlled 59.3 percent of the seats (Centro de Estudios Unión para la Nueva Mayoría 1994: 2).

But middle-class disaffection with the Pacto de Olivos, which was seen as an opportunistic deal between power-hungry politicians, allowed a new opposition front, the center-left Frente Grande, to garner a surprising 12.7 percent of the national vote. In the capital, which has always been distant from the Peronist Party, it obtained a striking 36 percent (Novaro and Palermo 1998: 94). Many of these votes came from former UCR supporters, who resented Alfonsín's collusion with Menem and his betrayal of the party's longstanding commitment to liberal-democratic principles of limited government, which called for the prohibition of presidential reelection.

The new opposition movement was unable, however, to keep Peronists and Radicals from passing the changes on which Menem and Alfonsín had agreed. The amended constitution therefore allowed for immediate reelection, while reducing the presidential term from six to four years. It also regulated the use of emergency decrees, which Menem had imposed in large numbers. These provisions legitimated presidential decrees in principle but allowed them only under "exceptional circumstances," restricted their application to certain issue areas, and introduced congressional oversight (Ferreira Rubio and Goretti 1998: 56–59). In sum, firm support from the Peronist Party and neopopulist pressure on the Radical opposition allowed Menem to remove the constitutional ban on presidential reelection, and to achieve this goal in democratic ways—though at the price of diminished presidential powers.

Fujimori, by contrast, pursued the same goal with illegal means. In April 1992, he took advantage of the strong popular aversion to the established political class to close a Congress that was beginning to oppose his policy initiatives in a more systematic and effective way and that would have refused to pass a reelection amendment. In typical neopopulist fashion, he attacked political parties as selfish cliques and charged congressional politicians and judges with rampant corruption. He claimed that he—as the popularly elected president—needed unrestricted power to combat the grave guerrilla threat and stabilize the economy (Fujimori 1992: 43–47). In line with my prospect-theory interpretation, the deep crisis afflicting Peru gave these arguments widespread appeal among the suffering population. Approval of the self-coup and its protagonist reached up to 82 percent in opinion polls

(Apoyo May 1992: 8; Conaghan 1995: 227, 236; see also fig. 5.3 above). Important sociopolitical groups, especially from the private sector, also offered firm backing;[1] two former presidents of the business peak association Confederación Nacional de Instituciones Empresariales Privadas (CONFIEP) entered the government at this point.

Yet while receiving massive domestic support, Fujimori's self-coup provoked widespread international opposition and protest. The United States, Japan, and European countries suspended financial aid and threatened Fujimori with additional sanctions. Economy Minister Carlos Boloña feared that the negative international reaction would keep Peru excluded from international financial markets and thus jeopardize the precarious stabilization achieved through two years of painful adjustment measures. Threatening to resign, Fujimori's top economic aide helped to persuade the president to cede to foreign demands and restore democracy (interviews with Boloña 1996 and De Soto 1996).

Compelled by strong external pressure, especially from the United States, Fujimori announced a gradual return to democracy and called constituent assembly elections for later in the year. The opposition disagreed on whether to participate in this contest and thus legitimate Fujimori's restructuring of the institutional order (interview with Flores 1999). Several old parties decided to stay on the sidelines. Their refusal to run probably helped the rest of the opposition, which formed new groupings and was therefore less identified with the established political class. Persistent popular misgivings about these old-time politicians; Fujimori's success in tackling the economic crisis and combating terrorism, especially the capture of the Shining Path leadership in September 1992; and adroit institutional engineering gave the incumbent's movement, Cambio 90/Nueva Mayoría, a clear plurality of votes and an absolute majority of seats.

The new unicameral body, called Congreso Constituyente Democrático (CCD), was charged with elaborating a new charter while fulfilling routine tasks of legislation and supervision of the executive. This accumulation of attributions left the CCD little time and energy to hold the president accountable. It also gave Fujimori the opportunity to influence the elaboration of the new charter by applying means—such as the provision of patronage—that ambitious politicians find attractive. Most importantly, the iron discipline inside the president's movement left the opposition minimal influence on the debates and the new constitution (Pease 1995: chaps. 3, 6).

The 1993 charter therefore enshrined many of the government's

---

[1] Confidential author interviews with two top business leaders, Lima, February 1995 and July 1999.

proposals, especially on institutional issues. Above all, it allowed for immediate presidential reelection. It also strengthened the institutional powers of the presidency, though less than the opposition had feared (Schmidt 1998: 113–14); for instance, Congress retained the right to censor ministers (article 132). Additional provisions paved the way for further neoliberal reforms by restricting the entrepreneurial role of the state, strengthening the protection of private property, and giving foreign owners the same rights as nationals (Torres y Torres Lara 1994: 30, 50).

In sum, both Menem and Fujimori took advantage of fresh memories of crisis and, especially, of successful recoveries to pave the way for extending their control over the government — a goal that is typical of personalistic, neopopulist rulers. But due to the differential strength and organization of their support base, they used different means to achieve this end.

The Struggle for Reelection

With the reelection provisions in place, Menem and Fujimori prepared their campaigns. Both incumbents commanded important political assets. First of all, their track records were impressive. Their risky and costly adjustment measures had eventually restored economic stability and fueled considerable growth. By getting the economic crisis under control, both presidents had also managed to resurrect the authority of the state and give the population a renewed sense of normality and order (Palermo and Novaro 1996; Mauceri 1995). The capture of the Shining Path leadership had greatly contributed to this accomplishment in Peru. Menem's and Fujimori's success in overcoming grave challenges put many people in the domain of gains and thus induced them to be favorably disposed toward the incumbent (figs. 5.1, 7.1). Risk aversion made these people reluctant to support the opposition, whose policy performance was much more uncertain. To maintain this popular support, the two presidents found it beneficial to keep the memory of the initial crises alive and to remind citizens of their accomplishments (e.g., Menem 1995: 15–22).

But Menem and Fujimori could not rest on their laurels if they wanted to guarantee reelection. They faced the danger that citizens would come to take the restored normality for granted and regard Menem's and Fujimori's continued stewardship as no longer necessary. Psychological decision theorists have consistently found that after receiving gains, most experimental subjects quickly raise their reference point for assessing gains and losses. Rather than continuing to appreci-

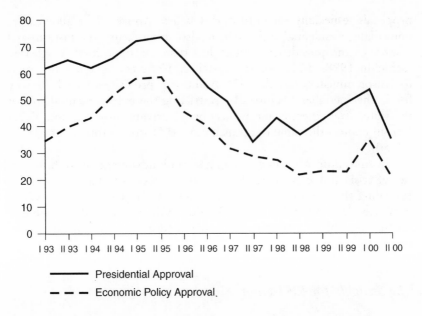

Figure 7.1. Popular Approval of Fujimori and His Economic Policy,
1993–2000. *Source:* Apoyo, *Informe de Opinión* (January 2001: 25, 31).
Note: Entries are averages for the respective six-month period. I thank Robert
Barr for giving me the data for 1999/2000.

ate these improvements, people soon take them for granted and give
their benefactors less and less credit. Thus, people rapidly absorb improvements, whereas they cling to the previous status quo after suffering losses.

People's quick adjustment to gains exposed Menem and Fujimori to
a "paradox of success" (Weyland 2000). By overcoming problems and
restoring normality, the two presidents diminished the motivation for
people to appreciate these successes. The incumbents' very achievements
in combating crises lowered the salience of these problems and redirected voters' attention to other, persisting problems. Therefore, these
accomplishments had ever lower weight in shaping citizens' assessment
of and support for the incumbents.

Fujimori was rudely alerted to the political danger created by this
paradox of success when his government won the plebiscite on the new
constitution in late 1993 with a surprisingly narrow margin—or, as
some observers suspect, only by resorting to fraud (interview with Belaúnde 1996). Especially in outlying provinces where poverty was deep
and widespread, a majority of voters rejected the new charter and, by
implication, the incumbent. Evidently, only one year after the decapita-

tion of the Shining Path and the recuperation of economic stability, these accomplishments no longer swayed a substantial sector of the population. Rather than displaying lasting gratitude, many people expected and demanded further improvements in their well-being. As the salience of terrorism and inflation declined, citizens redirected their concerns to issues like poverty, low wages, and the difficulties in finding well-paid employment (compare Apoyo June 1990: 35 with Apoyo April 1996: 32; see also Apoyo May 1997: 43–44; *IMASEN Confidencial* 43 [June 1996]: 13).

The constituent assembly election of 1994 sent Menem a similar message. The diminution of the Peronist vote compared with the 1993 legislative election (38.8 percent vs. 43.1 percent) and the rise of the center-left opposition movement Frente Grande showed the incumbent that his success in ending hyperinflation might not guarantee him lasting support nor ensure his victory in the presidential contest of 1995. Common people increasingly shifted their attention from the issue of economic stability to new problems. Rising unemployment was foremost among these concerns (Centro de Estudios Unión para la Nueva Mayoría 1997a: 4–6; 1999: 1–3).

Market reforms made it difficult for Menem and Fujimori to respond to these demands. For instance, large-scale employment programs or government-decreed wage raises were out of the question. Facing fiscal constraints, the two governments instituted targeted social assistance programs, through which they sought to benefit large numbers of people at relatively low cost. The external enforcers of financial discipline, especially the World Bank, actually recommended such programs and provided generous loans—especially to poor Peru—to enhance popular acceptance of neoliberalism. Specifically, these "safety nets" were designed to demonstrate to common people that they could benefit from the new development model (Graham 1994).

From 1992 onward, the Fujimori government allocated hundreds of millions of dollars to targeted antipoverty schemes (World Bank 1994: 39), especially a demand-driven social investment fund (Fondo Nacional de Compensación y Desarrollo Social, FONCODES), which spent a total of US$ 285 million until April 1995, the date of the presidential election (Schady 2000: 292); an education and health fund that engaged mostly in school building (Instituto Nacional de Infraestructura Educativa y de Salud, INFES) and that committed a total of US$ 334 million until April 1995 (Graham and Kane 1998: 95); and a nutrition program (Programa Nacional de Asistencia Alimentaria, PRONAA).[2] In

---

[2] On the scandalous political utilization of PRONAA in Fujimori's reelection campaign of 1999–2000, see "Mecánica Naranja," *Caretas* 24 June 1999: 33–36.

response to the near defeat in the plebiscite on the new constitution and in preparation for the 1995 election, expenditures reached especially high levels in 1994 and early 1995 (Graham and Kane 1998: 95; Roberts and Arce 1998: 233; Schady 2000: 293–94). As a result, the new discretionary programs controlled more resources than the corresponding line ministry in important areas, such as primary education.[3] They were coordinated and directed by the Ministry of the Presidency, an organizational arrangement that strengthened presidential powers.

On a more limited scale — given the lower level of destitution and the extensive existing social programs in Argentina[4] — the Menem administration announced a "social plan" in 1993 and allocated in subsequent years US\$ 1–200 million to antipoverty programs administered by the new Secretaría de Desarrollo Social, which — as in Peru — was directly subordinated to the presidency (Secretaría de Desarrollo Social 1995). In addition, a multitude of social programs executed by other government agencies were targeted toward poor people (SIEMPRO 1997). Furthermore, provincial governments established their own social programs. Above all, Governor Eduardo Duhalde of Buenos Aires province, which houses about one-third of all Argentines, used annual transfers of US\$ 4–700 million from the federal government to create a vast infrastructure and social program, the Fondo de Reparación Histórica del Conurbano Bonaerense (Prévôt Schapira 1996: 90–91; "Tres Años de Obras" 1994).

The focus of these social programs on very poor people suited both neoliberal experts and neopopulist leaders. From the perspective of neoliberal experts, this targeting guarantees a high marginal return because few dollars can make a significant difference to the destitute. As a result, large numbers of citizens receive substantial benefits, but the aggregate cost for the public budget remains limited. These new social programs therefore do not undermine economic adjustment. Furthermore, targeting channels public subsidies to people who on their own cannot attain much success in the market and who therefore "deserve" state support, even in the eyes of neoliberals. Indeed, some of the new programs sought to enhance the productive capacities of the poor so that they could obtain greater returns from the market and eventually work their way out of poverty. In all these ways, the design of targeted social schemes embodied neoliberal ideas and principles.

---

[3] Confidential author interview with a high-ranking official of the Ministry of Economy and Finance, Lima, 7 August 1996. Sectors inside the government sought to contain the hypertrophy of the new social funds, which other factions promoted (confidential conversations with a former government official, February 1995 and August 1996).

[4] Interview with Di Pietro (1997). See also Powers (1995) on Menem's longstanding efforts to "debate away" the problems of poverty in Argentina.

At the same time, targeting allowed neopopulist leaders to use social programs for their political purposes. Whereas universalist policies provide benefits indiscriminately to friends and enemies, targeted programs give the government considerable discretion over whom to favor and whom to exclude. In this way, the incumbent administration can reward its followers and hurt opponents (see Schady 2000: 298–302). Since the government has this discretion, anticipated reaction often induces aspiring beneficiaries to offer obedience and support and to refrain from backing the opposition. Targeting also permits neopopulist leaders to dole out goodies in a visible manner that has substantial political payoffs. For instance, festive donation or inauguration ceremonies give the president direct contact with common citizens and thus reinforce his image as a "man of the people." For all of these reasons, targeted antipoverty schemes are attractive both to neoliberal experts and to neopopulist presidents.[5]

These new social programs in fact reinforced popular support for neopopulist leaders. Fujimori's approval rating, which declined gradually in 1993, rose again after early 1994, when social spending expanded considerably.[6] When asked in opinion surveys why they backed Fujimori, 28.9 percent of the poorest respondents in Lima pointed to his "public works" and his "support for education"; the latter comments probably referred mainly to his high-profile school-building program. Popular appreciation for Fujimori's antipoverty and public works programs also helped the president win an overwhelming reelection victory in April 1995, as interviews and focus groups with poorer people suggest (Salcedo 1995: 67, 73, 80–81, 95; Valenzuela 1995: 30–31). Statistical analyses confirm that spending on antipoverty programs such as FONCODES and INFES had a significant effect on the vote for Fujimori (Roberts and Arce 1998: 233–38; Weyland 1998c: 557–58; see also Graham and Kane 1998: 85–97; Balbi 1996: 207–14).

Menem's targeted social spending also had important political payoffs by reinforcing the existing clientelist networks of the Peronist movement and making poor people grateful to their neopopulist leader.[7] Statistical analysis confirms that expenditures of the new Secretaría de

---

[5] See in general Weyland (1996c: 19–21). This congruence of interests further cements the alliance between these different forces, which chapter 6 discussed.

[6] Apoyo December 1994: 12, 18; IMASEN Confidencial January 1994: 13–15; January 1995: 11, 15–16. The following data are from IMASEN Confidencial September 1994: 11; see also Apoyo July 1995: 18.

[7] Auyero (1998); Repetto (1998: 17–20). Therefore, when Menem and Governor Duhalde clashed in later years over control of the Peronist movement and the presidential candidacy for 1999, these targeted social programs became one of the battlegrounds (interviews with Amadeo 1997 and Kohan 1997).

Desarrollo Social indeed had a significant impact on Menem's vote in 1995 (Weyland 1998c: 559–60). Also, Governor Duhalde's well-oiled patronage machine, funded by the Fondo del Conurbano, made a major contribution to Menem's victory by delivering the incumbent a disproportionate share of the vote in the governor's bailiwicks.[8]

The finding that antipoverty schemes strengthen presidential support are fully in line with the cognitive-psychological arguments advanced in this book. In times of recovery, targeted social programs visibly spread some of the benefits of renewed growth and thus helped to put large numbers of people more firmly into the domain of gains.[9] The resulting risk aversion induced many beneficiaries to prefer the incumbent with his substantial track record over the untried opposition, whose capacity to maintain the hard-won economic stability and to realize its promises of social improvements was uncertain.

In conclusion, targeted social programs that distributed some of the fruits of recovery boosted Menem's and Fujimori's electoral chances and helped them counteract the political fallout from the "paradox of success." Paradoxically, Menem also benefited electorally from the incipient problems that threatened Argentina as a result of Mexico's bungled peso devaluation. While his political advisers feared that the danger of a new crisis and the unavoidable adjustment measures taken by the government would turn many people against the incumbent,[10] in the short run the threat of renewed economic deterioration had the opposite effect by rallying people around the president. Above all, the fallout of the tequila effect counteracted the "paradox of success" by making economic stability again highly salient. Whereas in preceding years many Argentines had gradually shifted their attention to other concerns, such as unemployment and corruption, stability quickly became an overriding issue again and attracted firm support (Fraga 1995; Palermo and Novaro 1996: 447; Martínez Vivot 1995a, 1995b). Given the good track record of the government's economic team, the threat of a new crisis thus played into Menem's hands. Uncertainty about the future, which punctured the complacency prevailing before, made many citizens opt for the incumbent as the guarantor of stability (Martínez Vivot 1995a).

---

[8] *LAWR* (1995). When Duhalde ran as the Peronists' presidential candidate in 1999, 42 percent of respondents in an October 1999 survey justified their intention to vote for him with "public works" and "social assistance"; only 17 percent mentioned "party identity" (Estudio Graciela Römer 1999a: 8).

[9] Thus, targeted antipoverty schemes concentrated on creating "new winners," rather than compensating the principal losers from market reform (Graham 1994: 6–12).

[10] Confidential author interviews with two important Menem aides, Buenos Aires, March 1995.

The external origin of the new problems was crucial for allowing Menem to reap electoral benefits from the resurgence of economic difficulties. By depicting this threat as an exogenous shock, the government managed to deny responsibility and thus escape from the punishment in the polls that incumbents usually incur in times of economic deterioration. Furthermore, by the time of the election, the economic and social costs of the tequila effect and of the government's adjustment measures were only beginning to be felt by broader sectors of the population (Cavallo 1997: 214). Many people had not (yet) experienced losses, and they hoped that the competence of Menem's economic team could avert such losses (Palermo and Novaro 1996: 445–48, 457–58; see also Centro de Estudios Unión para la Nueva Mayoría 1995b: 5–6; Martínez Vivot 1995a). Thus, Menem was fortunate that the elections were held at a time when many voters were facing considerable uncertainty about the future but did not (yet) see themselves in the domain losses.[11]

In conclusion, Menem's and Fujimori's strong performance in economic stabilization, antipoverty programs, and the defeat of guerrilla forces gave them many advantages in their reelection campaigns.

The Opposition Campaigns

Whereas Menem and Fujimori emphasized economic and social issues in their campaigns, the major opposition candidates stressed political and moral themes, besides promising social improvements (as any critic of the government would do). José Octavio Bordón in Argentina, candidate of the new Frente del País Solidario (FREPASO), a successor to the Frente Grande, and Javier Pérez de Cuéllar in Peru, leader of the new Unión por el Perú (UPP), accepted the basic outlines of the new market model and focused much of their criticism on crucial features of neopopulism. Accordingly, their most distinctive promise was "liberal" and "republican" respect for democratic rules and values (cf. O'Donnell 1998: 113–15). By contrast, the denunciation of the social costs of neoliberalism, while important, was less central to and distinctive of the opposition campaigns, even in Argentina with its high unemployment.[12]

Neither Bordón nor Pérez de Cuéllar proposed a drastic reversal of neoliberal reform and an alternative type of socioeconomic policy. In

---

[11] See Estudio Graciela Römer (1997: T38.G8; 1999b: 5). Shortly after the election, these losses became visible, for instance, with the publication of the 18.2 percent unemployment rate in late May 1995. As many people therefore reentered the domain of losses, Menem's popularity plummeted, as analyzed in the next section.

[12] Novaro and Palermo (1998: 81–124). In fact, Argentina's unemployed ended up voting disproportionately *for* Menem (Gervasoni 1998: 27).

fact, Bordón pledged to maintain the convertibility plan (FREPASO 1995: 5–6, 10; Novaro and Palermo 1998: 123–28), which imposed a straitjacket on Argentina's economy and left the country exposed to external shocks, such as the tequila effect.[13] And Pérez de Cuéllar promised to reduce inflation, maintain fiscal discipline, and continue the privatization program (UPP 1995: 19–22; interview with Pease 1999). Both opposition candidates confined themselves to promising some modifications in the market model, especially greater attention to social problems. How they could achieve the latter goal within the constraints set by neoliberalism remained unclear.

To differentiate themselves from Menem and Fujimori, Bordón and Pérez de Cuéllar stressed political and moral themes. They criticized the concentration of power by the incumbents and accused Menem of bending and Fujimori of breaking the constitution and undermining the rule of law. Whereas Pérez de Cuéllar centered his attacks on Fujimori's autocratic tendencies, Bordón also pointed to the rampant corruption in Menem's entourage (UPP 1995: 1, 4–17; FREPASO 1995: 7, 23–25). Both opposition candidates thus took aim at the incumbents' neopopulist style and personalistic leadership and promised instead faithful respect for democratic and republican rules and norms.

These political principles, however, held major attraction mostly for middle sectors and — to a lesser extent — the organized working class (Novaro and Palermo 1998: 94–97; interview with Pennano 1996). A higher level of economic sustenance, more advanced education, and the resulting sense of political efficacy allowed and induced these segments to demand greater presidential accountability, more transparency in decision-making, and fair play in political competition.[14] Claiming higher status and a more refined style, these sectors also were averse to the populist tactics used by Menem and Fujimori, who often appealed to the "low" and "crude" elements in politics and society (see Ostiguy 1997: 1–8). In Argentina, middle-class sectors in sophisticated Buenos Aires saw Carlos Menem with contempt as a provincial buffoon. There was a similar cultural divide between Peru's white middle class and Alberto Fujimori, who had grown up in a tough lower-class neighborhood

---

[13] Radical Party candidate Horacio Massaccesi, who advocated a departure from the convertibility plan in the medium run, fared very poorly, winning a meager 17 percent of the vote.

[14] For instance, 21 percent of respondents in Greater Buenos Aires with tertiary education, but only 11 percent with primary education, named corruption as the most significant problem facing the country (Centro de Estudios Unión para la Nueva Mayoría 1997a: 5). And 18 percent of the upper and middle class mentioned as the worst aspect of Fujimori's fifth year in office "his dependence on the military," but only 8–10 percent of the two intermediate strata and a mere 3 percent of the poorest (Apoyo July 1995: 18).

and regularly used the dirty tricks he had learned in that setting (see Panfichi and Francis 1993: 236–37).

By contrast to these political and cultural considerations, destitution caused poorer groups to focus primarily on socioeconomic topics and to prefer strong leaders who could address these issues. These sectors did care about democracy and clean government, but as a secondary priority. In fact, they had a skeptical position toward formal institutions because "the law" too often protected middle- and upper-class groups while being turned against the poor. Also, formal rules and bureaucratic procedures often appeared as obstacles to fulfilling their pressing substantive concerns. Therefore, many of the poor were attracted to neopopulist leaders, who guaranteed economic stability, offered social benefits, exercised strong leadership, and displayed a "popular" cultural style (Balbi 1996: 187–206; Boggio, Romero, and Ansión 1991: 41–56; Catterberg 1991: 41–48; Lawton 1994: 18–20; Parodi and Twanama 1993: 63–87). As a result, the incumbents—especially Fujimori—received disproportionate support from less well-off segments of the population. By contrast, the middle sectors and the formal working class disproportionately preferred the opposition.

The upper class, however, strongly supported the incumbents. Businesspeople, in particular, appreciated the restoration of economic stability and growth and the reassertion of state authority, especially the strategic defeat of the Shining Path in Peru. In Argentina, they also praised Menem for discarding the anti–big business attitude that had traditionally characterized Peronism and that had created fierce political conflict in earlier decades. Top business leaders saw Menem's and Fujimori's neopopulist tactics as a necessary evil for garnering mass support for a reform program that, on balance, favored their interests.[15] Since they had direct, personal access to crucial decision-makers, they had only limited concern about the concentration of power by neopopulist leaders and their exclusionary decision-making style, especially the hermetic nature of the Fujimori government—problems that disturbed many people from the middle sectors.

As a result of the divergent priorities of different social strata, Menem and Fujimori assembled a support coalition that was very strong at the bottom and the top of the social pyramid, but weaker in the middle.[16] In a poll among Lima residents held right after the election, 78 percent of the wealthiest and 66 percent of the poorest stratum reported to have

[15] Confidential author interviews with top business leaders in Lima, February 1995, and Buenos Aires, March 1995.

[16] Gervasoni (1998: 10–19); Ostiguy (1997: 22–26); Roberts and Arce (1998: 236–38). Confidentially, an adviser to the Argentine presidency stressed this socially uneven support in March 1995.

voted for Fujimori, but only 60 percent of the two strata in the middle; by contrast, Pérez de Cuéllar received support from 26–32 percent of the two middle strata, but only 22 percent of the best-off and 19 percent of the worst-off.[17] And in Argentina's capital, Menem received 51.5 percent of the vote in better-off neighborhoods and 47.8 percent in the poorer areas, but only 35.7 percent in the intermediate sections of town (Centro de Estudios Unión para la Nueva Mayoría 1995a: 2–4; see also Mora y Araujo 1996). As in their first election, the two presidents thus appealed especially to the largely unorganized poor while finding less resonance in organized civil society. Contrary to their first campaigns, however, the incumbents now drew strong support from economic elites as well.

Given the different composition of Argentine and Peruvian society, the incumbents' similar campaign strategies had different outcomes. In Argentina, the middle class has remained fairly extensive; therefore, the opposition posed a real threat to Menem. In particular, if the incumbent had not won in the first round of the election, all the discontented sectors might have lined up behind the leading opposition candidate and defeated Menem. In early 1995, the president's political advisers were justifiably worried, especially about the rapid advance of the new FREPASO, which was not tainted by past failure like the UCR.

In Peru, by contrast, the middle class has always remained small while lower-class and very poor people have constituted a clear majority of the population. The severe economic decline of the 1980s further skewed this balance. As a result, the republican, democratic opposition never had a realistic chance of victory, and Fujimori was reelected in a landslide. Contrary to Argentina, where the UCR survived—though badly battered—all of Peru's established parties suffered the humiliation of garnering less than 5 percent of the vote. Abandoned by most of their supporters, they had to reapply for their registration as parties. The 1995 elections thus left behind an organizational wasteland in Peru, whereas they boosted a new opposition party coalition—FREPASO—in Argentina.[18] As a result, Fujimori managed to enhance his political predominance, whereas Menem continued to face significant political constraints. Thus, the political repercussions of dissimilar social structures put Argentina and Peru on different political trajectories.

[17] Apoyo April 1995: 12; similarly *IMASEN Confidencial* April 1995: 13, which unfortunately combines upper and middle class; see also Durand (1996: 113).

[18] On the significant though limited institutionalization of FREPASO as a party coalition, see Godio (1998: 105–6, 156–58, 190–92). The limitations are stressed by Abal Medina (1998: 19, 22, 26).

The Political Sustainability of Neoliberalism

Support for the New Market Model and Its Initiators in the Late 1990s

Immediately after Menem's reelection and a few months after Fujimori's victory, the Argentine and Peruvian economies deteriorated greatly. In Argentina, the population finally felt the full impact of the fallout from the Mexican peso crisis. As a result of plummeting investor confidence and of the government's austerity measures, the country slid into a pronounced recession. GDP contracted by 4.6 percent in 1995 (Llach 1997: 231), and unemployment soared to a stunning 18.4 percent in May 1995 (after having gradually increased to 12.2 percent by October 1994: Ministerio de Economía 1999: 198). In Peru, the Fujimori government also imposed a new round of adjustment measures in mid-1995. After stimulating the economy and expanding social programs in 1994 and early 1995, it had to shift course after the elections and adopt restrictive measures to prevent a serious overheating of the economy and imbalances in Peru's external accounts. As a result, growth slowed to a meager 2.6 percent in 1996 (Gonzales de Olarte 1998: 14), and the country's employment problems worsened further.

This new round of belt tightening disappointed popular (and governmental)[19] hopes that painful neoliberal adjustment would usher in sustained prosperity—hopes that the initial recoveries in Argentina (1991–94) and Peru (1993–95) had reinforced. It now became obvious that the new market model was subject to conjunctural problems similar to those plaguing ISI. In fact, the greater openness to the world economy and the restrictions imposed by neoliberal principles of budget austerity and balance in external accounts (which were particularly tight in Argentina's convertibility scheme) made growth more vulnerable to exogenous shocks and ruled out determined countercyclical policies.

These renewed economic problems put large numbers of people in the domain of losses. In Argentina, the proportion of poll respondents in Greater Buenos Aires who assessed the economic situation of the country as worse than at the inception of the convertibility plan rose

---

[19] An adviser to the Argentine presidency told this author confidentially in March 1995 that the political wing of the Peronist movement had accepted the initial adjustment as a necessary precondition for returning to Peronism's traditional distributional policies. That this hope was dashed right before the May elections caused virtual despair in these circles.

from 24 percent in April 1995 to 50 percent in May 1996 and 64 percent in September of that year (Estudio Graciela Römer 1997: T38.G8; 1999b: 5; see also Centro de Estudios Unión para la Nueva Mayoría 1995b: 5–6). From August 1995 through the end of the Menem administration, negative assessments of "how the economy was going" (*marcha de la economía*) consistently hovered around 36–44 percent in national-level samples (Estudio Graciela Römer 1999a: 4). Similarly, pessimism about the future of the country's economy consistently ran higher than optimism from July 1995 onward (Mora y Araujo 1997).

In Peru, from February 1996 onward, negative retrospective assessments of the economic situation of people's family were consistently and significantly higher among Lima residents than perceptions of recent gains (Apoyo November 1996: 28). After October 1996, these perceptions of recent losses rarely fell below 40 percent and reached almost 50 percent on several occasions in 1997 and early 1998. Another round of adjustment in 1998 further raised these negative assessments so that they hovered around the 50 percent mark from mid-1998 to mid-1999. Retrospective assessments of the country's economy also took a strong downturn in 1996. While 44 percent of respondents in Lima saw improvements in June 1995, only 20 percent did in December 1996, whereas 43 percent perceived losses (compared to 16 percent in June 1995). In 1998, these negative assessments rose further, reaching 60 percent in December of that year and 55 percent in June 1999. Expectations of improvements in people's economic situation also dropped, though more slowly; fears about future losses rose above hopes for improvements only from early 1997 onward (Apoyo 1999).

As a considerable proportion — sometimes a majority — of the population saw itself in the domain of losses, support for the incumbents diminished considerably, while approval for the opposition rose. Menem's presidential popularity dropped drastically from 47 percent in February 1995 to 36 percent in August of that year and fell further in subsequent years until reaching a low point of 24 percent in February 1998 (Estudio Graciela Römer 1999a: 2). In Greater Buenos Aires, Menem's performance ratings tracked assessments of the economy very closely; between February 1995 and March 1997, presidential approval and positive economic assessments were never more than three percentage points apart (Estudio Graciela Römer 1997: T38.G1; see fig. 5.1 above).

Fujimori's popularity, which had risen to much higher levels than Menem's, plummeted even more dramatically. After reaching 75 percent in January 1996, it dropped to around 60 percent by midyear and 45 percent in December. From mid-1997 onward, it generally hovered around 35 and 45 percent, whereas disapproval reached 50–63 percent

(Apoyo September 1997: 7; June 1999: 6; similarly *IMASEN Confidencial* March 1997: 8; April 98: 4; May 1999: 2). Survey respondents stressed that their diminishing support for the incumbent resulted from the economic deterioration. When those who disapproved of Fujimori were asked for the most important reason, 69 percent named "the economic situation" (Apoyo December 1998: 7; similarly Apoyo December 1996: 8).

Economic deterioration and widespread perceptions of loss also lowered support for the new market model. In Argentina, the proportion of respondents in Greater Buenos Aires who demanded a "total change" in the economic model increased from 24 percent in December 1994 to 43 percent in December 1995, whereas advocates of complete continuity diminished from 17 percent to 11 percent and those endorsing basic continuity, albeit with modifications, fell from 55 percent to 38 percent.[20] In Peru, the percentage of Lima residents who felt that "the state must leave productive activities to the private sector" diminished from a stable level of 56–59 percent between 1990 and 1994 to 48 percent in April 1997 and 49 percent in April 1998 (Apoyo September 1998: 45). Similarly, support for the privatization of public enterprises fell from about 50 percent in late 1995 to 42–43 percent in late 1996 and dropped further to about 30 percent from late 1997 onward, with disapproval fluctuating around 60 percent (Apoyo June 1999: 34).[21]

Interestingly, however, approval of the new market system in opinion surveys did not collapse but remained at reasonable levels and increased again in 1997 and 1998. Although in Argentina 44–48 percent of national-level poll respondents during 1998 and 1999 rated their personal economic situation as worse (Estudio Graciela Römer 1999b: 6), only 31–34 percent demanded a "total change" in the economic model, whereas 46–47 percent wanted to maintain its outlines, but introduce modifications. In May 1999, 60 percent preferred moderate, partial changes in economic policy, whereas only 33 percent demanded a radical change (Estudio Graciela Römer 1999b: 9). Similarly, rejection of the market system, which reached 48 percent in August 1997 (compared with 35 percent support), fell to 32–34 percent after mid-1998,

---

[20] Estudio Graciela Römer (1997: T38.G12). Interestingly, however, economic policy turned more orthodox as die-hard neoliberals like Carlos Rodríguez (interview with Rodríguez 1997) assumed crucial government positions.

[21] This decline has to be interpreted with caution, however, because respondents do not seem to express what absolute level of marketization they endorse, but whether they want more or less market than has already been instituted in the country; their point of reference is relative and changes over time. Therefore, considering the advance of market reform during the 1990s, popular support for neoliberal principles may actually have remained stable.

while support ranged from 38 to 48 percent (Estudio Graciela Römer 1999a: 11). Demands for a reversal of market reform garnered few adherents. For instance, only 14 percent of respondents in a 1998 poll among Greater Buenos Aires residents pleaded for restatizing recently privatized public enterprises, whereas 45 percent proposed more control and another 30 percent advocated more competition (Centro de Estudios Unión para la Nueva Mayoría 1998b: 1, 6). And 60 percent of Greater Buenos Aires residents preferred the maintenance of the cornerstone of Argentina's neoliberal model, the convertibility scheme, which only 12 percent wanted to abolish.[22]

In Peru, when asked in October 1997 about their vote intention for the presidential elections of 2000, 43 percent preferred a candidate "who would make adjustments in economic policy" but maintain its basic outline; another 10 percent opted for somebody "who would maintain the economic policy without modification"; only 42 percent chose a candidate who would "radically change the economic policy" pursued by Fujimori (Apoyo October 1997: 23). And the statement that "the market economy is best for the country," with which 62 percent of Lima residents had agreed in March 1994, found support among 66 percent in April 1997 and 58 percent (vs. 27 percent rejection) in April 1998 (Apoyo September 1998: 45–46). In fact, the statement that the government should determine prices lost support, from 42 percent in March 1994 to 34 percent in April 1997 (Apoyo April 1997: 39).

In sum, for reasons explained in the next section, substantial — though by no means overwhelming — adherence to the market model survived the conjunctural problems of the mid- to late 1990s. Demands for change concentrated more on specific aspects than on the underlying principles of the new development scheme, especially the predominance of private ownership and the centrality of the market as a mechanism of economic coordination. As a result, neoliberalism did not confront serious challenges in the political arena. Most importantly, no important partisan force proposed a frontal attack on the new market model; politicians who advocated such a radical stance failed to attract widespread backing. FREPASO in Argentina, which was gaining political strength, and UPP in Peru, which was growing weaker and more divided, maintained their support for the basic outlines of the new development scheme. The Radical Party in Argentina, which was gradually recuperating from its string of electoral defeats from 1991 to 1995, abandoned its proposal to loosen the convertibility plan in preparation for the legislative contest of October 1997. And new Lima mayor Alberto Andrade, who emerged as the leading opposition candidate to Fujimori,

[22] The remaining 28 percent did not voice an opinion (Centro de Estudios Unión para la Nueva Mayoría 1997b: 2).

remained true to his conservative political background and firmly supported market principles.

By contrast, more radical challengers to the new status quo, from both the right and the left, such as the reactionary Movimiento por la Dignidad y la Independencia (MODIN) of military renegade Aldo Rico in Argentina and the remaining splinters of Izquierda Unida in Peru, failed to attract many backers. Given that Peru's "party" system was highly inchoate and fluid and that even Argentina's more structured partisan arena allowed for the rise of new contenders (especially FRE-PASO and MODIN), the lack of support for attacks on the market system cannot be attributed to collusion among established elites. Fundamental opponents tried to win popular backing but clearly failed.

In conclusion, support for the market system had surprising strength and resilience in the face of serious economic problems. Thus, the basic outlines of the new development scheme had acquired considerable political sustainability.

Reasons for Continuing Acceptance of the New Market Model

Why did a good proportion of the population continue to endorse neoliberal principles despite the renewed economic problems of the mid-1990s, which put many citizens in the domain of losses? Why was support for the new development scheme stronger than purely economic factors would predict?

First, it seems that the difficulties of the mid-1990s appeared more as conjunctural than structural problems. Many people interpreted them not as indications of the market model's failure, but as temporary (though painful) problems that could be resolved within the confines of the new development scheme. This benign interpretation was plausible because Argentina's recession was triggered by an exogenous shock for which the Menem government denied responsibility.[23] Similarly, many Peruvians seemed to realize that the boom and bust of 1993–96 resulted in good part from Fujimori's electorally motivated manipulation of the economy, which caused a typical political business cycle.

In addition, the substantial drop in Menem's and Fujimori's popularity suggests that the popular discontent triggered by renewed economic deterioration focused first and foremost on the incumbents, not on the development model they had instituted. Citizens evidently hoped that a new government would eliminate the objectionable aspects of neoliberalism and allow for modifications in the market system. Since

---

[23] Obviously, however, the rigid convertibility scheme tied the government's hands in responding to this exogenous shock (Starr 1997: 97–99; Pastor and Wise 1999: 484–85).

democracy institutionalizes the possibility of regular alternation in power and thus provides the population with an easy opportunity to "throw the bums out," it operates as a protective device that concentrates discontent on the government and directs it away from underlying structural problems. The expectations attached to governmental turnover make people postpone demands for more deep-reaching change.

Furthermore, the very cost that market reform had imposed on the country during the early 1990s probably made many people reluctant to call for a fundamental transformation of the new development model. These costs functioned as a sunk investment that enveloped people in the prior-option bias and thus induced them to give the new scheme a full chance. As many citizens during the 1980s had been tempted to throw good money after bad, support the old ISI model, and object to neoliberal reform, they now — after the imposition of neoliberalism — refused to follow calls for a return to the old model or another round of profound changes. Such radical recipes were likely to entail further transitional costs, which most people refused to shoulder, given the painful memories of the sacrifices caused by neoliberal reform. Thus, the price they had already paid helped lock them into the new market model. The prior-option bias, which during the 1980s had obstructed market reform, now protected its results.

Many people also refused to depart from the new market model because there was no credible alternative that looked promising and realistic. While advancing a plethora of complaints and grievances, the radical critics of neoliberalism failed to propose a clear, coherent development scheme of their own. On the left, socialism was too discredited worldwide to hold much attraction to voters. On the right, constructive programs were conspicuous by their absence. The global ideological "hegemony" of neoliberal principles further protected the market model from serious political challenges.

Obviously, the absence of feasible alternatives resulted in part from the external constraints imposed by advancing economic globalization and continuing supervision from the international financial institutions. These restrictions greatly increased the costs of any attempt to abandon the market model. In particular, the volatility of capital markets, which react nervously to perceived threats to investor confidence, helped lock in the new orthodoxy. In and of themselves, however, these external restrictions cannot account for the reasonably strong acceptance of the new development scheme because external pressures could, in principle, backfire and unleash a nationalist reaction to the cosmopolitan project of neoliberalism. But by reinforcing the widespread perception of absent alternatives, this factor enhanced the sustainability of the new development model.

Finally, development models have distributional effects that over time tend to strengthen their beneficiaries and supporters and weaken the losers and opponents. For instance, business sectors that profit from trade liberalization, deregulation, and privatization prosper, expand, and gain in economic weight; by contrast, the sectors that are hurt shrink or go bankrupt, thus suffering a decline in their economic assets and political clout. Similarly, organized labor in uncompetitive sectors, which often led the opposition to neoliberalism, grows weaker due to labor market flexibilization and rising unemployment. These relative shifts in economic fortune can have major political repercussions; for instance, newly wealthy businesspeople may make generous campaign contributions that boost the political fortunes of the reform-initiating government. Thus, the distributional impact of neoliberal reform and the routine operation of the new market model shift the balance of economic weight in favor of the new winners and presumable supporters, and against the losers and likely opponents. Unless this redistribution is so skewed that it causes a powerful political backlash, it helps cement political support for the new development scheme.

For all these reasons, the market model survived the eruption of economic problems in the mid-1990s without facing dangerous political challenges. These conjunctural difficulties and the renewed adjustment measures greatly diminished Menem's and Fujimori's approval ratings but did not undermine support for market principles nor induce voters to back radical opponents of neoliberalism. The fact that the new market model did not fall from favor suggests that it has acquired considerable political sustainability in Argentina and Peru.

The Decline of Neopopulist Leaders

Does neopopulist leadership have similar staying power as the new market model, or is it a temporary phenomenon that begins to decline as plebiscitarian leaders succeed in resolving the initial crisis? Did Menem and Fujimori manage to maintain and further extend their autonomy and power, making politics in their countries revolve around their personalistic leadership? Or did they trade in part of their autonomy for a move toward institutional consolidation, which could bring about a "routinization" of neopopulism?[24] Alternatively, did they face increasing opposition and the threat of replacement?

---

[24] This process would be similar to Weber's (1976: 142–48, 681–87) "routinization of charisma."

The Disappearance of Opportune Issues

Neopopulist outsiders emerged in times of severe crisis, which allowed them to discredit the established political class and prove their charismatic capacity to save the country. Grave problems such as hyperinflation, which impose tremendous costs on large sectors of the population, but which can be ended quickly through bold (though painful) countermeasures, offer particularly good opportunities for the rise of charismatic leadership. But as another facet of the above-mentioned "paradox of success," their very achievements in combating these problems made it difficult for Menem and Fujimori to find important issues that could be resolved in similarly quick and striking ways during their second terms. The incumbents therefore proved unable to boost their neopopulist leadership further.

In the presidential campaign of 1995, Menem promised to "pulverize unemployment" as he had "pulverized hyperinflation" (*LAWR* 1995). But this promise proved impossible to fulfill. While a determined government can end skyrocketing price increases with a few bold measures, it cannot create millions of jobs by decree. In fact, whereas neoliberalism had provided a clear recipe for stopping hyperinflation, it hindered efforts to lower unemployment by limiting expansionary economic policies and ruling out large-scale public employment programs. As a result, joblessness hovered at a worrisome 14–18 percent during the second half of the 1990s. High unemployment remained Argentines' central concern and one of their most important criticisms of the Menem government (Estudio Graciela Römer 1999b: 3–4, 13).

Fujimori faced similar difficulties in identifying issues that he could successfully address with the bold measures befitting a neopopulist leader. The main concerns of most Peruvians in the second half of the 1990s, poverty, precarious employment, and low wages (Apoyo May 1997: 43–44; April 1998: 46–47; April 1999: 46–47; *IMASEN Confidencial* June 1996: 13), cannot be resolved by political fiat. Stressing the persistence of the terrorist threat was a double-edged sword because it diminished one of Fujimori's main accomplishments. The president therefore emphasized a new security issue, namely, growing common crime, which he combated with some of the tough measures used against the Shining Path (Apoyo April 1998: 35; Toche 1998). In addition, he took advantage of natural catastrophes, especially the extensive floods caused by El Niño in 1998, touring the affected regions and promising quick relief (Apoyo February 1998: 19; Grompone 1998: 36). But these new issues lacked the intensity of hyperinflation and massive insurgency.

The absence of catastrophic problems that imposed tremendous losses on large numbers of people and that bold countermeasures could quickly resolve weakened Menem's and Fujimori's standing in public opinion during the second half of the 1990s (figs. 5.1, 7.1). The strengths of these neopopulist leaders — their courage and willingness to run risks and override constraints — became ever less important. Their weaknesses — personalistic whims and concentration of power — therefore became less acceptable to many citizens. In particular, the corruption in Menem's entourage and the autocratic tendencies of Fujimori appeared more and more as *un*necessary evils.

For these reasons, as well as the renewed economic problems discussed above, the two neopopulist leaders were unable to maintain the massive backing they had garnered during their first terms. This diminishing support hindered pursuit of their most important goal, namely, a second immediate reelection. The first reelection drive was endorsed by large numbers of citizens and powerful interest groups, especially big business, which saw a second term for Menem and Fujimori as crucial for cementing economic and political stability. But the further consolidation of stability made the two presidents dispensable, and their desire to remain in office therefore appeared to many citizens as illegitimate, dangerous power hunger.[25] In fact, continued dependence on personalistic leadership, which would keep institutional structures fluid and weak, came to be seen as a source of future instability. Important sectors — including business — therefore perceived a change in top leadership as important for guaranteeing the institutionalization of the new market model.[26]

The Effort to Reconcile Conflictive Societies

Given the difficulty of identifying catastrophic issues that would justify bold neopopulist leadership, Menem and Fujimori modified their main appeal: They shifted from the determined enactment of drastic change

[25] In Peru, rejection ran as high as support (Apoyo September 1996: 24; October 1996: 22), and contrary to the government's desires, about 70 percent of survey respondents demanded a plebiscite to decide whether Fujimori could run in 2000 (Apoyo December 1997: 19; August 1998: 31; *IMASEN Confidencial* January 1997: 20). In Argentina, 84 percent held a negative view about another reelection; only 9 percent were positively disposed (Centro de Estudios Unión para la Nueva Mayoría 1997a: 7). In a potential plebiscite, 80 percent planned to deny Menem the right to run in 1999, while 15 percent would vote "yes" (Centro de Estudios Unión para la Nueva Mayoría 1998a: 1).

[26] Confidential author interview with an important business representative, Lima, August 1996; interview with Pennano (1996); Durand (1998: 34–35); Grompone (1998: 28).

to the pragmatic administration of the new development model. As analyzed in chapter 6, both presidents slowed down market reform after they entered the domain of gains. To legitimate their move to greater caution, Menem and Fujimori emphasized ever more an old populist appeal, namely the unity of the people, which calls for the reconciliation of old conflicts. From the beginning, Menem had left behind the antagonism inherent in traditional Peronism and had promised to overcome longstanding divisions and bring together the Argentine people, his "brethren" (Menem 1990: 7–8, 11–12, 29, 65; Menem and Duhalde 1989: chap. 2). Similarly, Fujimori had criticized ideology as the artificial creation of divisions and had instead promised to adopt a pragmatic posture and "put technical criteria ahead of politicking" (Fujimori 1991: 96–97). After defeating their initial enemies—such as the political class—both presidents reinforced these messages because they had a particular interest in preaching national harmony and thus delegitimating attacks on their own governments.

This message of unity held considerable appeal in Argentina and Peru, which had a long history of fierce conflict. By overcoming the antiliberal bias of his Peronist movement and making alliances with its former enemies, Menem overcame the longstanding cleavage between Peronism and anti-Peronism, which had agitated Argentine politics for decades and posed severe obstacles to the maintenance of democracy. In a similar vein, the Fujimori administration defeated dangerous, highly ideological guerrilla movements, completed the (self-)destruction of the radical left, and took important material and symbolic steps—such as antipoverty programs and innumerable presidential visits to long-neglected areas of the country—to give the "excluded" *cholo* majority of Peruvians a sense of national integration. Thus, both neopopulist leaders made great and ultimately successful efforts to turn fractious, conflict-ridden countries into more unified nations.[27]

Since the promise of unity and the end of political turmoil was attractive to many Argentines and Peruvians, Menem and Fujimori maintained considerable support. Even sectors that were critical of the two governments recognized their accomplishments in restoring economic stability and political calm. Given the widespread aversion to fierce conflict, the opposition forces that gained strength did not promote polarization by calling for fundamental change but promised a high degree of continuity, especially in economic policy. In sum, the efforts of neoliberal populists to ease old hostilities and avert new clashes achieved considerable success.

Interestingly, thus, the successful imposition of drastic, painful neo-

[27] I owe some of these ideas to María del Carmen Feijóo, Buenos Aires, July 1997.

liberal reform did not exacerbate political conflict in the medium run but ended up reducing it. An orthodox "vanguard" project surprisingly created substantial consensus on basic principles of the economic order. By pulling most of the opposition toward the center, effective market reform made countries that had been highly divided much more peaceful than they had long been, and more peaceful than nations without successful market reform—such as Brazil and Venezuela (not to speak of Ecuador)—continued to be.

The Divergent Fate of Neopopulist Leadership in Argentina and Peru

Despite the important similarities just analyzed, the political trajectories of Argentina and Peru differed in the last few years. Most importantly, the prospects for neopopulist leadership came to diverge considerably as Menem and Fujimori responded in dissimilar ways to the increasing constraints they faced. Whereas the Argentine leader failed to override these constraints and therefore did not manage to hold on to government power, his Peruvian counterpart combated these challenges head-on; to pave the way for another reelection, he applied means that compromised and even violated democratic rules and principles. And while infighting surprisingly brought down Fujimori's government soon after the beginning of his third term and while the transition government of Valentín Paniagua quickly restored full democracy, his successor Alejandro Toledo has few political options except for neopopulism. As a result, the prospects for democratic institutionalization improved in Argentina while the space for neopopulist leadership shrunk. In Peru, by contrast, the continued weakness of civil society and absence of organized political forces have kept the door wide open for neopopulism. While democracy recovered with Fujimori's fall, its future integrity is therefore far from assured; in particular, personalistic leadership is likely to be a recurrent phenomenon obstructing democratic institutionalization for the foreseeable future.

These differences arose from institutional, political, and societal factors. First, constitutional reform left less space for personalistic leadership in Argentina than in Peru. Whereas Menem negotiated the reelection provision in a functioning democracy, Fujimori imposed it after suspending democracy. As a result, Menem had to accept institutional limitations on presidential powers, whereas Fujimori succeeded in fortifying the presidency. In line with populist notions of democracy, Fujimori and his supporters also strengthened the majoritarian elements of Peru's constitution, especially by instituting a unicameral legislature with extensive powers, for instance vis-à-vis the judiciary.[28] For these reasons, Peru's new constitution provides a more propitious institutional setting for neopopulism than the reformed Argentine charter.

In addition, the constellation of partisan forces has been less favorable to neopopulist leadership in Argentina than in Peru. In Argentina, a new party coalition of center-left orientation — the FREPASO — emerged and quickly gained electoral strength and a minimum level of organization, and the old, seemingly moribund UCR rebounded. These two opposition forces formed the Alliance for Labor, Justice, and Education in 1997 and offered a serious, programmatic alternative to the incumbent and his party, achieving a clear victory in the midterm legislative elections of 1997. Emboldened by their political advance, the opposition parties — and groups in civil society — offered ever stronger resistance to Menem's initiatives.[29] Important sectors inside the Peronist movement, led by Governor Eduardo Duhalde of Buenos Aires province, also curtailed the incumbent's personal ambitions. After protracted internal conflicts, which further weakened the government, Menem eventually had to concede defeat on his central goal to achieve a second consecutive reelection.[30]

Distancing himself from Menem by emphasizing more traditional policy goals of Peronism, Duhalde managed to win his party's presidential candidacy for 1999. But this internal campaign tactic antagonized the conservative higher-status groups that Menem had won over with his market reforms and that now followed former Economy Minister Cavallo's third-party candidacy. The division of Menem's coalition helped the opposition alliance. Also, the UCR-FREPASO coalition had long benefited from the widespread aversion to Menem's neopopulist leadership, which many Argentines associated with arbitrariness, extravagance, and corruption. Its presidential candidate, former Buenos Aires mayor Fernando de la Rúa, was therefore attractive to many voters precisely because of his uncharismatic, boring personality, captured in his nickname *"el chupete"* — the baby pacifier. Renewed economic problems, exacerbated by Brazil's devaluation crisis of January 1999, further weakened the incumbent party and created greater resonance for the opposition's promises of social improvements. For these reasons, the UCR-FREPASO alliance won the presidential contest with 48.5 percent of the vote.

[28] Most of the transgressions of democratic rules and principles after 1995 were indeed carried out by the legislature, not the presidency (though clearly on behalf of — and most likely upon instigation by — the president).

[29] This stance reflected and reinforced attitudes in public opinion that were critical of the incumbent's efforts to extend his neopopulist leadership further (see note 25).

[30] This analysis of the continuing strength and rapid recuperation of Argentine parties is inspired partly by Novaro (1999).

Given de la Rúa's undynamic personality and the political limitations imposed on presidential latitude by continued Peronist control of the Senate, many provincial governments, and the Supreme Court, the new chief executive did not act like a neopopulist (Levitsky 2000). In fact, he quickly wasted the "political capital" stemming from his election victory with his weak leadership and Hamlet-like hesitations. Even after Argentina's worsening economic problems triggered de la Rúa's resignation in December 2001, and after social unrest and fierce rivalries inside the Peronist Party brought two weeks of unprecedented governmental instability (as analyzed below), Argentina's political class quickly regrouped and supported a government of national unity led by powerful PJ leader Eduardo Duhalde. While battered by the renewed crisis, Argentine parties have retained the organizational capacity to sustain the new government and prevent widespread popular disaffection from boiling over into an open challenge to the new administration's authority.

Thus, neopopulism predominated only temporarily in Argentina, rising and falling with Carlos Menem. Given the greater organizational strength of Argentina's main political forces, a revival is unlikely, unless the Duhalde administration fails to contain the current economic crisis and is also forced from office. If in that way Argentina's political class proves its incapacity to guarantee minimal economic and political stability, popular revulsion against party politicians could become so intense that an outsider might rise. But this worst-case scenario is unlikely to unfold because Duhalde can count on significant international support for his economic stabilization efforts and cooperation from many Argentine politicians, who fear the risks that a collapse of the new government would pose.

Whereas Argentina's parties continue to command significant organizational resources, Peru's political forces — most of which are too unorganized to deserve the label "party" — have remained weak and fragmented, as leading opposition politicians admit (interviews with Flores 1999, Pease 1999, Townsend 1999).[31] Also, the variety of groups in civil society that opposed Fujimori and supported his adversaries, especially current president Alejandro Toledo, have lacked organizational cohesion. For years, Fujimori therefore dared and managed to defy the growing opposition and pushed very hard for the opportunity to run

---

[31] The surprising resurgence of Alan García in the 2001 presidential elections confirms rather than contradicts this argument about party weakness in Peru. As vote intentions for the ex-president hovered below 5 percent four months before the first round (Datum 2001: 2), his dramatic comeback, which gave him 48.42 percent of the vote in the second round, was not based on longstanding organizational loyalties among APRA members, but on his personal charisma and skillful campaign. Thus, political commitments in Peru are highly volatile.

again in the 2000 presidential election. In fact, the majority in Congress that Fujimori controlled "reinterpreted" the constitution in 1996 to pave the way for his renewed candidacy; in 1997, it emasculated the Supreme Court, which struck down this distortion of the 1993 charter; and in another act of questionable legality, it prohibited in 1998 a plebiscite that the opposition called to take advantage of the aversion in public opinion to another reelection. These para-constitutional and undemocratic measures further discredited Fujimori and reinforced his autocratic image among middle-class groups. But they did not undermine his support among poorer sectors, which actually grew from late 1998 onward, pushing his approval ratings steadily higher and making a second reelection appear ever more unavoidable. Also, the opposition did not manage to develop an organized, programmatic alternative to Fujimori. Instead, the only serious rivals of the incumbent were themselves personalistic leaders, namely, first Lima mayor Alberto Andrade, then Luis Castañeda Lossio, a former official of the Fujimori government, and — at the very end of the election campaign — Alejandro Toledo (Carrión 2000: 6–14). While Toledo managed to pose a surprisingly strong challenge to the incumbent, his meteoric rise resembled Fujimori's own emergence from obscurity in 1990 and demonstrated the tremendous fluidity of political alignments and loyalties in Peru. In particular, Toledo also lacked organized backing and therefore used a populist political strategy to garner support.

With his controversial election victory in mid-2000, guaranteed with numerous irregularities and outright fraud, Fujimori seemed bound to prevail in Peruvian politics for years to come. But as a personalistic strategy that lacks institutionalization, neopopulism is always vulnerable and can collapse quickly. In fact, a severe power struggle between the autocratic president and his shady, unscrupulous, and utterly corrupt adviser Vladimiro Montesinos surprisingly imploded the government in the fall of 2000, prompting the ignominious flight of both protagonists (Balbi and Palmer 2001). Reacting to the widespread abuse, manipulation, and corruption under the Fujimori administration, Peruvian civil society then put a particularly high premium on the restoration of democratic principles and republican values. The transition administration of Valentín Paniagua indeed took important steps toward reinstituting the rule of law, guaranteeing greater accountability, and subordinating the military to civilian control; it also held clean elections in mid-2001.

Despite these efforts to deemphasize personalism and build democratic institutions, the door remains wide open for neopopulism. Since new president Alejandro Toledo lacks organized support and a congressional majority, he needs to maintain mass backing in order to promote his political initiatives. Given that he cannot draw on firm loyalties, he is resorting to typically populist tactics. In fact, with his special appeal to poorer, rural sectors and his heavy use of indigenous symbols, his initial governing style has striking resemblances to Fujimori's neopopulism. But the absence of opportune issues for proving charisma, which eroded Fujimori's leadership, keeps Toledo's support limited in extension and intensity. Thus, the new president seems to face a dilemma: He needs to — but cannot — become a successful neopopulist. In fact, his popularity — one of his most important bases of political sustenance — has dropped quickly, falling from 59 percent approval vs. 16 percent disapproval in August 2001 to 35 percent approval vs. 55 percent disapproval in January 2002 (Datum 2002: 3). Yet given the weakness of Peru's political society, Toledo's political difficulties will not produce organized alternatives, but strengthen other populist leaders, especially Alan García. Therefore, Peru will find it difficult to escape from personalistic, plebiscitarian leadership and institutionalize democracy.

Underlying Reasons for the Divergent Fate of Neopopulist Leadership

The divergent fate of neopopulist leadership in Argentina and Peru results from differences in the preexisting level of organizational strength, the depth of the crises facing both countries, and in their degree of economic and social development. First, Argentina had for decades had a more consolidated system of parties and interest groups than Peru (Mainwaring and Scully 1995: 17–20). The long predominance of two parties with fairly firm roots in society and the formal unity of the trade union confederation CGT gave Argentine society more organizational resources to withstand the troubles and travails of the 1980s and 1990s. By contrast, the inchoate nature and ideological division of the party system and the fragmentation of unions and social movements put Peruvian society in a more disadvantageous starting position.

Organizational continuities created important constraints on Menem's neopopulist leadership that Fujimori did not have to face. The Peronist Party has much greater strength than the fluid, unorganized groupings that backed Fujimori. As a result, whereas all of Fujimori's underlings depended on presidential discretion,[32] a number of Peronists

---

[32] As became obvious in late 2000, however, Fujimori's shady adviser Vladimiro Montesinos built up his own clandestine base of support, especially in the armed forces. This made it impossible for the president to dismiss Montesinos when striking evidence of his shameless bribery and his connections to Colombian guerrilla forces surfaced and the

maintained an independent power base that they used to limit or oppose Menem's ambitions and machinations. Above all, Eduardo Duhalde managed to build up his own support network as a Peronist alternative to the incumbent. Dependent upon Duhalde's backing for defeating an advancing partisan opposition in the 1995 election, Menem was unable to dislodge his internal rival. In subsequent years, Duhalde systematically used organizational loyalties and traditional Peronist slogans — such as demands for greater social justice — to distance himself from Menem's embrace of neoliberalism and further extend his backing inside the movement (Palermo and Novaro 1996: 432–44; Novaro and Palermo 1998: 59–62, 171–74, 189–92). Thus, the organizational and cultural network of Peronism provided cover for the survival and advance of an internal opponent to the incumbent neopopulist leader.

Similarly, longstanding organizational loyalties allowed the centenarian Radical Party to recuperate from its string of electoral defeats during the first half of the 1990s and make a strong comeback in the second half of the decade. These organizational resources also enabled the UCR to defeat its less institutionalized partner in the new opposition alliance, FREPASO, in the primary on the presidential candidacy for 1999 (Abal Medina 1998: 21–22). And they helped its uncharismatic, "boring" candidate de la Rúa win the general election. Thus, comparative organizational strength — on the side of both the governing party and the opposition — was important in hemming in Menem's personalistic leadership.

In Peru, by contrast, no sociopolitical force — except for APRA — ever had comparable organizational strength, and APRA was greatly weakened by Alan García's political and personal failures. Fujimori's neopopulist strategies therefore confronted few hurdles. The lack of organization among his own supporters also gave Fujimori virtually unlimited authority inside his movement.[33] Anybody who held a position of power in the government or its electoral vehicle Cambio 90/Nueva Mayoría owed his or her rise — and fall — exclusively to presidential discretion. Fujimori used this predominance to prevent the emergence of any internal rival. Jealously guarding his power, he systematically undermined potential challengers, such as former Minister of the Presidency Jaime Yoshiyama (Mauceri 1997: 907–8). In this way, Fujimori made himself indispensable to his own supporters, who lacked an alter-

---

U.S. government finally withdrew its support for him. The resulting internal stalemate — an important risk of a personalistic strategy such as neopopulism — brought down the Fujimori administration.

[33] The obvious exception was Montesinos.

native for the presidential contest of 2000 and therefore had to back his second reelection.

Similarly, the opposition to Fujimori always had little organizational strength and cohesion. For instance, the new UPP never defined party statutes nor held internal elections (interview with Pease 1999). The rapid rise and fall of opposition candidates for the 2000 elections — Andrade, Castañeda Lossio, and Toledo — demonstrates the resulting political volatility. This fluidity facilitated Fujimori's divide-and-rule strategies, including the effort to attract some members of established parties into his government.[34] Also, compared to Argentina, the opposition had less resilience to recover from the unsettling effects of drastic market reform. Even APRA, the party with the strongest organizational tradition, continued to suffer from the personalistic domination of ex-president Alan García, whose involvement in corruption long made him anathema to many Peruvians (Apoyo February 1999: 29). In fact, García's unexpected political resurrection in the presidential contest of 2001 derived mostly from his charismatic personality and skillful neopopulist tactics, not from APRA's organizational strength, as the very explosion of vote intentions for the ex-president suggests; longstanding party loyalties would have guaranteed García stronger support immediately upon entering the campaign. Last but not least, Alejandro Toledo, who came close to defeating Fujimori in 2000 and who edged out a narrow victory in 2001, has lacked any organized base of support. His followers constitute a loose, heterogeneous movement that cannot guarantee firm, cohesive backing for his government. This political fluidity leaves much room for plebiscitarian leadership; in fact, it gives the chief executive strong incentives to apply neopopulist strategies.

Besides starting out with fewer organizational resources than Argentina, Peru also suffered from significantly deeper, more complex crises and experienced more radical countermeasures, such as Fujimori's self-coup. The vibrant though weakly organized social movements, trade unions, and parties that formed in Peru during the 1980s were ravaged by the particularly profound economic deterioration of the 1980s, the radical neoliberal adjustment of the early 1990s, and the large-scale insurgency and counterinsurgency (Roberts 1998: chap. 8). In fact, the Shining Path deliberately sought to destroy community organizations in order to press the unprotected population into supporting its millenarian cause. Similarly, military repression deterred organiza-

---

[34] For instance, Fujimori's first prime minister, Hurtado Miller, hailed from Acción Popular (AP), which criticized as opportunistic his decision to cooperate with Fujimori immediately after the 1990 election, in which AP had supported Fujimori's rival Vargas Llosa (interview with Belaúnde 1996).

tional efforts by the left. Furthermore, Fujimori used the tremendous power and latitude that he gained from combating these grave crises to undermine established intermediary entities. These problems further corroded the weak institutional infrastructure of Peruvian society and eliminated all organized alternatives to personalistic leadership.

Finally, the greater opportunities for continued neopopulism in Peru reflect the country's lower level of economic development and social modernization. By contrast to Argentina, the social basis for the liberal-democratic, republican opposition to neopopulism is much weaker. Due to Peru's greater socioeconomic backwardness, the educational level of the population is lower than in Argentina. The middle class, which tends to be most strongly committed to liberal-democratic values, such as the rule of law and separation of powers (Catterberg 1989: chap. 4; Apoyo June 1997: 45; June 1999: 42; Dietz 1998: 187),[35] has a small size in Peru. The strong ethnic resentment of poor popular sectors against the white middle class and elite makes it even more difficult for the republican opposition to reach out and win mass support.[36]

Popular-sector groups that are susceptible to the appeals of neo-populist leaders are much larger than in Argentina. Given their desperate poverty, many Peruvians are tempted to accept small handouts from the government. While during the 1990s the resulting acquiescence was often tactical and did not reflect firm support for Fujimori, it did prevent many people from challenging the government and openly supporting the opposition. By creating new vertical links of patronage, these handouts also reinforced horizontal divisions among the popular sectors, hindering their collective organization (Cotler and Grompone 2000: 124–37; Degregori 2000: 91–97). For these reasons, it was exceedingly difficult to strengthen civil society and construct an organized alternative to neopopulist Fujimori, as opposition leaders recognized (interviews with Pennano 1996, Flores 1999, Pease 1999, Townsend 1999). And when the longstanding incumbent finally fell, the election of another neopopulist was difficult to avoid, as the advance of García and Toledo into the second round of the 2001 contest shows.

[35] While the middle class tends to be most strongly committed to democratic values, perceived threats from lower classes can induce it to support authoritarian solutions (Nun 1967: 98–118). But in the neoliberal era, such massive threats are unlikely, and the middle class is the mainstay of political liberalism and republicanism.

[36] In the 2000 contest, even Alejandro Toledo, who won surprisingly broad mass support by stressing his own *choledad* (nonwhite background), encountered particularly high disapproval among the most destitute, who disproportionately supported Fujimori; by contrast, the upper and middle class clearly preferred Toledo over the incumbent (Datum 2000: 1–2; Apoyo and IMASEN polls from mid-April 2000 available at <csd.queensu.ca/peru2000/polltrack/apr/poll1.shtml and poll2.shtml>).

By contrast, Argentina's more prosperous, better educated civil society gradually recovered from the economic crisis and social unrest of the 1980s and the radical shock therapies of the early 1990s (Peruzzotti 2001: 141–55). Contrary to Peru, its increasing vibrancy strengthened the party system, rather than producing additional personalistic leaders. Most importantly, civil society groups allied with small leftist parties and breakaway sectors of Peronism to form the Frente Grande, which soon turned into FREPASO. The new party coalition quickly built up some — albeit limited — organizational infrastructure.[37] And to achieve electoral success, it shifted its discourse from defending the victims of neoliberal adjustment — an unpromising, defensive strategy — to confronting Menem's neopopulist leadership with democratic, republican proposals, which were held in high esteem by the educated middle class (Novaro and Palermo 1998: 94–99). FREPASO therefore did well in elections, outpolling the UCR to place second in the presidential contest of 1995. The competitive challenge from FREPASO in turn helped to revive the old UCR, which had long based its appeal on republican, democratic principles. Thus, Argentina's more vigorous civil society provided fertile ground for the resurgent partisan opposition to neopopulist leadership.

For all these reasons, old and new democratic institutions ended up stifling populist leadership in Argentina, whereas Peru's longstanding personalistic leader trampled on democratic institutions for years; and when he finally fell, his anti-institutional tactics allowed another neopopulist to rise.

The de la Rúa Government: An Antipopulist Tied Down by Neoliberalism

The election of undynamic, drab de la Rúa, who benefited from widespread aversion to Menem's flashy, frivolous neopopulism, seemed to lead Argentine democracy into calmer waters. Many citizens hoped for greater respect for democratic and republican rules and principles. But the new president faced daunting political constraints. Besides Peronist majorities in the Senate, among provincial governors, and on the Supreme Court, his own coalition was fractious and even his UCR was internally divided. The president's notorious indecisiveness — a concomitant of his antipopulism — made it exceedingly difficult for him to deal

---

[37] A crucial institution-building step was that charismatic Frente Grande leader Carlos "Chacho" Álvarez accepted the narrow victory of José Octavio Bordón in FREPASO's internal primary for the presidential candidacy in 1995. Furthermore, Bordón, who sought to build up his own personalistic leadership, was forced out of FREPASO in early 1996 (Godio 1998: 139–41).

successfully with all these political challenges.[38] As a result, his presidency was so debilitated by early 2001 that proposals for a government of national unity and calls for new elections grew ever louder.

At the same time, de la Rúa faced a dire economic situation as Argentina has suffered from a stubborn recession since 1998. By raising the price of Argentina's exports, the strengthening of the U.S. dollar and the devaluation of January 1999 in Brazil, Argentina's main trading partner in the Common Market of the South (MERCOSUR), aggravated the problem. The currency peg, cornerstone of the convertibility plan, left Argentina defenseless against these external challenges. Upon taking office, de la Rúa initially responded with the boldness that is typical of presidents who face a domain of losses in the economic sphere. Taking advantage of the political strength resulting from his election victory, he enacted an important fiscal adjustment package. He also promoted a significant liberalization of labor laws (Corrales 2001: 12–13), which Menem had pursued with diminishing zeal and success during the 1990s. Displaying characteristic risk acceptance, de la Rúa's government pushed with all means — including the bribery of opposition politicians — for a change that was more neoliberal than Menem's reforms, although de la Rúa had promised a softening of neoliberalism in the campaign. This turnaround, and the questionable means with which it was pursued, harbored considerable political risks; in fact, de la Rúa's vice-president, FREPASO leader Carlos "Chacho" Álvarez, stepped down to protest the government's use of graft, deepening the rifts in the fragile governing coalition.

The labor reforms did little to ease the recession and the accompanying increase in unemployment, however. These problems, in turn, helped to erode de la Rúa's popularity with disturbing speed (see fig. 7.2). Greatly weakened, yet continuing to face a domain of losses, de la Rúa in March 2001 took the desperate step of appointing as his third economy minister none other than Domingo Cavallo, who had served in this position for five years under President Menem and who was anathema to many members of the UCR-FREPASO coalition. With this drastic step, de la Rúa took considerable political risks. Cavallo's nomination was bound to exacerbate tensions inside the ruling alliance and even inside de la Rúa's own UCR. After all, these forces had promised a softening of neoliberalism, yet the president handed over economic decision-making to the protagonist of neoliberalism in Argentina. De la Rúa's own authority as president was also likely to diminish further. Given Cavallo's power hunger, his appointment was widely seen as a partial abdication by the weak president. Thus, facing a domain of

---

[38] Confidential author conversation with a leading presidential adviser, April 2001.

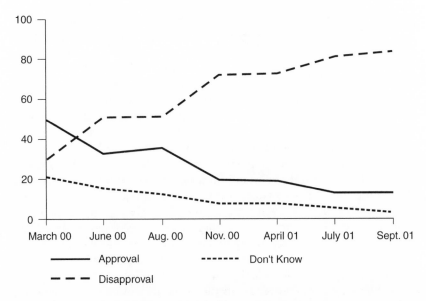

Figure 7.2. Popular Evaluation of de la Rúa's Presidential Performance, 2000–01. *Source:* Estudio Graciela Römer (2000; 2001).

losses, the new chief executive typically displayed risk acceptance in his economic policy decisions.

Observers speculated that Cavallo's appointment was the first step in a gradual loosening or a more decisive abandonment of the currency peg to the dollar, which most economists held responsible for the prolonged recession. Many of Argentina's exports had become too expensive to be internationally competitive, and cheap imports flooded the domestic market. In the long run, the parity with the U.S. dollar was therefore not sustainable, given especially the appreciation of the U.S. currency during the last few years and the devaluation enacted by Brazil. Cavallo indeed sought to soften the convertibility scheme by pegging the peso not only to the dollar, but also to the weakening euro. This limited and not very effective measure raised so much concern among international and domestic investors that the government shied away from further steps — not to speak of a whole-sale devaluation. These fears stemmed especially from the heavy indebtedness of Argentine firms and individuals in U.S. dollars; a substantial devaluation threatened to make many of these borrowers unable to service their obligations. Equally important, the convertibility plan was the symbol of Argentina's hard-won economic stability; popular support for this increasingly dysfunctional scheme therefore remained very high, despite the tight limitations that it imposed on the country's economic and social development. In November 2000, 67 percent of respondents in Greater Buenos Aires wanted the government to maintain the convertibility plan (Estudio Graciela Römer 2000b), and even in mid-2001 — after three years of recession — 64 percent of Argentines in major urban centers held this view.[39] Since the currency peg was unsustainable in the long run and caused considerable opportunity costs in the short run, advocating its preservation was not a fully rational choice; instead, this attitude arose from a prior-option bias at the mass level.

Given the strength of popular support for the convertibility scheme, weak de la Rúa could not enact a drastic change without undermining one of the last bases of trust in his government (cf. Estudio Graciela Römer 2001). In many ways, decision-makers were trapped by a self-fulfilling prophecy: Precisely because many Argentines believed the abandonment of currency parity would cause a catastrophe, such a step indeed threatened to bring about a meltdown as the panicked population would resort to individually rational but collectively disastrous defensive measures. The government therefore did not dare to give up the dollar peg. While de la Rúa initially made several economic policy choices that were surprisingly risk-acceptant for such a cautious, non-populist leader, he shied away from touching the mainstay of Argentina's economic stability. In this case, a prior-option bias at the mass level reinforced the personal aversion to run grave, potentially catastrophic risks displayed by a president who won office precisely because his cautious personality was the antithesis of Menem's neopopulist boldness.

The Recent Turmoil in Argentina and Duhalde's Efforts to Restore Stability

The de la Rúa government fell once the continuing deterioration in the economic situation made the populace lose trust in the sustainability of the currency peg. More and more people therefore withdrew their funds from the financial system to buy dollars. To prevent a run on the banks, Economy Minister Cavallo imposed tight limits on cash withdrawals. This defensive measure further depressed economic activity, squeezing especially the informal sector, which operates through cash transactions. Out of desperation, poor people soon started to loot stores, and politi-

---

[39] Gallup poll reported in "La convertibilidad, con un respaldo mayoritario," *La Nación* 2 August 2001 <www.lanacion.com.ar/01/08/02/dp−324531.asp>.

cal protests quickly spread as well. This more or less spontaneous out-burst of popular disaffection, to which the government responded with heavy-handed repression, destroyed the last remnants of de la Rúa's authority and legitimacy. As the powerful opposition, the Peronist Party, was unwilling to tarnish its political prospects by propping up the isolated and inept president, he resigned in December 2001.

The responsibility for forming a new government and leading the way out of the crisis fell to Argentina's strongest political force, the PJ, which had controlled both houses of Congress since the midterm elections of October 2001. But the Peronists were more divided than ever by rivalries among several presidential hopefuls. Therefore, they settled on the seemingly controllable governor of a small, poor province, Adolfo Rodríguez Saá, who was elected president to serve as a short-term caretaker until new elections could be held in March 2002. Rodríguez Saá, however, immediately sought to strengthen his precarious political position by promising significant economic and social benefits to the long-suffering population. As important economic sectors questioned the fiscal sustainability of these demagogic measures, and as powerful Peronist leaders worried that Rodríguez Saá intended to perpetuate himself in office beyond March 2002, support for his presidency collapsed and he had to step down before completing one week in office.

After the disastrous experience of the de la Rúa government had discredited the fractious UCR and FREPASO, the internecine infighting among Peronists in the midst of a grave national crisis threatened to cause profound popular revulsion against Argentina's political class. As continuing local revolts suggested the danger of large-scale unrest, politicians from all parties finally focused on their common interest in maintaining democratic stability. Therefore, a wide range of leaders supported a government of national unity led by old-timer Eduardo Duhalde, who had lost to de la Rúa in the 1999 presidential contest and who was now sworn in as chief executive for the remainder of de la Rúa's original term.[40] While selecting a predominantly Peronist cabinet, Duhalde also gave some posts to FREPASO and especially the UCR, thus cementing a broad base of partisan backing.

With the installation of Duhalde, Argentina's political class obtained another chance — perhaps its last chance — to restore political order and economic stability. To end the lengthy recession, allow the country to resume economic growth, and thus eventually alleviate the

---

[40] As a noteworthy indication of the democratic stability that Argentina has achieved, the military stayed completely on the sidelines during this period of unprecedented governmental instability.

serious social problems, Duhalde proceeded in the risk-acceptant fashion predicted by my prospect-theory interpretation. Rather than dollarizing Argentina's economy, as the Menem wing of the PJ as well as important domestic and international economists advocated (see, e.g., Sachs 2002), the new government immediately announced a significant devaluation of the currency and a general delinking of the economy from the U.S. dollar. Dollarization, which would have deepened the 1991 convertibility plan by substituting the domestic currency with the U.S. dollar, would have been less costly in the short run because the elimination of the peso would have boosted investor confidence, thus stimulating renewed growth. This economic effect could have stabilized the precarious political position of the Duhalde government, which continued to face frequent protests. But dollarization would have made it difficult for Argentina to enhance its international competitiveness and defend itself against future external shocks. Whereas dollarization offered immediate relief, yet limited future prospects, Duhalde's decision to end the convertibility scheme created high adjustment costs at a time of grave political problems but also held the uncertain promise of soon fueling more vigorous economic growth. Despite the serious political challenges he was facing, the new president typically responded to the crisis in a risk-acceptant fashion, choosing short-term pain for long-term gain over the less drastic strategy embodied in dollarization.

After making this bold strategic choice, however, the new government was confronting powerful cross-pressures. On the one hand, the international financial institutions, whose assistance Duhalde needs, have advocated a freely floating currency, that is, an unfettered devaluation, combined with extreme fiscal austerity. In their view, tough adjustment along these lines helped Mexico in 1995 and Brazil in 1999 to emerge from similar currency crises with surprising speed and resume fairly strong growth. Domestic experts, including new economy minister, Jorge Remes Lenicov, initially preferred the same purist strategy.[41] On the other hand, the failure of the convertibility plan and the experience of four years of recession have made many Argentines averse to a drastic intensification of market recipes; in fact, while not challenging the basic outlines of the market system, important sectors seem to advocate a move away from strict neoliberalism.[42] Duhalde himself, who had

[41] "Proponen una devaluación controlada del 30 por ciento," *La Nación* 3 January 2002 <www.lanacion.com.ar/02/01/03/de__363748.asp>.

[42] Unfortunately, new polls on Argentines' views about market principles are not available. Allegedly, the limits on cash withdrawals imposed by the government have made it impossible for pollsters to pay their interviewers; therefore, there has been a dearth of surveys in early 2002.

criticized Menem's zealous embrace of the market credo throughout the late 1990s, gave voice to these sentiments in his inaugural speech, promising to "end an exhausted [economic] model that has thrown into despair the enormous majority of our people."[43] Disturbed by these strong words, the IFIs and the international investment community feared that Argentina was experiencing a backlash against market reform, similar to the swing of the pendulum that affected Venezuela in 1993–94 and 1998–99 (see chapter 8). As a result, they redoubled their own pressures.

Exposed to these divergent tendencies and cross-pressures, the Duhalde government has so far pursued an unclear and halting course in defining the details of its bold devaluation strategy. In particular, the new administration did not let the peso float freely but temporarily instituted a dual exchange rate to forestall a resurgence of hyperinflation.[44] With this and other steps, it also sought to protect the numerous Argentines who had to service dollar-denominated loans and could therefore not bear a drastic drop in the value of the domestic currency. Giving in to antineoliberal sentiments, the president initially enacted some protectionist trade measures as well.

The international response to these deviations from strict free-market principles was hostile. The IFIs, in particular, feared a contagion effect throughout Latin America, given that Venezuela's populist president, Hugo Chávez, has also attacked "neoliberalism" and that the market-skeptical left seems to have a realistic opportunity to win the presidential elections of October 2002 in Brazil (see chapter 8). Furthermore, the IFIs remain convinced of the value of neoliberal recipes, which in their view worked in the cases of Mexico (1995) and Brazil (1999). For these reasons, the IMF, in particular, has pressed hard for more orthodox adjustment policies in Argentina. After gradually strengthening its hold on power, the Duhalde administration has signaled its willingness to comply, quickly scrapping the dual exchange-rate system, announcing the free flotation of the currency, and elaborating a very austere budget.[45] Urgently needed financial assistance from the IMF will make this new round of adjustment economically viable. Yet whether Duhalde can keep popular discontent under control and thus turn this painful recovery strategy politically viable remains to be seen.

[43] "'Este modelo arrasó con todo,'" La Nación 1 January 2002 <www.lanacion.com.ar/02/01/01/dp__363496.asp>.

[44] "Proponen una devaluación controlada del 30 por ciento," La Nación 3 January 2002 <www.lanacion.com.ar/02/01/03/de__363748.asp>.

[45] "Argentina Offers Economic Plan, Hoping to Sidestep Court," New York Times 4 February 2002: A6.

Conclusion

This chapter documents the advancing political sustainability of the new market model as well as the exhaustion and decline of neopopulist leadership in Argentina and Peru. As a result, the late 1990's saw the dissolution of the neoliberal/neopopulist combination that had been decisive for the initiation of market reform.

Although popular support for the orthodox version of neoliberalism imposed by Presidents Menem and Fujimori fell considerably with the renewed economic problems of the mid-1990's, calls for a radical change of the new development scheme failed to receive majority endorsement and diminished as the economy recovered again. By the end of the decade, acceptance of the basic outline of the market system, combined with calls for limited though significant modifications, predominated. The widespread reluctance to endorse a radical shift of course reflected the prior-option bias: The very costs of neoliberal adjustment constituted a "sunk investment" that induced many people to give the new market system a full chance and reject another round of fundamental change, which would entail further transitional costs and risks. Thus, the prior-option bias, which shielded the old development model against demands for neoliberal reform during the 1980's, now protected the new market model against its more radical detractors. As a result of this widespread support for basic continuity, Menem's and Fujimori's successors have not radically shifted the course of economic policy. In fact, de la Rúa maintained the convertibility scheme until the bitter end, despite the ever more obvious fetters it imposed on Argentina's economic development. And Duhalde quickly backed away from the limited deviations from neoliberal principles that he had enacted initially, under the impact of the final collapse of the Convertibility Plan.

The increased sustainability of the market system, combined with the strategic defeat of terrorism in Peru, made Menem's and Fujimori's neopopulist leadership ever more dispensable. In the mid-1990s, when economic stabilization and recovery together with new social programs placed a majority of the poulation in the domain of gains and therefore turned them risk-averse, the two chief executives, who had also assumed a more cautious, prudent posture, appeared as necessary for guaranteeing economic equilibrium and political tranquility, which were still precarious. But as the new economic problems after 1995 unleashed neither radical challenges to the market system nor serious political turmoil, and as most of the opposition kept moving toward the center, personalistic leaders turned from cornerstones of stability into threats to the new institutional order. Their tendency to transgress rules and norms, which had been decisive for the enactment of structural adjustment, now came to hinder the further institutionalization of the new development scheme and, especially, to impair the quality of democracy. Whereas the two presidents won convincing reelection victories in 1995, their desire even further to extend their power triggered strong resistance.

Since the opposition to neopopulism was more widespread in Argentina than Peru, the political fate of the two countries diverged at this point. The higher level of organization in Argentine society allowed for the rise of a powerful internal rival to Menem and the emergence of a partisan opposition that offered an organized, programmatic alternative to personalistic leadership. By contrast, the fragmentation and weakness of Peruvian society, combined with less advanced social modernization and more severe crises, prevented the formation of a well-organized opposition that could block Fujimori's para-constitutional efforts to engineer a second immediate reelection. Therefore, Peru's neopopulist leader managed to overpower democratic institutional constraints, whereas internal rivalry blocked and the democratic opposition defeated neopopulism in Argentina. And when grave internal conflicts brought down the personalistic Fujimori government, the weakness of civil society and the virtual absence of a party system did not allow the country to escape from neopopulist leadership, as shown by the election of Alejandro Toledo and, even more strikingly, the reemergence of Alan García, who had left office in 1990 in complete disrepute; this déja vu experience clearly demonstrates the troubled nature of Peruvian democracy.

By contrast, even the unprecedented period of governmental instability in Argentina in late 2001 did not allow for the resurgence of neopopulism. Instead, the country's better organized political class quickly regrouped, supporting a government of national unity led by old-timer Duhalde. In sum, democratic sustainability has been reaffirmed in Argentina, while Peru's more precarious democracy suffered a creeping involution in the late 1990s (Cameron 1997; McClintock 1998; Levitsky 1999), from which it has only partly recovered.

CHAPTER EIGHT

THE FITFUL COURSE OF MARKET REFORM IN BRAZIL AND VENEZUELA

The impeachment of presidents Collor and Pérez constituted an important setback for market reform. Their regular successors, Itamar Franco in Brazil (1992–94) and Rafael Caldera in Venezuela (1994–99),[1] had long criticized "neoliberalism." In addition, Collor's and Pérez's striking political failure demonstrated the tremendous risks involved in pursuing neoliberal programs against strong opposition. After taking office, Franco and Caldera therefore slowed down or reversed Collor's and Pérez's reform agenda and adopted more nationalist, state-interventionist measures. Learning from prior experiences thus caused a swing-of-the-pendulum effect, which was particularly pronounced in Venezuela.

Since these policy changes failed to get Brazil's and Venezuela's economic problems under control and since inflation rose steadily to ever higher levels, Franco and Caldera eventually had to change course again. Their determination to take bold market-oriented measures was hampered, however, by their earlier criticism of "neoliberalism." The prior-option bias limited their willingness to accept important elements of the neoliberal agenda. Their economic aides, who pushed for more drastic policy shifts, therefore saw the presidents themselves as a crucial obstacle to the adoption of resolute stabilization plans and profound structural reforms.

In Brazil, however, Fernando Henrique Cardoso, who governed the country like a prime minister during his tenure as finance minister (May 1993–April 1994) and who was in late 1994 elected president (1995–present), gave market reform a new impulse. The unstoppable advance of inflation in 1993 and early 1994 put both the government and many common people into the domain of losses and thus induced Cardoso to take the political risk of resuming the neoliberal agenda. Also, President Collor's initial popularity had shown that stopping exploding price rises could give the reform initiator tremendous popular support. Cardoso

---

[1] Interim President Ramón Velásquez in Venezuela, who served out the remaining months of Pérez's term, managed to enact some important measures that Congress had denied Pérez, such as a value-added tax, but Caldera quickly reversed or distorted these changes.

therefore turned his innovative stabilization plan into the mainstay of his presidential campaign, and he used his impressive first-round election victory to push for structural changes.

But Collor's political failure also showed the political risks of employing intransigent neopopulist tactics and an "imperial" decision-making style that hindered consultation with important socioeconomic groups. Learning from Collor's debacle, Cardoso has preferred negotiation and transaction. This caution has reduced the danger of a political backlash and reversal of reform but has also hampered the advance of controversial projects, especially administrative and social security reform. As Cardoso's fickle supporters have extracted ample patronage and sought to minimize losses, Brazil's public deficit and internal debt grew considerably. Contagion from the Asian financial crisis therefore pushed the country ever more deeply into economic trouble, which was contained, however, through a painful new round of adjustment in 1999.

In the absence of an exceptionally profound crisis, like that which plagued Peru in the late 1980s, the institutional fragmentation prevailing in Brazil and the resulting dispersal of political power have obstructed a decisive turnaround in the country's economic fate. As has been common for decades, muddling through has remained the modus operandi in the country.[2]

In Venezuela, renewed market reform advanced even more haltingly. In fact, the increase in petroleum prices in late 1996 further eroded the government's fickle determination to pursue budget austerity and structural reform. The sudden bonanza put many government officials — especially President Caldera and his political aides — into the domain of gains. They therefore shunned the political risks involved in pushing hard for the neoliberal agenda. As adjustment measures turned lax and public spending increased, Venezuela was ill prepared for the drastic fall of petroleum prices in early 1998, which threatened to produce an economic collapse.

This economic deterioration, barely contained by desperate budget cuts, put many citizens into the domain of losses and further exacerbated popular disaffection with the established political class. As a result, independent candidates — initially former beauty queen Irene Sáez,

---

[2] Thus, whereas neopopulist leadership can be unusually effective for advancing neoliberalism, as the experiences of Menem and Fujimori show, it is politically viable only when a profound conjunctural and structural crisis afflicts a country. Applied in less dire situations, it runs great risks of failing and thereby hindering the progress of market reform, as Collor's and Pérez's fall suggests. Under those conditions, only a less risky strategy of accommodation is promising, which pushes less hard for market reform but avoids a backlash.

and later coup monger Hugo Chávez—were the leaders in vote intentions for the presidential elections of December 1998, which Chávez won in a landslide. After taking office in February 1999, he pursued mixed economic policies, suspending and reversing some market reforms while tightening budget austerity and bringing inflation down. With the bonanza caused by skyrocketing petroleum prices, the new government soon engaged in higher spending yet eased its initial efforts to roll back neoliberalism. Which economic direction the Chávez administration will take in the long term remains unclear.

The government's unclear course has produced major costs. By causing considerable uncertainty among domestic and foreign investors, it has kept economic growth meager and thus maintained unemployment and poverty at high levels. As Chávez has failed to fulfill the exalted hopes for socioeconomic improvements that his followers had placed on him, his popularity—the main base of his neopopulist leadership—eroded substantially during 2001. The president's weakening political position has encouraged his opponents in organized civil society, especially among business, trade unions, and the Catholic church, to criticize his radical rhetoric more forcefully and increasingly resort to public protest. As discontent inside the armed forces has spread as well, the political fate of the Chávez government has become quite uncertain, as the coup attempt of April 2002 indicates.

The Slowdown or Reversal of Neoliberal Reform

The regular presidents who took office after the impeachment of Fernando Collor and Carlos Andrés Pérez learned from these political disasters and slowed down or reversed market reform. Both Itamar Franco and Rafael Caldera had long criticized their predecessors' strong commitment to neoliberalism, and Caldera had openly opposed market reform in his presidential campaign of 1993.

In Brazil, Franco—as Collor's vice-president—had remained true to his nationalist leanings, distanced himself from the push for market reform, and openly broken with Collor over the privatization of the steel industry in his home state and political base, Minas Gerais (Montero 1998: 50). Thus, Franco was acceptable to Collor's opponents, who led the impeachment drive. During the months in which Brazil's political class negotiated Collor's removal from office, Franco also tried to win the acquiescence of some Collor supporters, especially among Brazil's powerful business class. Wary of Franco's commitment to state-interventionism (Kingstone 1999: 190), these sectors long backed Collor. To make his own accession to the presidency politically viable, Franco reassured economic and political elites that he would not drastically change course. Also, the initially widespread support for Collor had demonstrated that minimal economic stability was politically indispensable. In addition, the Brazilian economy was beginning to recover from the long recession caused by Collor's tough stabilization measures. Prospects for growth — despite continuing high inflation — put the Franco administration in a mixed domain, inducing it to proceed in a risk-averse way. The new president therefore refrained from deviating drastically from his predecessor's economic policy and especially from decreeing a reversal of neoliberal reform.

For these reasons, President Franco slowed down market reform considerably but did not turn the clock back. The government did not initiate new sales of public enterprises but completed privatization deals prepared under Collor to mitigate pressing fiscal problems. And while it further raised the tax burden, through both new laws and a crackdown on tax evasion (Varsano et al. 1998: 39; interview with Bogéa 1994), it initially avoided budget cuts. On the contrary, Franco drastically raised public-sector salaries, which Collor had compressed substantially (MARE 1996: 25, 40). As a result, increasing tax revenues did little to alleviate Brazil's fiscal crisis. In contrast to these deviations from Collor's neoliberal policies, Franco maintained the schedule of import tariff reductions, through which his predecessor had begun to open the Brazilian economy to foreign competition.

In Venezuela, the backlash against neoliberalism was much more pronounced, although it did not start immediately. The interim government of Ramón Velásquez, who served out the last eight months of President Pérez's term, took advantage of the broad support created by the impeachment to pass the long-delayed tax reform, which created an efficient value-added tax. Velásquez's main goal was not, however, to speed up market reform, but to maintain a minimum of economic stability until the inauguration of the next regular president.

The presidential campaign of 1993 saw an unusual degree of party fragmentation and candidate proliferation for Venezuela. By putting many citizens into the domain of losses, persistent economic problems and the social unrest and political turmoil of the preceding years had further discredited established parties and boosted the fortunes of new forces and self-proclaimed outsiders. The trade-unionist Causa R (Radical Cause), which outside its regional home base had been a leftist splinter party in the 1980s, suddenly turned into a major vote-getter, garnering 20.80 percent of the final tally (Landman 1995: 101).

The eventual winner with 30.45 percent of the vote, Rafael Caldera, depicted himself as an independent and ran as the candidate of a heterogeneous, amorphous agglomeration of groupings and parties. Though a founder of COPEI and the first president hailing from the party (1969–74), Caldera broke with COPEI, which offered critical support to President Pérez, especially in the turbulent year 1992. Whereas the established COPEI leadership put the defense of democracy above partisan interests, Caldera gave a famous speech after the coup attempt of 4 February 1992 in which he seemed to make excuses for the military uprising (Caldera 1992). This discourse suddenly transformed Caldera, one of the mainstays of the post-1958 democracy, into an "outsider" and launched his presidential candidacy. During the campaign, the ex-president relentlessly attacked the other members of Venezuela's political class and the established parties and sharply criticized the neoliberal program initiated by the Pérez administration (Caldera 1993: 13, 39, 44).

By contrast to these "new" forces, AD and COPEI, which had received a combined 85–93 percent of the presidential vote in the 1970s and 1980s, garnered a mere 47.7 percent in 1993. COPEI, which in a stable two-party system would have had an excellent chance to return to power, was weakened by Caldera's exit and by tensions between the entrenched party apparatus and rising regional politicians. Supporting the general march toward market reform, it gained a disappointing 23.5 percent of the vote. Given how tainted AD was by the political debacle of Pérez's presidency, its second-place finish with 24.2 percent was a surprise—though a far cry from the party's earlier electoral dominance.

True to his campaign promises, President Caldera sharply deviated from orthodox economic policies and reversed important market reforms. His most drastic moves were triggered by a new problem that erupted shortly before he took office, namely, the virtual collapse of Venezuela's banking system (interview with Egaña 2000). The beneficiaries of radical deregulation under the Pérez government, many banks had engaged in imprudent, speculative, even fraudulent lending practices. As a result, the incipient recession of 1993 caused tremendous losses. When important credit institutions faced bankruptcy in early 1994, trust in the whole financial system evaporated. The resulting chain reaction forced the closure of seventeen banks that controlled two-thirds of all financial assets. To forestall a complete collapse, the new government enacted a US$ 7.1 billion bail-out package—equivalent to 12 percent of GDP (Nóbrega and Ortega 1996: 184)—that ripped a huge hole in the public budget.

These enormous problems, which destroyed any semblance of economic stability, put the new president clearly in the domain of losses. In a context of lingering sociopolitical discontent, the new economic challenge posed grave political dangers. The Caldera administration therefore acted in a highly risk-acceptant way and took bold and forceful policies that were arguably suboptimal and had lower expected value than more prudent alternatives.

The Caldera government adopted a series of draconian yet confused measures that sharply diverged from neoliberal precepts. For instance, it engaged in uncontrolled monetary emission, which drove up inflation. It hastily devalued the currency, hurting especially poorer sectors whom the new president had promised to benefit. And to stem capital flight, Caldera unprecedentedly imposed comprehensive foreign exchange controls. This drastic intervention in the market reached its main purpose only for a short period of time. Capital flight soon resumed, and the cumbersome controls provided ample opportunities for rent-seeking and corruption, which Caldera had pledged to root out (Nóbrega and Ortega 1996: 186–92; Palma 1999: 100–18).

To combat recession and inflation, the Caldera administration announced a number of stabilization plans whose theoretical inspiration diverged from the preceding market reform agenda. Whereas President Pérez had recruited many aides from the neoliberal think tank Instituto de Estudios Superiores de Administración (IESA), many of President Caldera's economic advisers in 1994 and 1995 hailed from the leftist Centro de Estudios del Desarrollo (CENDES). Claiming that neoliberalism had failed in Venezuela, these experts advocated a heterodox approach to Venezuela's deep economic crisis (CORDIPLAN 1994: 8–10, 37–38, 73, 88; CORDIPLAN 1995: 19–22, 48–49, 72, 77; Ministerio de Hacienda 1995: 2–5). They assumed that negotiations between the government and major social organizations could over time bring down inflation while stimulating production and employment and furthering social equity (CORDIPLAN 1994: 3, 43, 47–52, 88–95; CORDIPLAN 1995: 43–53, 72–79, 87–90, 99–100, 246–48, 256–59; *Compromiso Antiinflacionario* 1995: 5–8). Rejecting IMF conditionality, they hoped that Venezuela's oil wealth would provide the necessary resources for overcoming the fiscal crisis of the state (Nóbrega and Ortega 1996: 179–83). Thus, social learning, triggered by the perceived failure of neoliberalism, caused a clear swing of the pendulum in Venezuela.

Caldera crowned his rejection of neoliberalism and provided legal backing for other draconian measures — especially the foreign exchange controls — by suspending the guarantees of economic liberty enshrined in the 1961 constitution. These principles had been shelved for decades to allow for heavy-handed state interventionism. As part of his "Great Turnaround," Pérez had lifted this suspension, but Caldera renewed it by decree in July 1994. A severe constitutional crisis ensued. The congressional opposition, led by AD, sought to overturn Caldera's decree, and the president — taking advantage of his high popularity — threatened to call a plebiscite. Narrowly avoiding a dangerous showdown, the president and AD stalwarts cut a deal that guaranteed Caldera conditional support from the major opposition party in exchange for some policy influence and, especially, plentiful patronage (interview with Celli 1998; also interview with Alayón 1998). This pact gave the government a minimal base of parliamentary sustenance and ended the rumors that Caldera would follow Fujimori's example, close Congress, and rule by decree.

Since many Venezuelans also saw themselves in the domain of losses, a majority offered strong support for President Caldera's turn away from neoliberalism and his imposition of controls. For instance, 68–76 percent of respondents endorsed different aspects of the exchange controls in August 1994 (Consultores 21 1994a: 34, 38), and 66 percent qualified the government as very good, good, or okay tending toward good (Consultores 21 1994b: 91). At that point, "56% said they were as badly off or worse-off than [one year earlier] and 43% said they were better-off or equally well-off as before" (Consultores 21 1994b: 74). Thus, in line with what prospect theory would expect, perceptions of recent losses, which early in Caldera's government were probably attributed largely to his predecessors, led a clear majority of the population to approve of the new president's drastic—and in this case, highly interventionist—countermeasures. As a result, presidential popularity also ran at reasonably high levels (fig. 8.1)

In Venezuela, neoliberalism thus suffered a much more severe setback than in Brazil. Whereas President Franco slowed down the further advance of market reform, President Caldera reversed important neoliberal measures, imposed draconian controls on the market, and adopted a heterodox approach to stabilization. What accounts for this difference? First, neoliberalism had never proven popular in Venezuela, as shown by the massive rejection of Pérez's "Great Turnaround," compared with the outpouring of support for the first Collor Plan. As shown in chapter 5, this difference in turn reflects the much greater depth of the problems plaguing Brazil, especially hyperinflation. Second, Venezuela's fabulous oil wealth seemed to make a painful restructuring of the development model even less urgent than in Brazil. Since a magic solution to economic problems—namely, a sudden rise of the petroleum price—appeared to be possible, it was more difficult for a profound sense of crisis to take hold. Thus, the lower severity of Venezuela's crisis is crucial for explaining the stronger backlash against drastic market reform in the country.

Worsening Economic Problems

The first few economic teams appointed by presidents Franco and Caldera all failed to stem the further deterioration of the economy. Both

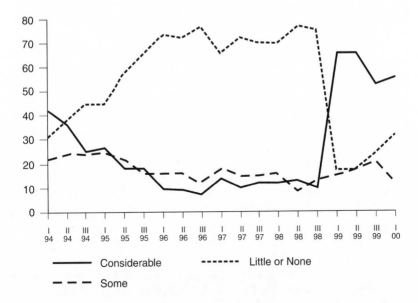

Figure 8.1. Trust in President's "Capacity to Manage the Country," Venezuela, 1994–2000. *Source:* Datos (2000: 21). *Note:* Time period is Quatrimester. President Caldera governed from I 94 to III 98; Hugo Chávez became president in early 1999.

Brazil and Venezuela saw a succession of economic plans and programs that did not manage to achieve stabilization. In Brazil, President Franco appointed four different finance ministers during his first eight months in office. In Venezuela, turnover in the Planning Ministry, which often spearheads governmental initiatives in the area of economics, was only slightly lower.

In addition to technical problems, such as the vague nature of the stabilization plans advanced by the Caldera administration, lack of confidence accounts for these recurring failures. The commitment of presidents Franco and Caldera to impose the unavoidable costs of stabilization and stand up to opposition was widely seen as questionable. For instance, the two administrations did little to fulfill their promises of budget austerity. And the efforts of both governments to stimulate growth put determined stabilization on the back burner. Political convenience and ideological divergence from neoliberalism thus prompted economic policies that obstructed the attainment of economic equilibrium.

As a result of these failures, important economic problems kept worsening in both countries. Certainly, Brazil experienced renewed growth fueled by more expansionary budget practices, which ended the recession prevailing under most of the Collor administration. But inflation continued to rise. While remaining at 22–25 percent per month in 1992 — despite the political turmoil caused by Collor's impeachment — it resumed its irresistible upward trend in 1993, reaching 33.9 percent in August of that year (Xavier and Costa 1993: 27). Despite widespread indexation, such accelerating price increases created losses for important actors, including the state, whose tax revenues were eroded by the Olivera-Tanzi effect. Poorer sectors who lacked access to indexed financial accounts and therefore used cash were especially hard hit. Demands for determined stabilization efforts therefore grew louder (see, e.g., Xavier and Costa 1993). Since many Brazilians assumed that, in response, the government might impose new shock plans, increasing inflation also created considerable economic uncertainty, which hindered investment and thus limited future growth. Thus, the need to stop further price increases became ever more obvious.

Venezuela's economic deterioration was even more severe (Palma 1999: 118–121). After sliding into a recession in 1993, the economy contracted by another 3.3 percent in 1994. And while inflation ran at much lower levels than in Brazil, reaching 71 percent per year in 1994, the absence of widespread indexation made the accelerating price rises costly for many sectors, especially poorer groupings. By failing to achieve stability, the heterodox efforts of the Caldera government, which were designed to protect the poor from the costs of adjustment, exposed precisely those groups to the substantial costs of nonadjustment. As a result, poverty spread so as to afflict up to 80 percent of the population. As inflation resumed its upward trend in late 1995 and reached 8.1 percent per month in January 1996, the social and political situation seemed to reach the limits of sustainability (interviews with Petkoff 1998 and Rojas Parra 1998).

The Resumption of Market Reform

The worsening economic problems, which threatened to push Brazil again into hyperinflation and to unleash renewed social and political turmoil in Venezuela, showed that the efforts to slow down or reverse the advance of neoliberalism were unsuccessful. Learning from this experience suggested another change of course, in this case, a resumption of market reform. The economic deterioration put the Franco and Caldera governments ever more clearly into the domain of losses, a perception that normally induces the enactment of drastic adjustment measures. Having appointed and dismissed three finance ministers during his first eight months in office, Franco seemed to be at wit's end by mid-1993 (Dimenstein and Souza 1994: 33). And in Venezuela, warnings of a social explosion in response to the deepening problems and calls for Caldera to step down became more frequent from late 1995 onward. Presiding over fragile democracies in which unsuccessful presidents had recently suffered impeachment, Franco and Caldera had reason to fear for their own political survival. Thus, the two presidents were clearly facing a domain of losses.

The tendency toward risk-seeking that such perceptions of negative prospects normally engender was mitigated by the prior-option bias, however. Both Franco and Caldera had criticized neoliberalism, and the Venezuelan president had taken important measures that diverged radically from neoliberal principles (Urbaneja 1996: 412). On record for their skepticism or hostility toward market reform, Franco and Caldera hesitated to shift course. In fact, Caldera and his inner political circle long refused to make such an embarrassing about-face (interviews with Alayón 1996, 1998). The large-scale riots that erupted in response to President Pérez's initiation of orthodox adjustment in 1989 and the persistent political problems that ensued heightened Caldera's obstinacy. Thus, even under the pressure of worsening economic problems, the prior-option bias prevented presidents Franco and Caldera from shifting course completely and from embracing the policy approach that they had attacked in the recent past.[3]

When the two presidents finally agreed to adopt a market-oriented agenda, they therefore did not appoint die-hard neoliberals. Both Finance Minister Fernando Henrique Cardoso in Brazil and Planning Minister Teodoro Petkoff in Venezuela, who took office in May 1993 and March 1996, respectively, had a leftist background and had kept their distance from neoliberal presidents Collor and Pérez (see, e.g., Cardoso 1994: 290–96). Although they had since come to accept market principles, their founding membership in the PSDB and the Movimiento al Socialismo (MAS), respectively, suggested to presidents Franco and Caldera that they would limit the impending about-face and provide a political cover for it.

Indeed, while having to grant these recently converted market reformers considerable latitude to combat increasing inflation effectively, presidents Franco and Caldera maintained their skepticism toward orthodox stabilization. Cardoso and Petkoff therefore remained in a precarious position. They could not count on full presidential support for the new adjustment plans and always had to fear that Franco's and

---

[3] Petkoff (interview 1998) mentioned that even after deciding to resume market reform, Caldera kept complaining about having to deviate from his earlier promises (as announced in Caldera 1993).

Caldera's antiliberal leanings would make the chief executives insist on measures that would undermine stabilization. For instance, Franco frequently pressed for wage concessions and lower interest rates (Dimenstein and Souza 1994: 13, 91, 159, 203–5, 228). Thus, the new economic teams had to fight a two-front battle: They needed both to win support in society and to protect themselves against being undermined from within the government.

As a result of their fragile political sustenance, the new economic teams had to concentrate on stabilization and postpone structural reform. This decision was especially consequential in Brazil, where the constitutional revision of late 1993 and early 1994 lowered the quorum and simplified the procedure for approving amendments. Minister Cardoso and his allies initially tried to take advantage of this golden opportunity to eliminate from the 1988 charter a host of rules that obstructed market reform. For this purpose, they prepared numerous proposals on important issues such as economic deregulation, tax simplification, and social security reform. Unwilling to convert to "neoliberalism," however, President Franco refused to push for this ambitious program and submit it as the administration's official project for the constitutional revision. Minister Cardoso and his allies in the government therefore advanced their proposals via sympathetic members of Congress, such as Cardoso's substitute in the Senate (Blay 1993).

The leftist opposition, however, offered strong resistance and used systematic obstruction. Furthermore, the government's official supporters in Congress were reluctant to pass unpopular reforms before the upcoming elections of late 1994. Minister Cardoso himself did not want to undermine his chances for becoming the government's presidential candidate and for winning the eventual contest (Dimenstein and Souza 1994: 124). He therefore made little effort to advance his structural reform agenda and let the opportunity opened up by the constitutional revision pass unused. Instead, Cardoso concentrated all of his energies on pushing for his stabilization plan, which could yield more immediate political payoffs.

A New Round of Determined Stabilization Measures

Given the dangerous economic deterioration and the political limitations set by presidents Franco and Caldera, the market-oriented teams in Brazil and Venezuela focused first and foremost on economic stabilization. They hoped that success in lowering inflation would boost their political clout and, as a result, allow them to push for a restructuring of the development model later on. These hopes prevailed especially in

Brazil, where Minister Cardoso was a precandidate for the upcoming presidential election of October 1994.

In two important ways, Collor's and Pérez's earlier reform efforts facilitated the task of the economic teams led by ministers Cardoso and Petkoff. First, these adjustment programs provided crucial learning experiences. The massive popular support for the first Collor Plan showed Cardoso that determined stabilization could have enormous political payoffs for his presidential candidacy.[4] Petkoff, by contrast, learned from the popular rejection of Pérez's shock program that in order to make his own plan politically viable, he needed to win over public opinion through extensive communication efforts and to prevent losses for strategic sectors by instituting targeted social measures (interviews with Petkoff 1998, Rojas Parra 1998, Alayón 1996).

Second, some of the neoliberal measures enacted or proposed by presidents Collor and Pérez made successful stabilization easier. Most importantly, the substantial lowering of trade barriers allowed ministers Cardoso and Petkoff to use the threat of cheap foreign imports to force domestic prices down (Oliveira 1996: 77–80, 112). Also, trade liberalization had induced businesses to modernize and become more productive — or to close. Thus, since a good part of the costs of adjustment had already been paid, resistance to renewed market reform was weaker.

Brazil

By late 1993, Minister Cardoso and his team clearly saw themselves in the domain of losses (interview with Franco 1996). Inflation stubbornly kept rising as his first stabilization proposal, which focused on fiscal adjustment (Ministério da Fazenda 1993), faced considerable resistance and failed to restore economic equilibrium. The minister and his aides therefore realized that a more comprehensive effort was indispensable. They considered three main options (interview with Oliveira 1996; similarly Bacha 1998: 15–16; see also Dimenstein and Souza 1994: 97, 203–4), namely, a gradual approach designed to muddle through until the end of President Franco's term; a drastic approach, such as a shock program or a rigid dollarization à la Argentina; and a "gradual shock" (interview with Franco 1996) designed to enact some crucial elements of the drastic option, yet in a sequenced and flexible fashion. The economic team's insistence on maintaining a margin of maneuver and the

---

[4] Interviews with Franco (1996) and Oliveira (1996); Oliveira (1996: 117–18, also 106, 115, 181). Cardoso's team also learned from the failure of the Cruzado Plan of 1986, discarding a price freeze and pursuing strict fiscal adjustment (Oliveira 1996: 36–38, 106–10; interview with Veras 1996).

widespread rejection of shock programs in Brazilian society made Cardoso's team reject dollarization and other radical measures as economically unpromising or politically infeasible (Cardoso 1995: 58–60; interviews with Franco 1996 and Oliveira 1996). Thus, learning from prior experiences restricted the available choices.

In line with my prospect-theory interpretation, Cardoso and his aides refused to muddle through and chose the more daring approach among the feasible options.[5] Thus, the perception that Brazil was in a domain of losses once again triggered risk acceptance in economic policy-making. This boldness also shaped Cardoso's political calculations. A "gradual shock" promised to end accelerating inflation and thus boost the minister's chances in the upcoming presidential election of late 1994. But it also threatened to unleash a disaster, especially hyperinflation, which would have destroyed Cardoso's prominent standing in Brazil's political class. By contrast, muddling through probably did not offer the big prize of winning the presidency, but it also avoided the danger of a catastrophe, thus preserving Cardoso's reputation.[6] Seeing himself in the domain of losses, Cardoso typically shunned safety and pursued the riskier course of action.

In his sequential approach, Cardoso—learning from the failures of earlier adjustment efforts—pushed first for an alleviation of the state's fiscal problems.[7] After managing to enact some budget cuts in late 1993 (Bacha 1998: 13–14), the minister used the constitutional revision to propose a fiscal package that permitted the federal government to retain part of the revenues transferred by the 1988 charter to states and municipalities. To enhance its political acceptability, the government misnamed this initiative the Emergency Social Fund—Fundo Social de Emergência (Cardoso 1996: 4). But given the upcoming elections of 1994, in which patronage resources were bound to play a crucial role, this proposal faced strong resistance from congressional politicians and state governors. Starting the adjustment plan with a measure that imposed only costs without promising any immediate benefits thus was a politically risky endeavor. Congressional obstruction, exacerbated by

[5] Cardoso (1996: 4). Interestingly, the IMF did not support this decision, denouncing the initial fiscal adjustment as insufficient and precarious because the "Emergency Social Fund" would expire in December 1995 (Bacha 1998: 11, 17–18; Cardoso 1996: 5).

[6] President Sarney's last finance minister, Maílson da Nóbrega, who pursued such muddling through with limited economic success in most of 1988 and 1989, has nevertheless retained a prominent place among economic commentators and business consultants.

[7] Cardoso (1995: 54–58). Important leaders of the political wing of Cardoso's PSDB resisted this priority to avoid the political costs and risks of fiscal adjustment (interview with Franco 1996; Dimenstein and Souza 1994: 119–21). On Cardoso's political strategy in pushing for economic stabilization and reform, see Gómez (1998).

political rivalries among different precandidates for the presidential election, could well have nipped Cardoso's gradual shock in the bud.

The impending presidential contest also gave Cardoso a strong argument to garner support, however. In early 1994, Luís Inácio Lula da Silva from the socialist PT was the clear leader in vote intentions with up to 42 percent of preferences (Datafolha data presented in Almeida 1996: 39). Further economic deterioration would have ensured his victory. This threat induced the centrist and rightist politicians aligned with the government to guarantee a minimum of economic stability (Dimenstein and Souza 1994: 129–30). Therefore, they begrudgingly — and in exchange for plentiful patronage — passed a revised version of Cardoso's fiscal adjustment proposal (Afonso, Carvalho, and Spíndola 1995).

The next step in the stabilization plan was to expunge the backward-looking component of indexation, which kept inflation from ever falling. For this purpose, Cardoso's team dramatically accelerated indexation by creating a new indicator for expressing economic value — a proto-currency called Unidade Real de Valores (URV) — which was readjusted daily and pegged to the dollar. By greatly reducing the institutionalized memory of inflation, the URV's introduction prepared for the restoration of stability. While prices expressed in the old currency could increase daily, prices expressed in URV would remain stable. At the same time, the URV served to eliminate the distortions in the relative price system that indexation had created. These distortions resulted from the fact that different prices were readjusted at different moments. At any point in time, some prices were thus outdated, whereas others had just been raised. These distortions were bound to undermine any sudden stabilization effort because sectors with outdated prices would seek to recuperate their relative loss, thus triggering a new spiral of inflation. Since it was difficult for the government to define an acceptable solution for this problem (as the problems experienced under the Cruzado Plan of 1986 had shown — see chapter 4 above), Cardoso's economic team used mostly market mechanisms and government-mediated negotiations among societal sectors to even out these inflation-fueling distortions. Specifically, the government urged economic actors to adopt the URV, which minimized lags in readjustment and thus ended distortions in the relative price system (Bacha 1998: 20–21; Cardoso 1995: 58–60; Franco 1995: 34–49; Oliveira 1996: 43–48).

While crucial for preparing the eventual return to stability, however, the very acceleration of readjustments also held tremendous risks. Precisely by minimizing the inertial element of inflation, which perpetuated price rises but also limited their further increase, the introduction of virtually instantaneous readjustments could have triggered uncontrolled hyperinflation (interviews with Franco 1996 and Veras 1996; Cardoso 1995: 59; 1996: 3; Bacha 1998: 24; Oliveira 1996: 46, 49–52). This move practically eliminated the inertia that could keep price increases in check and discourage their explosion. In fact, "several economies tried this system before . . . but . . . it was a disaster since inflation accelerated during the transition" (Silva and Andrade 1996: 443). These dangers were exacerbated by Cardoso's failure to achieve a permanent fiscal adjustment, which he had depicted as a necessary precondition for the further steps in the stabilization effort (Cardoso 1995). Thus, Cardoso and his team clearly made a risky choice.

To prevent catastrophic hyperinflation, the government used a number of safeguards and considerable arm-twisting to restrain the price increases adopted by powerful business sectors (interviews with Franco 1996, Oliveira 1996, Veras 1996; Bacha 1998: 27–31). It also managed to win the acquiescence of trade unions and persuade other government ministers and Congress to stipulate moderate wage adjustments by law. In these ways, Cardoso's team succeeded in passing the danger zone of immediate indexation unharmed.

After economic agents translated their prices into URV and thus created a stable relative price system, the government ended the daily readjustments and transformed the URV on 1 July 1994 into a new currency, the *real*. The U.S. dollar served as a nominal anchor for the stabilization program. To minimize inflation in the new currency, the government also reduced trade barriers, thus disciplining domestic business with the threat of cheap foreign imports (interview with Veras 1996). Inflation in fact dropped quickly, falling from 47.7 percent in June to 6.1 percent in July and 2.8 percent in August (Ministério da Fazenda 1996: 3).

As prospect theory would expect, a population afflicted by incipient hyperinflation offered massive support for the decisive stage of Minister Cardoso's gradual shock. In late 1993 and early 1994, many Brazilians saw themselves in the domain of losses. For instance, a whopping 91 percent of respondents rated Brazil's economic situation as fairly poor or very poor in August 1993 (USIA 1993: 7), and 48 percent were pessimistic or very pessimistic about Brazil's future in September (IBOPE 1993). And in December, 55.7 percent rated the country's economic situation as bad and thought it would stay that way or get even worse in 1994 (Arruda 1994). Brazilians perceived rising inflation as the single gravest problem confronting them (USIA 1993: 8, 10; CESOP 1994: 15). Facing negative prospects, they had long demanded bold measures to stop the economic deterioration (Xavier and Costa 1993). Since Cardoso's step-wise adjustment plan appeared as hesitant and indecisive, it received limited popular endorsement during the first half of 1994 (CESOP 1994: 12–13; Figueiredo 1994: 76). Only when Cardoso's team directly attacked the main problem plaguing the population by introducing the *real* did a majority of people offer strong support (Almeida 1996: 94–110).

The success of the Real Plan in lowering inflation, which quickly transferred many people from the domain of losses into the domain of gains (Almeida 1996: 94–100), also boosted popular support for its initiator, the government's candidate for president. In the weeks following the introduction of the new currency, Cardoso displaced "Lula" as the leader in vote intentions. Whereas the former finance minister had trailed by 19 percent to 41 percent in mid-June, he pulled almost even in late July (29 percent to 32 percent) and established his clear leadership (41 percent to 24 percent) in mid-August (Almeida 1996: 39 and chap. 8; Mendes and Venturi 1994). Risk aversion among the large number of people who had suddenly entered the domain of gains (Almeida 1996: 107–8; Figueiredo 1994: 79–80) indeed gave the government's candidate—the guarantor of continuity—a first-round victory with an impressive 54.3 percent of the vote. By contrast, socialist Lula, who criticized the shortcomings of the stabilization plan and promised additional improvements—a risky option—garnered only 27 percent,[8] a drastic drop from the 42 percent of vote intentions he had received when many Brazilians still saw themselves in the domain of losses.

Venezuela

By contrast to Brazil's innovative Real Plan, Venezuela's new economic team applied conventional recipes because domestic technocratic capacity was less developed and the IMF had therefore much stronger influence.[9] To confront the worsening economic difficulties,[10] the Caldera government decreed, essentially, a tougher version of the stabilization program that Carlos Andrés Pérez had initiated in February 1989. Specifically, it chose the most drastic option among the alternatives considered in early 1996 (interviews with Petkoff 1998 and Alayón 1998). This new plan, called Agenda Venezuela, was centered around eco-

[8] Lula based his campaign strategy on a poll suggesting that economic stability constituted only people's fourth priority, ranking below unemployment, poverty, and education (Fritz 1995: 35). But while this finding applied to PT voters, it was incorrect for Brazilians in general (see Almeida 1996: 70–71).

[9] Alayón (interview 1996) and Rojas Parra (interview 1998) stressed IMF influence in the elaboration and enactment of the Agenda Venezuela. Rojas Parra reported that the economic team never considered more drastic solutions, such as a convertibility scheme à la Argentina.

[10] Petkoff (1997: 21, 77–78) stresses the severity of the crisis looming in early 1996: "My perception at that point was that we were approaching the abyss."

nomic liberalization and fiscal adjustment. President Caldera lifted the exchange controls, enacted a massive devaluation, raised public-sector prices (including the politically sensitive price of gasoline), and announced budget cuts and the dismissal of public officials (CORDIPLAN 1996a; Matos Azócar 1996).

Yet while these economic measures closely followed IFI recommendations and repeated the basic outline of President Pérez's ill-fated shock program, the Caldera government learned from the social unrest that had erupted on 27 February 1989. The new leader of the economic team, Planning Minister Teodoro Petkoff, made a concerted effort to prepare public opinion for the painful adjustment measures. By crisscrossing the country and speaking to numerous societal and party organizations, Petkoff sought to project an image of frankness and honesty and dispel any sense of surprise and betrayal, which in his view had proven fatal for Pérez's shock program (interviews with Petkoff 1998, Rojas Parra 1998, Alayón 1996). The government also created a social safety net to protect strategic groups from the costs of stabilization and compensate groups that would get hurt. For instance, before the gasoline price increase took effect, providers of public transportation, who had been decisive in triggering the riots of 27 February 1989, received a subsidy that covered the higher cost.[11]

Despite these efforts to prevent a recurrence of popular protest, leading decision-makers knew they were taking considerable risks and were quite concerned on the day the new stabilization plan took effect (interviews with Petkoff 1998 and Alayón 1996). Their fears of a new *Caracazo* did not come true, however. Even in subsequent weeks, there were only a few sporadic outbursts of violence. But neither did Venezuelans offer the massive support that the initial adjustment programs announced by presidents Menem, Collor, and Fujimori had received. Instead, the popular reaction was divided and contradictory, with dull acquiescence as the prevailing sentiment. When asked about the Agenda Venezuela in June 1996, for instance, only 32 percent of survey respondents expressed "trust" and willingness to accept sacrifice, whereas 61 percent thought that President Caldera was mistaken in imposing such costs (Consultores 21 1996: question 38). In a later question, the same survey found willingness to accept sacrifice among 41 percent, rejection among 34 percent, and confusion among 20 percent.[12] Furthermore,

[11] CORDIPLAN (1996b: 9–10); interview with Petkoff (1998). Yet 75 percent of respondents denied in June 1996 that "these compensatory measures were sufficiently compensating for the effect of the economic [stabilization] measures" (Consultores 21 1996: question 54).

[12] Consultores 21 (1996: question 56); similarly Mercanálisis (1996: 47); Datos (1996: 117–21); "Del Gran Viraje a la Agenda Venezuela," *El Universal* 18 April 1996: 2/10–2/11; Murua (1996: 5).

President Caldera had an approval rating of only 25 percent, against 63 percent disapproval—worse than ex-President Pérez (Consultores 21 1996: questions 88–89; similar Datos 1998: 35; Mercanálisis 1997: 1; Cosar Grupo Comunicacional 1996: 4–11, 19; Murua 1996: 19; see fig. 8.1).

This unenthusiastic response reflected the state of the Venezuelan economy, which—while having suffered substantial deterioration in the preceding years—was not plagued by hyperinflation. Price increases reached a worrisome 8 percent per month in early 1996, but not the explosive levels prevailing in Argentina, Brazil, and Peru during the late 1980s and in Brazil again in 1993–94. More importantly, since Caldera had failed for more than two years to stem the economic deterioration, large numbers of citizens questioned his capacity to overcome these problems now. When asked in June 1996 "how much the current government was working to resolve the main problems of the country," 28 percent answered "little" and another 51 percent "not at all" (Consultores 21 1996: question 9). Some 55 percent of respondents therefore thought the government was a failure when it finally enacted the Agenda Venezuela (Consultores 21 1996: question 39).

In sum, although up to 82 percent of respondents reported a recent deterioration in their well-being and thus saw themselves in the domain of losses (Consultores 21 1996: question 4), many people doubted that the Caldera administration could successfully combat the severe problems and therefore refused to endorse the new stabilization plan. Thus, the political impact of perceptions of losses was mediated in this case by widespread skepticism about the government's capacity to turn the country around.[13]

The Limited Push for Structural Reform

In the wake of pursuing stabilization, the economic teams led by Cardoso and Petkoff also sought to advance an ambitious agenda of market reforms. In fact, they tried to enact many of the changes that the political weakness and eventual impeachment of presidents Collor and Pérez had obstructed. Thus, there was a good deal of substantive continuity to these earlier efforts, although for political reasons, the new teams emphasized the differences and disputed the neoliberal label that the leftist opposition—especially in Brazil—tried to make stick. Also, Minister Petkoff and President Cardoso deliberately deviated from the neopopulist strategy and imperious decision-making style that presidents

---

[13] Thus, Caldera's bad track record kept many citizens from applying an "antidotal" posture in assessing the Agenda Venezuela (cf. Stokes 2001b: 15–17).

Pérez and particularly Collor had applied. Instead, the renewed reform efforts proceeded by ample consultation, negotiation, and parliamentary debate. This choice of strategy—a product of learning from the political failures of presidents Collor and Pérez—made the advance of market reform more cumbersome and difficult, but also less reversible.

Due to the massive support for the Real Plan and his impressive electoral mandate, President Cardoso had more political capital than the Venezuelan reformers, who depended on lukewarm presidential backing. In Venezuela, the temporary bonanza caused by the petroleum price increase of late 1996 also stiffened opposition to austerity measures. By prematurely putting many decision-makers—especially President Caldera and his political aides—into the domain of gains, this windfall diminished the government's willingness to take further political risks and thus weakened the impulse for market reform. Therefore, the structural components of the Agenda Venezuela advanced only haltingly, especially in the area of fiscal reform, where budget cuts and the downsizing of the state proved exceedingly difficult.

The Cardoso government also faced greater obstacles than its promising starting position suggested. While it managed in 1995 to have Congress pass a number of constitutional amendments that deregulated important sectors of the economy, its proposals for administrative, social security, and tax reform triggered stubborn passive resistance from its own supporters and active opposition from interest groups and leftist parties. Since the government therefore did not manage to limit public expenditures, the fiscal situation of the Brazilian state and, as a result, economic stability remained precarious.

Brazil

President Cardoso seemed to command enviable strength upon taking office in January 1995. The stabilization plan he had initiated continued to receive massive support from political parties, interest groups, and public opinion (85 percent approval in February, IBOPE 1995: question 07; see fig. 8.2). It had also ensured him a convincing victory in the first round of the presidential election and dealt another defeat to the left, which had appeared bound to win. Furthermore, the parties that backed Cardoso's candidacy and their new coalition partners held a clear majority of 75 percent in Congress (Power 1998a: 52), which seemed sufficient for passing constitutional amendments. Finally, politicians from the president's PSDB or close allies won the governorships of important states, such as São Paulo, Minas Gerais, and Rio de Janeiro. Thus, Car-

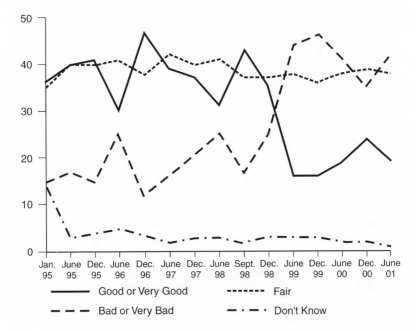

Figure 8.2. Popular Evaluation of President Cardoso's Performance. *Source:* Toledo (1999); Datafolha (2001).

doso had a strong base of support with which to counteract the institutional fragmentation prevailing in Brazil's new democracy.

Trusting in its political strength, the new government quickly submitted a number of structural reform proposals to Congress. Some projects intended to lift state monopolies and deregulate important areas of the economy, including the politically sensitive petroleum sector. In this way, the Cardoso administration sought to attract new investment, especially from foreign sources, and thus boost growth (Pojo de Rego and Peixoto 1998: 143–156). In addition, it elaborated wide-ranging constitutional amendments on social security and administrative reform and announced a similar effort in the area of taxation (Câmara dos Deputados 1995, 1996; Presidência 1995). These initiatives sought to produce permanent fiscal adjustment and thus put the Real Plan on more solid ground than the Emergency Social Fund of early 1994, which was scheduled to expire in December 1995. As in Argentina, Peru, and Brazil under Collor, structural reforms thus pursued the goals of both short-term stabilization and long-term development (see chapter 6 above).

Invoking its electoral mandate, distributing plentiful patronage, and drawing support from powerful transnationally oriented business sectors, the Cardoso administration engineered congressional approval for the lifting of state monopolies. But administrative, social security, and tax reforms made little headway because they threatened crucial interests of Brazil's political class, especially legislators and public bureaucrats (interviews with Moreira Franco 1996 and Santana 1996). The undisciplined nature of Brazilian parties also hindered the formation of the three-fifths majority required for passing constitutional amendments. A multitude of interest groups took advantage of party fragmentation to block many reform proposals and defend — even extend — their privileges (Fleischer 1998; Jolowicz 1999; Kingstone 1999: 203–27; Weyland 1996b). As a result, Congress greatly watered down the amendments that were crucial for definite fiscal adjustment. Even the few changes that eventually passed — for instance, the abolition of the unconditional job tenure of civil servants — were difficult to implement because dismissals have a high political cost (interview with Santana 1996). Thus, widespread active and passive resistance posed tremendous obstacles to the structural reform agenda of the Cardoso government.

In addition, the increase in tax revenues caused by economic stabilization and strong growth in 1994 and 1995 (see Varsano et al. 1998: 39) seemed to make determined efforts to reduce long-term public expenditures and reform the tax system less urgent (interview with Bogéa 1995). The return of investor confidence also allowed Brazil to cover eventual revenue shortfalls by augmenting the public debt. This alleviation of the state's fiscal problems — together with the success of the Real Plan in guaranteeing economic stability and stimulating moderate growth — put the government into the domain of gains. As a result, it soon became risk-averse and further moderated its push for structural reforms. Whereas the threat of imminent hyperinflation had induced Cardoso to make an all-out effort to garner congressional approval for the Emergency Social Fund in February 1994, he and his ministers fought much less hard for administrative and social security reform from 1995 onward.[14] Similarly, resistance against reform in society and Congress grew stronger (interview with Considera 1999). Eventually, the president's political interests also came to limit the pressure for permanent fiscal adjustment: Cardoso used the unfinished reform agenda

---

[14] For instance, the government significantly scaled down its proposal for social security reform even before sending it to Congress (confidential author interview with a leading official of the Social Security Ministry, Brasília, June 1995). Certainly, pension reform is difficult because there are clear, well-organized losers, whereas winners are diffuse and unorganized. But the same argument applies to the stabilization of inflation, which helps most of the population but hurts the financial sector, which earned huge profits from accelerating price rises (Armijo 1996).

to justify his desire for immediate reelection. And to win support for a reelection amendment, he could not afford to antagonize Brazil's political class by pushing hard for painful changes in 1997 (Flynn 1999: 291, 294). Thus, a confluence of factors — especially Cardoso's preference for negotiation over confrontation and the further turn to caution triggered by economic stabilization — accounts for the minimal progress of the structural initiatives that sought to limit public expenditures. As a result, the Real Plan continued to have a precarious fiscal foundation.

Temporarily, the enormous resources from privatization alleviated these fiscal problems. During Cardoso's first term, the federal government received US$ 72.7 billion through the privatization of public enterprises and the concession of services. In 1997 and 1998 alone, when the main mining firm (Companhia Vale do Rio Doce) and the telecommunications sector were sold off, these revenues added up to US$ 66.5 billion (Pêgo, Lima, and Pereira 1999: 13). But since this sale of assets could not continue for long, it did not put the Real Plan on a firmer fiscal footing.

Venezuela

Once the stabilization measures of the Agenda Venezuela succeeded in lowering inflation considerably, the new economic team proposed important structural reforms, especially the privatization of public enterprises, the elimination of budget rigidities and other fiscal reforms, and an overhaul of the complicated system of social obligations and benefits in the private and public sectors (CORDIPLAN 1996a: 3, 11–13). These initiatives had two main goals, namely, to make the economy more efficient and competitive and to give the Venezuelan state a firmer fiscal basis.[15]

But weak popular support for the stabilization plan did not give the market reformers much leverage with interest groups nor great clout vis-à-vis the political wing of the government itself, especially President Caldera. In addition, the rise of petroleum prices in the fall of 1996, which was triggered by a U.S. attack on Iraq, lifted the political wing of the government quickly out of the domain of losses, turned it more cautious, and thus diminished the reform impulse greatly (see Palma 1999: 154–55). This shift to risk aversion made the president and his political aides even less willing to incur the short-term costs of adjustment and structural change.

[15] Petkoff (1997: 59–60) was convinced that "Venezuela's crucial problem . . . [was] the fiscal problem."

The turn to caution jeopardized continued economic stability because it induced the government to loosen budget austerity and increase public spending (interviews with Petkoff 1998 and Alayón 1998; García Osío et al. 1998: 22). Besieged by a wave of strikes in early 1997, it made fairly generous concessions to sectors that sought compensation for the costs caused by the preceding economic crisis and by the adjustment measures of the Agenda Venezuela (interviews with Petkoff 1998, Rojas Parra 1998, Navarro 1998; Palma 1999: 126–27, 136). As the government granted substantial salary raises to public employees, risk aversion in the domain of gains created commitments for permanent spending increases (see interviews with Petkoff 1998 and Alayón 1998). This leniency threatened to cause severe fiscal problems if the temporary oil boom were followed by a bust—as happened in 1998.

Risk aversion in the domain of gains also slowed down important structural reform initiatives. The privatization program, for instance, quickly fell behind schedule as entrenched parties defended the patronage resources that public employment provided and as unions worried about job losses for their members. As a result, the state received fewer revenues than expected.[16] The ambitious plans to overhaul and slim down the public administration also advanced very little. Resistance by government bureaucrats, trade unionists, and clientelist politicians, especially from AD, made it virtually impossible to reorganize ministries and eliminate countless other public agencies—Minister Petkoff's priority project (interviews with Petkoff 1998, Alayón 1996, 1998, Rojas Parra 1998).

In the area of taxation, the Agenda Venezuela also brought little progress. But the Caldera administration now reaped the benefits of the institution of a value-added/sales tax in 1993–94 and the creation of a modern tax agency (Servicio Nacional Integrado de Administración Tributaria—SENIAT) in 1994, which sought to combat the rampant tax evasion. Therefore, tax revenues, which had run at a very low 4–4.7 percent of GDP from 1990 to 1992, rose to 6.8–7 percent in 1993 and 1994, 7.9–8.2 percent in 1995 and 1996, and 9.5 percent in 1997 (data provided by SENIAT, 10 July 1998). In 1995, for the first time in fifty years, tax revenues were higher than the state's income from petroleum sales (Solórzano 1997: 97). But although the fiscal position of the Venezuelan state improved, it remained dependent on oil income (García

---

[16] Interview with Castillo (1998); *LAWR* (1998). On the important "opening" of the petroleum industry to foreign investment, which was enacted in 1994–95—before the Agenda Venezuela—to provide additional resources and thus alleviate the severe economic problems, see Arrioja (1998) and Philip (1999: 370–73).

Osío et al. 1998: 9) and therefore vulnerable to the volatility of the international petroleum market.

In the area of social obligations and benefits, the reformers did make progress toward resolving an issue that had eluded agreement for years, but this success created a short-term fiscal cost. Since 1989, businesspeople and neoliberal experts had sought to change the system of severance payments, which multiplied workers' last — usually, highest — wage by their years of service. Especially in times of high inflation, this "retroactivity" saddled private and public enterprises with huge nominal obligations, which hindered dismissals during economic recessions (interview with Castillo 1998). Labor, which had long opposed reform, finally gave in because governmental expedients to cope with increasing inflation had substantially eroded the real value of severance pay for workers (interview with Navarro 1998). Tripartite negotiations therefore yielded an agreement that capped these benefits in the future while obligating private and public employers to pay out their accumulated value immediately (Ministerio del Trabajo 1997: 13–21; Ellner 1999). This pact turned the state's fiscal position more solid in the long run, but it further raised public expenditure commitments in the short run (interview with Alayón 1998; Palma 1999: 136).

In sum, lax budget control and the halting and uneven advance of structural reforms kept the fiscal situation of the state precarious in Venezuela — similar to Brazil. This limited progress stemmed from governments' weak pressure for profound restructuring, which reflected risk aversion in the domain of gains, and from the resistance of vested interests, especially the political class.

The Politics of Market Reform

Learning from earlier experiences — especially the impeachment of presidents Collor and Pérez — also shaped the political strategies applied to propel renewed market reform in Brazil and Venezuela. To avoid such a debacle, President Cardoso and Planning Minister Petkoff deliberately refrained from using neopopulist tactics and proceeded instead by negotiation and compromise. Risk aversion in the domain of gains soon reinforced this preference for a nonconfrontational approach. This choice of a cautious strategy made it impossible for Cardoso and Petkoff to establish the political predominance and autonomy that Menem and Fujimori had managed to attain, but it also weakened the partisan opposition to their political projects and avoided the damage that neopopulist strategies commonly inflict on party systems.

Brazil

Instead of boldly imposing a host of drastic measures, President Cardoso, who learned from Collor's political failure, sought to garner support for important changes through constant bargaining and frequent concessions. Many citizens, interest groups, and politicians also felt burned by Collor's dramatic fall, which dashed the high expectations that his meteoric rise had initially elicited. Reluctant to believe in another savior who made exorbitant promises but had an obscure track record, they preferred the safer option of an established politician who was experienced and seemed reasonable (Dimenstein and Souza 1994: 157, 196; Figueiredo 1994: 77, 79). This predisposition was boosted by the promise and rapid success of the Real Plan in bringing down inflation, which lifted large numbers of citizens from the domain of losses into the domain of gains. The resulting turn to risk aversion induced many voters in the presidential contest of 1994 to choose the "established" Cardoso over his more radical rival Lula from the PT. Thus, after Brazil's political class had defeated a neopopulist upstart in bringing down Collor, under the leadership of Cardoso it now managed to stabilize the economy and recapture the presidency.

To garner electoral support from the poor, uneducated, and largely unorganized sectors of the hinterland whom Collor had won over with his neopopulist appeals, Cardoso made an alliance with the clientelist PFL, which has particularly solid backing in the backward areas of the Northeast. But for the better-off, educated sectors of urban areas, the president deliberately emphasized his democratic, republican credentials and his international prestige as a renowned sociologist. Whereas Collor had acted like a tempestuous *enfant terrible*, Cardoso depicted himself as an elder statesman. Instead of resorting to imposition, he sought to resolve problems and conflicts by discussion and negotiation. Thus, whereas Collor had combined economic liberalism with political populism, Cardoso embraced political liberalism while promoting market reform.

Cardoso's liberal political approach limited the opportunities available to the partisan opposition, particularly the PT. Through his democratic, republican appeal, the president occupied a political space that UPP in Peru and—with particular success—FREPASO in Argentina filled.[17] While involved in some scandals, such as alleged vote buying for the reelection amendment, the president and his close aides were tainted

---

[17] The following two paragraphs are inspired by Novaro and Palermo (1998: chap. 4) but diverge substantially from their analysis of the PT's difficulties.

neither by the autocratic tendencies of President Fujimori nor by the rampant corruption of President Menem's entourage. Leftist opposition parties therefore could not easily use democratic principles and calls for clean government to undermine popular support for the Cardoso administration.[18]

The lack of opportunity for shifting their main appeal to democratic, republican slogans reinforced the tendency among the left, especially the PT, to cling to socialist principles, frontally attack Cardoso's turn to "neoliberalism," and defend groups that bore high adjustment costs.[19] The Cardoso administration skillfully exploited this defensive posture to depict the PT as an outdated, antimodern force that sought to maintain a status quo rejected by many Brazilians (e.g., Cardoso 1996: 8). Whereas the PT had been the most modern, progressive force in Brazilian politics during the 1980s, it now appeared as opposed to "modernization." And despite its egalitarian rhetoric, the PT defended relatively better-off sectors such as public employees, who enjoyed benefits that ordinary Brazilians — especially the poor, whose cause the PT officially espoused — could only dream of (Weyland 1996b: 74, 76). To exploit the resulting resentment, the government presented its proposals for administrative and social security reform as progressive efforts to eliminate these privileges. While this "mobilization of bias" did not persuade Congress to pass the projects, it left the PT ill-positioned in public opinion and disoriented in its political actions. Conflicts between radical, socialist sectors and proponents of a renovation of the PT's ideology and program have therefore run high (e.g., PT 1999). These difficulties weakened the electoral appeal of the PT and the left as a whole.

Cardoso's liberal political style, especially the preference for negotiation over imposition, and the economic stability and political normality that this posture maintained, also helped to stabilize the Brazilian party system. The concessions that parties received in exchange for backing governmental initiatives satisfied their key constituents and demonstrated to the broader public their influence and contribution to preserving economic stability. Although Brazilian parties and electoral politicians continued to score low on democratic representation and accountability, and although their hunger for patronage disgusted many citizens, especially from the middle class, their politicking at least did not keep the country mired in crisis. Thus, the economic recovery and

---

[18] The left sought to use these themes in the presidential campaign of 1998 (União do Povo 1998: 5, 7), but with limited emphasis — most of its program focused on social issues (ibid. 10–15) — and with limited success.

[19] See, e.g., PT (1995: especially 7–8). Therefore, there has been a profound gulf between the left and Brazil's other parties (Power 1998a: 61, 66–67).

restoration of governability under Cardoso reflected well on the parties supporting the government.

Thus, whereas Collor's attacks on established politicians had helped to lower parties' prestige in the early 1990s, his political failure raised their image in 1992, and—after a renewed deterioration under incompetent President Franco—Cardoso's success in lowering inflation and administering the country stabilized their standing in the second half of the decade.[20] And whereas President Fujimori's neopopulist style and autocratic tendencies greatly weakened Peru's established parties (Tanaka 1998), Brazil's party system stabilized in the 1994 and 1998 elections. A number of bigger parties, especially the PSDB, PFL, PMDB, and PPB, established a more solid electoral base and a cooperative—though competitive—relationship in Congress. In fact, the effective number of parties fell slightly from 8.69 in 1990 to 7.45 in 1994 and 7.07 in 1998 (Ames and Power 2000). While still highly divided, the Brazilian party system was therefore less fluid in the late 1990s than eight to ten years earlier (see Mainwaring 1999: 96–98; Kinzo and Rodrigues 1999: 259–60).

Venezuela

Similar to Brazil, renewed market reform was not accompanied by neopopulist politics in Venezuela. President Caldera, who had applied neopopulist strategies from 1993 to 1995, was a reluctant follower, not the initiator, of the Agenda Venezuela. Since he had to make an embarrassing about-face and deviate from his earlier rejection of "neoliberalism," his standing in public opinion remained weak from 1996 on. In mid-1997, 70 percent of respondents classified his government as bad, only 27 percent as good—including 17 percent who begrudgingly rated it "okay tending toward good" (Consultores 21 1997: 15; similarly Mercanálisis 1997: question 2a; see fig. 8.1). And *dis*trust in Caldera's capacity to "manage the country well during the remainder of his term" ran between 66 percent and 77 percent from early 1996 through 1998 (Datos 1998: 35). Caldera was therefore unwilling and unable to revive his neopopulist tactics (interview with Petkoff 1998) and lead the new market reform effort.

Like President Cardoso, the main protagonist of the Agenda Vene-

---

[20] After party identification in Datafolha surveys fell from 48 percent in 1989 to 43.8 percent in 1990, rose to 57.2 percent in 1992, and fell to 43 percent in mid-1994 (Meneguello 1994: 159; Mainwaring 1999: 113), it remained more stable thereafter, reaching 42.4 percent in June 1996 (Mainwaring, Meneguello, and Power 1999: 38) and 41 percent in 1999 (IBOPE 1999: 17).

zuela, Planning Minister Petkoff, deliberately avoided a neopopulist strategy and preferred negotiation with interest groups and parties in order not to suffer a political disaster like Carlos Andrés Pérez. The limited commitment of President Caldera also kept the economic team from enacting a comprehensive neoliberal program through decree and imposition. The government's lack of a majority in Congress therefore made constant bargaining necessary. In addition, the continued organizational strength of Venezuela's business peak association Federación Venezolana de Cámaras y Asociaciones de Comercio y Producción (FEDE-CAMARAS) and the trade union confederation Confederación de Trabajadores de Venezuela (CTV) made tripartite negotiations on changes in the system of social protection feasible, which in turn facilitated Congressional approval of important reform initiatives.

Minister Petkoff's nonpopulist, cooperative strategy built on political agreements that Venezuelan political leaders had forged earlier to avert the risks created by presidential neopopulism. At the beginning of his term, President Caldera had governed in a rather autocratic fashion and engaged in frequent confrontations with Congress. In turn, the two "established" parties, AD and COPEI, had offered strong resistance to the government's drastic measures and intransigent style. To avert a dangerous showdown, the president and AD leaders eventually cut a deal that provided the government with minimal support. AD President Luis Alfaro Ucero hoped to use the resulting influence to improve his chances for the presidential race of 1998. In particular, access to ample patronage allowed AD to grease its party machine, which provided it with a hard core of voters. The electoral value of this core constituency rose with the growing fragmentation of the party system. In fact, the subnational elections of December 1995 brought a recovery of the AD vote that gave the party control over the important mayoralty of Caracas and ten governorships.[21] This success strengthened AD's resolve to maintain its conditional support for the government.

As a result, the economic team led by Minister Petkoff could count on good will from Venezuela's major party for enacting the stabilization measures of the Agenda Venezuela (interviews with Hospedales 1996 and Lauría 1998). In particular, the AD leadership had an interest in preventing an economic collapse, which would further delegitimate the established political class. The other traditional party, COPEI, actually had more ideological affinity to the renewed push for market reform, but continued aversion to President Caldera made its cooperation less

---

[21] I owe these insights to survey researcher Friedrich Welsch, Universidad Simon Bolívar. The proportion of respondents who declared themselves adherents of AD rose from 17 percent in early 1994 to 21 percent in late 1995 (Consultores 21 1997: 21).

predictable. Finally, MAS and Convergencia had supported Caldera's candidacy in 1993 and had significant participation in the government. For these reasons, the economic team could count on the conditional backing or neutrality of Venezuela's major parties. Petkoff's effort to use persuasion and negotiation to build support for determined stabilization measures therefore achieved considerable success in mid-1996.

Since the Agenda Venezuela lowered inflation, the parties backing this plan saw their standing with the electorate enhanced slightly, although they remained at an extremely low level of trust. Net assessments of parties' "contribution to solving the country's problems" rose from a dismal −85 percent in the second trimester of 1996 to −72 percent one year later (Consultores 21 1997: 18).[22] And the proportion of respondents identifying as adherents of AD rose from 17 percent at the beginning of the Caldera government to 25 percent in mid-1997 (Consultores 21 1997: 21). Thus, as the Real Plan helped to stabilize Brazil's party system, the Agenda Venezuela temporarily slowed down party erosion in Venezuela.

But the weak popular support for the Agenda Venezuela made it impossible for the political head of the economic team to launch his own bid for the top leadership. In 1996, many observers suspected that Planning Minister Petkoff had the ambition to follow Fernando Henrique Cardoso's example and use a successful stabilization of the economy as a launching pad for a presidential candidacy in 1998. But the meager public approval of the adjustment plan and the obstacles faced by the Agenda Venezuela's structural reform proposals obstructed any such ambition. Petkoff's avoidance of a neopopulist style and his preference for negotiation over imposition posed further obstacles to whipping up massive support for an eventual bid for the presidency.

In sum, political leaders — and in Brazil, citizens — learned from the political failure of neoliberal populism under presidents Collor and Pérez. Therefore, the resumption of market reform was not accompanied by a revival of neopopulist politics. Instead, the protagonists of the adjustment efforts were established politicians who shied away from confrontation and relied instead on negotiations with parties and interest groups. As a result, major parties managed to solidify their hold on the electorate in Brazil and temporarily stem its further erosion in Venezuela because they proved their effectiveness by supporting economically successful stabilization plans, exerting policy influence, and distributing patronage.

---

[22] The polling institute computes these net assessments by subtracting the percentage of people who respond "little" or "not at all" from those who respond "much" or "some" when asked how much an institution works to resolve the main problems afflicting the country.

Renewed Problems

While bolstering economic and political stability in the short run, the cautious, risk-averse strategies of President Cardoso and Minister Petkoff left Brazil and Venezuela vulnerable to new challenges in the medium run. Above all, the slow advance of market reform kept public spending high, perpetuated fiscal problems, and thus exposed the two nations more than other Latin American countries to exogenous shocks, especially the Asian and Russian financial crises and the steep drop of international petroleum prices after late 1997.

Brazil

The failure to put the Brazilian state on a firmer fiscal foundation, especially by revamping public administration and social security (Velloso 1998), forced President Cardoso's economic team to rely primarily on monetary instruments to keep inflation low (Arida 1996: 35–38). The government therefore kept the currency closely pegged to the dollar, maintaining a significant appreciation of the exchange rate that worsened Brazil's trade balance. To attract the foreign capital required to finance the resulting current account deficit, the Central Bank maintained high interest rates. This expedient raised the cost of the public debt that the government used to sterilize the influx of foreign capital. The resulting public deficit was financed by more public debt, which therefore grew dramatically (Presidência 1999a: 18–19).

After the initial boom caused by the end of hyperinflation, the control of inflation therefore had high costs. Throttled by high interest rates, economic growth slowed down to 3 percent in 1996 and 3.2 percent in 1997. Thus, the Real Plan certainly did not put Brazil back on its historic growth trajectory of 6–7 percent per year, which it had attained during the decades before the debt crisis. Anemic growth — combined with business efforts to adapt to increased foreign competition — exacerbated Brazil's longstanding employment problems (Delfim 1998: 93–100; Mercadante 1998: 150–61).

Furthermore, the precarious fiscal situation, rapidly rising public debt, and growing overvaluation of the *real* exposed Brazil to external shocks, especially contagion from the Asian financial crisis. Shaken by a sudden drop in investor confidence, the government in late 1997 announced an adjustment package that sought to raise taxes and reduce public spending. But it proved impossible to win congressional approval for significant budget cuts in a pre-electoral year. Also, Brazil's pronounced fiscal federalism made it difficult for the federal government to induce state administrations to cooperate with its adjustment efforts. Therefore, fiscal problems kept worsening in the course of 1998. The high interest rates that the government used to keep attracting foreign capital ended up further exacerbating the fiscal problems.

When Russia's debt default in mid-1998 threatened to cause a panic in global financial markets, the U.S. government and the IMF engineered a large crisis preemption package, which offered Brazil US$ 41.5 billion in financial support conditional upon determined adjustment efforts. In line with my application of prospect theory, this promise of a bailout prematurely lowered negative prospects, turned political actors more cautious, and therefore made sectors of the government, congressional politicians, and state governors more averse to incurring the political risks of tough stabilization measures. The Finance Ministry's stabilization plan therefore elicited only lukewarm support and made limited progress in Congress (Presidência 1999b: 9; Flynn 1999: 299–300).

The looming crisis also had a seemingly paradoxical political effect. While the government parties feared for President Cardoso's reelection in the upcoming contest of October 1998, the danger of renewed economic problems actually boosted support for the incumbent. At the time of the electoral campaign, the costs of the new crisis and of the government's adjustment measures had not yet hit in full force. A majority of Brazilians still had a positive or neutral assessment of recent changes in their well-being.[23] Since they did not see themselves in the domain of losses, they cautiously preferred continuity over change and therefore opted for the incumbent, rather than the leftist opposition.[24] The specter of renewed economic problems probably boosted the salience of economic stability, an area in which Cardoso had a proven track record.[25] By contrast, the main concerns raised by the opposition — unemployment and social justice (União do Povo 1998: 10–15) — seem to have become less immediately urgent. As in President Menem's reelection in May 1995 (see chapter 7), an externally originating threat of economic deterioration, coming after a successful stabilization and

[23] CNI (1998: 3–4, 9); "Para maioria, novo governo de FHC será melhor," *Estado de São Paulo* 8 January 1999: A4.

[24] For the correlation between economic assessments and vote intention, see Datafolha (1998a: question 20). Baker (2000: 24, 27, 37) confirms that respondents who held positive economic assessments disproportionately voted for Cardoso, but his survey was conducted after the devaluation crisis of January 1999.

[25] Flynn (1999: 288–90, 298); Kinzo and Rodrigues (1999: 257–58). In October 1998, 68 percent of respondents thought "the government had the capacity to confront the crisis in a responsible manner" (Vox Populi 1999b). Popular approval of the Real Plan increased significantly as it faced threats in August/September 1998 (Datafolha 1998b: question 15). Also, 61 percent of respondents — more than ever before — thought the Real Plan had improved "their lives" (CNI 1998: 20).

recovery, solidified electoral backing for the incumbent—the guarantor of stability—and hurt the opposition, whose inexperience in economic governance and demands for change now appeared as too risky. After running neck and neck with his main rival, the PT's Lula, in May and June (Datafolha 1998b: question 9), President Cardoso therefore won a convincing reelection victory with 53.1 percent of the vote in October (see also fig. 8.2).

This first-round victory did not, however, sufficiently boost Cardoso's leverage with the recalcitrant Congress, which rejected some crucial items of the fiscal adjustment plan (Presidência 1999b: 9). As investor confidence remained shaky, the internal debt moratorium declared by Itamar Franco, now a renegade state governor, triggered large-scale capital flight, which forced the Central Bank to devalue the currency and drastically raise interest rates in January 1999. These measures caused a recession and threatened to unleash a new inflationary spiral. As a result, large numbers of Brazilians now entered the domain of losses, lost their faith in the Real Plan, and came to reject President Cardoso (Albuquerque 1999; CNI 1999: 7, 13; Vox Populi 1999a; fig. 8.2). Thus, the problems not addressed by President Cardoso's cautious strategy of negotiation soon came to haunt Brazil.

Responding to this drastic deterioration and seeking to avert an economic collapse, the government now put much stronger pressure on Congress, which therefore approved fiscal adjustment measures that it had rejected a mere weeks before (Presidência 1999b: 10; interview with Delfim 1999). Thus, by putting the government in the domain of losses, the renewed crisis triggered risk acceptance and therefore prompted intensified reform efforts. Finance Minister Pedro Malan (1999: 3) declared that "the times of gradualism" were over. As in Argentina in 1995, a new threat to economic stability brought a stronger push to pursue the market reform program. Interestingly, facing the danger of an economic collapse—i.e., clear prospects of losses—Congress now supported the government's stabilization effort. Since this shift in posture reflects a change in perceived domain and a resulting change in propensity toward risk among pivotal groups of parliamentarians, it corroborates my prospect-theory interpretation. By contrast, advocates of rational choice would have difficulty explaining this surprising shift because the "logic of collective action" (Olson 1971) suggests that a crisis threatening the whole country should not affect the individual actions of self-interested politicians from undisciplined parties. Mechanisms of electoral accountability are too weak in Brazil to create a rational incentive for individual politicians to approve painful, politically costly stabilization measures in order to contribute to the collective good of rescuing the country.

The new crisis passed much faster than expected, however. The Brazilian economy adjusted quickly and emerged from the recession in mid-1999. Therefore, more and more people, interest groups, and politicians began again to foresee prospects of gains. This quick recovery led to a premature relaxation of the adjustment efforts,[26] including a reversal of some decisions taken in early 1999. Throughout the year, the government's proposals for additional changes, especially in taxation and social security, therefore elicited ever stronger resistance. In fact, the government itself soon lowered its ambitions, focusing on initiatives to guarantee fiscal stability while moderating its push for additional structural reforms. Cardoso did persuade Congress to pass the Fiscal Responsibility Law, which disciplines expenditures by state and municipal governments and constrains their capacity to incur debt, thus making it easier for the federal government to guarantee fiscal equilibrium at the national level (Mora and Varsano 2001: 22–23). But in other areas, the administration has stepped back from proposing drastic changes. For instance, the Social Security Ministry introduced "notional accounts" in the deficit-ridden pension system to preempt any further consideration of full-scale social security privatization (Pinheiro 2000). Thus, as a result of the rapid turnaround in Brazil's economic fate, caution has prevailed. In sum, rapidly changing economic conjunctures led to shifting propensities toward risk and the corresponding oscillations in the government's economic policy approach.

With the magic of the Real Plan shattered and his popularity at unprecedentedly low levels (see figure 8.2), President Cardoso began his second term on a weak footing. In fact, even Brazil's quick recovery from the devaluation crisis did little to boost the president's approval ratings. His status as a lame duck who cannot be reelected any more also diminished his political clout as his allies have begun to maneuver in preparation for the 2002 presidential contest (interview with Delfim 1999). In particular, while Cardoso's PSDB—after significant internal debates—promoted Health Minister José Serra as its candidate, the PFL, the other core party of the governing alliance, closed ranks behind Roseana Sarney, the governor of a poor Northeastern state and daughter of former president José Sarney. These electoral rivalries further diminish the cohesion of the governing coalition, thus posing additional obstacles to the further advance of market reform. Yet these political tensions are unlikely to endanger the economic stability restored after the devaluation crisis.

The more precarious political standing of the governing coalition

[26] Interview with Considera (1999). Finance Minister Malan (1999: 4) foresaw and warned against this tendency.

during Cardoso's second term will probably not jeopardize Brazil's commitment to the basic principles of the new market system either. Certainly, the shock of the devaluation crisis and the resulting drop in presidential popularity shifted political preferences toward the left, making Lula, the leader of the leftist PT, the frontrunner of vote intentions for the 2002 presidential contest. Center-left politicians also gained support, whereas representatives of the governmental alliance long trailed in the list of potential candidates; even the rise of Roseana Sarney, ranked second in the January 2002 polls (Fleischer 2002: 1–3), did not reverse the overall movement of opinion toward the left. But the left, even the socialist PT, has toned down its criticism of "neoliberalism" and accepted some of its basic principles, as the party's new economic program shows (PT 2001). After all, the new development model guarantees stability, which Brazilians continue to value highly. And as the lack of contagion from Argentina's severe problems suggests, a grave new crisis, which could trigger a return to widespread risk acceptance, is unlikely to erupt. Thus, support for a radical backlash against market principles will remain limited; even a leftist victory in the 2002 contest will probably not endanger the basic continuity of the economic policies adopted since 1994. The market system appears to have considerable political sustainability in contemporary Brazil.

Venezuela

Given the insufficient success in putting the state on a firmer fiscal foundation, Venezuela also proved vulnerable to an external shock (Corrales 2000; Palma 1999: 139–51). Its temporary economic recovery came to a crushing halt with the precipitous drop of international petroleum prices after late 1997. The resulting fall in fiscal revenues, which still depended to a substantial degree on oil income (García Osío et al. 1998: 9), caused a severe budget crisis. Three rounds of desperate spending cuts forestalled a new jump in inflation, but at the cost of a deepening recession. As investment and consumer spending dropped, unemployment rose, exacerbating the poverty afflicting many Venezuelans.

The resurgence of grave economic problems right after the temporary recovery of 1997 pushed many people back into the domain of losses. The proportion of respondents who reported a recent deterioration in their personal economic situation increased from 33 percent in November 1997 to 48 percent in April 1998 (Mercanálisis 1998: question 5a). These negative perceptions induced more and more people to become risk-acceptant and advocate drastic change; in May 1998, for instance, 82.8 percent advocated "profound reforms or changes in

Venezuela's system of government" (Subero 1998). As a result, they rejected the established political class and embraced newcomers and outsiders as candidates for the presidential contest of December 1998. After former beauty queen and mayor of a fancy Caracas suburb, Irene Sáez, had been ahead in vote intentions from late 1996 to early 1998, with the further aggravation of the economic problems a more radical outsider, Hugo Chávez Frías, the leader of the failed coup of 4 February 1992, displaced her as the front-runner in the polls (McCoy 1999: 66).

Heading a heterogeneous movement that allegedly included a militia wing, Chávez promised a profound renovation of Venezuelan politics and an end of neoliberal reform. To give these proposals a democratic facade, the candidate called for a constituent assembly to revamp the established institutional framework and conclusively break the stranglehold of the entrenched political class (Pottelá and Decarli 1998). To critics, this proposal looked suspiciously similar to President Fujimori's suspension of Congress in April 1992 and the convocation of a constituent assembly that strengthened presidential powers. Chávez's calls for drastic change found broad resonance among the suffering population, however, and the former coup monger won the presidency with 56 percent of the vote (McCoy 1999: 71).

Thus, Venezuela's persistent economic difficulties, which many citizens attributed to political factors, especially the corruption and stifling predominance of the traditional parties (Keller 1996), prompted an abrupt political renewal and a dangerous "jump in the dark." Whereas the 1988 election, which resulted in the victory of an insider acting like an outsider (Carlos Andrés Pérez), was preceded by three years of recovery and modest income growth, the 1998 contest occurred in a setting of clear losses, which dashed the hopes instilled by the growth achieved in 1997. After suffering a string of losses that established political forces proved unable to stop, many voters typically chose the riskiest option among the available choices, namely, a radical antisystem outsider. Once again, risk-seeking in the domain of losses accounts for this striking outcome, which has created the danger of an involution of democracy in Venezuela.

The Chávez Government—Another Reversal of Neoliberalism?

When President Chávez took office in February 1999, many economic and political forces, especially private business and its allies, feared a new effort to roll back market reform. Chávez's Fifth Republic Movement (Movimiento V República—MVR), which included many leftists, had relentlessly criticized neoliberalism during the campaign. His massive electoral mandate and the disrepute into which established socio-political forces had fallen gave Chávez the power to enact drastic changes in economic policy.

Many of these expectations have not come true, however. During a good part of 1999, the new government maintained a surprisingly orthodox economic policy, slashing the budget and controlling inflation at the expense of a severe recession. And while Chávez has further slowed down structural reforms and his new constitution seems to mandate a reversal of some market-oriented changes, the government has hesitated to enact those anti-neoliberal provisions.

Despite announcing a "revolution," President Chávez initially maintained striking continuity in macroeconomic policy. In fact, he kept Finance Minister Maritza Izaguirre, who had served his predecessor since July 1998. The decision to retain this former official of the Inter-American Development Bank signaled to domestic and foreign investors that the new government intended to pursue responsible economic measures. Under the pressure of falling oil prices, Chávez's economic team indeed cut the budget by 10 percent. And it took additional steps to lower inflation, which had reached 29.9 percent in 1998, a relatively high level in contemporary Latin America.

These austerity measures and orthodox economic policies contributed to a severe recession. GDP dropped by 7.2 percent in 1999 (Poder Legislativo Nacional 2000: 49). This weak performance is particularly striking because from mid-1999 on, international oil prices increased dramatically; on prior occasions, the resulting windfall always caused a boom in Venezuela. The economic contraction had severe social repercussions, especially by driving up unemployment. In mid-2000, up to 23 percent of the economically active population was out of work; another 40 percent labored unprotected in the informal sector (CENDA 2000; 1999: 33–37). As a result of these problems, consumption of foodstuffs fell by 11.6 percent in early 1999 (CENDA 1999: 38). While these negative outcomes resulted not from governmental policies alone, but also from drastic investment cuts and capital flight by private business, the Chávez administration displayed an unexpected willingness to impose considerable sacrifices on an already suffering population.

What accounts for Chávez's surprising embrace of economic orthodoxy in early 1999? First, despite rhetorical attacks on "neoliberalism," the new president lacked a clear economic vision and project. Concentrating all his energies on the transformation of Venezuela's political-institutional system, he gave his economic aides considerable latitude to pursue "pragmatic" policies that responded to present conjunctures. Second, in early 1999, Venezuela faced profound economic difficulties, which resulted from the collapse of international oil prices in 1998. As is common, these pressing problems induced the new government to incur the social costs and political risks involved in enacting tough countermeasures.[27] Finally, Chávez's status as an outsider without links to established interest groups and parties allowed him to slash the budget without having to target his own allies. In sum, since ideology did not limit Chávez's economic policy options and since the prior-option bias did not tie down the new president, risk-seeking in the domain of losses prompted the surprising adoption of painful adjustment measures.

Typically, the tremendous rise in world petroleum prices during 1999 quickly moved the Chávez government from the domain of losses into the domain of gains in the economic sphere. As a result, it became unwilling to persist with socially costly and politically risky austerity policies and adopted instead expansionary measures. It greatly increased budget outlays from late 1999 onward, relying on the flood of petrodollars and on considerable debt (Poder Legislativo Nacional 2000: 2–4, 11–20). These "Keynesian" policies were designed to lift the country out of its prolonged recession and thus lower the social and political cost that the Chávez administration had incurred with its initial orthodoxy.[28] In fact, large sectors of the population rated governmental performance in important areas of economic and social policy as low, and this discontent slowly began to erode presidential popularity, causing a more substantial decline from early 2001 onward (Datanálisis 2000: 9–12, 16; Datos 2000: 21, 26–27; Aróstegui 2001; Naím 2001: 28, Consultores 2001b: 3, 8, 23–34; Toledo 2001a). Thus, moving into the domain of gains and assuming a more cautious stance, the government sought to reduce this discontent by pursuing economic stimulation, but it had only limited and diminishing success.

While Chávez's macroeconomic policies have responded to changing economic conjunctures in the way predicted by prospect theory, the new administration has failed to chart a clear course in the area of structural reforms. It has further decelerated privatization but hesitated to act on the principles enshrined in the new constitution and to overturn the social policy reforms adopted in 1997–98. Even on privatization itself, the government's stance remains unclear. While constitutionally banning private participation in the state oil company PDVSA, the president followed some of his market-oriented advisers and resumed the privatization of aluminum and electricity companies. But more nationalist aides managed to make the process so complicated and

---

[27] Chávez's continuous rhetorical attacks on business show that these orthodox policies were not motivated by the goal of winning investor confidence.

[28] A leading economic policy-maker used the Keynesian label in a confidential interview with the author, Caracas, June 2000.

unattractive for business that it will probably not lead to the sale of these public enterprises.[29]

The future of Venezuela's extensive system of social protection is even less clear. As mentioned above, the Caldera government had enacted profound change by lowering the burden of severance payments for business and by allowing for private participation in pension insurance and health care. Critical of this neoliberal transformation, Chávez's supporters included in the new constitution of 1999 provisions that seemed to mandate a return to the prereform system, for instance by precluding private health insurance with the stipulation of cost-free attention (articles 80–93). Yet these rule changes drew protest from business (FEDECAMARAS 1999; interview with Calvo 2000) and "concern" from international financial institutions. Market-oriented experts inside the state apparatus have also sought to convince the new political leadership to avoid a reversal of the reform.[30] But the National Assembly, dominated by Chávez supporters, has been heading precisely in that direction. After years of debates, the final outcome of this tortuous decision-making process remains uncertain.

In sum, President Chávez has enacted much less of a break with market reform than his rhetoric suggested. His government has pursued a rather unclear and shifting course in its economic policy (see business complaints in FEDECAMARAS 2000: 1–6; 2001) because the new president has focused most of his energies on a thorough overhaul of Venezuela's political-institutional system. This "revolution" has focused on removing the established political elite, especially the traditionally predominant parties AD and COPEI, strengthening presidential powers, and introducing plebiscitarian procedures. In pursing those goals, Chávez has applied a typically neopopulist strategy.

Chávez has relentlessly attacked the old political class and its institutional bastions, Congress and the courts (Carrasquero, Maingon, and Welsch 2001). He convoked a Constituent Assembly in order to purge the judiciary and sideline Parliament, in which the opposition held majorities. The new charter, masterminded by Chávez and his closest aides, also allowed for immediate presidential reelection and extended the chief executive's attributions in a number of ways (articles 225, 230, 236). Finally, the 1999 constitution instituted direct-democratic mechanisms — for instance, the possibility of revoking electoral mandates by

[29] Confidential author interview with a high-ranking ministerial official, Caracas, June 2000.

[30] Confidential author interview with a high-ranking ministerial official, Caracas, June 2000; "Sector privado cuestiona ley realizada por la asamblea: El sistema de reparto se queda," El Universal 12 November 2001 <www.eluniversal.com/2001/11/12/12201AA.shtml>.

referendum (article 72) — that a populist president like Chávez can use to discipline the opposition, for instance by unseating its representatives in the new National Assembly.

Chávez's attacks, which the widespread aversion to established socio-political forces gave strong resonance among the population, further weakened the formerly hegemonic parties and their allies among interest groups, especially the trade union confederation CTV. Thus, Chávez has managed to undermine many of the intermediary organizations that used to give Venezuelan democracy such solidity — and eventually, rigidity.

In typical neopopulist fashion, Chávez has based his own person-alistic leadership on a largely unmediated, seemingly direct relationship with a heterogeneous, virtually unorganized mass of followers. His own MVR comprises variegated groupings of cadres but — occupied with one election or referendum after the other — has not managed to create a solid organization encompassing the president's numerous followers (in-terview with Armas 2000). Instead of working through organizational channels, Chávez uses the media and large-scale public meetings to reach his mass base.

Through his neopopulist strategy, Chávez established a hegemonic position in Venezuelan politics from early 1999 until mid-2001. He clearly predominated inside his own movement, commanded great pop-ularity among the population (fig. 8.3), and faced an opposition that was divided and weak. The institutional changes he effected accumu-lated power in the presidency. With his own new prerogatives and his control over the majority in the legislature, he had the capacity to abuse power and exercise it in less than fully democratic ways. Thus, through early 2001, Chávez enjoyed unchallenged political predominance.

But the government's weak socioeconomic performance and its fail-ure to combat the crime wave that has plagued Venezuela since the late 1990s lowered presidential popularity substantially in the course of 2001 (see fig. 8.3). Many Venezuelans came to doubt that Chávez could fulfill the exalted expectations of concrete improvements that his mete-oric rise had stimulated; therefore, he began to lose their support. To forestall the further erosion of his political base, this neopopulist leader decided to radicalize his "revolution," using the MVR's control over the National Assembly to impose a package of forty-nine laws. Several of these changes, especially a redistributive land reform and tighter rules for private investments in the petroleum industry, elicited fierce criticism from ample sectors of business and other groupings in civil society. A wave of protests resulted, which revealed the increasing isolation of the government and led to the coalescence of the opposition. As calls for Chávez's resignation or his removal by plebiscite grew louder and rest-lessness in the armed forces increased, the political future of the govern-ment quickly turned highly uncertain. If Chávez's mass support — his

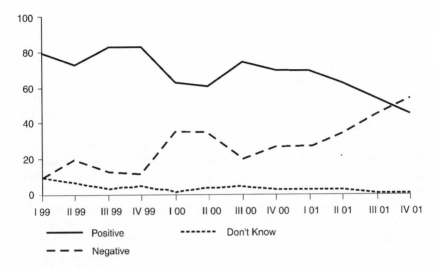

Figure 8.3. Popular Evaluation of Chávez's Governmental Performance.
Source: Consultores 21 (2001a: question 41); Toledo (2001a: 3; 2001b: 2–3).

main base of sustenance—continues to melt away, he could well suffer the fate of several other neopopulist leaders, such as Collor, Pérez, and—eventually—Fujimori, and be forced out of office long before the end of his term, which officially lasts until 2007.

In sum, Chávez's neopopulism is very similar to the political tactics and strategies applied by Menem in Argentina and especially Collor in Brazil and Fujimori in Peru; in particular, the lack of organized support exposes the Venezuelan leader to considerable political risks.[31] Yet due to the widespread aversion to market reform in Venezuela, the absence of a hyperinflationary crisis, and the revenue windfall resulting from high international petroleum prices, Chávez has not embraced "neoliberalism," in contrast to Menem, Collor, and Fujimori.

Conclusion

The shifting propensities toward risk stressed by prospect theory, combined with learning from prior experiences, explain the tortuous path of structural adjustment in Brazil and Venezuela from the mid-1990s onward. The political disaster striking neoliberals Collor and Pérez inspired a deceleration or reversal of market reform, which failed, however, to bring economic stability. Worsening problems sooner (Brazil) or

[31] On similarities and differences between Chávez's movement and other cases of political transformation throughout history, see Vivas (1999: 85–141).

later (Venezuela) put chief executives and the leaders of their economic teams in the domain of losses. The resulting turn to risk acceptance induced them to shift course and resume market reform. Since Brazil was once again on the verge of hyperinflation, Fernando Henrique Cardoso's successful stabilization plan yielded much stronger popular support and greater political payoffs than the program promoted by Teodoro Petkoff, which lowered price increases that were high, but far removed from hyperinflationary levels. Since economic recovery soon put both governments in the domain of gains, their push for structural reform weakened quickly and progress remained limited, especially in the fiscal arena. Both countries therefore were vulnerable to external shocks, which indeed hit at the end of the decade.

Since President Cardoso managed to forestall great losses before the presidential contest of 1998, he won a convincing reelection victory. As a result, Brazil's political class maintained its predominance and continued its ever more cautious pursuit of market reform. In Venezuela, by contrast, where a new round of severe open problems exacerbated popular discontent with the established political class, a radical outsider and critic of neoliberalism was swept into office in that year. President Chávez has moved exactly in the opposite direction compared to President Cardoso: He has applied a neopopulist political strategy while not embracing market reform. Thus, the political and economic fate of Brazil and Venezuela, which had oscillated in broadly similar ways during the 1990s—though at a consistently lower level of support for neoliberalism in Venezuela—came to diverge considerably.

At the turn of the millenium, Venezuela became, in political terms, more similar to Peru, whereas Brazil became more similar to Argentina. In the former two countries, neopopulist leaders—Fujimori and Chávez—overpowered and undermined established democratic institutions and revamped constitutions to create more room for their personal leadership; even after Fujimori's fall, Peru therefore remains trapped in neopopulism, and the same outcome is likely to prevail in Venezuela if Chávez is forced out of office. In the latter two nations, by contrast, democratic institutions and parties defeated neopopulist leaders sooner (Collor) or later (Menem), and more republican, politically liberal leaders—Cardoso and de la Rúa—won the chief executive office; even after de la Rúa's downfall, Argentina's political class quickly managed to reconsolidate its hold on power by forming a government of national unity led by political old-timer Eduardo Duhalde, thus averting the risk of a resurgence of neopopulism for the time being. Therefore, Peru and Venezuela are potentially headed toward the involution of democracy, whereas democratic sustainability has advanced in Brazil and—despite recent threats—in Argentina.

CHAPTER NINE

THEORETICAL IMPLICATIONS AND CROSS-REGIONAL PERSPECTIVES

Theoretical Implications

Central Findings

To explain the initiation of drastic neoliberal adjustment in four fragile democracies and account for the divergent advance and outcome of market reform programs, this study has stressed the different severity of the problems confronting Argentina, Brazil, Peru, and Venezuela in the 1980s. These problems had two dimensions, namely, pressing conjunctural issues and structural difficulties of the established development model.

In all four countries, serious conjunctural disequilibria induced new presidents to enact tough, costly stabilization measures. Where these problems were so grave as to unleash hyperinflation, as in Argentina, Brazil, and Peru, the bold, risky adjustment plans of presidents Menem, Collor, and Fujimori elicited widespread support. In Venezuela, by contrast, where inflation was limited and the outgoing government had hidden worsening problems from the population, a similar stabilization program triggered massive — even violent — rejection, thus weakening President Pérez, who had sought to preempt a full-scale conjunctural crisis.

The desire to restore conjunctural stability also induced the four presidents to begin a fundamental restructuring of their countries' development models, which had run into increasing difficulties over the preceding decades. The differential severity of these structural problems accounts for the varying degree of support that these bold, risky reform efforts elicited and, as a result, for their faster and farther advance in Argentina and Peru than in Brazil and Venezuela. Where the established development model had produced decades of stagnation, as in Argentina, or caused tremendous impoverishment, as in Peru, presidents found considerable backing for their efforts to push through wide-ranging, profound market reforms. By contrast, where the development model had continued to produce substantial growth, as in Brazil, the president proved unable to win approval for crucial changes (which could in turn have contributed to stabilization). Similarly, where an exogenous solution to economic decline seemed to exist, as in petroleum-rich Venezuela, governmental proposals for overhauling the fiscal system made little headway. In addition, President Pérez was weakened by popular rejection of his initial stabilization plan.

Thus, chief executives succeeded in enacting a large part of the market reform program where both aspects of the crisis—conjunctural and structural problems—were acute and grave. By contrast, where conjunctural or structural problems were less severe, as in Venezuela and Brazil, respectively, neoliberalism ran into serious political difficulties.

Prospect theory provides a novel, empirically based microfoundation for these findings. In particular, risk-seeking in the domain of losses accounts for the enactment of bold reforms during serious crises. Under such adverse conditions, presidents shun the risk aversion of their predecessors and make determined efforts to restore stability and growth. And many people who confront pressing problems and have suffered recent losses endorse such daring rescue efforts.

These choices mirror the experimental situations designed by prospect theorists. Due to disproportionate loss aversion, people's main goal under crisis conditions is the return to normalcy, that is, the restoration of the status quo ante ("breaking even," Thaler and Johnson 1990). People focus on reverting recent losses and preventing future losses, while seeking further improvements with much less zeal. In its effort to restore order, this goal is essentially conservative. During crises, people are most interested in stability, rather than pursuing more ambitious goals, such as a social transformation. But they accept great risks in trying to recover stability. Rather than embracing cautious options, they prefer daring moves. Rejecting the permanent losses that risk-averse strategies would likely entail, they take a gamble in the uncertain hope of avoiding and reverting all losses, even at the danger of incurring much greater losses. Thus, people choose bold means to attain a conservative end. This situationally driven risk acceptance helps explain why attempts to restore stability often have a modernizing outcome because they boldly break longstanding obstacles to change and combat established sociopolitical groupings that seek to maintain the decaying old development model. Thus, my prospect-theory interpretation captures the odd mixture of backward and forward orientation that often characterizes reform efforts and is encapsulated in terms like "reconstruction" and "regeneration," which the initiators of market reform used frequently.[1]

---

[1] For instance, Collor called his electoral vehicle "Partido de Reconstrução Nacional" and his structural reform program "Projeto de Reconstrução Nacional" (Collor 1991a); Fujimori entitled his 1992 report to Congress, which extolled his initial accom-

Once the crisis passes, the economy stabilizes, and recovery sets in, political leaders and common citizens move into the domain of gains and shift from risk acceptance to risk aversion. As a result, presidents who boldly advanced market reforms when confronting deep crises now push much less hard for completing the neoliberal program. And a majority of the people support this turn to greater caution and reelect these neoliberal reformers, contrary to expectations derived from rational-choice principles (presented in Acuña and Smith 1994: 31–41).

These shifting propensities toward risk are influenced by other factors — particularly the prior-option bias — and triggered by context conditions, especially changing economic conjunctures, learning from prior experiences, and institutional structures. The prior-option bias ties down chief executives who have enacted well-defined policy approaches and keeps them from drastically shifting course when they face worsening problems. It thus introduces an obstacle to change that prevents established leaders from acting upon risk-seeking in the domain of losses. Therefore, only new presidents, especially political outsiders, proceed in the risk-acceptant fashion predicted by prospect theory, whereas incumbents or their handpicked successors tend to persist with unpromising policy approaches, keep muddling through, and thus throw good money after bad.

Furthermore, learning from prior experiences shapes the framing of the decision options that leaders and citizens consider. Specifically, perceived success prompts imitation. By contrast, perceived failure induces chief executives to embark on new departures. Since such innovative solutions are risky, learning does not necessarily improve policy-making; instead, it can lead to a sequence of failures. Negative feedback can thus trigger a "swing of the pendulum" as subsequent decision-makers move back and forth between alternative policy approaches.

Moreover, economic conjunctures and structural developments lead government officials and common citizens to see themselves in the domain of losses or the domain of gains, thus shaping the choice between different decision options. Specifically, the debt crisis of the 1980s created severe problems for all four countries and eventually contributed to hyperinflation in Argentina, Brazil, and Peru, but not in Venezuela. And the established development model had produced long stagnation in Argentina and severe income losses in Peru, whereas Brazil had continued to achieve substantial growth and many Venezuelans hoped for a renewed windfall from higher international oil prices.

---

plishments, "Hacia la Reconstruccíon Nacional" (Fujimori 1992); and Menem announced early on in his inaugural speech: "Argentina is broken. In this historic hour, its reconstruction begins" (Menem 1990: 8).

Finally, institutions condition the effective political impact of the individual choices elucidated by prospect theory. Specifically, Latin America's presidential systems make the decision of a single chief executive ultimately decisive in economic policy-making. And redemocratization and the advance of opinion polling give the aggregation of individual choices in elections and surveys an enormous political role. The neopopulist strategy that often accompanied market reform makes the application of a theory of individual decision-making particularly appropriate.

In sum, this study has advanced an argument rooted in cognitive-psychological findings and embedded it in an economic, political-institutional, and ideational context.

Bolstering and Improving Crisis Arguments

This book advances a crisis argument. In my prospect-theory interpretation, severe pressing problems faced by new leaders trigger bold, costly reforms, which hold the uncertain promise of saving the country from continuing deterioration but risk unleashing a full-scale catastrophe. And the deeper the crisis, the greater the latitude for pushing through structural reforms that transform the country's development model. Such crisis arguments are common in the literature on policy reform (e.g., Bates and Krueger 1993: 452–54; Bienen 1990; Grindle and Thomas 1991; Haggard and Kaufman 1995; Waterbury 1993). They hold great plausibility, and a glance at the evidence yields many confirmatory cases.

But crisis arguments have theoretical and operational problems and have therefore faced strong criticism (Rodrik 1996; Corrales 1996: chap. 4). In theoretical terms, the mechanisms through which crises trigger rescue efforts are often not well specified.[2] In particular, many crisis arguments lack clear microfoundations; they postulate aggregate effects but fail to elucidate the decisions of individual actors that would produce those effects. Specifically, they do not fully explain why chief executives, who have conflicting goals and would therefore like to avoid adjustment, decide to adopt painful, politically costly reforms. And they do not adequately show how reform initiators overcome collective-action problems among societal actors and elicit sufficient cooperation to make these reforms work. Given these lacunae, crisis arguments face charges of logically problematic "functionalism." In the eyes of critics,

---

[2] The interesting discussion in Haggard and Kaufman (1995: chap. 6) constitutes an exception to this claim.

they rest on the facile assumption that challenges automatically trigger solutions.

Crisis arguments also have the operational difficulty of determining when problems are sufficiently severe to qualify as a crisis. Most problems worsen in a continuous fashion, not through a sudden explosion. Such gradual deterioration poses a hard question: At what point does a problem turn into a crisis, which then triggers bold reform and makes this painful rescue effort acceptable to the citizenry? The difficulty of determining this threshold exposes crisis arguments to the danger of tautology. Their advocates can explain away the absence of reform — or of popular support for reform — by resorting to the auxiliary argument that problems had not yet reached crisis proportions. This flexible measurement of the independent variable makes crisis arguments hard to test.

This study strengthens crisis arguments by addressing several of these difficulties. As regards the threshold issue, it points to hyperinflation as the crucial trigger for the popular acceptance of drastic adjustment efforts. Price increases above 50 percent per month — economists' definition of hyperinflation — have a dramatic psychological impact. They signal a loss of control and threaten large sectors of the population with grave, potentially catastrophic losses. Hyperinflation completely unsettles the relative price system, undermines notions of economic value, and creates a pervasive sense of uncertainty and danger.[3] The eruption of hyperinflation thus ushers in a deep open crisis, which induces many people to accept great sacrifices in order to support their leaders' rescue efforts.

Once the outbreak of hyperinflation has prompted widespread popular support for neoliberal adjustment, the advance of structural reforms depends on the differential depth of a country's economic and political difficulties. After the crisis threshold has been passed, relative differences in problem severity turn crucial. Thus, my crisis argument uses both nominal comparison, which requires a binary classification of crisis vs. noncrisis, and ordinal comparison, which draws inferences from the differential depth of the crises facing different countries (cf. Mahoney 1999). The threshold problem thus does not confine crisis theorists to binary categories and crude "all-or-nothing" arguments.

What about the crucial first step, however: Namely, what level of economic difficulty induces chief executives to initiate drastic adjustment? Unfortunately, the exact point at which worsening problems turn

---

[3] This immediate psychological effect occurs even in economies with widespread indexation. In a situation of dramatic increases of inflation, indexation, which compensates for past inflation, cannot prevent current losses.

into a crisis in leaders' eyes is impossible to determine objectively. This threshold varies across countries, depending on prior experiences.[4] In fact, crisis perceptions reflect leaders' level of information and understanding; a sophisticated chief executive worries about early signs of looming danger that his or her uninformed counterpart may overlook.

In subjective terms, however, a crisis is always characterized by a pervasive sense of loss of control, deep uncertainty, and looming catastrophe (Vierhaus 1978: 312–24; Grindle and Thomas 1991: 75). This crisis perception can be gauged with reasonable reliability through interviews with decision-makers and the analysis of contemporary media accounts, opinion polls, memoirs, and country risk ratings. Thus, the presence of a crisis can be ascertained independently of its presumed impact, the initiation of drastic reform. Therefore, crisis arguments are not inherently tautological.

Furthermore, my study has made one contribution to addressing the threshold issue for leaders by invoking the political calendar for purposes of punctuation. The assumption of power by a new chief executive constitutes a necessary precondition for pressing problems to prompt bold reform efforts; by contrast, the prior-option bias induces incumbents to keep pursuing established policies. Leadership turnover thus creates a crucial discontinuity in the context of worsening economic difficulties. This emphasis on discrete political change eases the threshold problem plaguing crisis arguments.

As regards the criticism that crisis arguments lack a theoretical microfoundation, my application of prospect theory fills precisely this gap. Risk-seeking in the domain of losses makes new chief executives respond to crises with bold, risky rescue efforts. It also induces common citizens to support these drastic adjustment programs, at least initially. Relying on a well-corroborated psychological finding, this explanation operates at the individual level. It thus constitutes a microfoundation, as demanded by rational-choice theorists. But it breaks the monopolistic claim that only rational-choice arguments qualify as microfoundations.

In sum, this study proposes solutions for important problems that beset crisis arguments. By addressing several aspects of the threshold problem and by proposing a novel microfoundation, it strengthens crisis arguments against their detractors.

---

[4] For instance, in the late 1980s and early 1990s, 150 percent annual inflation would have constituted a crisis in Venezuela, but a considerable success in Brazil. In addition, political improvements can occasionally mitigate perceptions of economic crisis. Argentina, for instance, was suffering from deep economic problems in 1983, but the restoration of democracy inspired the hope that these difficulties could be easily overcome, inducing President Alfonsín to adopt traditional Keynesian policies (Machinea 1993: 124).

Prospect Theory and the Aufhebung of Functionalism into Reactionism

In bolstering crisis arguments, prospect theory makes a more general contribution by offering a Hegelian *Aufhebung* of functionalism. An *Aufhebung* preserves the positive elements of a theoretical approach, discards its problematic features, and introduces improvements that qualitatively transform an approach and give it greater validity.[5]

Functionalism deserves to undergo such an *Aufhebung*. Probably *the* dominant mode of social-scientific explanation forty or fifty years ago, it has suffered strong criticism due to its logical and methodological problems. But functionalism did make important contributions that have been lost by the approaches superseding it. In particular, functionalism's postulate of homeostatic tendencies recognized the capacity of social systems to self-regenerate and overcome accumulating problems. Functionalism thus managed to account for reversals of ongoing negative trends and for surprising turnarounds in social systems' fate.[6] By contrast, currently prevailing approaches, especially different versions of institutionalism, rest on linear assumptions, which induce scholars to extrapolate present trends. They thus expect that tendencies toward deterioration will continue, whereas functionalism predicts an eventual turnaround, recovery, and resolution of the underlying problems.

Certainly, many criticisms advanced against functionalism are correct (Hempel 1965; Nagel 1979). Above all, functionalists greatly overestimated the integrated nature and automatic equilibrating tendency of social systems. As a result, they were overly optimistic in expecting a quick and necessarily positive adjustment to strains and stresses. Contrary to this postulate of flexible, "functional" responses to challenges, many problems remain in fact unresolved; and if remedial efforts are made, they often fail — or make things worse. A revival of functionalism is therefore completely out of the question. Instead, the proposed *Aufhebung* discards the problematic elements of functionalism but preserves its valuable insights and bases them on elements of prospect theory. In this way, it proposes a new approach — "reactionism" — that is qualitatively superior to functionalism.

Such an *Aufhebung* is crucial because in demolishing functionalism, the social sciences have thrown out the baby with the bath water. By stressing the questionable elements of functionalism, they have covered

[5] The label "reactionism" — as in a challenge triggering a *reaction* — is meant to indicate clearly that I am not advocating a resuscitation of functionalism.

[6] Easton (1979: chap. 23); Binder et al. (1971); similarly, Gerschenkron (1962: chap. 1) used Arnold Toynbee's functionalist "challenge and response" scheme to account for countries' efforts to overcome backwardness.

up its important contributions. This purge of functionalism—combined with the discrediting of Marxian dialectics—has left the social sciences incapable of accounting for drastic departures from ongoing trends. The approaches predominating in the postfunctionalist era are committed to linear thinking:[7] They predict the continuation of current trends because they emphasize constraints on innovative action and impediments to change. In this vein, the situational equilibrium analysis advanced by rational choice (Murphy 1996),[8] especially game theory, expects continuity, not qualitative change. For instance, actors who are stuck in a "prisoners' dilemma" find it exceedingly difficult to escape from mutual defection and achieve cooperation. An even stronger linear tendency prevails in historical institutionalism and culturalism, which predict inertia, if not rigidity.[9]

While these approaches make important contributions to elucidating the established patterns of normal politics, they are at a loss to explain the bold and innovative rescue efforts often evident in crisis situations, and their sometimes striking success. For instance, rational choice, historical institutionalism, and culturalism did not expect the drastic market reforms adopted in a wide range of countries. Adherents of rational choice assumed that narrow self-interests—such as the desire to garner support by doling out patronage—would prevent political leaders from addressing national-level problems and enacting politically costly changes (Bates 1981; Geddes 1994b; criticism in Grindle 1991). Similarly, historical institutionalism and culturalism stress constraints that prevent flexible adjustment to challenges (e.g., Skowronek 1982), such as the worsening economic problems facing many countries in the 1980s. All of these approaches predicted continuing deterioration and failed to foresee the sudden wave of neoliberal adjustment ex ante.[10]

To account for these unexpected developments ex post, many authors have resorted to crisis arguments. As the preceding subsection shows, crisis arguments usually embody a functional—not purely causal—

[7] For a new challenge to this linearity assumption, see Kiel and Elliott (1996).

[8] Since the equilibrium of "games" of rational interaction changes with any change in actor preferences, it is purely situational and thus lacks the strong homeostatic tendencies of the dynamic equilibrium of functionalism (as stressed by Van den Berghe 1963: 697).

[9] Krasner (1984); March and Olsen (1984). Eckstein (1988) admits this static bias and seeks to rectify it, but rather than explaining cultural change, he discusses its effects. As in Eckstein's argument, change is exogenous to Krasner's "punctuated equilibrium" model (1984: 240–43); it interrupts the rigidity that Krasner's institutional argument predicts, but remains unexplained.

[10] For a similar discussion of the insufficiency of rational choice and historical institutionalism in explaining the "audacious reforms" that instituted decentralization in many Latin American countries, see Grindle (2000: chap. 9).

logic. Thus, the gaping holes in currently prevailing approaches have stimulated a recourse to functionalist reasoning. Functionalist elements have crept back even into explicitly antifunctionalist approaches. For instance, rational-choice authors have slipped into their arguments functionalist claims that clearly conflict with their methodologically individualist premises and their usual insistence that divergent self-interests and the resulting collective action dilemmas obstruct the resolution of systemic problems (see criticism by Granovetter 1985: 503–5; Hall and Taylor 1996: 952; see also Moe 1990: 215–20).

The surreptitious reappearance of functionalism suggests that this discredited approach made contributions that are in fact useful, maybe even indispensable. Specifically, functionalism's "challenge and response" mechanism provided a theoretical explanation for the fact that some countries do escape from linear trends of deterioration, for instance by overcoming collective-action dilemmas or by bending or breaking rigid institutional constraints or stifling traditions. But functionalism exaggerated this insight by postulating the automatic adjustment to challenges and the successful resolution of difficulties. As critics correctly noted, such flexible action and positive outcomes are by no means guaranteed. Functionalism therefore requires fundamental reformulation.[11]

Psychological decision theories suggest such an *Aufhebung* of functionalism. Specifically, risk-seeking in the domain of losses accounts for bold efforts by political leaders to overcome grave problems facing their country. The underlying motivation — strong loss aversion — explains why serious difficulties trigger rescue efforts that may stop continuing deterioration and produce a recovery. But the risk acceptance predicted by prospect theory also implies that these bold efforts do by no means succeed necessarily. Instead, they may well lead to dramatic failures and worsen the situation. As my application of prospect theory stresses, they hold lower expected value than more prudent, gradual measures, which leaders and citizens discard due to risk-seeking in the domain of losses. For instance, the serious problems plaguing Weimar Germany prompted the rise of Adolf Hitler, who promised a dramatic turnaround and initiated a bold, risky program of change — with absolutely disastrous consequences. Thus, my application of prospect theory predicts an eventual reaction to problems but stresses that this reaction is not necessarily adaptive and "functional."[12] And the prior-option bias explains why

---

[11] For other attempts to resurrect some aspects of functional reasoning, see Jervis (1997) and Lane (1994).

[12] The quality of learning from prior experiences — another factor stressed in this study — helps explain how promising and "functional" governmental responses to crises are.

this reaction is much less timely and automatic than functionalism had expected.

Psychological decision theories thus yield a profound reformulation of functionalism that preserves its positive insights while discarding its problematic, overoptimistic claims. This *Aufhebung* of functionalism into reactionism differs qualitatively from "elaborations" that seek to shore up functionalism by resorting to arguments on competition and selection (à la "survival of the fittest"; see Cohen 1986: 227–30; Stinch-combe 1968: 85–91). Whereas such elaborations retain claims of func-tionality, the present reformulation stresses the dangerous nature of leaders' bold reactions to challenges: These countermeasures have lower expected value than feasible alternatives because they hold a serious risk of making the situation worse, rather than bringing improvements.

Psychological Decision Theories vs. Rational Choice

As stated previously, psychological decision theories such as prospect theory provide a microfoundation for political analysis that diverges from conventional rational-choice approaches. Thus, they constitute an alternative to the paradigm that has been on the advance in political science, including the subfield of comparative politics. While sharing a number of similarities, such as a focus on individual choice, the two approaches differ on other dimensions. Whereas rational choice excels in parsimony, deductive rigor, and formal elaboration—for instance, in the form of game theory—psychological decision theories are much more complex and do not form a well-integrated paradigm. But this lack of coherence results from one of their principal strengths: They rest on solid empirical foundations, whereas rational choice starts from un-realistic assumptions about human problem-solving. Psychological deci-sion theories start from substantive knowledge about the complicated ways in which people do in fact act, not from simplifying ideal-typical postulates (Tversky and Kahneman 1986). Due to their strong empirical basis, psychological decision theories hold special promise for elucidat-ing the actual regularities of political life. By analyzing how real people act, they privilege empirical accuracy over parsimony and logical rigor. For an empirical field like political science, this priority appears entirely appropriate—indeed, imperative.

To claim that despite their ideal-typical premises, rational-choice models are in fact realistic, their advocates invoke several arguments, especially individual learning, collective aggregation, and "natural" se-lection (Tsebelis 1990: 31–39). But as these authors themselves admit, such arguments apply mostly in stable settings that guarantee minimal predictability and a reasonable time horizon. Under such regular conditions, actor identities and interests are clear and fixed, allowing for careful cost-benefit calculations. By contrast, rational choice is much less applicable to crisis situations, when extreme uncertainty makes it exceedingly difficult for actors to process information systematically and anticipate other actors' responses — in fact, even to rank-order their own preferences. For instance, is the maintenance of governmental stability more important in a severe crisis than determined adjustment? Thus, rational choice is better at analyzing normal politics that proceeds inside established institutional parameters than at unraveling the chaotic complexities of crisis politics.[13] In those unclear, fluid situations, rational incentives and constraints have much less determining force than under normal circumstances.

Psychological decision theories, especially prospect theory, help to fill this important gap. As argued above, prospect theory's central finding of risk-seeking in the domain of losses provides a strong foundation for crisis arguments. This insight diverges starkly from the predictions of conventional expected-utility theories, which tend to postulate risk aversion under all circumstances,[14] including crisis conditions. Due to this premise, authors oriented toward rational choice, such as Bates (1981), Ames (1987), and Geddes (1994b), did not foresee the wave of neoliberal reforms under democracy but claimed instead that in precarious institutional settings, politicians would prefer caution and shy away from determined adjustment. Prospect theory improves greatly on these accounts by providing a systematic explanation for presidents' shift from the risk aversion observed during the 1980s to the risk acceptance displayed in the initiation of neoliberal adjustment. Thus, psychological decision theories make a particularly important contribution to analyzing crisis situations, which are not infrequent in Latin America and which — as critical junctures — can shape institutional structures and policy patterns for decades (Collier and Collier 1991: chap. 2; Krasner 1984: 240–43).

Certainly, prospect theory claims greater empirical accuracy than rational choice in all situations, including normal politics; its finding of risk aversion in the domain of gains also deviates from conventional expected-utility arguments. But since those theories assume risk aversion in general, their predictions for the domain of gains are more difficult to test against prospect-theory arguments. Observers cannot easily

---

[13] Tsebelis (1990: 32–33). Naím (interview, 2000) confirmed this argument from the perspective of a key decision-maker.

[14] Risk aversion is implied by the assumption of diminishing marginal returns (McDermott 1998: 16).

determine whether in complex real-life situations, risk aversion was rationally justified and appropriate, or excessive and suboptimal. Thus, while arguments derived from prospect theory seem more accurate than rational-choice models even in noncrisis situations, as the slowdown of market reform after economic recovery in Argentina, Peru, and Brazil suggests (see chapters 6 and 8), it offers less "value added" for analyzing normal politics than for investigating crisis conditions. But since the bold reform efforts triggered by crises often reshape the parameters of normal politics, insights derived from prospect theory are — indirectly — crucial for understanding political actions and interactions in noncrisis situations as well.

By drawing on prospect theory and other cognitive-psychological insights to develop a new explanation of adjustment politics, the present book is part of a broader movement in political science to design alternatives to conventional rational-choice approaches, which have advanced greatly in the discipline during the last two decades. Yet ironically, while political scientists who adhere to rational choice have taken their main inspiration from economics, that discipline has in recent years been deeply affected by the influx of cognitive-psychological theories. Under the label of "behavioral economics," a good deal of the most interesting and promising recent work in economics has drawn on prospect theory, findings about status quo biases, and many other cognitive-psychological deviations from conventional rationality postulates (Camerer 2000; *Economist* 1999; Lowenstein 2001; McFadden 1999; Thaler 1992, 2000; Uchitelle 2001). Thus, principles and approaches of economics that are still being depicted as cutting edge in political science are quickly being challenged and superseded in economics itself. As more and more political scientists become aware of these new developments in the "dismal science," and as the wave of behavioral economics thus reaches the shores of our discipline, political science may soon experience a cognitive-psychological turn and a move away from conventional rationality approaches as well.

Cross-Regional Perspectives on the Politics of Market Reform

Does the explanation advanced in this book have broader validity beyond the four countries under investigation? Since space constraints preclude a comprehensive assessment, the following analysis concentrates on the most novel arguments, which are derived from the cognitive-psychological findings of shifts in people's propensity toward risk.[15]

[15] This section is a profoundly revised version of Weyland (1998b) reproduced with

Do these arguments apply to other nations in Latin America, Africa, and Eastern Europe? This section discusses a pragmatically delimited sample of cases. Since assessing psychological arguments requires a great deal of qualitative information, for instance on leaders' crisis perceptions, only cases on which there is substantial secondary literature can be included. Because scholars like to investigate change more than continuity, this sample is skewed toward reform efforts and underrepresents instances of nonreform. But this sample includes all possible combinations of outcomes: cases of reform and nonreform, and successful change as well as reform failure. Thus, while inappropriate for statistical investigation, this sample is unproblematic for qualitative comparative analysis, which merely requires cases that represent different combinations of factors and is not affected by the relative frequency of cases (Ragin 1987).

The Initiation of Adjustment: New Leaders Facing Deep Crises

Countries in this broader sample in fact initiate drastic adjustment when two conditions coincide, namely, a profound economic crisis and leadership turnover. When a country suffers from deep, acute problems and further deterioration is imminent, there is a tendency toward bold choices designed to save the nation, even at great risk. New leaders act on this impulse and initiate draconian adjustment while discarding more cautious and arguably more promising alternatives (cf. Bresser Pereira, Maravall, and Przeworski 1993; Murrell 1993). By contrast, the prior-option bias makes longstanding leaders reluctant to admit the failure of their earlier policies, acknowledge the losses they have caused, and drastically shift course. Only new leaders who face deep crises therefore adopt drastic neoliberal programs (see table 9.1).[16]

Leaders choose risky shock plans only when they confront severe problems, such as imminent hyperinflation, spiraling fiscal deficits, or deepening imbalances in external accounts. Incipient or full-scale hyperinflation triggered bold and painful market reforms in Bolivia and Poland, as in Argentina, Brazil, and Peru. Similarly, skyrocketing fiscal deficits, enormous imbalances in foreign trade, or widening shortages of goods led to determined adjustment efforts in Chile (1975), Ghana, Mexico (mid-1980s), Senegal, Russia, Tanzania, and Zambia (early

---

permission from Blackwell Publishers. Weyland (1999) extends the arguments in chapter 6 on neoliberal populism to a wide range of Latin American and East European countries.

[16] Czechoslovakia constitutes an exception as the new post-Communist government enacted shock therapy although the country was not suffering from a severe open crisis. The reasons for this deviation are discussed below, toward the end of this section.

TABLE 9.1 DRASTIC REFORM INITIATION

	Deep Crisis	No Deep Crisis
New Leader	*Menem (Argentina 1989)*	Alfonsín (Argentina 1984)
	Paz Est. (Bolivia 1985)	Paz Zamora (Bolivia 1989)
	Collor (Brazil 1990)	Aylwin (Chile 1990)
	Franco/Cardoso (Brazil 1994)	Sanguinetti (Uruguay 1985)
	Pinochet (Chile 1975)	Pérez (Venezuela 1974)
	Fujimori (Peru 1990)	Moi (Kenya 1978)
	Pérez (Venezuela 1989)	Shagari (Nigeria 1980)
	Rawlings (Ghana 1983)	*Havel (Czechoslovakia 1991)*
	Babangida (Nigeria 1986)	Antall (Hungary 1990)
	Diouf (Senegal 1984)	Gierek (Poland 1971)
	Mwinyi (Tanzania 1986)	Iliescu (Romania 1991)
	Chiluba (Zambia 1992)	
	Mazowiecki (Poland 1989)	
	Yeltsin (Russia 1992)	
	Kuchma (Ukraine 1994)	
Incumbent	Alfonsín (Argentina 1988)	Aylwin (Chile 1993)
or Insider	Sarney (Brazil 1988, 1989)	Frei (Chile 1994)
	De la Madrid (Mexico 1985)	Rawlings (Ghana 1993)
	García (Peru 1988, 1989)	Kaunda (Zambia 1974)
	Biya (Cameroon 1988)	Mugabe (Zimbabwe 1985)
	Limann (Ghana 1992)	Husák (Czechoslovakia 1988)
	Moi (Kenya 1991)	Gierek (Poland 1975)
	Shagari (Nigeria 1982)	Brezhnev (Russia 1975–82)
	Kaunda (Zambia 1985–90)	
	Mugabe (Zimbabwe 1990)	
	Gierek (Poland 1979)	
	Rakowski (Poland 1988)	
	Gorbachev (Russia 1989, 1990)	
	Kravchuk (Ukraine 1992, 1993)	

Note: The initiation of radical reforms is marked by italics.

1990s). Ghana, for instance, was teetering on "the brink of total collapse" (Chazan 1991: 21; similar Callaghy 1990: 274; Herbst 1993: 7, 14, 17, 29). After the boom and bust of raw-material prices in the mid-1970s, the sharpest drop in per capita income occurred from 1981 on, right before Jerry Rawlings' shift of course (Herbst 1993: 18).[17] In the absence of deep crises, by contrast, governments adopted more prudent, gradual adjustment measures in Chile (1990), Colombia,[18] Hungary, and Zimbabwe. Thus, severe, acute economic problems bring forth bold responses; otherwise, caution prevails.

The tendency toward risk acceptance in the domain of losses only comes to the fore, however, if a leader has some distance from the policies that caused — or failed to prevent — the deep crisis. Political outsiders who can disassociate themselves from recent mistakes and blame their predecessors are especially likely to adopt drastic adjustment.[19] By contrast, incumbents who are responsible for these failures refuse to admit the losses they caused and cling to their old policy approach as much as possible. For instance, although "among all the nations of Sub-Saharan Africa, Zambia . . . suffered one of the greatest — and most rapid — economic declines" (Bates and Collier 1993: 388), longstanding President Kenneth Kaunda (1964–91) abandoned in 1987 an orthodox stabilization program recommended by the IMF and adopted instead a homegrown, more heterodox adjustment plan, which predictably failed to stop economic deterioration (Bates and Collier 1993: 407–30; Callaghy 1990: 291–302). Félix Houphouët-Boigny of Côte d'Ivoire, in power from the country's independence in 1960 until his death in 1993, refused to enact determined adjustment measures, despite serious economic problems caused by drastic overspending in the 1970s (Demery 1994: 72–73, 97–100, 114, 127–30). Other established leaders in Africa, such as Cameroon's Paul Biya, Kenya's Daniel arap Moi, Nigeria's Shehu Shagari, and Zimbabwe's Robert Mugabe, also avoided serious stabilization or evaded the commitments made under pressure from international financial institutions (Van de Walle 1993; Lofchie 1993: 435–43; Herbst and Olukoshi 1994: 458–67; Herbst 1989; Knight 1996).

[17] Herbst (1993: 29–32, 41–43) stresses the political and economic risks of Rawlings' stabilization measures. On Senegal, see Ka and van de Walle (1994: 309–14); on Tanzania, Lofchie (1993, 446–54); on Zambia, Bates and Collier (1993: 388); Simutanyi (1996: 828–29).

[18] The trade liberalization initiated by President Virgilio Barco in 1989 was "tentative" and "gradual" (Urrutia 1994: 285, 301, 303), but new President César Gaviria (1990–94) unexpectedly radicalized it, especially to combat rising inflation (Urrutia 1994: 296–97).

[19] Based on different premises, Geddes (1994a: 115–17), Ravenhill (1993: 46), and Remmer (1993: 403–5) advance similar arguments.

Given the fundamental divergence of Communist central planning from market capitalism, the prior-option bias had a particularly strong hold on East European countries. Thus, despite economic stagnation, severe shortages, and rising inflation, General Wojciech Jaruzelski in Poland (1981–90) merely tinkered with the socialist command economy and refused to adopt profound reforms. Facing similar, though less urgent problems, party leaders Gustáv Husák of Czechoslovakia and Erich Honecker of East Germany were even more reluctant to change their fossilized Communist systems. In all these cases, a strong prior-option bias prevented longstanding incumbents from admitting failure, disavowing their efforts to shore up the established development model, and embracing market reforms that they had condemned before.

By contrast, new leaders are not tied down by association with the existing development model. Since their actions have not committed them to established policies, discarding old programs and adopting new measures does not constitute an admission of failure. They therefore respond to deep crises in the risk-acceptant fashion predicted by prospect theory. When facing the failures of state-interventionist, protectionist policies, they boldly adopt drastic market reform. In this vein, Bolivia's Víctor Paz Estenssoro (1985–89), an opponent of his predecessor Hernán Siles Suazo, adopted a dramatic shock program right after taking office in 1985 to combat full-scale hyperinflation (Malloy 1991: 48–53). Chilean dictator Augusto Pinochet, who removed the socialist government of Salvador Allende in a bloody coup in late 1973, enacted tough stabilization measures in early 1975 to reduce skyrocketing price rises.[20]

Similarly, Zambia's Frederick Chiluba, who ended President Kaunda's twenty-seven-year rule with a decisive election victory in 1991, and Ghana's Jerry Rawlings, who dislodged the established political elite through a coup in late 1981, sought to revert their countries' deepening economic crisis by adopting determined stabilization measures that their predecessors had long rejected. Senegal's Abdou Diouf and Tanzania's Ali Hassan Mwinyi, who emerged from the pragmatic or technocratic wing of dominant parties and replaced long-governing "socialist" leaders,[21] and Nigeria's Ibrahim Babangida, who took power through a coup, proceeded likewise (Herbst and Olukoshi 1994: 471–79; Ka and van de Walle 1994: 309–14; Lofchie 1993: 446–54; Camp-

---

[20] Colombia's Barco initiated neoliberal reform at the end of his term, but Gaviria, the standard-bearer of a former dissident faction of the ruling party, "encouraged the Barco economic team to start the liberalization process when he was a presidential candidate" (Urrutia 1994: 304).

[21] On the refusal of Tanzania's longtime leader Julius Nyerere to adopt adjustment measures, see Mans (1994: 354–69).

bell and Stein 1992: 7–9, 14–16; Faruqee 1994: 238, 245–46, 259). In a similar vein, successful opponents to Communist rule, such as Tadeusz Mazowiecki and Lech Wałęsa in Poland and Boris Yeltsin in Russia, confronted the tremendous problems caused by the decaying central command economy—especially widespread shortages and incipient or imminent hyperinflation—with the "big bang" of radical market reform (Johnson and Kowalska 1994: 191–199; Kowalik 1994: 139; Åslund 1995: chaps. 2–3; Yeltsin 1995: 124–27).

As in Argentina, Brazil, Peru, and Venezuela, the choice of these draconian adjustment measures mirrored the risk acceptance displayed by experimental subjects in the domain of losses. Compared to more cautious stabilization policies, shock therapy held great economic and political dangers, but also the uncertain prospect of quickly reverting past losses and avoiding future deterioration. As regards economic risks, far-reaching price liberalization and drastic currency devaluation threatened to fuel, rather than contain, rapid inflation; the slashing of tariffs and elimination of other protectionist measures endangered the survival of domestic industry; and large-scale, rapid privatization threatened to cement oligopolies and monopolies, rather than ensuring competition. Even more clearly, shock therapy carried enormous political risks by imposing further immediate costs on the suffering population while promising uncertain future benefits, which people commonly discount heavily (cf. Thaler 1992: 94). In fact, earlier adjustment measures had often been obstructed by opposition, protest, and sometimes the overthrow of the government. Political forces that had not campaigned on neoliberal programs—such as Bolivia's Paz Estenssoro, Zambia's Chiluba, and Poland's Solidarity movement—ran particular risks due to their betrayal of popular expectations.

Decision-makers were aware of the dangers inherent in drastic market reform. For instance, Yeltsin (1995: 146, 149) admits in his candid autobiography that shock therapy "can lead to catastrophe, to complete collapse" and describes "the grave second thoughts, the insomnia and headaches in the middle of the night" that plagued him after he liberalized prices in Russia.[22] Among Paz Estenssoro's team, "all were also aware that the shock [treatment they considered] held the grave risk of awakening the sense of rebellion and social unrest of the population" (Cariaga 1997: 96; also 102, 197; similar Conaghan and Malloy 1994: 149), which had prompted frequent strikes that obstructed the preceding government's stabilization efforts. Similarly, Rawlings knowingly took a grave risk by devaluing the currency, given the association

[22] See also Yeltsin's conversation with Balcerowicz (1995: 366–67); and Gaidar (1999: chaps. 6–7).

in Ghana between devaluations and the overthrow of the government (Herbst 1993: 41).

Due to the instability plaguing many countries, which threatened to turn protest deadly for a government, shock therapy embodied greater political dangers than less drastic policies. But contrary to more cautious stabilization measures, it held the uncertain promise of recouping past losses ("breaking even," cf. Thaler and Johnson 1990) and of paving the way for renewed growth. The hope to escape from losses quickly—even at the risk of unleashing a catastrophe—made decision-makers prefer drastic neoliberal reform to more prudent measures that would keep economic and especially political risks limited, but that did not offer the (uncertain) prospect of a quick recovery.

Leszek Balcerowicz, the architect of Poland's shock therapy, states this tendency toward risk-seeking in the domain of losses: "[A]ttractive for me was the best variant from the available set, even if it was a very difficult, or a very risky one" (cited in Kozielecki 1995: 191). Specifically, "I tended to prefer those policy options which were associated with the higher risk of being rejected by society but which, if implemented, promised to bring better economic results than those that were socially less risky but economically also less promising" (Balcerowicz 1995: 344). Thus, Balcerowicz accepted great risk in pursuing the option that could potentially yield the highest economic benefit, but that due to political dangers had uncertain prospects of overall success. In the terms of prospect theory, he preferred the lottery that comprised widely divergent outcomes—ranging from the highest potential payoff to the danger of complete, politically caused failure—over safer options that had a more narrow band of outcomes but did not promise a dramatic economic turnaround.[23]

In line with my prospect-theory interpretation, new leaders thus tackled severe problems with particularly bold policy changes, rather than selecting prudent alternatives. Two cases, however, constitute partial exceptions to this argument, which underpredicts determined adjustment (table 9.1): Czechoslovakia and Mexico. Although Czechoslovakia was not suffering from a severe open crisis, the new post-Communist government enacted shock therapy. Two factors account for this deviation from the general pattern. The strong desire to rejoin "Europe" and quickly become a prosperous country, which was inspired in

---

[23] For the latter reason, Balcerowicz (1995: 225) sometimes claims that "a radical approach involving forceful stabilization measures and rapid liberalization is almost surely the least risky option." In these passages, however, he seems to understand "risk" as the inverse of the chance of attaining the highest possible outcome, thus diverging from the definition of risk in prospect theory, which considers the spread among the whole bundle of the potential outcomes a choice may entail.

part by territorial contiguity to an advanced capitalist country (Germany), strengthened the impulse to implement drastic change. And the absence of a monetary overhang, resulting from the "conservative" economic policies of the preceding hard-line Communist administration, limited the danger that instant liberalization would trigger high inflation, thus diminishing the cost of bold reform.

In Mexico, President Miguel de la Madrid (1982–88) imposed a shock stabilization plan in 1983 (Lustig 1992: 29–34) and initiated determined structural reform in 1985 although he was not an outsider but hailed from the long-governing Partido Revolucionario Institucional (PRI) and had been handpicked by his predecessor. Mexico's unique authoritarian regime, which had a high level of institutionalization and thus guaranteed resilience in the face of challenges, helps account for this exception. The political risks of neoliberalism were lower in Mexico, and they could be more easily contained by the incumbent elite, as in the disputed election of 1988 (in which the leftist opposition may have outpolled the PRI candidate but was prevented from taking over the government). The institutionalization of Mexico's authoritarian regime also gave presidents a long time horizon, making them more willing to impose short-term pain for long-term gain. Furthermore, the technocratic wing of the PRI had the incentive to enact market reform and thus establish predominance over its "political" wing (Centeno 1994). This competition inside the ruling party resembles the emergence of "factional outsiders" mentioned in chapter 3 and exemplified by Carlos Andrés Pérez in Venezuela. Finally, territorial contiguity to an advanced capitalist country, which also operated in the Czechoslovakian case, reinforced the push for drastic market reform in Mexico. This stark contrast reinforced perceptions of losses and thus heightened risk acceptance. It also provided concrete incentives to enact profound change, which could pave the way for economic integration. Thus, the exceptional cases of Czechoslovakia and Mexico deviate from the specific arguments advanced in this study but are compatible with the underlying logic of my explanation.

Popular Responses to Neoliberal Adjustment

These painful adjustment plans found majority endorsement where citizens faced a deep, open crisis, saw themselves in the domain of losses, and therefore accepted the risks inherent in shock programs. As mentioned above, the eruption of hyperinflation is the clearest threshold for widespread perceptions of a severe crisis, which in turn trigger a massive shift to risk acceptance. In the absence of a deep visible crisis, by

TABLE 9.2 INITIAL POPULAR REACTION TO DRASTIC REFORM

	Popular Support	Popular Rejection
Hyperinflation	*Argentina (1989)*	
	Bolivia (1985)	
	Brazil (1990, 1994)	
	Peru (1990)	
	Poland (1989–90)	
No Hyperinflation		Chile (1975)
		Mexico (1985)
		Venezuela (1989)
		Ghana (1983)?
		Nigeria (1986)
		Bulgaria (1991)
		Russia (1992)

contrast, a majority of citizens had a positive or neutral outlook on the recent past and the foreseeable future, preferred caution, and rejected shock programs. Thus, the severity of the initial crisis—especially the presence or absence of hyperinflation—shapes citizens' reaction to leaders' bold choices (see table 9.2).

Immediately before the enactment of draconian stabilization measures, a majority of Bolivians and Poles—like Argentines, Brazilians, and Peruvians—saw themselves in a domain of losses. Above all, inflation was spiraling out of control. Monthly price increases reached 66.3 percent in July 1985 in Bolivia (after a staggering 182.8 percent in February) and 54.8 percent in October 1989 in Poland. As a result, a majority of poll respondents in Poland, where surveys were conducted, reported a recent decline in their economic well-being. Due to exploding inflation, expectations of further deterioration were widespread. Thus, hyperinflation put many people in the domain of losses (Przeworski 1993: 160).

A clear majority of the suffering population therefore supported draconian adjustment plans and their initiators—even *before* beneficial results appeared. They approved of risky efforts to end the crisis and recoup recent losses, rather than demanding gradual stabilization efforts

designed to limit and slowly reverse the decline. This massive endorsement prevailed although tough adjustment often imposed tremendous
additional costs on the population, such as price increases for basic necessities by up to 900 percent and a currency devaluation by 93 percent,
as in Bolivia. By contrast to these immediate costs, the promised benefits of neoliberal programs — stabilization and eventual recovery — were
quite uncertain. Indeed, earlier adjustment measures, which had been
announced with similar promises, had invariably failed. Nevertheless,
many people abandoned the healthy skepticism that these disappoint-
ments would have justified. The uncertain hope to be "saved" from a
deep crisis made them disregard the common tendency to discount future benefits heavily (cf. Thaler 1992: 94). Thus, in approving of shock
treatment, a majority of people accepted great risks.

In Poland, endorsement of the draconian Balcerowicz plan outnumbered rejection by about 30 percentage points during the first two
months (Przeworski 1993: 158–60; see Frentzel-Zagorska and Zagorski
1993: 709, 725; Johnson and Kowalska 1994: 211–12). In Bolivia, the
lack of survey data makes it more difficult to assess the popular reaction
to Paz Estenssoro's shock program. But the general strike called immediately by the powerful peak union Central Obrera Boliviana (COB)
found limited adherence and was about to fizzle out when the government imposed a state of siege to break the labor movement. "The weary
middle classes . . . support[ed] Paz's austerity programme. Equally decisive in [the COB's] defeat was the lack of peasant support for the
strike" (*LAWR* 1985). Thus, the available evidence suggests "an explicit
or implicit consensus in favor of harsh macroeconomic measures" (Pastor 1992: 92; cf. Gamarra 1994: 110).

In sum, where people confronted a deep, open crisis, especially hyperinflation, they endorsed drastic, painful stabilization measures, at
least initially. While this support diminished thereafter when the costs of
shock programs became intense and — in some cases — inflation returned, it often rose again when leaders enacted new, even more determined, stabilization plans.

By contrast, in countries that experienced economic problems below the level of hyperinflation, such as Bulgaria, Russia, Senegal, and
Zambia, many people rejected their leaders' adjustment measures, and
protests sometimes erupted (Przeworski 1993: 132, 145–46; Baglione
and Clark 1995: 221–22; Ka and van de Walle 1994: 334–39; Bratton
and Liatto-Katundu 1994: 544, 549). In Hungary in 1995, the new
Socialist Party government anticipated a serious financial crisis and
therefore adopted a radical stabilization plan, but since the imminent
danger had not yet tangibly affected the general public, these painful
measures elicited widespread disapproval (Kornai 1996: 969, 973, 976,

1012–13; Cook and Orenstein 1999: 92–96). In Nigeria, the hope for an easy escape from problems via a sudden rise of petroleum prices — the country's main export — prevented many citizens from seeing themselves in the domain of losses. As a result, they opposed the stabilization measures proposed by the government of Ibrahim Babangida (Herbst and Olukoshi 1994: 473–86). These cases confirm that a majority of the population will endorse painful, risky adjustment plans only if it clearly faces prospects of losses, especially due to hyperinflation.[24]

Leaders' Turn to Caution in Cases of Economic Recovery

Like presidents Menem and Fujimori, reform-initiating chief executives shifted to risk aversion when and where the acute crisis passed, the economy stabilized, and growth resumed. As leaders moved from the domain of losses into the domain of gains, they switched from risk acceptance to risk aversion. This noteworthy turn to caution led chief executives to push for market reforms much less hard than they had done when facing severe, open crises. Leaders who had initially enacted tremendously bold measures and had run roughshod over opponents turned ever more cautious, risk-averse, and reluctant to engage in confrontation. Neoliberal experts and international financial institutions, ideologically committed to completing the market reform program, complained that change was getting stuck in midstream and kept reminding chief executives of the many tasks that remained unfinished, but to no avail.

Indicating this shift to risk aversion, government leaders now started to take the political costs of market reforms much more seriously than at the beginning of their terms. This change in the decision-making calculus resulted not only from the electoral calendar; even after winning reelections, getting a new mandate, and disposing again of a medium-term time horizon, chief executives did not speed up the reform process with renewed energy. Diminished political capital or electoral expediencies were not decisive for slowing down market reform; the turn toward risk aversion that arose from the very success in combating deep initial crises played a critical role, as was obvious above in the cases of Menem and Fujimori.

---

[24] The absence of opinion polls makes it difficult to ascertain popular reactions to adjustment in Ghana and other African countries. Yet the eruption of protests — despite repression — suggests that the stabilization measures initially encountered considerable rejection, at least in cities. Authoritarian rule, however, allowed Rawlings to persist in his reform course until economic recovery produced growing support for the market model (Jeffries 1992: 214–16; Herbst 1993: 65–71).

This striking shift from risk acceptance to risk aversion also shows that the initial boldness displayed by chief executives in enacting drastic neoliberal programs did not reflect inherent personality traits, but the situational conditions emphasized by prospect theory, namely, leaders' perception of domain. Some chief executives commented openly on their change of attitude. For instance, Ghana's Rawlings said in mid-1999: "I have to admit that the fierce pride of determination which was characteristic of the hard days of the early 1980's has given way to a certain degree of complacency[, which arises as] social and economic conditions improve" (cited in Boateng 1999).

In the cases of economic recovery, the shift to risk aversion is obvious. For instance, as the Czech economy quickly emerged from its transitional recession and entered a period of sustained growth in the mid-1990s, Václav Klaus, who had insisted on drastic liberalization in 1990 and 1991, became reluctant to pursue the restructuring of enterprises with equal determination. Therefore, the tough bankruptcy law passed in late 1991 was never implemented; instead, the Czech government bailed out many failing firms (Hoen 1996: 14–16; see also 10–11; Stark and Bruszt 1998: 154–59). Most banks, which through long-standing credit relationships and control over voucher privatization funds maintained great influence over the large enterprise sector, were not included in the privatization program but remained in state hands. And to avoid high unemployment, the Klaus government never forced the banks to impose hard budget constraints on firms, which therefore postponed painful restructuring. This delay in enterprise adjustment limited productivity, competitiveness, and exports, caused external imbalances, and triggered a currency crisis in 1997 and a recession in 1998 (World Bank 1999: 4–7, 135–45). Thus, the initial success of the Czech transition led to complacency and excessive caution, which soon caused serious problems.[25]

In a similar vein, the government led by the Hungarian Socialist Party, which in early 1995 combated the threat of "a major financial crisis" with "the most radical structural adjustment program ever attempted" in the country (Cook and Orenstein 1999: 92), soon moderated its push for further market reform as the economy recovered. For instance, "the initiative to restructure public finances . . . lost momentum" (Csaba 1998: 1389) after 1996. The radical reform of the social

---

[25] Similarly, the Czech(oslovak) government enacted a radical health care reform in 1991 (World Bank 1999: 219–21), but in 1994 instituted changes in the pension system that were much less drastic than the mandatory privatization introduced in Poland and Hungary. See Charlton, McKinnon, and Konopielko (1998: 1419–20, 1423–24) and compare Cook and Orenstein (1999: 87–89, 97–98) with Rueschemeyer and Wolchik (1999: 132–33) and World Bank (1999: 205).

security system that Finance Minister Lajos Bokros proposed at the height of the crisis was gradually watered down as privatization was limited to an ever smaller share of pension funding (Bokros 1998: 549–51; Cook and Orenstein 1999: 97–98). Thus, whereas the threat of a severe crisis had prompted very bold measures, economic recovery inspired risk aversion and political caution.

The shift to risk aversion prompted by economic improvement is also evident in African cases. Most notably, the Rawlings government in Ghana, which had taken drastic, politically risky adjustment measures to avert the country's collapse in the early 1980s, relaxed its fiscal discipline and shied away from further structural change as the economy achieved stability and sustained growth. For instance, Rawlings never privatized Ghana's inefficient public enterprises (Leith and Lofchie 1993: 276–77; Verlet 1997: 43), thus limiting the influx of much-needed foreign investment. And while this ruthless leader had not hesitated to unleash repression during the initial crisis, stabilization and recovery made him much more willing to accommodate to political pressures. Accordingly, he responded to expressions of discontent in 1986 with a social compensation program (discussed below). And he gave in to domestic and international pressures for democratization, which predictably triggered a loosening of adjustment as the government engaged in considerable patronage spending before the presidential elections of 1992 and 1996 (Morna 1995: 38–39; Sandbrook and Oelbaum 1997: 627–30). Thus, the country that the IFIs had held up as the model of structural adjustment in Africa came to succumb to adjustment fatigue as—and because—the painful early reforms attained considerable success.

Similarly, the military government of Ibrahim Babangida in Nigeria loosened its adjustment policies not only in 1988 in response to opposition and protest, but also in 1990–91 due to the oil price boom caused by the Iraq/Kuwait conflict. This unexpected windfall quickly alleviated economic difficulties and eased the sense of crisis prevailing among decision-makers (Faruqee 1994: 239, 245–48, 252, 266–67). By putting government leaders into the domain of gains, it induced them to adopt a cautious stance and push less hard for structural adjustment.

Due to this turn to caution, governments that had forcefully initiated drastic stabilization and neoliberal restructuring hesitated to complete the reform process. Economic experts and international financial institutions therefore pointed to many unfinished tasks that in their view kept the recovery precarious and obstructed self-sustained growth. For instance, Bolivia's former finance minister, Juan Cariaga, lists a number of reform deficits as obstacles to more dynamic development (1997: 209, 214–22). Similarly, his Hungarian colleague Bokros (1998:

549) outlines "the unfinished agenda," stressing, for instance, that "the Hungarian pension reform is far from complete."

In sum, as in Argentina and Peru, chief executives in Latin America, Eastern Europe, and Africa turned to caution as their initial drastic stabilization and reform measures attained success. Improvement in economic indicators triggered a switch from risk acceptance to risk aversion.

People's Turn to Risk Aversion and the Political Sustainability of the New Market System

As countries emerged from acute crises; as the economy stabilized and returned to growth; and as more and more people benefited from the improving economy or expected to do so in the near future, an ever larger number of citizens also turned from risk acceptance to risk aversion and therefore tended to accept the new status quo. While unwilling to risk further neoliberal changes, they embraced the basic outline of the new market model despite its remaining flaws. Indeed, the steep transitional costs that many people had to pay reinforced their determination to give the new development scheme a chance, rather than trying out untested alternatives. These costs constitute a sunk investment that — analogous to the prior-option bias affecting leaders — makes citizens reluctant to support a new round of painful, risky experiments, such as a radical reversal of neoliberal programs. Thus, the current benefits and hopes for future payoffs as well as the past costs of market reform create a tendency toward caution and inertia that protects the basic features of the recently instituted neoliberal model from immediate challenges.

Two conditions are crucial for this shift to risk aversion and the resulting increase in the political sustainability of the new market model: Does it achieve economic stabilization and recovery? And do governments distribute some fruits of the economic turnaround to large numbers of people? The first condition depends on several political and economic factors, yet the character of the initial crisis seems especially important. Where hyperinflation devastated an economy, as in Bolivia and Poland, drastic, painful adjustment can also produce benefits, at least by averting an imminent catastrophe. Furthermore, stabilization constitutes a necessary — though not sufficient — condition for renewed growth. By contrast, in countries that suffered from repressed inflation, such as Russia, neoliberal reforms unleash a torrent of price increases that discredits the new policies, spurs opposition, and thus hinders stabilization and recovery.

In Bolivia and Poland, the end of hyperinflation brought quick relief to the suffering population. The restoration of minimal economic stability lifted the inflation tax, which had imposed particularly steep losses on large numbers of poorer people. And by reestablishing predictability, it eased the prevailing sense of uncertainty and facilitated the planning of daily life. Furthermore, development eventually resumed. While Bolivia achieved only low growth for several years, the first half of the 1990s saw significant expansion, averaging 4.1 percent per year. And after the Polish economy emerged from a deep transitional recession in 1993, it attained one of the highest growth rates in Europe at a yearly average of 5.4 percent (World Bank 1999: 2). Thus, in countries plagued by hyperinflation, shock treatment can — despite its tremendous transitional costs — end the acute crisis quickly and eventually produce recovery.

By contrast, neoliberal adjustment worsened the problems of nations plagued by repressed inflation. In Russia, for instance, inflation shot up by 245 percent immediately after price liberalization in January 1992 and then hovered around 20–25 percent per month from October 1992 through November 1993 (Åslund 1995: 184). This explosion of inflation undermined stabilization efforts, strengthened resistance to neoliberal reforms, and turned economic recovery precarious. In fact, Russia's GDP contracted by a combined 38 percent from early 1992 to late 1994 (Åslund 1995: 278). This collapse, combined with persistent price rises, fueled discontent with market-oriented change. People who remained in the domain of losses were more likely to cast a risk-acceptant vote for the opposition in parliamentary and presidential elections (Whitefield and Evans 1994: 53–59; Kim and Sidorenko-Stephenson 1999: 475–80).

The corrective inflation resulting from price liberalization does not always create widespread hardship, however. In prereform Ghana, for instance, products used to be unavailable at the official controlled prices, and consumers had to resort to the burgeoning black market, which charged outrageous premiums. The nominal inflation unleashed by price liberalization thus had little effective impact (Jeffries 1991: 161; Herbst 1993: 31, 67–68). Market reform in Ghana indeed led to an economic recovery that produced growth of 5–6 percent from 1983 to 1991.

Furthermore, price liberalization does not cause exploding inflation where the economy enjoys relative equilibrium. Due to a limited monetary overhang, the Czechoslovak government, for instance, managed to free prices in one fell swoop without triggering dramatic price rises. Since the fiscally conservative policies of the preceding Communist regime had safeguarded economic stability, the shock treatment adopted at the instigation of Finance Minister Klaus had less painful repercussions than in Russia. With low unemployment and the resumption of growth in 1993, the Czech economy seemed to emerge from the transition in rather good shape.

Economic recovery provides governments with the resources to engage in social policies that extend some fruits of renewed growth to large numbers of people (Nelson 1992; Graham 1994; Waterbury 1993: 197–208). By putting more and more citizens in the domain of gains and thus turning them risk-averse, social programs enhance the acceptance of the newly established market model, create support for its initiators, and prevent the less well-off from giving the opposition a try.[26] Spending programs therefore substantially enhance the political sustainability of market reform.

Due to their own shift to risk aversion, which made them more interested in "buying" support, all governments that achieved an economic recovery created social programs to benefit large numbers of voters. For instance, Rawlings instituted in 1986 "the most ambitious [social compensation] program on the [African] continent" (Herbst 1993: 53). The government used these antipoverty measures to reduce opposition to economic reform (Callaghy 1990: 284; Herbst 1993: 149). Similar spending programs adopted in the early 1990s, especially significant improvements in rural infrastructure, helped Rawlings win clear victories in the presidential elections of 1992 and 1996 (Jeffries 1998: 194–95, 203–5).

The governments appointed by Lech Wałęsa also instituted and maintained social programs to mitigate the costs of dismantling Poland's central command economy, particularly skyrocketing unemployment, which reached 15.7 percent of the labor force in December 1993. These compensation measures accounted for 29 percent of government spending in 1991 and 35 percent in 1992 (Graham 1994: 217, 223). Certainly, these social programs did not eliminate discontent; unemployment was the factor that most clearly diminished support for the government and its neoliberal reforms (Przeworski 1993: 164–66, 180–81; Gibson and Cielecka 1995: 777–781). Nevertheless, the recovery beginning in 1993 and the above-mentioned social programs enhanced popular backing for the market model so much that its outline was not at stake in the 1995 presidential campaign (Juchler 1996: 273, 282).

Due to the absence of large-scale unemployment, the Klaus govern-

[26] Especially where clientelism is entrenched, as in much of Latin America and Africa, people's political choices — such as votes — depend not only on sociotropic considerations, but also on pocketbook concerns.

ment in the Czech Republic did not institute a social compensation program. But it distributed benefits to broad sectors of the population by maintaining some price and rent controls, disbursing generous social expenditures, and ensuring through negotiations with labor and business that real wages kept rising (Rueschemeyer and Wolchik 1999: 132; World Bank 1999: 81, 206, 221; Stark and Bruszt 1998: 183–87). The government used these traditional social policies to strengthen its political base and boost support for the new development scheme.

Due to economic recovery and social programs, many Poles, Ghanaians, and — temporarily — Czechs entered the domain of gains (European Commission 1998: 44, figs. 74, 81; Jeffries 1992: 214–16; Jeffries and Thomas 1993: 360, 362; Cline and Fisher 1994: 33–35). They therefore turned risk-averse and accepted the newly established market model, rather than experimenting with alternatives (European Commission 1998: 39, figs. 71, 81; Nugent 1999: 297; Verlet 1997: 42–43). No significant contender in recent presidential and parliamentary elections therefore advocated a turnaround in economic policy. Even the opposition candidates promised to maintain the neoliberal model and proposed only limited modifications.[27] Given the fluid, fragmented party systems in these countries, which allowed for the rise of new challengers,[28] this absence of a fundamental attack on neoliberalism provides evidence of considerable popular support or at least acquiescence. In fact, Czech reform initiator Klaus achieved election victories in 1992 and 1996, a rare accomplishment in post-Communist Eastern Europe (Schneider 1997: 154–55, 158). This strong base of agreement suggests that the new market model has become politically sustainable.

By contrast, the presidential election of 1996 in Russia, which has continued to suffer from severe economic problems,[29] saw a confrontation between the unreliable guarantor of market reform and a stalwart of the old system. Russia's Communist Party has refused to revamp its program, as successor parties in many other post-Communist countries have done, and has continued to attack the new market system frontally (Cook and Orenstein 1999: 53–55). Thus, where economic recovery is weak or social policies lag, many people remain stuck in the domain of losses, reject neoliberalism, and search for alternative solutions to the persistent crisis (Whitefield and Evans 1994: 53–59; Kim and Sidorenko-Stephenson 1999: 475–80; Grant 1999).

[27] This reasoning also applies to the founding election of Chile's new democracy (Weyland 1996c: 199–200).

[28] Witness, for instance, the rise of Stanislaw Tyminski in Poland (1990), Vladimir Zhirinovsky in Russia (1993), and Adu Boahen in Ghana (1992).

[29] Market reforms have also been heavily distorted, especially through nomenklatura privatization (McFaul 1995).

Further Extensions of the Prospect-Theory Argument

The basic logic of the crisis argument that the present study derives from prospect theory is applicable to a range of issues besides the enactment of market reform. In particular, risk acceptance in the domain of losses can account for a variety of drastic policy changes that often had a lasting impact on economic, social, and political development in large numbers of countries.

First of all, economic crises that preceded the severe problems of the 1980s also triggered dramatic, risky policy changes. In this vein, the Great Depression of 1929, which caused a collapse in international trade and entailed large-scale unemployment, induced many governments to initiate daring reforms that had uncertain economic prospects and were politically controversial, such as the New Deal in the United States, social-democratic Keynesianism in Sweden, and a militaristic economic reactivation in Germany (Gourevitch 1986: chap. 4). And since the Great Depression "assumed catastrophic proportions" in Latin America (Furtado 1976: 54), it prompted the embrace of untested policies of import-substitution industrialization throughout the region (Furtado 1976: 107–17; Kaufman 1990a). Since this grave crisis seemed to prove the failure of economic liberalism, social learning inspired the embrace of pronounced state interventionism in a typical swing of the pendulum. Since this move to economic nationalism had unforeseeable consequences, it constituted a risky policy choice. In fact, by hindering international economic exchange and aggravating conflict among countries, protectionism actually made the crisis worse. Risk-seeking in the domain of losses helps account for this suboptimal outcome.

My prospect-theory based crisis argument also sheds light on the many instances in which grave social and political difficulties triggered dramatic, bold, and highly risky political and institutional transformations. As many authors have noted, serious sociopolitical conflict and the resulting perceptions of threat to the established order tend to provoke drastic responses, including military coups (see seminal discussion in O'Donnell 1978, 1979; and recently Bellin 2000). The armed overthrow of the political regime is, obviously, a risky course of action, given that the response of political adversaries is difficult to predict and that the coup makers cannot be assured of firm support within their own ranks;[30] in fact, many rebellions fail, and the consequences for their initiators can be dire indeed. Yet where perceptions of profound threat

---

[30] For military perceptions of these risks, see, e.g., D'Araujo, Soares, and Castro (1994: 16–18, 39–44, 48, 85, 102–8).

are widespread, many otherwise cautious actors—such as business groups—become risk-acceptant and support the installation of an authoritarian regime, despite the tremendous concentration of power that makes the new leaders unaccountable and enables them to act arbitrarily. For instance, dictators may for political or personal reasons (e.g., graft) decide to encroach on the economic interests of entrepreneurs—or even endanger their families by torturing relatives who support the opposition. Despite these grave risks, however, military coups in countries plagued by stark polarization tend to elicit widespread popular support because they hold the uncertain promise of ending turmoil and chaos (e.g., Skidmore 1967: 294–302; Sigmund 1977: chap. 11).

The depth of the precoup crisis and the severity of the perceived threat also help account for the character and duration of the authoritarian regime. Where these problems were limited, military leaders are often willing—even eager—to return to the barracks soon; they may ban some partisan forces from electoral participation but do not try to revamp the whole political system. By contrast, where the coup initiators perceived a grave danger to the established order, authoritarian rulers often pursue a long-term project of profound economic, social, and political transformation aimed at reliably preventing the recurrence of crises in the future (Garretón 1983: chaps. 3, 7). Thus, different levels of threat to the sociopolitical order affect the extent of political change under military regimes in similar ways as the depth of structural problems conditions the advance of market reform, as analyzed in chapter 6.

In sum, the crisis argument that this study derives from prospect theory elucidates a range of political events and issues, far beyond economic policy-making. Obviously, however, the operational criteria specified in the discussion of crisis arguments above cannot be directly transferred. Whether it is possible to specify objective criteria for identifying such a variety of crises or whether scholars have to rely on subjective accounts is a topic for future research. Regardless of the results of those efforts, the danger of tautology stressed by critics of crisis arguments (e.g., Remmer and Merkx 1982) can be avoided because even *perceptions* of threats can be ascertained independently of their alleged outcomes. In sum, my prospect-theory interpretation promises to have broad applicability.

Conclusion

This study has explained how four fragile democracies managed to enact costly, risky neoliberal reforms, though with different degrees of economic and political success. Argentina and Peru have thoroughly restructured their development models, and Brazil has advanced quite far in this direction; even in Venezuela, where neoliberalism has faced the strongest challenges, substantial change has taken hold, for instance trade liberalization and privatization. Contrary to scholarly expectations in the 1980s, democracy — defined in minimal, procedural ways — survived these painful and risky transformations in Argentina, Brazil, and Venezuela and, after a temporary interruption, was quickly restored in Peru. And the recent threats of democratic involution in Peru and Venezuela did not coincide with the initial imposition of neoliberalism, as skeptics had hypothesized (Przeworski 1991: 180–87; Conaghan and Malloy 1994: chap. 8). Thus, democracy has proven surprisingly resilient, despite the costs and conflicts associated with neoliberal reform.

One main reason for the survival or rapid resurrection of democracy is, of course, strong pressure from First World countries, particularly the United States. After the end of the Cold War, democracy has become the incontestable norm for the capitalist countries of Latin America, as President Fujimori learned after his self-coup in 1992. In fact, neoliberalism has furthered the maintenance of democracy because deeper integration into the world economy exposes Latin American countries more than ever to external pressures. For instance, whereas Guatemala's military regime flatly rejected President Carter's pressure for human right improvements in 1977, when the country's economy was inward-oriented, President Jorge Serrano had to give in to international threats and retreat from his self-coup in 1993, after Guatemala had become more export-oriented.

Yet while international pressures can overcome occasional challenges to democracy, they could not stem a wave of coups, as it swept across Latin America in the early 1960s. Threats of sanctions work if they target an isolated country. But in case of an authoritarian chain reaction, the cost of sanctions would increase dramatically, and their limited effectiveness — as evident in the survival of many "rogue states" — would become apparent, undermining their deterrent effect. Thus, the international protection of democracy in Latin America works precisely because domestic challenges to elected government have been few and far between. Why, then, have the troubles and travails associated with neoliberal reforms rarely produced such challenges?

Prospect theory helps to account for this surprising tranquility. By triggering risk acceptance in the domain of losses, deep crises allowed presidents to garner widespread support for or acquiescence to their daring rescue efforts and the subsequent transformation of the development model. In line with the above-mentioned *Aufhebung* of functionalism, grave challenges did in fact elicit a reaction, from both political leaders and common citizens. Therefore, the initiators of neoliberalism provoked less rejection and received more approval than expected; where they managed to beat the odds and bring about stabilization and recovery, as in Argentina, Peru, and eventually Brazil, they even achieved democratic reelection. Only where severe economic problems coincided with a violent insurgency, as in Peru,[31] did the "savior" have the latitude to overthrow the established institutional framework, change the constitution, and manipulate the new rules to guarantee his complete political predominance and perpetuation in power—though not indefinitely.

This book thus suggests that democracy and the enactment of neoliberalism are compatible in situations of grave, yet not extreme, crisis. By contrast, worsening problems that do not reach such severity do not allow for the successful implementation of the neoliberal program under democracy, as the cases of Venezuela and Ecuador suggest. Under those conditions, threats to democracy block market reforms, and democracy allows for the rise of leaders who oppose such reforms. Thus, democracy and neoliberalism can be combined, but not under all circumstances.

Under conditions of severe crisis, especially hyperinflation, democracy actually provides a strong impetus for determined stabilization and structural reform. The reason is that democratization empowers the biggest losers from hyperinflation—the large numbers of poorer people—and in this way eventually helps to break the deadlock of contending interests that helps to obstruct adjustment. This deadlock arises because political actors face a collective action dilemma when witnessing economic disequilibria. While they would benefit from restored stability, they seek to avoid the sacrifices that serious adjustment plans entail because the necessary contributions of other actors are not guaranteed. Distributional conflicts further exacerbate this problem (Alesina and Drazen 1991). In fact, some groups—especially the financial sector—actually benefit from high inflation and therefore dislike stabilization (Armijo 1996).

Authoritarian rule suppresses some of these actors, especially trade unions, but others—such as powerful business sectors—retain considerable clout. Therefore, Latin America's bureaucratic-authoritarian regimes faced great difficulties to reach their announced goal of forcing inflation down. In fact, military rulers in Argentina, Brazil, and Peru

---

[31] Whereas in Peru, a large-scale insurgency was crucial for legitimating Fujimori's self-coup, in Venezuela, the deficient performance of the established political elite since the late 1970s and its extensive malfeasance gradually eroded popular support for the liberal-democratic regime, making it vulnerable to attack by radical populist Hugo Chávez. Support for this outsider was driven mostly by political and economic discontent, not by the rejection of Venezuela's uneven and halting embrace of neoliberalism (Weyland 2003).

never achieved inflation rates as low as those prevailing under democracy in recent years. Admittedly, democratization initially made things worse: It first fueled increases in inflation by conceding political voice to previously excluded groups, such as unions. As those sectors refused to shoulder the burden of stabilization and instead pressed their pent-up demands, the spiral of price rises accelerated greatly during and after the transition to democracy.

But as this book shows, the very explosion of inflation eventually caused a backlash as the demand for stability grew ever stronger, especially among the largely unorganized mass of poorer voters. These sectors, who are at the margins of the formal economy, suffered the greatest cost from skyrocketing inflation. Without access to indexed bank accounts and without bargaining power, they lacked individual or collective mechanisms of protection against the erosion of their purchasing power. Yet while their economic clout was minimal, they commanded a power capability that became decisive with democratization: large numbers of votes. The regime change turned this "silent majority," which had been disenfranchised under authoritarian rule and drowned out by the clamor of interest groups, into the ultimate sovereign. Under democracy, all contenders for the presidency are well-advised to consider its most basic demand: economic and political stability, including price stability. In fact, the rapid spread of opinion polling made this majority, which even under democracy used to speak only on rare—though politically decisive—occasions (namely, in elections), an ever-present sounding board for political initiatives. On issues of high salience and visibility, nowadays public opinion often speaks louder than the special demands of interest groups.

The imposition of determined, costly stabilization efforts designed to bring down skyrocketing inflation would be unimaginable under democracy without the support or acquiescence of this largely unorganized mass. And without the widespread aversion to entrenched interest groups and the political class that has prevailed among common people in recent years, it would be difficult to enact costly, risky structural reforms through democratic procedures. In sum, by empowering the populace, the institution of democracy—in the context of severe crises—paved the way for market reform. In this way, democratization eventually helped to resolve the problem of skyrocketing price rises that it had initially exacerbated.

In conclusion, neoliberalism is indeed compatible with democracy, but only under certain conditions. In severe crises, chief executives can win widespread support for innovative, risky reforms and effect dramatic change in liberal, pluralist regimes that under normal circumstances make such transformations very difficult by dispersing power.

Political agency is thus capable of overcoming the obstacles posed by institutional constraints, but not under conditions of its own choosing. Also, this window of opportunity for thoroughgoing reform closes if presidents manage to end the grave crisis. Ironically, due to this success, leaders who initially commanded great latitude and power see their clout diminish and demands for participation, accountability, and alternation in office intensify. So while democracy is flexible enough to allow for determined efforts to overcome grave problems, it is also usually resilient enough to gradually limit the power of plebiscitarian leaders who spearheaded such drastic change. Even in Third World countries buffeted by multiple serious challenges, democracy therefore balances freedom and governability better than skeptics claim.

Abad, Alberto. 1997. Author interview with Secretario de Control Estratégico, Jefatura de Gabinete de Ministros. Buenos Aires: 27 June.

Abal Medina Jr., Juan Manuel. 1998. Viejos y Nuevos Actores en el Escenario Posmenemista. Paper for 21st Latin American Studies Association Congress, Chicago, 24–26 September.

Abugattás, Javier. 1999. Author interview in Ministerio de Economía y Finanzas. Lima: 8 July.

Acuña, Carlos. 1994. Politics and Economics in the Argentina of the Nineties. In William Smith, Carlos Acuña, and Eduardo Gamarra, eds. *Democracy, Markets, and Structural Reform in Latin America*, 31–73. New Brunswick: Transaction.

Acuña, Carlos, and William Smith. 1994. The Political Economy of Structural Adjustment. In William Smith, Carlos Acuña, and Eduardo Gamarra, eds. *Latin American Political Economy in the Age of Neoliberal Reform*, 17–66. New Brunswick: Transaction.

Afonso, José Roberto, Luiz Carvalho, and Lytha Spíndola. 1995. *Fundo Social de Emergência*. Nota Técnica 11. São Paulo: Instituto de Economia do Setor Público (May).

Aguirre Roca, Juan Antonio. 1995. Author interview with former Presidente, Confederación Nacional de Instituciones Empresariales Privadas. Lima: 14 February.

Ahumada, Hildegart, et al. 1992. *Efectos Distributivos del Impuesto Inflacionario*. Proyecto ARG 91/016. Buenos Aires: Ministerio de Economía. Secretaría de Programación Económica.

Alayón, Javier. 1998. Author interview with Director General Sectorial de Política Económica, CORDIPLAN. Caracas: 3 July.

———. 1996. Author interview with Director General Sectorial de Política Económica (Encargado), CORDIPLAN. Caracas: 19 June.

Albuquerque, Liége. 1999. Despenca aprovação de FHC e cresce pessimismo. *Estado de São Paulo* (11 March): A4.

Alesina, Alberto, and Allan Drazen. 1991. Why Are Stabilizations Delayed? *American Economic Review* 81:5 (December): 1170–88.

Almeida, Jorge. 1996. *Como Vota o Brasileiro*. São Paulo: Casa Amarela.

Almond, Gabriel. 1991. Capitalism and Democracy. *PS: Political Science & Politics* 24:3 (September): 467–74.

Alsogaray, Alvaro. 1995. Author interview with former Asesor Especial to President Menem. Buenos Aires: 20 March.

———. 1993. *Experiencias de Cincuenta Años de Política y Economía Argentina*. Buenos Aires: Planeta.

Alvarez, Angel. 1996. La Crisis de Hegemonía de los Partidos Políticos Venezolanos. In Alvarez, ed. *El Sistema Político Venezolano*, 131–54. Caracas: Universidad Central de Venezuela.

Alvarez de Stella, Ana. 1988. Economic Crisis and Foreign Debt Management in Venezuela. In Stephany Griffith-Jones, ed. *Managing World Debt*, 211–44. New York: St. Martin's Press.

Álvarez Rodrich, Augusto. 1997. Balance (Preliminar) del Proceso de Privatización en el Perú. *Socialismo y Participación* 77 (January): 9–20.

Amadeo, Eduardo. 1997. Author interview with Secretario de Desarrollo Social, Presidencia de la Nación. Buenos Aires: 1 July.

———. 1995. Author interview with Secretario de Desarrollo Social, Presidencia de la Nación. Buenos Aires: 21 March.

Amat y León, Carlos. 1996. Author interview with former Ministro de Agricultura (1990–91). Lima: 15 August.

Amato, Mário. 1992. Author interview with Presidente, Federação das Indústrias do Estado de São Paulo. São Paulo: 9 June.

Ames, Barry. 2001. *The Deadlock of Democracy in Brazil.* Ann Arbor: University of Michigan Press.

———. 1987. *Political Survival.* Berkeley: University of California Press.

Ames, Barry, and Timothy Power. 2000. Parties and Governability in Brazil. In Paul Webb, Stephen White, and David Stansfield, eds. *Political Parties in Transitional Democracies.* Oxford: Oxford University Press, forthcoming.

Andrei, Cristian, Fernando Azevedo de Arruda Sampaio, and José Geraldo Portugal Jr., eds. 1995. *Gestão Estatal no Brasil. Limites do Liberalismo 1990–1992.* São Paulo: Instituto de Economia do Setor Público.

Angell, Alan, and Carol Graham. 1995. Can Social Sector Reform Make Adjustment Sustainable and Equitable? *Journal of Latin American Studies* 27:1 (February): 189–219.

Angeloz, Eduardo. 1989. *La Argentina de los '90.* Buenos Aires: n.p.

Apoyo. *Informe de Opinión,* various issues. Lima: Apoyo.

Apoyo. 1999. *Situación Familiar respecto a hace 12 Meses,* etc. (data compilation for the author from *Informe de Opinión*). Lima: Apoyo.

Arida, Pérsio. 1996. Esclarecimentos do ex-Presidente do Banco Central, Pérsio Arida, a respeito do Programa de Estabilização Monetária. In Câmara dos Deputados. *Debate Econômico. Audiências Públicas 1995,* vol. 2, 13–115. Brasília: Câmara dos Deputados.

Arkes, Hal, and Catherine Blumer. 1985. The Psychology of Sunk Cost. *Organizational Behavior and Human Decision Processes* 35:1 (February): 124–40.

Armas, Alejandro. 2000. Author interview with leader of Movimiento V República. Caracas: 27 June.

Armijo, Leslie. 1999. Balance Sheet or Ballot Box? In Philip Oxhorn and Pamela Starr, eds. *Markets and Democracy in Latin America,* 161–203. Boulder: Lynne Rienner.

———. 1996. Inflation and Insouciance. *Latin American Research Review* 31:3: 7–46.

Armijo, Leslie, Thomas Biersteker, and Abraham Lowenthal. 1994. The Problems of Simultaneous Transitions. *Journal of Democracy* 5:4 (October): 161–75.

Aróstegui, María del Carmen. 2001. Yo Prometo. *Percepción 21* (May) <www.consultores21.com/domino/html/articulos>.

Arrioja, José Enrique. 1998. *Clientes Negros.* Caracas: Libros de El Nacional.

Arruda, Roldão. 1994. Entrevistados acreditam mais no esforço pessoal do que no País. *Estado de São Paulo* (3 January): A10.

Ashoff, Guido. 1993. Wirtschaftspolitik in Venezuela 1973–1992. *Lateinamerika* 9:21: 17–55.

Åslund, Anders. 1995. *How Russia Became a Market Economy*. Washington, DC: Brookings.

Assis, Luis Eduardo. 1995. Author interview with former Diretor do Banco Central do Brasíl. São Paulo: 23 June.

Austerlitz, Marcelo. 1995. Author interview with Jefe de Gabinete, Ministerio de Trabajo y Seguridad Social. Buenos Aires: 8 March.

Auyero, Javier. 1998. Todo por Amor, o lo que Quedó de la Herejía. In Felipe Burbano de Lara, ed. *El Fantasma del Populismo*, 81–118. Caracas: Nueva Sociedad.

Bacha, Edmar. 1998. O Plano Real. In Aloizio Mercadante, ed. *O Brasil Pós-Real*, 11–69. Campinas, SP: Universidade Estadual de Campinas. Instituto de Economia.

Baer, Werner, and Paul Beckerman. 1989. The Decline and Fall of Brazil's Cruzado. *Latin American Research Review* 24:1: 35–64.

Baer, Werner, and Joseph Love, eds. 2000. *Liberalization and Its Consequences*. Cheltenham, UK: Edward Elgar.

Baglione, Lisa, and Carol Clark. 1995. Participation and the Success of Economic and Political Reforms. *Journal of Communist Studies and Transition Politics* 11:3 (September): 215–48.

Baizan, Mario. 1993. *Conversaciones con Carlos Menem*. Buenos Aires: Fundación de Integración Americana.

Baker, Andy. 2000. Economic Policy Debates and Voter Choice in Brazil. Paper for 22nd Latin American Studies Association Congress, Miami, 16–18 March.

Balbi, Carmen Rosa. 1996. El Fujimorismo. *Pretextos* 9: 187–223.

———. 1993. El Desaparecido Poder del Sindicalismo. In Augusto Álvarez Rodrich, ed. *El Poder en el Perú*, 97–104. Lima: Editorial Apoyo.

Balbi, Carmen Rosa, and David Scott Palmer. 2001. Political Earthquake: The 70 Days That Shook Peru. *LASA Forum* 31:4 (Winter): 7–11.

Balcerowicz, Leszek. 1995. *Socialism, Capitalism, Transformation*. Budapest: Central European University Press.

Bank of Boston. 1990. Plano Brasil Novo. *Newsletter Brazil* 28:8 (26 March): 1–4.

Barros de Castro, Antônio. 1994. Renegade Development. In William Smith, Carlos Acuña, and Eduardo Gamarra, eds. *Democracy, Markets, and Structural Reform in Latin America*, 183–213. New Brunswick: Transaction.

Bartlett, David. 1997. *The Political Economy of Dual Transformations*. Ann Arbor: University of Michigan Press.

Bates, Robert. 1981. *Markets and States in Tropical Africa*. Berkeley: University of California Press.

Bates, Robert, and Paul Collier. 1993. The Politics and Economics of Policy Reform in Zambia. In Robert Bates and Anne Krueger, eds. *Political and Economic Interactions in Economic Policy Reform*, 387–443. Oxford: Blackwell.

Bates, Robert, Avner Greif, Margaret Levi, Jean-Laurent Rosenthal, and Barry Weingast. 1998. *Analytic Narratives*. Princeton: Princeton University Press.

Bates, Robert, and Anne Krueger. 1993. Generalizations Arising from the Country Studies. In Bates and Krueger, eds. *Political and Economic Interactions in Economic Policy Reform*, 444–72. Oxford: Blackwell.

Belaúnde Terry, Fernando. 1996. Author interview with former Presidente de la República. Lima: 2 August.

Bellin, Eva. 2000. Contingent Democrats: Industrialists, Labor, and Democratization in Late-Developing Countries. *World Politics* 52:2 (January): 175–205.

Benavides, Roque. 1999. Author interview with Presidente, Confederación Nacional de Instituciones Empresariales Privadas. Lima: 8 July.

Berejikian, Jeffrey. 1997. The Gains Debate. *American Political Science Review* 91:4 (December): 789–805.

———. 1992. Revolutionary Collective Action and the Agent-Structure Problem. *American Political Science Review* 86:3 (September): 647–57.

Bienen, Henry. 1990. The Politics of Trade Liberalization in Africa. *Economic Development and Cultural Change* 38:4 (July): 713–32.

Biglaiser, Glen. 1999. Military Regimes, Neoliberal Restructuring, and Economic Development. *Studies in Comparative International Development* 34:1 (Spring): 3–26.

Binder, Leonard, et al. 1971. *Crises and Sequences in Political Development.* Princeton: Princeton University Press.

Birle, Peter. 1995. *Argentinien: Unternehmer, Staat und Demokratie.* Frankfurt am Main: Vervuert.

———. 1991. Vom "Plan Bunge & Born" zum "Plan Cavallo." *Lateinamerika.* Supplement 9 (July): 1–24.

Bitar, Sergio. 1989. Más Industrialización. In Moisés Naím and Ramón Piñango, eds. *El Caso Venezuela,* 5th ed., 102–21. Caracas: Instituto de Estudios Superiores de Administración.

Blanco, Carlos. 1996. Author interview with former Presidente, Comisión Presidencial para la Reforma del Estado (1989–92). Caracas: 12 June.

Blay, Eva. 1993. *Proposta Revisional, No. 13869 a 13936.* Brasília: Congresso Nacional. Revisão da Constituição Federal.

Boateng, Osei. 1999. Bold March into the Millenium. *New African* 375 (June): 1–2 (www.africalynx.com/icpubs/na/jun99/nasf0601.htm).

Bogéa, Mauro. 1994/1995. Author interviews with Coordenador Geral de Estudos Tributários, Secretaria da Receita Federal, Ministério da Fazenda. Brasília: 18 and 26 October 1994, 16 June 1995.

Boggio, María, Fernando Romero, and Juan Ansión. 1991. *El Pueblo es Así . . . y también Asá.* Lima: Instituto Democracia y Socialismo.

Bokros, Lajos. 1998. The Unfinished Agenda. In Lajos Bokros and Jean-Jacques Dethier, eds. *Public Finance Reform during the Transition,* 535–68. Washington, DC: World Bank.

Boloña, Carlos. 1996. Author interview with former Ministro de Economía y Finanzas (1991–93). Lima: 14 August.

———. 1993. *Cambio de Rumbo.* Lima: Instituto de Economía de Libre Mercado.

Bornhausen, Roberto Konder. 1991. *Reflexões sobre o Brasil.* Cadernos do Instituto Roberto Simonsen no. 18. São Paulo: Federação das Indústrias do Estado de São Paulo.

Bottom, William, and Gary Miller. 1997. *"Take It or Leave It": Prospect Theory and Coalition Formation.* Working Paper no. 339. St. Louis: Department of Political Science, Washington University.

Branco, Flávio Castelo, and Maria Beatriz de Albuquerque David. 1989. A Aceleração Inflacionária e as Políticas de Estabilização nos Anos 80. In

Instituto de Pesquisas, ed. *Perspectivas da Economia Brasileira, 1989*, 149–75. Rio de Janeiro: Instituto de Planejamento Econômico e Social.

Bratton, Michael. 1994. Economic Crisis and Political Realignment in Zambia. In Jennifer Widner, ed. *Economic Change and Political Liberalization in Sub-Saharan Africa*, 101–28. Baltimore: Johns Hopkins University Press.

Bratton, Michael, and Beatrice Liatto-Katundu. 1994. A Focus Group Assessment of Political Attitudes in Zambia. *African Affairs* 93:373 (October): 535–63.

Bresser Pereira, Luiz Carlos. 1994. Brazil. In John Williamson, ed. *The Political Economy of Policy Reform*, 333–54. Washington, DC: Institute for International Economics.

———. 1991. *Os Tempos Heróicos de Collor e Zélia*. São Paulo: Nobel.

Bresser Pereira, Luiz Carlos, José María Maravall, and Adam Przeworski. 1993. *Economic Reforms in New Democracies*. Cambridge: Cambridge University Press.

Bruhn, Kathleen. 1996. Social Spending and Political Support. *Comparative Politics* 28:2 (January): 151–77.

Bruno, Michael. 1992. Stabilization and Reform in Eastern Europe. *IMF Staff Papers* 39:4 (December): 741–77.

Buendía, Jorge. 1995. Economics, Presidential Approval, and Party Choice in Mexico. Paper for 19th Latin American Studies Association Congress, Washington, DC, 28–30 September.

Bueno de Mesquita, Bruce. 1981. *The War Trap*. New Haven: Yale University Press.

Burns, James MacGregor. 1978. *Leadership*. New York: Harper & Row.

Butori, Paulo. 1992. Author interview with former Coordenador, Pensamento Nacional das Bases Empresariais. São Paulo: 12 June.

Caldera, Rafael. 1993. *Mi Carta de Intención con el Pueblo de Venezuela*. Caracas: n.p.

———. 1992. Discurso del Doctor Rafael Caldera en la Sesión Conjunta del Congreso de la República, el día 4 de Febrero de 1992. *Politeia* 15: 437–42.

Callaghy, Thomas. 1990. Lost between State and Market. In Joan Nelson, ed. *Economic Crisis and Policy Choice*, 257–319. Princeton: Princeton University Press.

Callaghy, Thomas, and John Ravenhill. 1993. How Hemmed In? In Callaghy and Ravenhill, eds. *Hemmed In*, 520–63. New York: Columbia University Press.

Calvo, Juan. 2000. Author interview with Presidente, Conindustria. Caracas: 23 June.

Câmara dos Deputados. 1996. *Proposta de Emenda à Constituição no. 33-D, de 1995*. Brasília: Câmara dos Deputados.

———. 1995. *Proposta de Emenda à Constituição no. 173-A, de 1995*. Brasília: Câmara dos Deputados.

Camargo, José Márcio, and Carlos Ramos. 1988. *A Revolução Indesejada*. Rio de Janeiro: Campus.

Cambio 90. 1990. *Lineamientos del Plan de Gobierno 1990*. Lima: n.p.

Camerer, Colin. 2000. Prospect Theory in the Wild. In Daniel Kahneman and Amos Tversky, eds. *Choices, Values, and Frames*, 288–300. New York: Russell Sage Foundation.

Cameron, Maxwell. 1997a. Political and Economic Origins of Regime Change in Peru. In Maxwell Cameron and Philip Mauceri, eds. *The Peruvian Labyrinth*, 37–69. University Park: Pennsylvania State University Press.

———. 1997b. *Uncivil Democracy in Peru*. Ottawa: Carleton University.

Cameron, Maxwell, and Philip Mauceri, eds. 1997. *The Peruvian Labyrinth*. University Park: Pennsylvania State University Press.

Campbell, Horace, and Howard Stein. 1992. The Dynamics of Liberalization in Tanzania. In Campbell and Stein, eds. *Tanzania and the IMF*, 1–19. Boulder: Westview.

Cardoso, Fernando Henrique. 1996. Discurso do Presidente da República, Fernando Henrique Cardoso, na Abertura do Seminário: Dois Anos do Plano Real. Brasília: Presidência da República. Assessoria de Imprensa.

———. 1995. Plano Fernando Henrique Cardoso. Exposição de Motivos no. 395, de 7 de Dezembro de 1993. Reprinted in *Lateinamerika. Supplement* no. 15: 52–60.

———. 1994. *Mãos à Obra, Brasil*. Brasília: n.p.

Cariaga, Juan. 1997. *Estabilización y Desarrollo*, 2d ed. Mexico and La Paz: Fondo de Cultura Económica.

Carrasquero, José, Thais Maingon, and Friedrich Welsch, eds. 2001. *Venezuela en Transición*. Caracas: CDB Publicaciones.

Carrera, Jorge. 1994. La Política Económica de la Delegación. *Anales de la Asociación Argentina de Economía Política. XXIX Reunión Anual*, vol. 2., 339–63. La Plata: Universidad Nacional de La Plata.

Carrión, Julio. 2000. La Campaña Electoral y la Opinión Pública en el Perú Actual. Paper for 22nd Latin American Studies Association Congress, Miami, 16–18 March.

———. 1995. The Transformation of Public Opinion under the Fujimori Administration. Paper for 19th Latin American Studies Association Congress, Washington, DC, 28–30 September.

———. 1994. The "Support Gap" for Democracy in Peru. Paper for 18th Latin American Studies Association Congress, Atlanta, GA, 10–12 March.

Cassullo, Eduardo. 1995. Author interview with Director Ejecutivo, Unión Industrial Argentina. Buenos Aires: 23 March.

Castillo, Leopoldo. 1998. Author interview with Director Ejecutivo, Federación Venezolana de Cámaras y Asociaciones de Comercio y Producción. Caracas: 19 June.

Catterberg, Edgardo. 1991. *Argentina Confronts Politics*. Boulder: Lynne Rienner.

———. 1989. *Los Argentinos frente a la Política*. Buenos Aires: Planeta.

Cavallo, Domingo. 1997. *El Peso de la Verdad*. Buenos Aires: Planeta.

———. 1995. Palabras del Ministro de Economía, Seminario de FORO, Club Americano. Buenos Aires: 16 March.

Cavallo, Domingo, and Joaquín Cottani. 1997. Argentina's Convertibility Plan and the IMF. *American Economic Review* 87:2 (May): 17–22.

Cavarozzi, Marcelo, and María Grossi. 1992. Argentine Parties under Alfonsín. In Edward Epstein, ed. *The New Argentine Democracy*, 173–202. Westport, CT: Praeger.

CEA (Consejo Empresario Argentino). 1997. *Un Trabajo para Todos*. Buenos Aires: CEA.

Celli, Humberto. 1998. Author interview with Acción Democrática politician. Caracas: 2 July.

———. 1996. Author interview with former Secretario General and Presidente, Acción Democrática. Caracas: 31 May.

———. 1993. *Dos Discursos y un Sólo Pensamiento*. Caracas: n.p.

CENDA (Centro de Documentación y Análisis para los Trabajadores). 2000. *Indicadores* 36 (May).

———. 1999. *Informe Social del CENDA, Enero 1998 – Agosto 1999*. Serie Azul no. 43. Caracas: CENDA.

Centeno, Miguel. 1994. *Democracy within Reason: Technocratic Revolution in Mexico*. University Park: Pennsylvania State University Press.

Centro de Estudios Unión para la Nueva Mayoría. 1999. Marcado Aumento de la Prioridad por el Desempleo. Buenos Aires: Centro de Estudios <dns2.sminter.com.ar/nmayoria/agosto99.html>.

———. 1998a. Predomina el Voto por le No en un Eventual Plebiscito sobre la Reelección. Buenos Aires: Centro de Estudios <dns2.sminter.com.ar/ nmayoria/Informes/1998/11–1998.html>.

———. 1998b. Si Bien Sólo una de Cada Siete Personas Piensa que las Empresas Públicas Deben Ser Reestatizadas, casi la Mitad Requiere un Mayor Control sobre Ellas. Buenos Aires: Centro de Estudios <dns2.sminter.com.ar/nmayoria/Informes/1998/08–1998.html>.

———. 1997a. *Percepciones de la Opinión Pública al Comenzar 1997*. Cuaderno no. 229. Buenos Aires: Centro de Estudios.

———. 1997b. Pese a la Disconformidad con la Política Económica, Predomina la Opinión de que es Conveniente Mantener la Convertibilidad. Buenos Aires: Centro de Estudios <dns2.sminter.com.ar/ nmayoria/Informes/1997/43–1997.html>.

———. 1995a. *Análisis Socio-Político de la Elección del 14 de Mayo*. Cuaderno no. 130. Buenos Aires: Centro de Estudios.

———. 1995b. *Imagen de la Política Económica*. Cuaderno no. 148. Buenos Aires: Centro de Estudios.

———. 1994. *Análisis de la Elección de Constituyentes*. Cuaderno no. 78. Buenos Aires: Centro de Estudios.

———. 1993. *La Afiliación a Partidos Políticos en la Argentina*. Cuaderno no. 52. Buenos Aires: Centro de Estudios.

CESOP (Centro de Estudos de Opinião Pública. Universidade Estadual de Campinas). 1994. O Brasil através de Pacotes Econômicos. *Opinião Pública: Encarte de Dados* 2:3 (June): 3–16.

Chalmers, Douglas. 1977. The Politicized State in Latin America. In James Malloy, ed. *Authoritarianism and Corporatism in Latin America*, 23–45. Pittsburgh: University of Pittsburgh Press.

Charlton, Roger, Roddy McKinnon, and Lukasz Konopielko. 1998. Pensions Reform, Privatisation and Restructuring in the Transition. *Europe-Asia Studies* 50:8 (December): 1413–46.

Chazan, Naomi. 1991. The Political Transformation of Ghana under the PNDC. In Donald Rothchild, ed. *Ghana: The Political Economy of Recovery*, 21–47. Boulder: Lynne Rienner.

Cline, Mary, and Sharon Fisher. 1994. Czech Republic and Slovakia. *RFE/RL Research Report* 3:27 (8 July): 33–39.

CNI (Confederação Nacional da Indústria). 1999. *Pesquisa de Opinião CNI/ IBOPE. Aspectos Econômicos*. (April). Rio de Janeiro: CNI.

———. 1998. *Pesquisa de Opinião CNI/IBOPE. Aspectos Econômicos*. (September). Rio de Janeiro: CNI.

Cohen, Gerald. 1986. Marxism and Functional Explanation. In John Roemer, ed. *Analytical Marxism*, 221–34. Cambridge: Cambridge University Press.

Collier, David. 1998. Comparative Method in the 1990s. *Newsletter of the APSA Organized Section in Comparative Politics* 9:1 (Winter): 1–4.

Collier, David, Henry Brady, and Jason Seawright. 2002. Eliminating Rival Explanations: Evaluating Sources of Leverage. In Henry Brady and David Collier, eds. *Rethinking Social Inquiry*. Lanham: Rowman & Littlefield, forthcoming.

Collier, David, and James Mahoney. 1996. Insights and Pitfalls. *World Politics* 49:1 (October): 56–91.

Collier, Ruth Berins, and David Collier. 1991. *Shaping the Political Arena*. Princeton: Princeton University Press.

Collor de Mello, Fernando. 1995. Author interview with former Presidente da República (1990–92). Brasília: 9 June.

———. 1991a. *Brasil: Um Projeto de Reconstrução Nacional*. Brasília: Presidência.

———. 1991b. *Mensagem no. 523*. Brasília: Presidência (4 October).

Comisión Presidencial para el Enfrentamiento de la Pobreza. 1989. *Plan para el Enfrentamiento de la Pobreza*. Caracas: n.p.

Compromiso Antiinflacionario: Declaración de Intención. 1995. Caracas: n.p.

Conaghan, Catherine. 1997. Estrellas de la Crisis. *Pensamiento Iberoamericano* 30: 177–205.

———. 1996. *Public Life in the Time of Alberto Fujimori*. Working Paper no. 219. Washington, DC: Woodrow Wilson Center.

———. 1995. Polls, Political Discourse, and the Public Sphere. In Peter Smith, ed. *Latin America in Comparative Perspective*, 227–55. Boulder: Westview.

Conaghan, Catherine, and James Malloy. 1994. *Unsettling Statecraft*. Pittsburgh: University of Pittsburgh Press.

CONASSEPS (Consejo Nacional para Supervisión y Seguimiento de los Programas Sociales del Ejecutivo Nacional). 1994. *Seguimiento de la Ejecución Física y Financiera de los Programas Sociales Compensatorios, 1989–1992*. Caracas: CONASSEPS.

Considera, Claudio. 1999. Author interview with Secretário de Acompanhamento Econômico, Ministério da Fazenda. Brasília: 8 June.

Consultores 21. 2001a. *Estudio de Temas Económicos* (April/May). Caracas: Consultores 21.

———. 2001b. *Presentación PERFIL 21 (Estudio de Temas Económicos) no. 51* (November). Caracas: Consultores 21.

———. 1997. *Estudio de Temas Económicos. Informe Analítico de Resultados* (2d trimester). Caracas: Consultores 21.

———. 1996. *Estudio de Temas Económicos* (June). Caracas: Consultores 21.

———. 1994a. *Estudio de Temas Económicos. Informe Analítico de Resultados* (3rd trimester). Caracas: Consultores 21.

———. 1994b. *Estudio de Temas Económicos. Informe Analítico de Resultados* (4th trimester). Caracas: Consultores 21.

———. 1994c. *Indice de Contenidos y Resultados Lineales de los Temas Continuos. Temas Económicos 1989–1993*. Caracas: Consultores 21.

———. 1989a. *Encuesta Nacional de Evaluación de la Campaña Electoral de 1988 (IPR-12189)*. Caracas: Consultores 21.

———. 1989b. *Estudio de Temas Económicos. Informe Analítico de Resultados* (April). Caracas: Consultores 21.

———. 1988. *Estudio Nacional de Opinión Pública sobre Temas Económicos: Informe (ICR08188)*. Caracas: Consultores 21.

Cook, Karen Schweers, and Margaret Levi, eds. 1990. *The Limits of Rationality*. Chicago: University of Chicago Press.

Cook, Linda, and Mitchell Orenstein. 1999. The Return of the Left and Its Impact on the Welfare State in Poland, Hungary, and Russia. In Linda Cook, Mitchell Orenstein, and Marilyn Rueschemeyer, eds. *Left Parties and Social Policy in Postcommunist Europe*, 47–107. Boulder: Westview.

Cook, Maria. 2000. Contrasting Rounds: Democratic Transitions, Neoliberal Economies, and Labor Law Reform in Argentina and Brazil. Paper for 22d Latin American Studies Association Congress, Miami, 16–18 March.

Coppedge, Michael. 1994a. Prospects for Democratic Governability in Venezuela. *Journal of Interamerican Studies and World Affairs* 36:2 (Winter): 39–64.

———. 1994b. *Strong Parties and Lame Ducks*. Stanford: Stanford University Press.

CORDIPLAN (Oficina Central de Coordinación y Planificación. Presidencia de la República). 1996a. *Agenda Venezuela (Segunda Compilación)* (December). Caracas: CORDIPLAN.

———. 1996b *Síntesis de la Economía Venezolana y Oportunidades de Inversión* (September). Caracas: CORDIPLAN.

———. 1995. *Un Proyecto de País. Documentos del IX Plan de la Nación.* Caracas: CORDIPLAN.

———. 1994. *Programa para la Estabilización y la Recuperación de la Economía.* Caracas: CORDIPLAN.

———. 1990. *El Gran Viraje. Lineamientos Generales del VIII Plan de la Nación.* Caracas: Oficina Central de Estadística e Informática.

———. 1989a. *Bases Metodológicas para la Elaboración del VIII Plan de la Nación.* Caracas: CORDIPLAN (January).

———. 1989b. *Crecimiento sin Inflación en la Década de los Noventas [sic]. Programa Macroeconómico del Gobierno de Venezuela.* Caracas: CORDIPLAN (February).

———. 1989c. *VIII Plan de la Nación: El Gran Viraje. Presentación de los Lineamientos Generales del VIII Plan de la Nación. Resumen Ejecutivo.* Caracas: CORDIPLAN (13 October).

Cornelius, Wayne, Ann Craig, and Jonathan Fox, eds. 1994. *Transforming State-Society Relations in Mexico.* San Diego: Center for U.S.-Mexican Studies, University of California.

Corrales, Javier. 2001. The Political Causes of Argentina's Recession. Washington, DC: Woodrow Wilson Center. Ms.

———. 2000. Reform-Lagging States and the Question of Devaluation. In Carol Wise and Riordan Roett, eds. *Exchange Rate Politics in Latin America*, 123–158. Washington, DC: Brookings.

———. 1998. Coalitions and Corporate Choices in Argentina, 1976–1994. *Studies in Comparative International Development* 32:4 (Winter): 24–51.

———. 1997. Why Argentines Followed Cavallo. In Jorge Domínguez, ed. *Technopols*, 49–93. University Park: Pennsylvania State University Press.

———. 1996. From Market-Correctors to Market-Creators: Executive–Ruling Party Relations in the Economic Reforms of Argentina and Venezuela, 1989–1993. Ph.D. dissertation, Harvard University.

Cosar Grupo Comunicacional. 1996. *Estudio Cuántitativo de la Agenda Venezuela: Resultados Preliminares.* N.p.

Cotler, Julio. 1998. *Los Empresarios y las Reformas Económicas en el Perú.* Documento de Trabajo no. 91. Lima: Instituto de Estudios Peruanos.

Cotler, Julio, and Romeo Grompone. 2000. *El Fujimorismo.* Lima: Instituto de Estudios Peruanos.

Crabtree, John. 1992. *Peru under García.* Pittsburgh: University of Pittsburgh Press.

————. 1991. The Collor Plan. *Bulletin of Latin American Research* 10:2 (May): 119–32.

Crotto, Enrique. 1995. Author interview with Presidente, Sociedad Rural Argentina. Buenos Aires: 6 March.

Csaba, László. 1998. A Decade of Transformation in Hungarian Economic Policy. *Europe-Asia Studies* 50:8 (December): 1381–91.

Cuánto. 1994. Perú 1994: El Perfil de la Pobreza. *Cuánto* 6:68: 5–14.

Curia, Eduardo Luis. 1995. Author interview with former Secretario de Gestión Económica, Ministerio de Economía. Buenos Aires: 7 March.

————. 1991. *Dos Años de la Economía de Menem.* Buenos Aires: El Cronista.

Damill, Mario, and Roberto Frenkel. 1991. Argentina. Hiperinflación y Estabilización. In Guillermo Rozenwurcel, ed. *Elecciones y Política Económica en América Latina,* 1–82. Buenos Aires: Tesis.

Dancourt, Oscar, et al. 1990. *Una Propuesta de Reforma Monetaria para Acabar con la Hiperinflación.* Documento de Trabajo no. 90 (July). Lima. Departamento de Economía. Pontificia Universidad Católica del Perú. Publicaciones CISEPA.

D'Araujo, Maria, Gláucio Soares, and Celso Castro, eds. 1994. *Visões do Golpe.* Rio de Janeiro: Relume-Dumará.

Datafolha. 2001. Aumenta Reprovação ao Governo Fernando Henrique Cardoso (June). São Paulo: Datafolha <www.uol.com.br/folha/datafolha/eleicoes2000/ult333u236.shtml>.

————. 1998a. *Avaliação do Governo Fernando Henrique. PO 2434/2436/2461.* (August). São Paulo: Datafolha.

————. 1998b. *Intenção de Voto Presidente. PO 2484/2485/2486.* (September). São Paulo: Datafolha.

————. 1991. *Plano Collor 2 — Avaliação — 1 Semana (08/02/91).* São Paulo: Datafolha.

————. 1990. *Plano Collor 1 — Avaliação III (11/04/90).* São Paulo: Datafolha.

Datanálisis. 2000. *Escenarios Dinámicos de Venezuela 2000–2002.* Caracas: Datanálisis. [= *Escenarios Datanálisis* 3:3 (March).]

Datos. 2000. *Pulso Opinión Pública 1er Cuatrimestre del 2000.* Caracas: Datos.

————. 1998. *Pulso Nacional I/98.* Caracas: Datos.

————. 1996. *Estudio Pulso Nacional 96–2* (July–August). Caracas: Datos.

Datum. 2002. *Estudio de Opinión Pública — Nivel Nacional — Mes de Enero 2002.* No. 0002-REE/JNE. Lima: Datum.

————. 2001. *Informe Técnico. Elecciones Políticas Generales 2001.* Lima: Datum.

————. 2000. *Informe de Opinión Pública Post-Electoral, Segunda Vuelta Presidencial — A Nivel Nacional — Junio de 2000.* Lima: Datum.

————. 1990a. *Estudio de Opinión Pública. April 1990. Post-Test.* Lima: Datum.

———. 1990b. *Estudio de Opinión Pública. Gran Lima—Julio 1990*. Lima: Datum.

———. 1990c. *Estudio de Opinión Pública. Gran Lima—Septiembre 1990*. Lima: Datum.

———. 1990d. *Estudio de Opinión Pública. Gran Lima—Diciembre 1990*. Lima: Datum.

Degregori, Carlos Iván. 2000. *La Década de la Antipolítica*. Lima: Instituto de Estudios Peruanos.

Degregori, Carlos Iván, and Romeo Grompone. 1991. *Elecciones 1990. Demonios y Redentores en el Nuevo Perú*. Lima: Instituto de Estudios Peruanos.

De la Balze, Felipe. 1995. *Remaking the Argentine Economy*. New York: Council on Foreign Relations.

Delfim Netto, Antônio. 1999. Author interview with federal deputy from Partido Progressista Brasileiro. Brasília: 9 June.

———. 1998. O Plano Real e a Armadilha do Crescimento Econômico. In Aloizio Mercadante, ed. *O Brasil Pós-Real*, 89–100. Campinas, SP: Universidade Estadual de Campinas. Instituto de Economia.

———. 1995. Author interview with federal deputy from Partido Progressista Brasileiro. Brasília: 21 June.

Demery, Lionel. 1994. Côte d'Ivoire: Fettered Adjustment. In Ishrat Husain and Rashid Faruqee, eds. *Adjustment in Africa*, 72–152. Washington, DC: World Bank.

Demmers, Jolle, Alex Fernández Jilberto, and Barbara Hogenboom, eds. 2001. *Miraculous Metamorphoses: The Neoliberalization of Latin American Populism*. London: Zed Books.

De Pablo, Juan Carlos. 1987. Transición hacia las Urnas, Confusión Inicial y Plan Austral. *Económica* (La Plata) 33:2 (July–December): 213–44.

De Soto, Hernando. 1996. Author interview with former Asesor Especial del Presidente de la República Fujimori (1990–92). Lima: 20 August.

———. 1989. *The Other Path*. New York: Harper & Row.

De Souza, Amaury. 1992. Sindicatos e Greves. In Bolívar Lamounier, ed. *Ouvindo o Brasil*, 117–36. São Paulo: Editora Sumaré.

Deutsch, Karl. 1961. Social Mobilization and Political Development. *American Political Science Review* 55:3 (September): 493–513.

Dietz, Henry. 1998. *Urban Poverty, Political Participation, and the State*. Pittsburgh: University of Pittsburgh Press.

Dimenstein, Gilberto, and Josias de Souza. 1994. *A História Real*, 3d ed. São Paulo: Editora Ática.

Di Pietro, Leonardo. 1997. Author interview with Subsecretario de Políticas Sociales, Secretaría de Desarrollo Social, Presidencia de la Nación. Buenos Aires: 30 June.

Diretrizes de Ação do Governo Fernando Collor de Mello. 1989. Brasília: n.p.

Domínguez, Jorge. 1997. Technopols. In Domínguez, ed. *Technopols*, 1–48. University Park: Pennsylvania State University Press.

Dornbusch, Rüdiger, and Sebastian Edwards, eds. 1991. *The Macroeconomics of Populism in Latin America*. Chicago: University of Chicago Press.

Dowding, Keith. 1994. The Compatibility of Behaviouralism, Rational Choice and 'New Institutionalism'. *Journal of Theoretical Politics* 6:1 (January): 105–117.

Drake, Paul. 1991. Comment. In Rüdiger Dornbusch and Sebastian Edwards, eds. *The Macroeconomics of Populism in Latin America*, 35–40. Chicago: University of Chicago Press.

Drazen, Allan, and Vittorio Grilli. 1993. The Benefit of Crises for Economic Reforms. *American Economic Review* 83:3 (June): 598–607.

DuBois, Fritz. 1999. Author interview with former Asesor Especial del Ministerio de Economía y Finanzas under Ministers Carlos Boloña (1991–93) and Jorge Camet (1993–98). Lima: 7 July.

Durán, Viviana, and Juan Gómez Sabaini. 1994. *Lecciones sobre Reformas Fiscales en Argentina*. Buenos Aires: Centro Interamericano de Tributación y Administración Financiera.

Durand, Francisco. 1998. The Transformation of Business-Government Relations under Fujimori. Paper for 21st International Congress, Latin American Studies Association, Chicago, 24–26 September.

———. 1996. El Fenómeno Fujimori y la Crisis de los Partidos. *Revista Mexicana de Sociología* 58:1 (January–March): 97–120.

———. 1990. The National Bourgeoisie and the Peruvian State. Ph.D. dissertation, University of California, Berkeley.

Durand, Francisco, and Rosemary Thorp. 1998. Reforming the State. *Oxford Development Studies* 26:2: 133–51.

Dyba, Karel, and Jan Svejnar. 1991. Economic Developments and Prospects in Czechoslovakia, Yugoslavia, and Germany. *American Economic Review* 81:2 (May): 185–90.

Easton, David. 1979. *A Systems Analysis of Political Life*. Chicago: University of Chicago Press.

Echegaray, Fabián, and Carlos Elordi. 2001. Public Opinion, Presidential Popularity, and Economic Reform in Argentina, 1989–1996. In Susan Stokes, ed. *Public Support for Market Reforms in New Democracies*, 187–214. Cambridge: Cambridge University Press.

Eckstein, Harry. 1988. A Culturalist Theory of Change. *American Political Science Review* 82:3 (September): 789–804.

Economist. 1999. Rethinking Thinking. *Economist* 353:8150 (16 December): 63–65.

Edwards, Sebastian. 1995. *Crisis and Reform in Latin America*. Oxford: Oxford University Press.

Egaña, Fernando. 2000. Author interview with former Director, Oficina Central de Información (1994–99) and political confidant of President Rafael Caldera. Caracas: 28 June.

Ellner, Steve. 1999. The Assault on Benefits in Venezuela. *NACLA Report on the Americas* 32:4 (January–February): 18–19.

Elster, Jon. 1986. Further Thoughts on Marxism, Functionalism, and Game Theory. In John Roemer, ed. *Analytical Marxism*, 202–20. Cambridge: Cambridge University Press.

———, ed. 1982. Marxism, Functionalism, and Game Theory. *Theory and Society* 11:4 (July): 453–539.

Eris, Ibrahim. 1992. Author interview with former Presidente, Banco Central do Brasil (1990–91). São Paulo: 27 May.

Estudio Graciela Römer & Asociados. 2001. Actitudes de la Población sobre el Mantenimiento de la Convertibilidad. Buenos Aires: Estudio Graciela Römer <www.romer.com.ar/informes/convertibilidad—03-01.htm>.

———. 2000a. Informe Junio de 2000: El Contexto Político Económico. Buenos Aires: Estudio Graciela Römer <www.romer.com.ar/informes/lanacion—junio—2000.htm>.

————. 2000b. *Informe Noviembre de 2000: Principales Conclusiones*. Buenos Aires: Estudio Graciela Römer <www.romer.com.ar/informes/nov2000.htm>.

————. 1999a. *El País que Recibe De la Rúa* (December). Buenos Aires: Estudio Graciela Römer <www.romer.com.ar/Informe/top53/inf53.htm>.

————. 1999b. *Orientaciones Político Económicas y Tendencias Electorales* (May). Buenos Aires: Estudio Graciela Römer <www.romer.com.ar/info9907/informe.htm>.

————. 1997. *Informe Mensual* (March) (excerpt prepared specifically for the author). Buenos Aires: Estudio Graciela Römer.

Etchemendy, Sebastián. 2000. Constructing Reform Coalitions. *Latin American Politics and Society* 43:3 (Fall): 1–35.

Etchemendy, Sebastián, and Vicente Palermo. 1998. Conflicto y Concertación. *Desarrollo Económico* 37:148 (January–March): 559–90.

European Commission. Education and Culture Directorate-General. 1998. *Central and Eastern Eurobarometer*, no. 8. Brussels: European Commission. <europa.eu.int/comm/dg10/epo/ceeb8/ceeb08.pdf>.

Farnham, Barbara, ed. 1994. *Avoiding Losses/Taking Risks*. Ann Arbor: University of Michigan Press.

Faro, Clovis de, ed. 1991. *A Economia Pós-Plano Collor II*. Rio de Janeiro: Livros Técnicos e Científicos.

————, ed. 1990. *Plano Collor. Avaliações e Perspectivas*. Rio de Janeiro: Livros Técnicos e Científicos.

Faruqee, Rashid. 1994. Nigeria: Ownership Abandoned. In Ishrat Husain and Rashid Faruqee, eds. *Adjustment in Africa*, 238–85. Washington, DC: World Bank.

FEDECAMARAS (Federación Venezolana de Cámaras y Asociaciones de Comercio y Producción). 2001. Declaración Final, 57ª Asamblea Nacional (28 July) <www.fedecamaras.org.ve/documento.html>.

————. 2000. *Nuestra Visión de Futuro. Documento Presentado a los Candidatos Presidenciales*. Caracas: FEDECAMARAS. <www.fedecamaras.org.ve/elecion/elecciones.htm>.

————. 1999. Observaciones al Proyecto de Constitución que Será Sometido a Referendum. Informe de Comisión de Aspectos Sociales y Laborales. Caracas: FEDECAMARAS (22 November).

————. 1993. *Proceso de Ajuste Estructural, 1989–1993*. Caracas: ACIDE.

Fernandes, José Augusto Coelho, et al. 1994. A Indústria: Perfil e Perspectivas. In João Paulo dos Reis Velloso, ed. *Estabilidade e Crescimento*, 185–216. Rio de Janeiro: José Olympio.

Ferreira Rubio, Delia, and Matteo Goretti. 1998. When the President Governs Alone. In John Carey and Matthew Shugart, eds. *Executive Decree Authority*, 33–61. Cambridge: Cambridge University Press.

Ferreres, Orlando. 1995. Author interview with former Secretario de Programación Económica, Ministerio de Economía. Buenos Aires: 8 March.

Figueiredo, Rubens. 1994. Opinião Pública, Intencionalidade e Voto. *Opinião Pública* 2:2 (December): 73–82.

Figueroa, Adolfo. 1996. Author interview with economic advisor to presidential candidate and President-elect Fujimori (1990). Lima: 30 July.

Fishlow, Albert. 1989. A Tale of Two Presidents. In Alfred Stepan, ed. *Democratizing Brazil*, 83–119. New York: Oxford University Press.

————. 1986. Latin American Adjustment to the Oil Shocks of 1973 and

1979. In Jonathan Hartlyn and Samuel Morley, eds. *Latin American Political Economy*, 54–84. Boulder: Westview.

Fleischer, David. 2002. *Brazil Focus. Weekly Report* (26 January–1 February).

———. 1998. The Cardoso Government's Reform Agenda. *Journal of Interamerican Studies and World Affairs* 40:4 (Winter): 119–36.

Flores Nano, Lourdes. 1999. Author interview with congresswoman and leader of Partido Popular Cristiano. Lima: 3 July.

Flynn, Peter. 1999. Brazil: The Politics of Crisis. *Third World Quarterly* 20:2: 287–317.

FONCODES (Fondo Nacional de Compensación y Desarrollo Social). 1995a. *El Mapa de la Inversión Social*. Lima: FONCODES.

———. 1995b. Plan Operativo Institucional 1995. Resumen Ejecutivo. Lima: FONCODES.

———. 1994. *Nota Mensual* 8 (September).

Foxley, Alejandro. 1983. *Latin American Experiments in Neoconservative Economics*. Berkeley: University of California Press.

Fraga, Rosendo. 1995. Para Vencer a Menem, Bordón Deberá Tener un Discurso Económico Preciso. *Cronista Comercial* (27 March): 13.

Franco, Gustavo. 1996. Author interview with Diretor de Assuntos Internacionais, Banco Central do Brasil. Brasília: 10 July.

———. 1995. *O Plano Real e Outros Ensaios*. Rio de Janeiro: Francisco Alves.

Frentzel-Zagorska, Janina, and Krzysztof Zagorski. 1993. Polish Public Opinion on Privatisation and State Interventionism. *Europe-Asia Studies* 45:4: 705–28.

FREPASO (Frente del País Solidario). 1995. *Propuesta de los Equipos Programáticos* (May). Buenos Aires: FREPASO.

Friedman, Jeffrey, ed. 1996. *The Rational Choice Controversy*. New Haven: Yale University Press.

Fritz, Barbara. 1995. Stabilisierung in Brasilien. *Lateinamerika. Supplement* no. 15: 3–41.

Fujimori, Alberto. 1992. *Hacia la Reconstrucción Nacional. Mensaje a la Nación y Memoria Anual, 2° Año de Gobierno*. Lima: Secretaría General de la Presidencia.

———. 1991. Mensaje al País del Presidente Fujimori el 8 de Agosto de 1990. *Encuentro* (Lima) 58 (May): 96–97.

Furtado, Celso. 1976. *Economic Development of Latin America*, 2d ed. London: Cambridge University Press.

Gaidar, Yegor. 1999. *Days of Defeat and Victory*. Seattle: University of Washington Press.

Gamarra, Eduardo. 1994. Crafting Political Support for Stabilization. In William Smith, Carlos Acuña, and Eduardo Gamarra, eds. *Democracy, Markets, and Structural Reform in Latin America*, 104–27. New Brunswick: Transaction.

Garcia, Márcio. 1996. Avoiding Some Costs of Inflation and Crawling toward Hyperinflation. *Journal of Development Economics* 51:1 (October): 139–59.

García Osío, Gustavo, et al. 1998. *La Sostenibilidad de la Política Fiscal en Venezuela*. Documento de Trabajo R-317. Caracas: Instituto de Estudios Superiores de Administración/Inter-American Development Bank.

Garretón, Manuel Antonio. 1983. *El Proceso Político Chileno*. Santiago: Facultad Latinoamericana de Ciencias Sociales.

Geddes, Barbara. 1994a. Challenging the Conventional Wisdom. *Journal of Democracy* 6:4 (October): 104–18.

———. 1994b. *Politician's Dilemma*. Berkeley: University of California Press.

Gélineau, François. 2000. Explaining Popular Support for Market Reform Programs and Their Implementers. Paper for 22d Latin American Studies Association Congress, Miami, 16–18 March.

George, Alexander. 1979. Case Studies and Theory Development. In Paul Lauren, ed. *Diplomacy*, 43–68. New York: Free Press.

Gereffi, Gary, and Donald Wyman, eds. 1990. *Manufacturing Miracles*. Princeton: Princeton University Press.

Gerschenkron, Alexander. 1962. *Economic Backwardness in Historical Perspective*. Cambridge: Harvard University Press.

Gervasoni, Carlos. 1998. Del Distribucionismo al Neoliberalismo. Paper for 21st Latin American Studies Association Congress, Chicago, 24–26 September.

Ghio, José María. 1999. The Politics of Administrative Reform in Argentina. Forthcoming in Blanca Heredia and Ben Schneider, eds. *The Political Economy of Administrative Reforms in Developing Countries*.

Gibson, Edward. 1997. The Populist Road to Market Reform. *World Politics* 49:3 (April): 339–70.

Gibson, John, and Anna Cielecka. 1995. Economic Influences on the Political Support for Market Reform in Post-Communist Transitions. *Europe-Asia Studies* 47:5: 765–85.

Giussani, Pablo. 1987. ¿Por Qué, Doctor Alfonsín? Buenos Aires: Sudamericana-Planeta.

Godio, Julio. 1998. *La Alianza*. Buenos Aires: Grijalbo.

Goldstein, Judith, and Robert Keohane, eds. 1993. *Ideas and Foreign Policy*. Ithaca: Cornell University Press.

Gómez, Eduardo. 1998. Small Institutions in Big Systems. Paper for 21st Latin American Studies Association Congress, Chicago, 24–26 September.

Gonçalves, José Francisco. 1995. Author interview with former Assessor Especial da Ministra da Economia, da Fazendo e do Planejamento, Zélia Cardoso de Mello (1990–91). São Paulo: 30 June.

Gonzales de Olarte, Efraín. 1998. *El Neoliberalismo a la Peruana*. Lima: Instituto de Estudios Peruanos.

Gonzales de Olarte, Efraín, and Lilian Samamé. 1994. *El Péndulo Peruano*, 2d ed. Lima: Instituto de Estudios Peruanos.

González, Antonio Erman. 1995. Author interview with former Ministro de Economía (1989–91). Buenos Aires: 24 March.

González, Rosa. 1995. La Reforma Impositiva en Venezuela. Paper for 19th Latin American Studies Association Congress, Washington, DC, 28–30 September.

González Izquierdo, Jorge. 1991. Las Nuevas Medidas. *Moneda* (Lima) 3:32 (February): 31–33.

Gourevitch, Peter. 1986. *Politics in Hard Times*. Ithaca: Cornell University Press.

Graham, Carol. 1994. *Safety Nets, Politics, and the Poor*. Washington, DC: Brookings.

———. 1993. Economic Austerity and the Peruvian Crisis. *SAIS Review* 31:1 (Winter–Spring): 45–60.

Graham, Carol, Merilee Grindle, Eduardo Lora, and Jessica Seddon. 1999. *Improving the Odds*. Washington, DC: Inter-American Development Bank.

Graham, Carol, and Cheikh Kane. 1998. Opportunistic Government or Sustaining Reform? *Latin American Research Review* 33:1: 67–104.

Graham, Carol, and Stefano Pettinato. 1999. *Assessing Hardship and Happiness*. Working Paper no. 7. Washington, DC: Brookings Institution and Johns Hopkins University. Center on Social and Economic Dynamics.

Granovetter, Mark. 1985. Economic Action and Social Structure. *American Journal of Sociology* 91:3 (November): 481–510.

Grant, Steven. 1999. Is Economic Reform in Russia Dead? USIA Opinion Analysis M-42-99 (March 15).

Graziano, Walter. 1990. *Crónica de Dos Hiperinflaciones*. Buenos Aires: Fundación Gabriel y Dario Ramos.

Green, Donald, and Ian Shapiro. 1994. *Pathologies of Rational Choice Theory*. New Haven: Yale University Press.

Grindle, Merilee. 2000. *Audacious Reforms*. Baltimore: Johns Hopkins University Press.

———. 1999. *In Quest of the Political*. Working Paper no. 17. Cambridge: Harvard University Center for International Development.

———. 1991. The New Political Economy. In Gerald Meier, ed. *Politics and Policy Making in Developing Countries*, 41–67. San Francisco: Institute for Contemporary Studies Press.

Grindle, Merilee, and John Thomas. 1991. *Public Choices and Policy Change*. Baltimore: Johns Hopkins University Press.

Grompone, Romeo. 1998. *Fujimori, Neopopulismo y Comunicación Política*. Documento de Trabajo no. 93. Lima: Instituto de Estudios Peruanos.

Grosh, Margaret. 1994. Through the Structural Adjustment Minefield. In Jennifer Widner, ed. *Economic Change and Political Liberalization in Sub-Saharan Africa*, 29–46. Baltimore: Johns Hopkins University Press.

Guevara, Pedro. 1989. *Concertación o Conflicto*. Caracas: Universidad Central de Venezuela.

Guillermoprieto, Alma. 1990. Letter from Lima. *New Yorker* (29 October): 116–29.

Gyimah-Boadi, E. 1996. Explaining the Economic and Political Success of Rawlings. In John Harriss et al., eds. *The New Institutional Economics and Third World Development*, 306–22. London: Routledge.

Haas, Mark. 2001. Prospect Theory and the Cuban Missile Crisis. *International Studies Quarterly* 45:2 (June): 241–70.

Haggard, Stephan, and Robert Kaufman. 1995. *The Political Economy of Democratic Transitions*. Princeton: Princeton University Press.

———. 1989. Economic Adjustment in New Democracies. In Joan Nelson, ed. *Fragile Coalitions*, 57–77. New Brunswick: Transaction.

Haggard, Stephan, and Steven Webb. 1994. Introduction. In Haggard and Webb, eds., *Voting for Reform*, 1–36. New York: Oxford University Press.

Hagopian, Frances. 1998. *Negotiating Economic Transitions in Liberalizing Polities*. Paper no. 98-5. Cambridge: Harvard University. Weatherhead Center for International Affairs.

Hall, John. 1993. Ideas and the Social Sciences. In Judith Goldstein and

Robert Keohane, eds. *Ideas and Foreign Policy*, 31–54. Ithaca: Cornell University Press.

Hall, Peter. 1993. Policy Paradigms, Social Learning, and the State. *Comparative Politics* 25:3 (April): 275–96.

———, ed. 1989. *The Political Power of Economic Ideas*. Princeton: Princeton University Press.

Hall, Peter, and Rosemary Taylor. 1996. Political Science and the Three New Institutionalisms. *Political Studies* 44:5 (December): 936–57.

Haller, Brandon, and Helmut Norpoth. 1994. Let the Good Times Roll. *American Journal of Political Science* 38:3 (August): 625–50.

Hauser, Heinz-Michael. 1990. Wie gelingt wirtschaftliche Anpassung? *Vierteljahresberichte* 120 (June): 163–75.

Hausmann, Ricardo. 1995. Quitting Populism Cold Turkey. In Louis Goodman et al., eds. *Lessons of the Venezuelan Experience*, 252–82. Washington, DC: Woodrow Wilson Center Press.

———. 1990. Venezuela. In John Williamson, ed. *Latin American Adjustment*, 224–44. Washington, DC: Institute for International Economics.

Hellman, Joel. 1998. Winners Take All. *World Politics* 50:2 (January): 203–34.

Hempel, Carl. 1965. The Logic of Functional Analysis. In Hempel, *Aspects of Scientific Explanation*, 297–330. New York: Free Press.

Herbst, Jeffrey. 1993. *The Politics of Reform in Ghana, 1982–1991*. Berkeley: University of California Press.

———. 1989. Political Impediments to Economic Rationality. *Journal of Modern African Studies* 27:1 (March): 67–84.

Herbst, Jeffrey, and Adebayo Olukoshi. 1994. Nigeria. In Stephan Haggard and Steven Webb, eds. *Voting for Reform*, 453–502. Oxford: Oxford University Press.

Heredia, Blanca, and Ben Ross Schneider. 1998. The Political Economy of Administrative Reform. Paper for 21st Latin American Studies Association Congress, Chicago, 24–26 September. Forthcoming in Heredia and Schneider, eds. *The Political Economy of Administrative Reforms in Developing Countries*.

Hirschman, Albert. 1971. The Political Economy of Import-Substituting Industrialization in Latin America. In Hirschman, *A Bias for Hope*, 85–123. New Haven: Yale University Press.

Hoen, Herman. 1996. "Shock versus Gradualism" in Central Europe Reconsidered. *Comparative Economic Studies* 38:1 (Spring): 1–20.

Hogarth, Robin, and Melvin Reder, eds. 1987. *Rational Choice: The Contrast between Economics and Psychology*. Chicago: University of Chicago Press.

Hospedales, Arístides. 1996. Author interview with Subsecretario General, Acción Democrática. Caracas: 29 May.

Hunter, Wendy. 1997a. Continuity or Change? Civil-Military Relations in Democratic Argentina, Chile, and Peru. *Political Science Quarterly* 112:3 (Fall): 453–75.

———. 1997b. *Eroding Military Influence in Brazil*. Chapel Hill: University of North Carolina Press.

Hunter, Wendy, and David Brown. 2000. World Bank Directives, Domestic Interests, and the Politics of Human Capital Investment in Latin America. *Comparative Political Studies* 33:1 (February): 113–43.

Huntington, Samuel. 1991. *The Third Wave*. Norman: University of
Oklahoma Press.
——. 1968. *Political Order in Changing Societies*. New Haven: Yale
University Press.
Hurtado Miller, Juan Carlos. 1996. Author interview with former Presidente
del Consejo de Ministros and Ministro de Economía y Finanzas (1990–
1991). Lima: 6 August.
——. 1992. *201 Días de Gestión*. Lima: n.p.
——. 1990. *Mensaje al País, 8 Agosto*. Lima: Ministerio de Economía y
Finanzas.
IADB (Inter-American Development Bank). 2000. *Development Beyond
Economics: 2000 Report*. Washington, DC: IADB.
IBOPE (Instituto Brasileiro de Opinião Pública e Estatística). 1999. *Pesquisa
de Opinião Pública sobre Assuntos Políticos. Brasil, Maio de 1999. OPP
046*. Rio de Janeiro: IBOPE.
——. 1995. *Pesquisa de Opinião Pública sobre Assuntos Políticos/
Administrativos. Brasil, Fevereiro de 1995. OPP 014*. Rio de Janeiro:
IBOPE.
——. 1993. *Pesquisa de Opinião Pública sobre Assuntos Políticos. Brasil,
Setembro de 1993. OPP 171*. Rio de Janeiro: IBOPE.
——. 1990a. *Questionário OPP 553–Brasil* (May). Rio de Janeiro: IBOPE.
——. 1990b. *Questionário OPP 602–Brasil* (August). Rio de Janeiro:
IBOPE.
——. 1990c. *Questionário OPP662/90–Brasil* (December). Rio de Janeiro:
IBOPE.
——. 1989. National Voter Survey 0 Wave 18. BRIBOPE89-OPP601 (20–
22 November). Rio de Janeiro: IBOPE.
IDESP (Instituto de Estudos Econômicos, Sociais e Políticos de São Paulo).
1989. *Projeto Democratização, Crise Política e Opinião Pública. Eleições
de 1989 em Niterói (04-11-89–23-12-89)*. São Paulo: IDESP.
Iguíñiz, Javier. 1991. Perú: Ajuste e Inflación en el Plan Fujimori. In Guillermo
Rozenwurcel, ed. *Elecciones y Política en América Latina*, 387–432.
Buenos Aires: Tesis.
IMASEN 1991. *Estudio de Opinión Pública, Agosto 1991, Gran Lima*. Lima:
IMASEN.
——. 1990. *Investigación Sociológica y de Mercado* (October). Lima:
IMASEN.
IMASEN Confidencial, various issues. Lima: IMASEN.
INFES (Instituto Nacional de Infraestructura Educativa y de Salud). 1995.
Memoria 1994. Lima: INFES.
Inglehart, Ronald. 1997. *Modernization and Postmodernization*. Princeton:
Princeton University Press.
Istoé Senhor. 1991. Adeus às Bases. 13 February: 24–25.
Iturbe de Blanco, Eglée. 1996. Author interview with former Ministra de
Hacienda (1989–90). Caracas: 17 June.
Jara, Antonio. 1997. Author interview with Coordinador Técnico de
Relaciones Internacionales, Secretariado Nacional, Unión Obrera
Metalúgica. Buenos Aires: 2 July.
Jefatura de Gabinete de Ministros. Secretaría de Control Estratégico. 1997.
Reforma del Estado II. Buenos Aires: Jefatura.
Jeffries, Richard. 1992. Urban Popular Attitudes towards the Economic

Recovery Programme and the PNDC Government in Ghana. *African Affairs* 91:363 (April): 207–26.

———. 1991. Leadership Commitment and Political Opposition to Structural Adjustment in Ghana. In Donald Rothchild, ed. *Ghana: The Political Economy of Recovery*, 157–71. Boulder: Lynne Rienner.

Jeffries, Richard, and Clare Thomas. 1993. The Ghanaian Elections of 1992. *African Affairs* 92:368 (July): 331–66.

Jervis, Robert. 1997. *System Effects.* Princeton: Princeton University Press.

———. 1992. Political Implications of Loss Aversion. *Political Psychology* 13:2 (June): 187–204.

———. 1976. *Perception and Misperception in International Politics.* Princeton: Princeton University Press.

Johnson, John. 1958. *Political Change in Latin America.* Stanford: Stanford University Press.

Johnson, Simon, and Marzena Kowalska. 1994. Poland. In Stephan Haggard and Steven Webb, eds. *Voting for Reform*, 185–241. Oxford: Oxford University Press.

Jolowicz, Claudio. 1999. Verfassungsreformen und Krisenmanagement in Brasilien am Beispiel der Rentenreform 1998. *Lateinamerika* 16:40 (September): 55–70.

Jongkind, Fred. 1993. Venezuelan Industry under the New Conditions of the 1989 Economic Policy. *European Review of Latin American and Caribbean Studies* 54 (June): 65–93.

Juarez, Carlos. 1993. Trade and Development Policies in Colombia. *Studies in Comparative International Development* 28:3 (Fall): 67–97.

Juchler, Jakob. 1996. Machtwechsel — die Präsidentschaftswahlen in Polen. *Osteuropa* 46:3 (March): 267–83.

Ka, Samba, and Nicolas van de Walle. 1994. Senegal. In Stephan Haggard and Steven Webb, eds. *Voting for Reform*, 290–359. Oxford: Oxford University Press.

Kahler, Miles. 1992. External Influence, Conditionality, and the Politics of Adjustment. In Stephan Haggard and Robert Kaufman, eds. *The Politics of Economic Adjustment*, 89–136. Princeton: Princeton University Press.

———. 1990. Orthodoxy and Its Alternatives. In Joan Nelson, ed. *Economic Crisis and Policy Choice*, 33–61. Princeton: Princeton University Press.

Kahneman, Daniel, Jack Knetsch, and Richard Thaler. 1990. Experimental Tests of the Endowment Effect and the Coase Theorem. *Journal of Political Economy* 98:6 (December): 1325–48.

———. 1986. Fairness as a Constraint on Profit Seeking. *American Economic Review* 76:4 (September): 728–41.

Kahneman, Daniel, and Amos Tversky. 1984. Choices, Values, and Frames. *American Psychologist* 39:4 (April): 341–50.

———. 1979. Prospect Theory. *Econometrica* 47:2 (March): 263–91.

———, eds. 2000. *Choices, Values, and Frames.* New York: Russell Sage Foundation.

Kameda, Tatsuya, and James Davis. 1990. The Function of the Reference Point in Individual and Group Risk Decision Making. *Organizational Behavior and Human Decision Processes* 46:1 (June): 55–76.

Kandir, Antônio. 1995. Author interview with former Secretário de Política Econômica, Ministério da Economia, Fazenda e Planejamento (1990–91). Brasília: 13 June.

Karl, Terry. 1997. *The Paradox of Plenty*. Berkeley: University of California Press.

Katznelson, Ira. 1997. Structure and Configuration in Comparative Politics. In Mark Lichbach and Alan Zuckerman, eds. *Comparative Politics*, 81–112. Cambridge: Cambridge University Press.

Kaufman, Robert. 1990a. How Societies Change Developmental Models or Keep Them. In Gary Gereffi and Donald Wyman, eds. *Manufacturing Miracles*, 110–38. Princeton: Princeton University Press.

———. 1990b. Stabilization and Adjustment in Argentina, Brazil, and Mexico. In Joan Nelson, ed. *Economic Crisis and Policy Choice*, 63–111. Princeton: Princeton University Press.

Kaufman, Robert, and Barbara Stallings. 1989. Debt and Democracy in the 1980s. In Stallings and Kaufman, eds. *Debt and Democracy in Latin America*, 201–23. Boulder: Westview.

Keeler, John. 1993. Opening the Window for Reform. *Comparative Political Studies* 25:4 (January): 433–86.

Keller, Alfredo. 1996. Motivación Electoral y Participación Política. In Ricardo Combellas, ed. *Gobernabilidad y Sistemas Políticos Latinoamericanos*, 63–83. Caracas: Fundación Konrad Adenauer.

Kennamer, David. 1995. Argentina: Polling in an Emerging Democracy. *The Public Perspective* 6:6 (October–November): 62–64.

Kennedy, Paul. 1987. *The Rise and Fall of the Great Powers*. New York: Random House.

Kenney, Charles. 1996. ¿Por qué el Autogolpe? In Fernando Tuesta Soldevilla, ed. *Los Enigmas del Poder*. Lima: Fundación Friedrich Ebert.

Keohane, Robert, and Helen Milner, eds. 1996. *Internationalization and Domestic Politics*. Cambridge: Cambridge University Press.

Kiel, Douglas, and Euel Elliott, eds. 1996. *Chaos Theory in the Social Sciences*. Ann Arbor: University of Michigan Press.

Kim, Byung-Yeon, and Svetlana Sidorenko-Stephenson. 1999. Economic Experience and Market Commitment in the 1996 Russian Presidential Election. *Europe-Asia Studies* 51:3 (May): 467–82.

Kinder, Donald, and Roderick Kiewiet. 1981. Sociotropic Politics. *British Journal of Political Science* 11:2 (April): 129–61.

King, Gary, Robert Keohane, and Sidney Verba. 1994. *Designing Social Inquiry*. Princeton: Princeton University Press.

Kingstone, Peter. 1999. *Crafting Coalitions for Reform*. University Park: Pennsylvania State University Press.

Kinzo, Maria D'Alva, and Simone Rodrigues. 1999. Politics in Brazil. *Government and Opposition* 34:2 (Spring): 243–62.

Knight, Jack. 1992. *Institutions and Social Conflict*. Cambridge: Cambridge University Press.

Knight, Virginia. 1996. Zimbabwe's Reluctant Transformation. *Current History* 95:601 (May): 222–27.

Kohan, Alberto. 1997. Author interview with Secretario General de la Presidencia. Buenos Aires: 1 July.

———. 1995. Author interview with former Secretario General de la Presidencia. Buenos Aires: 22 March.

Kornai, János. 1996. Paying the Bill for Goulash Communism. *Social Research* 63:4 (Winter): 944–1040.

Kornblith, Miriam. 1989. Deuda y Democracia en Venezuela. *Cuadernos del CENDES* 10 (January–April): 17–34.

Kowalik, Tadeusz. 1994. A Reply to Maurice Glasman. *New Left Review* 206 (July–August): 133–44.

Kozielecki, Jozef. 1995. The Polish Economic Reform. *Journal of Economic Psychology* 16:2 (July): 175–204.

Krasner, Stephen. 1984. Approaches to the State. *Comparative Politics* 16:2 (January): 223–45.

Kruse, Sabine. 1992. Peru. *Lateinamerika. Supplement* 11 (August): 1–70.

Kuhn, Thomas. 1970. *The Structure of Scientific Revolutions.* Chicago: University of Chicago Press.

Lago, Ricardo. 1991. The Illusion of Pursuing Redistribution through Macropolicy. In Rüdiger Dornbusch and Sebastian Edwards, eds. *The Macroeconomics of Populism in Latin America*, 263–23. Chicago: University of Chicago Press.

Lamounier, Bolívar, and Alkimar Moura. 1986. Economic Policy and Political Opening in Brazil. In Jonathan Hartlyn and Samuel Morley, eds. *Latin American Political Economy*, 165–96. Boulder: Westview.

Landman, Todd. 1995. "El Chiripero" Wins. *Electoral Studies* 14:1 (March): 100–104.

Lane, Robert. 1996. What Rational Choice Explains. In Jeffrey Friedman, ed. *The Rational Choice Controversy*, 107–26. New Haven: Yale University Press.

Lane, Ruth. 1994. Structural-Functionalism Reconsidered. *Comparative Politics* 26:4 (July): 461–77.

LARS (Latin American Regional Reports — Southern Cone). 1995. Menem Backers Suggest Third Term. (6 July): 6.

LASA (Latin American Studies Association). 1995. *The 1995 Electoral Process in Peru.* N.p.

Latinobarómetro. 1995. *Latinobarómetro 1995. Datos Preliminares.* Santiago de Chile: Latinobarómetro.

Lauría, Carmelo. 1998. Author interview with congressman from Acción Democrática. Caracas: 17 June.

LAWR (Latin American Weekly Report). 1998. Aluminium Sell-off Fails Once Again. (28 July): 346–47.

———. 1995. No Jobs Yet; Just More Benefits. (27 July): 326.

———. 1989. Lusinchi Leaves the Mess to CAP. (5 January): 4–5.

———. 1988. No Austerity Package — Yet. (8 September): 9.

———. 1985. Strike Likely to Fizzle Out. (20 September): 11.

———. 1982. Bolívar Comes under Pressure. (26 March): 6.

———. 1981. Herrera Gets Conflicting Advice on Timing of Economic Recovery. (27 February): 5–6.

———. 1980. Consumer Spending to Receive Boost from Extra Oil Revenue. (21 March): 4.

Lawton, Judy. 1994. Clientelist Politics and Peronism in the Squatter Settlements of Greater Buenos Aires. Paper for 18th Latin American Studies Association Congress, Atlanta, 10–12 March.

Leith, J.Clark, and Michael Lofchie. 1993. The Political Economy of Structural Adjustment in Ghana. In Robert Bates and Anne Krueger, eds. *Political and Economic Interactions in Economic Policy Reform*, 225–293. Oxford: Blackwell.

Levitsky, Steven. 2000. The "Normalization" of Argentine Politics. *Journal of Democracy* 11:2 (April): 56–59.

————. 1999. Fujimori and Post-Party Politics in Peru. *Journal of Democracy* 10:3 (July): 78–92.

————. 1998. Crisis, Party Adaptation and Regime Stability in Argentina. *Party Politics* 4:4 (October): 445–70.

Levy, Jack. 1997. Prospect Theory, Rational Choice, and International Relations. *International Studies Quarterly* 41:1 (March): 87–112.

————. 1992. Prospect Theory and International Relations. *Political Psychology* 13:2 (June): 283–310.

Lewis, Paul. 1990. *The Crisis of Argentine Capitalism*. Chapel Hill: University of North Carolina Press.

Lewis-Beck, Michael. 1988. *Economics and Elections*. Ann Arbor: University of Michigan Press.

Lichbach, Mark. 1997. Social Theory and Comparative Politics. In Mark Lichbach and Alan Zuckerman, eds. *Comparative Politics*, 239–76. Cambridge: Cambridge University Press.

Lieberson, Stanley. 1991. Small N's and Big Conclusions. *Social Forces* 70:2 (December): 307–20.

Lijphart, Arend, and Carlos Waisman. 1996. Institutional Design and Democratization. In Lijphart and Waisman, eds. *Institutional Design in New Democracies*, 1–11. Boulder: Westview.

Lima Figueiredo, Ney. 1992. Imagem do Empresariado. In Bolívar Lamounier, ed. *Ouvindo o Brasil*, 81–94. São Paulo: Editora Sumaré.

Linz, Juan, and Alfred Stepan. 1996. *Problems of Democratic Transition and Consolidation*. Baltimore: Johns Hopkins University Press.

Lipset, Seymour Martin. 1981. *Political Man*. Baltimore: Johns Hopkins University Press.

Loayza Galván, Francisco. 1998. *El Rostro Oscuro del Poder*. Lima: San Borja Ediciones.

Lofchie, Michael. 1993. Trading Places. In Thomas Callaghy and John Ravenhill, eds. *Hemmed In*, 398–462. New York: Columbia University Press.

Looney, Robert. 1986. Venezuela's Economic Crisis. *Journal of Social, Political and Economic Studies* 11 (Fall): 327–337.

López Maya, Margarita. 1999. Venezuela: Formas de la Protesta Popular entre 1989 y 1994. *Revista Venezolana de Economía y Ciencias Sociales* 5:4 (October–December): 11–41.

Lowenstein, Roger. 2001. Exuberance Is Rational or at Least Human. *New York Times Magazine* (11 February): 68–71.

Lustig, Nora. 1992. *Mexico: The Remaking of an Economy*. Washington, DC: Brookings.

Llach, Juan. 1997. *Otro Siglo, Otra Argentina*. Buenos Aires: Ariel.

————. 1995. Author interview with Secretario de Programación Económica, Ministerio de Economía. Buenos Aires: 15 March.

————. 1990. *Las Hiperestabilizaciones sin Mitos*. Buenos Aires: Instituto Torcuato Di Tella. Centro de Investigaciones Económicas. Serie Documentos de Trabajo. DTE 168 (November).

Llanos, Mariana. 1998. El Presidente, el Congreso y la Política de Privatizaciones en la Argentina (1989–1997). *Desarrollo Económico* 38:151 (October–December): 743–70.

McClintock, Cynthia. 1998. Should the Authoritarian Regime Label Be

Revived? Paper for 21st Latin American Studies Association Congress, Chicago, 24–26 September.

———. 1994a. The Breakdown of Constitutional Democracy in Peru. Paper for 18th Latin American Studies Association Congress, Atlanta, 10–12 March.

———. 1994b. Classifying the Regime Types of El Salvador and Peru in the 1980s and the 1990s. Paper for 90th American Political Science Association meeting, New York, 1–4 September.

McCoy, Jennifer. 1999. Chavez and the End of "Partyarchy" in Venezuela. *Journal of Democracy* 10:3 (July): 64–77.

McDermott, Rose. 1998. *Risk-Taking in International Politics.* Ann Arbor: University of Michigan Press.

Macedo, Roberto. 1995. Author interview with former Secretário de Política Econômica, Ministério da Economia, Fazenda e Planejamento. São Paulo: 3 July.

McFadden, Daniel. 1999. Rationality for Economists? *Journal of Risk and Uncertainty* 19:1–3: 73–105.

McFaul, Michael. 1995. State Power, Institutional Change, and the Politics of Privatization in Russia. *World Politics* 47:2 (January): 210–43.

McGuire, James. 1997. *Peronism without Perón.* Stanford: Stanford University Press.

Machiavelli, Niccolò. 1532; 1947. *The Prince*, translated by Thomas Bergin. Arlington Heights, IL: Harlan Davidson.

Machina, Mark. 1987. Choice Under Uncertainty. *Journal of Economic Perspectives* 1:1 (Summer): 121–154.

Machinea, José Luis. 1993. Stabilisation under Alfonsín. In Colin Lewis and Nissa Torrents, eds. *Argentina in the Crisis Years (1983–1990)*, 124–143. London: Institute of Latin American Studies, University of London.

McKeown, Timothy. 1999. Case Studies and the Statistical Worldview. *International Organization* 53:1 (Winter): 161–90.

Mahoney, James. 1999. Nominal, Ordinal, and Narrative Appraisal in Macrocausal Analysis. *American Journal of Sociology* 104:4 (January): 1154–96.

Mainwaring, Scott. 1999. *Rethinking Party Systems in the Third Wave of Democratization.* Stanford: Stanford University Press.

———. 1992–93. Brazilian Party Underdevelopment in Comparative Perspective. *Political Science Quarterly* 107:4 (Winter): 677–707.

———. 1992. Transitions to Democracy and Democratic Consolidation. In Scott Mainwaring, Guillermo O'Donnell, and Samuel Valenzuela, eds. *Issues in Democratic Consolidation*, 294–341. Notre Dame: University of Notre Dame Press.

Mainwaring, Scott, Rachel Meneguello, and Timothy Power. 1999. *Conservative Parties, Democracy, and Economic Reform in Contemporary Brazil.* Working Paper no. 264. Notre Dame: Kellogg Institute.

Mainwaring, Scott, and Timothy Scully. 1995. Introduction: Party Systems in Latin America. In Mainwaring and Scully, eds. *Building Democratic Institutions*, 1–34. Stanford: Stanford University Press.

Majluf, Salvador. 1996. Author interview with former Presidente, Sociedad Nacional de Industrias. Lima: 6 August.

Malan, Pedro. 1999. Transcrição da Palestra do Ministro Pedro Malan no XI

Fórum Nacional (17 May). Brasília: Ministério da Fazenda
<www.fazenda.gov.br/portugues/document/1999/P990517.html>.

Malloy, James. 1991. Democracy, Economic Crisis, and the Problem of
Governance. *Studies in Comparative International Development* 26:2:
37–57.

Mans, Darius. 1994. Tanzania: Resolute Action. In Ishrat Husain and Rashid
Faruqee, eds. *Adjustment in Africa*, 352–426. Washington, DC: World
Bank.

Manzetti, Luigi. 1999. *Privatization South American Style*. Oxford: Oxford
University Press.

March, James, and Johan Olsen. 1984. The New Institutionalism. *American
Political Science Review* 78:3 (September): 734–49.

MARE (Ministério da Administração Federal e Reforma do Estado). 1996.
Boletim Estatístico Mensal 1 (May).

Márquez, Gustavo. 1995. Venezuela: Poverty and Social Policies in the 1980s.
In Nora Lustig, ed. *Coping with Austerity*, 400–52. Washington, DC:
Brookings.

Marta Sosa, Joaquín. 1989. La Apuesta por el Presente con la Magia de los
Equilibrios y los Cambios. In Manuel Caballero et al. *Las Elecciones
Presidenciales*, 167–221. Caracas: Grijalbo.

Martínez, Alfonso. 1997. Author interview with Director Ejecutivo, Consejo
Empresario Argentino. Buenos Aires: 3 July.

Martínez Móttola, Fernando. 1996. Author interview with former Ministro de
Transporte y Comunicaciones. Caracas: 26 June.

Martínez Vivot, Adriana. 1995a. La Estabilidad y el Voto por Menem. *La
Avispa* 2:8 (May): 14.

———. 1995b. La Opinión Pública Frente a la Crisis Económica. *La Avispa*
2:6 (March): 13.

Martins, Luciano. 1990. A Autonomia Política do Governo Collor. In Clovis
de Faro, ed. *Plano Collor*, 27–33. Rio de Janeiro: Livros Técnicos e
Científicos Editora.

Martz, John. 1984. The Crisis of Venezuelan Democracy. *Current History*
83:490 (February): 73–77, 89.

Matos Azócar, Luis Raúl. 1996. *Agenda Venezuela*. Caracas: Ministerio de
Hacienda.

Mauceri, Philip. 1997. Return of the *Caudillo*. *Third World Quarterly* 18:5:
899–911.

———. 1995. State Reform, Coalitions, and the Neoliberal *Autogolpe* in Peru.
Latin American Research Review 30:1: 7–37.

Medina Ayala, Andrés. 1996. Pobreza, Crecimiento y Desigualdad. In Gilberto
Moncada and Richard Webb, eds. *¿Cómo Estamos?* Lima: Instituto
Cuánto.

MEFP (Ministério da Economia, Fazenda e Planejamento). Comissão
Executiva de Reforma Fiscal. 1992. *Projeto de Emenda à Constituição
(Versão atual-26/06/92)*. Brasília: MEFP.

Mello, Zélia Cardoso de. 1995. Author interview with former Ministra da
Economia, Fazenda e Planejamento (1990–91). Rio de Janeiro: 7 July.

Mendes, Antonio Teixeira, and Gustavo Venturi. 1994. Eleição Presidencial.
Opinião Pública 2:2 (December): 39–48.

Meneguello, Rachel. 1994. Partidos e Tendências de Comportamento. In
Evelina Dagnino, ed. *Os Anos 90*, 151–72. São Paulo: Brasiliense.

Menem, Carlos. 1995. *Mensaje Presidencial*. Buenos Aires: Presidencia.
——. 1990. *La Esperanza y la Acción*. Buenos Aires: Emecé.
Menem, Carlos, and Eduardo Duhalde. 1989. *La Revolución Productiva*, 2d ed. N.p.: Fundación Lealtad.
Mercadante, Aloizio. 1998. Plano Real e Neoliberalismo Tardio. In Mercadante, ed. *O Brasil Pós-Real*, 131–67. Campinas: Universidade Estadual de Campinas. Instituto de Economia.
Mercanálisis. 1998. *Estudio de la Opinión Pública Urbana II* (April). Caracas: Mercanálisis.
——. 1997. *Estudio de la Opinión Pública Urbana II* (May–June). Caracas: Mercanálisis.
——. 1996. *Estudio de la Opinión Pública Urbana III* (August–September). Caracas: Mercanálisis.
——. 1989. *Estudio Opinión Pública Urbana I, 23/02 al 16/03/89*. Caracas: Mercanálisis.
Merton, Robert. 1968. Manifest and Latent Functions. In Merton, *Social Theory and Social Structure*, 73–138. New York: Free Press.
Midré, Georges. 1992. Bread or Solidarity? *Journal of Latin American Studies* 24:2 (May): 343–73.
Miguel, Lorenzo. 1995. Author interview with Presidente, Unión Obrera Metalúrgica. Buenos Aires: 27 March.
Ministério da Fazenda. 1996. *O Plano Real: Vigésimo Quarto Mês*. Brasília: Ministério da Fazenda.
——. Gabinete do Ministro. Assessoria de Comunicação Social. 1993. *Programa de Ação Imediata*. Brasília: Ministério da Fazenda.
Ministerio de Economía (Buenos Aires). 1999. *Informe Económico* 8:29 (July).
——. 1996. *Informe Económico* 5:18 (October).
——. 1994. *Informe Económico* 3:10 (October).
Ministerio de Hacienda. 1995. *Estabilización Macroeconómica, Transformaciones Estructurales, Desarrollo de la Competitividad y Estímulos al Crecimiento Sostenido*. Caracas: Ministerio de Hacienda.
Ministerio del Trabajo. 1997. *Acuerdo Tripartito sobre Seguridad Social Integral y Política Salarial (ATSSI)*. Caracas: Ministerio del Trabajo.
Moe, Terry. 1990. Political Institutions. *Journal of Law, Economics, and Organization* 6 (special issue): 213–53.
Moisés, José Alvaro. 1993. Democratization and Political Culture. In Maria D'Alva Kinzo, ed. *Brazil: The Challenges of the 1990s*, 155–84. London: Institute of Latin American Studies, University of London.
Molinar Horcasitas, Juan, and Jeffrey Weldon. 1994. Electoral Determinants and Consequences of National Solidarity. In Wayne Cornelius, Ann Craig, and Jonathan Fox, eds., *Transforming State-Society Relations in Mexico*, 123–41. San Diego: Center for U.S.-Mexican Studies, University of California.
Montero, Alfred. 1998. State Interests and the New Industrial Policy in Brazil. *Journal of Interamerican Studies and World Affairs* 40:3 (Fall): 27–62.
Mora, Mônica, and Ricardo Varsano. 2001. *Fiscal Decentralization and Subnational Fiscal Autonomy in Brazil*. Texto para Discussão no. 854. Rio de Janeiro: Instituto de Pesquisa Econômica Aplicada (December).
Mora y Araujo, Manuel. 1993. Las Demandas Sociales y la Legitimidad de la Política de Ajuste. In Felipe de la Balze, ed. *Reforma y Convergencia*, 301–33. Buenos Aires: Manantial.

———. 1991. *Ensayo y Error*. Buenos Aires: Planeta.

Mora y Araujo, Noguera y Asociados. 1997. Nivel de Optimismo/Pesimismo País, Personal. Capital Federal y Gran Buenos Aires. (Data compilation for author). Buenos Aires: Mora y Araujo.

———. 1996. *Análisis Socio-Político de la Coyuntura Argentina* (February). Buenos Aires: Mora y Araujo.

———. 1995. *Análisis Socio-Político de la Coyuntura Argentina* (February). Buenos Aires: Mora y Araujo.

———. 1990. *Análisis Socio-Político de la Coyuntura Argentina* (September). Buenos Aires: Mora y Araujo.

———. 1989. *Informe General 89/2* (March). Buenos Aires: Mora y Araujo.

———. 1989. *Informe General 89/3* (April). Buenos Aires: Mora y Araujo.

Moreira, Marcílio Marques. 1995. Author interview with former Ministro da Economia, Fazenda e Planejamento (1991–92). Rio de Janeiro: 7 July.

———. 1992. Author interview with Ministro da Economia, Fazenda e Planejamento. Brasília: 9 July.

Moreira, Maurício Mesquita, and Paulo Guilherme Correa. 1998. A First Look at the Impacts of Trade Liberalization on Brazilian Manufacturing Industry. *World Development* 26:10 (October): 1859–74.

Moreira Franco, Wellington. 1996. Author interview with Deputado Federal (PMDB-Rio de Janeiro) and Relator on administrative reform. Brasília: 4 July.

Morley, Samuel. 1995. Structural Adjustment and the Determinants of Poverty in Latin America. In Nora Lustig, ed. *Coping with Austerity*, 42–70. Washington, DC: Brookings.

Morley, Samuel, and Carola Alvarez. 1992. Recession and the Growth of Poverty in Argentina. Washington, DC: Inter-American Development Bank.

Morna, Colleen. 1995. Interview: Kwesi Botchwey, Ghana's Finance Minister. *Africa Report* 40:2 (March–April): 38–40.

Morrow, James. 1995. A Rational Choice Approach to International Conflict. Stanford: Hoover Institution.

Moura, Alkimar. 1993. Stabilization Policy as a Game of Mutual Distrust. In Maria D'Alva Kinzo, ed. *Brazil: The Challenges of the 1990s*, 5–23. London: Institute of Latin American Studies, University of London.

MTSS (Ministerio de Trabajo y Seguridad Social). 1994. *Proyecto de Ley para Pequeñas y Medianas Empresas*. Buenos Aires: MTSS.

Müller Rojas, Alberto. 1989. Las Fuerzas del Orden en la Crisis de Febrero. *Politeia* 13: 115–54.

Murillo, María Victoria. 2001. *Labor Unions, Partisan Coalitions, and Market Reforms in Latin America*. Cambridge: Cambridge University Press.

Murphy, James. 1996. Rational Choice Theory as Social Physics. In Jeffrey Friedman, ed. *The Rational Choice Controversy*, 155–74. New Haven: Yale University Press.

Murrell, Peter. 1993. What Is Shock Therapy? *Post-Soviet Affairs* 9:2 (April–June): 111–40.

Murua, Mario. 1996. *Pulsando la Opinión en Mérida*. Mérida: Instituto de Investigaciones Económicas y Sociales, Universidad de los Andes.

Muszynski, Judith, and Antonio Teixeira Mendes. 1990. Democratização e Opinião Pública no Brasil. In Bolívar Lamounier, ed. *De Geisel a Collor*, 61–80. São Paulo: Editora Sumaré.

Myers, David. 1993. Percepciones de una Democracia Bajo Presión. In Andrés

Serbin et al., eds. *Venezuela: La Democracia Bajo Presión*, 43–68. Caracas: Nueva Sociedad.

Nagel, Ernest. 1979. Teleology Revisited. In *Teleology Revisited and Other Essays in the Philosophy and History of Science*, 275–316. New York: Columbia University Press.

Naím, Moisés. 2001. The Real Story Behind Venezuela's Woes. *Journal of Democracy* 12:2 (April): 17–31.

———. 2000. Author interview with former Ministro de Fomento (1989–90). Washington, DC: 30 March.

———. 1995. *Latin America's Journey to the Market*. San Francisco: Institute for Contemporary Studies.

———. 1993a. The Launching of Radical Policy Changes, 1989–1991; and The Political Management of Radical Economic Change. Both in Joseph Tulchin, ed. *Venezuela in the Wake of Radical Reform*, 39–94, 147–78. Boulder: Lynne Rienner.

———. 1993b. *Paper Tigers and Minotaurs*. Washington, DC: Carnegie Endowment.

Navarro, Carlos. 1998. Author interview with Secretario General of Confederación de Trabajadores de Venezuela. Caracas: 8 July.

Navarro, Juan Carlos. 1994. Reforming Social Policy in Venezuela. Paper for 18th Latin American Studies Association Congress, Atlanta, 10–12 March.

Navarro, Mario. 1995. Democracia y Reformas Estructurales. *Desarrollo Económico* 35:139 (October–December): 443–65.

Nelson, Joan. 1997. Reforming Social Sector Governance. Paper for Conference on Governance, Poverty Eradication, and Social Policy, United Nations Development Program/Harvard Institute for International Development, Harvard University, 12–14 November.

———. 1992. Poverty, Equity, and the Politics of Adjustment. In Stephan Haggard and Robert Kaufman, eds., *The Politics of Economic Adjustment*, 221–69. Princeton: Princeton University Press.

———. 1990. Introduction: The Politics of Economic Adjustment in Developing Nations. In Nelson, ed. *Economic Crisis and Policy Choice*, 3–32. Princeton: Princeton University Press.

Nêumanne, José. 1989. *Atrás do Palanque*. São Paulo: Siciliano.

Nóbrega, Maílson da. 1992. Presença do Estado na Economia e na Sociedade. In Bolívar Lamounier, ed. *Ouvindo o Brasil*, 15–47. São Paulo: Editora Sumaré.

Nóbrega, Tobías, and Guillermo Ortega. 1996. La Agenda Venezuela. *Nueva Economía* 5:7 (October): 169–216.

Norden, Deborah. 1998. Democracy and Military Control in Venezuela. *Latin American Research Review* 33:2: 143–65.

North, Douglass. 1981. *Structure and Change in Economic History*. New York: Norton.

Novaro, Marcos. 1999. Crisis y Renovación de los Partidos. In Novaro, *Entre el Abismo y la Ilusión*, 63–157. Buenos Aires: Grupo Editorial Norma.

———. 1994. *Pilotos de Tormentas*. Buenos Aires: Ediciones Letra Buena.

Novaro, Marcos, and Vicente Palermo. 1998. *Los Caminos de la Centroizquierda*. Buenos Aires: Losada.

Nugent, Paul. 1999. Living in the Past. *Journal of Modern African Studies* 37:2 (June): 287–319.

Nun, José. 1967. The Middle-Class Military Coup. In Claudio Véliz, ed. *The Politics of Conformity in Latin America*, 66–118. London: Oxford University Press.

Nylen, William. 1993. Small Business Owners Fight Back. Ph.D. dissertation, Columbia University.

Obando, Enrique. 1998. Fujimori and the Military. In John Crabtree and Jim Thomas, eds. *Fujimori's Peru*, 192–208. London: Institute of Latin American Studies, University of London.

OCI (Oficina Central de Información). 1989. *¡Saldremos Adelante!* Caracas: OCI.

O'Donnell, Guillermo. 1998. Horizontal Accountability in New Democracies. *Journal of Democracy* 9:3 (July): 112–26.

———. 1994. Delegative Democracy. *Journal of Democracy* 5:1 (January): 55–69.

———. 1993. On the State, Democratization, and Some Conceptual Problems. *World Development* 21:8 (August): 1355–69.

———. 1985. External Debt. *CEPAL Review* 27 (December): 27–33.

———. 1979. *Modernization and Bureaucratic-Authoritarianism*, 2d ed. Berkeley: Institute of International Studies, University of California.

———. 1978. Reflections on the Patterns of Change in the Bureaucratic-Authoritarian State. *Latin American Research Review* 13:1: 3–38.

O'Donnell, Guillermo, and Philippe Schmitter. 1986. *Transitions from Authoritarian Rule: Tentative Conclusions about Uncertain Democracies*. Baltimore: Johns Hopkins University Press.

Offe, Claus. 1991. Capitalism by Democratic Design? *Social Research* 58:4 (Winter): 865–92.

Oliveira, Gesner. 1996. Author interview with former Secretário-Adjunto de Política Econômica, Ministério da Fazenda. Brasília: 10 July.

———. 1996. *Brasil Real*. São Paulo: Mandarim.

Olsen, Örjan. 2000. Encuestas en Brasil. In Friedrich Welsch and Frederick Turner, eds. *Opinión Pública y Elecciones en América*, 65–100. Caracas: Universidad Simón Bolívar.

Olson, Mancur. 1982. *The Rise and Decline of Nations*. New Haven: Yale University Press.

———. 1971. *The Logic of Collective Action*. Cambridge: Harvard University Press.

Oquaye, Mike. 1995. The Ghanaian Elections of 1992. *African Affairs* 94:375 (April): 259–75.

Ostiguy, Pierre. 1997. Peronism and Anti-Peronism. Paper for 20th Latin American Studies Association Congress, Guadalajara, 17–19 April.

Ovalles, Caupolicán. 1996. *Usted me debe esa Cárcel*. Caracas: Rayuela.

Oxhorn, Philip. 1998. The Social Foundations of Latin America's Recurrent Populism. *Journal of Historical Sociology* 11:2 (June): 212–46.

Oxhorn, Philip, and Pamela Starr, eds. 1999. *Markets and Democracy in Latin America*. Boulder: Lynne Rienner.

Packenham, Robert. 1994. *The Politics of Economic Liberalization*. Working Paper no. 206. Notre Dame: Kellogg Institute.

Palacios, Leonardo. 1996. Author interview with former Coordinador del Proyecto de Reforma Tributaria under President Pérez. Caracas: 25 June.

Palermo, Vicente, and Marcos Novaro. 1996. *Política y Poder en el Gobierno de Menem*. Buenos Aires: Grupo Editorial Norma.

Palma, Pedro. 1999. La Economía Venezolana en el Quinquenio 1994–1998. *Nueva Economía* 8:12 (April): 97–158.

Palmer, David Scott. 1995. Peru's 1995 Elections. *LASA Forum* 26:2 (Summer): 17–20.

Panfichi, Aldo, and César Francis. 1993. Liderazgos Políticos Autoritarios en el Perú. *Debates en Sociología* 18: 227–47.

Panizza, Francisco. 2000. Neopopulism and Its Limits in Collor's Brazil. *Bulletin of Latin American Research* 19:2 (April): 177–92.

Paredes, Carlos. 1999. Author interview with Jefe del Gabinete de Asesores, Ministerio de Economía y Finanzas. Lima: 5 July.

———. 1991. Epilogue: In the Aftermath of Hyperinflation. In Carlos Paredes and Jeffrey Sachs, eds. *Peru's Path to Recovery*, 299–322. Washington, DC: Brookings.

Parodi, Jorge, and Walter Twanama. 1993. Los Pobladores, la Ciudad y la Política. In Jorge Parodi, ed. *Los Pobres, la Ciudad y la Política*. Lima: Centro de Estudios Democracia y Sociedad.

Pastor, Manuel. 1992. *Inflation, Stabilization, and Debt*. Boulder: Westview.

Pastor, Manuel, and Carol Wise. 1999. Stabilization and its Discontents. *World Development* 27:3 (March): 477–503.

———. 1992. Peruvian Economic Policy in the 1980s. *Latin American Research Review* 27:2: 83–117.

Payne, John, James Bettman, and Eric Johnson. 1992. Behavioral Decision Research. *Annual Review of Psychology* 43: 87–131.

Paz, Pedro. 1989. La Gestión Económica del Radicalismo. *Nuevo Proyecto* 5–6: 79–112.

Pease, Henry. 1999. Author interview with congressman and leader of Unión por el Perú. Lima: 6 July.

———. 1996. Author interview with congressman for Unión por el Perú. Lima: 12 August.

———. 1995. *Remando a Contracorriente*. Lima: Congreso Constituyente Democrático.

Pêgo Filho, Bolívar, Edilberto Pontes Lima, and Francisco Pereira. 1999. *Privatização, Ajuste Patrimonial e Contas Públicas no Brasil*. Texto para Discussão no. 668. Brasília: Instituto de Pesquisa Econômica Aplicada.

Pennano, Guido. 1996. Author interview with former Ministro de Industria y Comercio (1990–91) and leader of Unión por el Perú. Lima: 7 August.

———. 1990. Política Económica en el Perú. In Alfredo Barnechea, ed. *Posible: El Perú de los 90*. Lima: Instituto del Sur para la Cooperación Democrática.

Pérez, Carlos Andrés. 1996. Author interviews with former Presidente de la República (1989–93). Oripoto: 5 June and 28 June.

———. 1990. *El Gran Viraje*. Caracas: Oficina Central de Información (7 March).

———. 1989. *Manos a la Obra. Textos de Mensajes, Discursos y Declaraciones del Presidente de la República*. Tomo I, vol.1: *2 de Febrero a 25 de Mayo de 1989*. Caracas: Oficina Central de Información.

Peruzzotti, Enrique. 2001. The Nature of the New Argentine Democracy. *Journal of Latin American Studies* 33:1 (February): 133–155.

Petkoff, Teodoro. 1998. Author interview with Ministro Jefe de Oficina Central de Coordinación y Planificación. Caracas: 3 July.

———. 1997. *Por Qué Hago lo Que Hago*. Caracas: Alfadil Editores.

Petras, James. 1997. Latin America: The Resurgence of the Left. *New Left Review* 223 (May–June): 17–47.

Philip, George. 1999. When Oil Prices Were Low. *Bulletin of Latin American Research* 18:3 (July): 361–76.

Pinheiro, Vinícius. 2000. *A Política da Reforma da Previdência no Brasil.* Paper for conference on Learning from Foreign Models in Latin American Policy Reform, Woodrow Wilson Center, Washington, DC, 14 September.

Pion-Berlin, David. 1983. Political Repression and Economic Doctrines. *Comparative Political Studies* 16:1 (April): 37–66.

Poder Legislativo Nacional. Oficina de Asesoría Económica y Financiera (OAEF). 2000. *Informe de Coyuntura Cuarto Trimestre de 1999.* Caracas: OAEF.

Pojo de Rego, Antonio. 1995. Author interview with former Chefe de Gabinete, Ministro da Justiça Bernardo Cabral (1990) and Jarbas Passarinho (1990–91). Brasília: 20 June.

Pojo de Rego, Antonio and João Paulo Peixoto. 1998. *A Política das Reformas Econômicas no Brasil.* Rio de Janeiro: Editora Expressão e Cultura.

Polanyi, Karl. 1957. *The Great Transformation.* Boston: Beacon.

Pottellá, Luis A., and Humberto Decarli. 1998. *Para Qué una Asamblea Nacional Constituyente,* 2d ed. Caracas: Funda Historia.

Power, Timothy. 1998a. Brazilian Politicians and Neoliberalism. *Journal of Interamerican Studies and World Affairs* 40:4 (Winter): 51–72.

———. 1998b. The Pen Is Mightier than the Congress. In John Carey and Matthew Shugart, eds. *Executive Decree Authority,* 197–230. Cambridge: Cambridge University Press.

Powers, Nancy. 1995. The Politics of Poverty in Argentina in the 1990s. *Journal of Interamerican Studies and World Affairs* 37:4 (Winter): 89–137.

Presidência da República. 1999a. *Brazil's Macroeconomic Outlook.* Brasília: Presidência.

———. 1999b. *Brazil's Macroeconomic Stability Program 1999–2001.* Brasília: Presidência.

———. 1995. *Proposta de Reforma Tributária.* Brasília: Presidência.

Prévôt Schapira, Marie-France. 1996. Las Políticas de Lucha contra la Pobreza en la Periferia de Buenos Aires, 1984–1994. *Revista Mexicana de Sociología* 59:2 (April–June): 73–94.

Programa de Gobierno 1989 en adelante—PROMENEM. 1989. Buenos Aires: N.p. (5 July).

Proyecto de Ley de Creación del Nuevo Sistema Monetario Argentino. 1989. N.p.

Przeworski, Adam. 1997. Una Defensa de la Concepción Minimalista de la Democracia. *Revista Mexicana de Sociología* 59:3 (July-September): 3–36.

———. 1993. Economic Reforms, Public Opinion, and Political Institutions. In Luiz Carlos Bresser Pereira, José María Maravall, and Adam Przeworski, eds. *Economic Reforms in New Democracies,* 132–98. Cambridge: Cambridge University Press.

———. 1991. *Democracy and the Market.* Cambridge: Cambridge University Press.

———. 1985. *Capitalism and Social Democracy.* Cambridge: Cambridge University Press.

Przeworski, Adam, et al. 1996. What Makes Democracies Endure? *Journal of Democracy* 7:1 (January): 39–55.

Przeworski, Adam, and Henry Teune. 1970; 1982. *The Logic of Comparative Social Inquiry*. Malabar, FL: Robert E. Krieger.

PT (Partido dos Trabalhadores). 2001. Programa Econômico <PT.uol.com.br/site/jornalismo/openew.asp>.

———. 1999. *II Congresso. 1° Caderno de Debates*. São Paulo: PT.

———. 1995. *10° Encontro Nacional do PT. Documento para Discussão de Base*. São Paulo: PT.

Quattrone, George, and Amos Tversky. 1988. Contrasting Rational and Psychological Analyses of Political Choice. *American Political Science Review* 82:3 (September): 719–36.

Quenan, Carlos. 1990. Venezuela: Crise Économique et Ajustement. *Notes et Études Documentaires* 4916 (3d quarter): 99–122.

Ragin, Charles. 1987. *The Comparative Method*. Berkeley: University of California Press.

Ramos, Joseph. 1986. *Neoconservative Economics in the Southern Cone of Latin America, 1973–1983*. Baltimore: Johns Hopkins University Press.

Ranis, Peter. 1995. The New Menem Peronism. In Ranis, *Class, Democracy, and Labor in Argentina*, ix–xxxv. New Brunswick: Transaction.

Rapanelli, Néstor. 1997. Author interview with former Ministro de Economía (1989). Buenos Aires: 24 June.

Ravenhill, John. 1993. A Second Decade of Adjustment. In Thomas Callaghy and John Ravenhill, eds. *Hemmed In*, 18–53. New York: Columbia University Press.

Recomendaciones del Consejo Consultivo al Presidente de la República. 1992. *Politeia* 15: 449–80.

Remmer, Karen. 1996. The Sustainability of Political Democracy. *Comparative Political Studies* 29:6 (December): 611–34.

———. 1995. New Theoretical Perspectives on Democratization. *Comparative Politics* 28:1 (October): 103–22.

———. 1993. The Political Economy of Elections in Latin America, 1980–1991. *American Political Science Review* 87:2 (June): 393–407.

———. 1991. The Political Impact of Economic Crisis in Latin America in the 1980s. *American Political Science Review* 85:3 (September): 777–800.

Remmer, Karen, and Gilbert Merkx. 1982. Bureaucratic-Authoritarianism Revisited. *Latin American Research Review* 17:2: 3–40.

Repetto, Fabián. 2001. La "Política" de las Reformas Administrativas en la Argentina. Paper for 23d Latin American Studies Association Congress, Washington, DC, 6–8 September.

———. 1998. Capacidad de Gestión Pública y Gobernabilidad. Paper for 21st Latin American Studies Association Congress, Chicago, 24–26 September.

Roberts, Kenneth. 1998. *Deepening Democracy?* Stanford: Stanford University Press.

———. 1995. Neoliberalism and the Transformation of Populism in Latin America. *World Politics* 48:1 (October): 82–116.

Roberts, Kenneth, and Moisés Arce. 1998. Neoliberalism and Lower-Class Voting Behavior in Peru. *Comparative Political Studies* 31:2 (April): 217–46.

Roca, Santiago. 1996. Author interview with top economic adviser to presidential candidate Alberto Fujimori (1990). Lima: 22 August.

Rodríguez, Carlos. 1997. Author interview with Jefe de Asesores, Ministerio de Economía. Buenos Aires: 3 July.

Rodríguez, Miguel. 1996. Author interview with former Jefe de la Oficina Central de Coordinación y Planificación (1989–92). Caracas: 6 June.

———. 1994. Comment. In John Williamson, ed. *The Political Economy of Policy Reform*, 376–81. Washington, DC: Institute for International Economics.

Rodrik, Dani. 1996. Understanding Economic Policy Reform. *Journal of Economic Literature* 34:2 (March): 9–41.

———. 1994. The Rush to Free Trade in the Developing World. In Stephan Haggard and Steven Webb, eds. *Voting for Reform*, 61–88. New York: Oxford University Press.

———. 1989. Promises, Promises. *Economic Journal* 99:397 (September): 756–72.

Rojas Parra, Freddy. 1998. Author interview with Ministro de Hacienda. Caracas: 16 June.

Römer, Graciela. 1997. Author interview with pollster. Buenos Aires: 2 July.

Rosa e Silva, Cláudio Humberto. 1993. *Mil Dias de Solidão*. São Paulo: Geração Editorial.

Rosas, Pedro. 1996. Author interview with former Vice-Ministro, Oficina Central de Coordinación y Planificación (1990–91), and Ministro de Hacienda (1992–93). Caracas: 11 June.

Rospigliosi, Fernando. 1992. Las Elecciones Peruanas de 1990. In Instituto Interamericano de Derechos Humanos (IIDH), ed. *Una Tarea Inconclusa*. San José, Costa Rica: IIDH.

Rueschemeyer, Dietrich, Evelyne Huber Stephens, and John Stephens. 1992. *Capitalist Development and Democracy*. Chicago: University of Chicago Press.

Rueschemeyer, Marilyn, and Sharon Wolchik. 1999. The Return of Left-Oriented Parties in Eastern Germany and the Czech Republic and Their Social Policies. In Linda Cook, Mitchell Orenstein, and Marilyn Rueschemeyer, eds. *Left Parties and Social Policy in Postcommunist Europe*, 109–43. Boulder: Westview.

Sabino, Fernando. 1991. *Zélia, uma Paixão*. Rio de Janeiro: Record.

Sachs, Jeffrey. 2002. Duhalde's Wrong Turn. *Financial Times* (11 January): 13.

———. 1989. Una Política para la Hiperinflación. Seminario Extraordinario (28 June). Buenos Aires: Foro Ciencia, Empresa y Política.

Salamanca, Luis. 1997. *Crisis de la Modernización y Crisis de la Democracia en Venezuela*. Caracas: Universidad Central de Venezuela.

Salcedo, José María. 1995. *Terremoto: ¿Por Qué Ganó Fujimori?* Lima: Editorial Brasa.

Salgado, René. 1987. Economic Pressure Groups and Policy-Making in Venezuela. *Latin American Research Review* 22:3: 91–105.

Samuelson, William, and Richard Zeckhauser. 1988. Status Quo Bias in Decision Making. *Journal of Risk and Uncertainty* 1:1 (March): 7–59.

Sandbrook, Richard, and Jay Oelbaum. 1997. Reforming Dysfunctional Institutions through Democratisation? *Journal of Modern African Studies* 35:4 (December): 603–646.

Santana, Angela. 1996. Author interview with Secretária de Reforma do Estado, Ministério da Administração Federal e Reforma do Estado. Brasília: 10 July.

Santoro, Daniel. 1994. *El Hacedor*. Buenos Aires: Planeta.

Sardenberg, Carlos Alberto. 1987. *Aventura e Agonia*. São Paulo: Companhia das Letras.

Schady, Norbert. 2000. The Political Economy of Expenditures by the Peruvian Social Fund (FONCODES), 1991–95. *American Political Science Review* 94:2 (June): 289–304.

Schamis, Hector. 1999. Distributional Coalitions and the Politics of Economic Reform in Latin America. *World Politics* 51:2 (January): 236–68.

Scharpf, Fritz. 1997. *Games Real Actors Play*. Boulder: Westview.

Schattschneider, Elmer. 1975. *The Semisovereign People*. Hinsdale, IL: Dryden.

Schaubroeck, John, and Elaine Davis. 1994. Prospect Theory Predictions When Escalation Is Not the Only Chance to Recover Sunk Costs. *Organizational Behavior and Human Decision Processes* 57:1 (January): 59–82.

Schmidt, Gregory. 1998. Presidential Usurpation or Congressional Preference? In John Carey and Matthew Shugart, eds. *Executive Decree Authority*, 104–41. Cambridge: Cambridge University Press.

———. 1996. Fujimori's 1990 Upset Victory in Peru. *Comparative Politics* 28:3 (April): 321–54.

Schmitter, Philippe. 1992. The Consolidation of Democracy and Representation of Social Groups. *American Behavioral Scientist* 35:4–5 (March–June): 422–49.

Schneider, Ben. 1991. Brazil Under Collor. *World Policy Journal* 8:2 (Spring): 321–47.

Schneider, Eleonora. 1997. Ende der politischen Stabilität? *Osteuropa* 47:2 (February): 150–59.

Schvarzer, Jorge. 1986. *La Política Económica de Martínez de Hoz*. Buenos Aires: Hyspamérica.

Schydlowsky, Daniel. 1986. The Tragedy of Lost Opportunity in Peru. In Jonathan Hartlyn and Samuel Morley, eds. *Latin American Political Economy*, 217–42. Boulder: Westview.

Secretaría de Desarrollo Social. Presidencia de la Nación. 1995. *Plan Social 1995*. Buenos Aires: Secretaría de Desarrollo Social.

Selznick, Philip. 1957. *Leaderhip in Administration*. Evanston, IL: Row, Peterson.

Seminario, Bruno. 1995. *Reformas Estructurales y Política de Estabilización*. Documento de Trabajo no. 22. Lima: Centro de Investigación, Universidad del Pacífico.

Sheahan, John. 1994. Peru's Return Toward an Open Economy. *World Development* 22:6 (June): 911–23.

———. 1987. *Patterns of Development in Latin America*. Princeton: Princeton University Press.

Shugart, Matthew, and John Carey. 1992. *Presidents and Assemblies*. Cambridge: Cambridge University Press.

Shugart, Matthew, and Scott Mainwaring. 1997. Presidentialism and Democracy in Latin America. In Mainwaring and Shugart, eds. *Presidentialism and Democracy in Latin America*, 12–54. Cambridge: Cambridge University Press.

SIEMPRO (Sistema de Información, Monitoreo y Evaluación de Programas Sociales). Secretaría de Desarrollo Social. 1997. *Base de Datos de*

Programas Nacionales Destinados a la Población en Situación de Pobreza-1997. Buenos Aires: SIEMPRO.

Sigmund, Paul. 1977. *The Overthrow of Allende and the Politics of Chile, 1964–1976.* Pittsburgh: University of Pittsburgh Press.

Silva, Eduardo, and Francisco Durand, eds. 1998. *Business Peak Associations in Latin America.* Miami: North-South Center Press.

Silva, Maria Luiza Falcão, and Joaquim Pinto de Andrade. 1996. Brazil's New Currency. *Revista Brasileira de Economia* 50:4 (October–December): 427–67.

Simutanyi, Neo. 1996. The Politics of Structural Adjustment in Zambia. *Third World Quarterly* 17:4: 825–39.

SIP (Secretaría de Ingresos Públicos. Ministerio de Economía). 1995. *La Recaudación Tributaria en el Cuarto Trimestre de 1994.* Buenos Aires: Dirección Nacional de Investigaciones y Análisis Fiscal, SIP.

Skidmore, Thomas. 1967. *Politics in Brazil, 1930–1964.* London: Oxford University Press.

Skocpol, Theda. 1979. *States and Social Revolutions.* Cambridge: Cambridge University Press.

Skowronek, Stephen. 1982. *Building a New American State.* Cambridge: Cambridge University Press.

Smith, William. 1991. State, Market and Neoliberalism in Post-Transition Argentina. *Journal of Interamerican Studies and World Affairs* 33:4 (Winter): 45–82.

———. 1990. Democracy, Distributional Conflicts and Macroeconomic Policymaking in Argentina, 1983–89. *Journal of Interamerican Studies and World Affairs* 32:2 (Summer): 1–42.

———. 1989. *Authoritarianism and the Crisis of the Argentine Political Economy.* Stanford: Stanford University Press.

Sola, Lourdes. 1994. The State, Structural Reform, and Democratization in Brazil. In William Smith, Carlos Acuña, and Eduardo Gamarra, eds. *Democracy, Markets, and Structural Reform in Latin America*, 151–81. New Brunswick: Transaction.

———. 1988. Choque Heterodoxo e Transição Democrática sem Ruptura. In Sola, ed. *O Estado da Transição*, 13–62. São Paulo: Vértice.

Solimeo, Marcel Domingos. 1995. Author interview with Diretor, Instituto de Economia Gastão Vidigal, Associação Comercial de São Paulo. São Paulo: 26 June.

Solnik, Alex. 1987. *Os Pais do Cruzado Contam Por Que Não Deu Certo.* Porto Alegre: L&PM Editores.

Solórzano, Rafael. 1997. Política y Administración Tributaria en Venezuela y Agenda para los Años Noventa. In Raúl Angulo Anselmi, ed. *Serie Ensayos "3er Aniversario,"* 79–101. Caracas: SENIAT.

Stallings, Barbara. 1992. International Influence on Economic Policy. In Stephan Haggard and Robert Kaufman, eds. *The Politics of Economic Adjustment*, 41–88. Princeton: Princeton University Press.

Stambouli, Andrés. 1989. Encuestas, Resultados y Tendencias en las Elecciones de Diciembre de 1988. In Manuel Caballero et al. *Las Elecciones Presidenciales*, 223–37. Caracas: Grijalbo.

Stark, David, and László Bruszt. 1998. *Postsocialist Pathways.* Cambridge: Cambridge University Press.

Starr, Pamela. 1997. Government Coalitions and the Viability of Currency

Boards. *Journal of Interamerican Studies and World Affairs* 39:2 (Summer): 83–133.

Stein, Janice Gross, and Louis W. Pauly, eds. 1993. *Choosing to Co-operate.* Baltimore: Johns Hopkins University Press.

Stinchcombe, Arthur. 1968; 1987. *Constructing Social Theories.* Chicago: University of Chicago Press.

Stokes, Susan. 2001a. *Mandates and Democracy.* Cambridge: Cambridge University Press.

———. 2001b. Public Opinion of Market Reforms. In Stokes, ed. *Public Support for Market Reforms in New Democracies*, 1–32. Cambridge: Cambridge University Press.

Stokes, Susan, and John Baughman. 1998. Is Neoliberalism a Mass Ideology in Latin America? Paper for 94th American Political Science Association meeting, Boston, 3–6 September.

Strange, Susan. 1996. *The Retreat of the State.* Cambridge: Cambridge University Press.

Subero, Carlos. 1998. Asamblea Constituyente: 53% y Congreso: 41%. *El Universal* (15 June): 1–14.

SUNAT (Superintendencia Nacional de Administración Tributaria). 1996. Principales Impuestos: 1987–96. Lima: SUNAT.

Tacchi, Carlos. 1997. Author interview with former Secretario de Ingresos Públicos, Ministerio de Economía (1990–95). Buenos Aires: 19 June.

Tanaka, Martín. 1998. *Los Espejismos de la Democracia.* Lima: Instituto de Estudios Peruanos.

Taylor, Michael. 1996. When Rationality Fails. In Jeffrey Friedman, ed. *The Rational Choice Controversy*, 223–234. New Haven: Yale University Press.

Taylor, Shelley, and Jonathon Brown. 1988. Illusion and Well-Being. *Psychological Bulletin* 103:2 (March): 193–210.

Teichman, Judith. 2001. *The Politics of Freeing Markets in Latin America.* Chapel Hill: University of North Carolina Press.

Templeton, Andrew. 1995. The Evolution of Popular Opinion. In Louis Goodman et al., eds. *Lessons of the Venezuelan Experience*, 79–114. Washington, DC: Woodrow Wilson Center Press.

Temporal, Amaury. 1992. Author interview with former Presidente, Confederação das Associações Comerciais do Brasil. Rio de Janeiro: 20 July.

Thaler, Richard. 2000. From Homo Economicus to Homo Sapiens. *Journal of Economic Perspectives* 14:1 (Winter): 133–41.

———. 1992. *The Winner's Curse.* Princeton: Princeton University Press.

Thaler, Richard, and Eric Johnson. 1990. Gambling with the House Money and Trying to Break Even. *Management Science* 36:6 (June): 643–60.

Thorp, Rosemary. 1987. The APRA Alternative in Peru. *Bulletin of Latin American Research* 6:2 (April): 163–82.

Toche, Eduardo. 1998. La Emergencia Permanente. *Quehacer* 113 (May–June): 30–34.

Toledo, José. 1999. FHC Volta a Bater Recorde de Rejeição. *Folha de São Paulo* (20 June): 1–12

Toledo, Nicolás. 2001a. El Punto de Quiebra de la Hegemonía Chavista. Caracas: Consultores 21 (December).

———. 2001b. Siete Mitos sobre Hugo Chávez y su Gobierno que a la

Oposición le Haría Bien Desechar. *Percepción 21* (March) <www.consultores21.com/domino/articulos/html>.

Toledo Segura, Rafael. 1993. *El Programa de Estabilización y las Reformas Estructurales en el Perú en 1993.* Buenos Aires: Centro Interdisciplinario de Estudios sobre el Desarrollo Latinoamericano. Konrad Adenauer Stiftung.

Torre, Juan Carlos. 1998. *El Proceso Político de las Reformas Económicas en América Latina.* Buenos Aires: Paidós.

———. 1993. Conflict and Cooperation in Governing the Economic Emergency. In Colin Lewis and Nissa Torrents, eds. *Argentina in the Crisis Years (1983–1990),* 73–89. London: Institute of Latin American Studies, University of London.

Torres y Torres Lara, Carlos. 1999. Author interview with leading congressman of Cambio 90/Nueva Mayoría. Lima: 8 July.

———. 1996. Author interview with former Ministro de Trabajo y Promoción Social and Presidente del Consejo de Ministros (1990–91) and leading congressman of Cambio 90/Nueva Mayoría. Lima: 18 July.

———. 1994. *La Constitución Económica en el Perú.* Lima: Desarrollo y Paz.

———. 1992. *Los Nudos del Poder.* Lima: Desarrollo y Paz.

Townsend, Anel. 1999. Author interview with independent congresswoman and opposition leader. Lima: 30 June.

"Tres Años de Obras." 1994. *Clarín,* special advertising supplement (29 December).

Tsebelis, George. 1990. *Nested Games.* Berkeley: University of California Press.

Tuesta Soldevilla, Fernando, ed. 1996. *Los Enigmas del Poder: Fujimori 1990–1996.* Lima: Fundación Friedrich Ebert.

Tulchin, Joseph, and Gary Bland, eds. 1994. *Peru in Crisis?* Boulder: Lynne Rienner.

Turner, Frederick, and Carlos Elordi. 1995. Economic Values and the Role of Government in Latin America. *International Social Science Journal* 145 (September): 473–88.

Tversky, Amos, and Daniel Kahneman. 1992. Advances in Prospect Theory. *Journal of Risk and Uncertainty* 5:3 (October): 297–323.

———. 1986. Rational Choice and the Framing of Decisions. *Journal of Business* 59:4: S251–78.

Ubaldini, Saúl. 1995. Author interview with former Secretario General, Confederación General del Trabajo. Buenos Aires: 15 March.

Uchitelle, Louis. 2001. Following the Money, but Also the Mind. *New York Times* (11 February): BU 1, 11.

União do Povo. 1998. *Um Brasil para os Brasileiros. Diretrizes do Programa de Governo.* N.p.

UPP (Unión por el Perú). 1995. *Prosperidad y Paz hacia el Siglo XXI. Lineamientos Generales del Plan de Gobierno.* Lima: UPP.

Urbaneja, Diego Bautista. 1996. Esquema Interpretativo del Actual Período de Gobierno. In Angel Alvarez, ed. *El Sistema Político Venezolano,* 407–18. Caracas: Instituto de Estudios Políticos, Universidad Central de Venezuela.

Urrutia, Miguel. 1994. Colombia. In John Williamson, ed. *The Political Economy of Policy Reform,* 285–315. Washington, DC: Institute for International Economics.

USIA (U.S. Information Agency). Office of Research. 1993. *Widespread Discontent in Brazil, but no Political Beneficiary* (30 November). Washington, DC: USIA.

Vacs, Aldo. 1994. Convergence and Dissension. In William Smith, Carlos Acuña, and Eduardo Gamarra, eds. *Latin American Political Economy in the Age of Neoliberal Reform*, 67–100. New Brunswick: Transaction.

Valenzuela, Cecilia. 1995. Corazones Jalados. *Caretas* 1359 (20 April): 28–31.

Valenzuela, Samuel. 1992. Democratic Consolidation in Post-Transitional Settings. In Scott Mainwaring, Guillermo O'Donnell, and Samuel Valenzuela, eds. *Issues in Democratic Consolidation*, 57–104. Notre Dame: University of Notre Dame Press.

Van den Berghe, Pierre. 1963. Dialectic and Functionalism. *American Sociological Review* 28:5 (October): 695–705.

Van de Walle, Nicolas. 1993. The Politics of Nonreform in Cameroon. In Thomas Callaghy and John Ravenhill, eds. *Hemmed In*, 357–97. New York: Columbia University Press.

Vargas Llosa, Mario. 1994. *A Fish in the Water*. New York: Farrar, Strauss and Giroux.

Vargas Llosa, Mario, and Alberto Fujimori. 1990. *El Debate*. Lima: Centro de Investigación, Universidad del Pacífico.

Varsano, Ricardo, et al. 1998. *Uma Análise da Carga Tributária do Brasil*. Texto para Discussão no. 583. Rio de Janeiro: Instituto de Pesquisa Econômica Aplicada.

Vasconcelos, Jorge. 1997. Author interview with former Asesor Especial del Ministro de Economía Domingo Cavallo. Buenos Aires: 20 June.

Velarde, Julio. 1996. Author interview with former Director, Banco Central de Reserva del Perú (1990–92). Lima: 15 August.

Velarde, Julio, and Martha Rodríguez. 1994. *El Programa de Estabilización Peruano: Evaluación del Período 1991–1993*. Documento de Trabajo no. 18. Lima: Centro de Investigación, Universidad del Pacífico (CIUP).

———. 1992a. *Lineamientos para un Programa de Estabilización de Ajuste Drástico*. Documento de Trabajo no. 1. Lima: CIUP.

———. 1992b. *El Programa Económico de Agosto de 1990*. Documento de Trabajo no. 2. Lima: CIUP.

Velasco e Cruz, Sebastião. 1984. Empresários e o Regime no Brasil. Ph.D. dissertation, Universidade de São Paulo.

Velloso, João Paulo dos Reis. 1986. *O Último Trêm para Paris*. Rio de Janeiro: Nova Fronteira.

Velloso, Raul. 1998. A Situação das Contas Públicas após o Real. In João Paulo dos Reis Velloso, ed. *O Brasil e o Mundo no Limiar do Novo Século*, vol. 2, 101–35. Rio de Janeiro: José Olympio.

Veras, Beni. 1996. Author interview with senator (PSDB-Ceará) and former Ministro-Chefe, Secretaria de Planejamento (March–December 1994). Brasília: 9 July.

Verbitsky, Horacio. 1991. *Robo para la Corona*. Buenos Aires: Planeta.

Verlet, Martin. 1997. Ghana: "L'Effet Rawlings." *Afrique Contemporaine* 182 (2d quarter): 32–46.

Vierhaus, Rudolf. 1978. Zum Problem historischer Krisen. In Karl-Georg Faber and Christian Meier, eds. *Historische Prozesse*, 313–29. München: Deutscher Taschenbuch Verlag.

Viguera, Aníbal. 2000. *La Trama Política de la Apertura Económica en la Argentina*. La Plata: Ediciones Al Margen.

Vivas, Leonardo. 1999. *Chávez: La Última Revolución del Siglo*. Caracas: Editorial Planeta Venezolana.

Vox Populi. 1999a. Avaliação de Governos. Poderes Executivo, Legislativo e Judiciário. Belo Horizonte: Vox Populi <www.voxpopuli.com.br/pesquisa1.html>.

———. 1999b. A Situação Econômica do Brasil (April). Belo Horizonte: Vox Populi <www.voxpopuli.com.br/pesquisa1.html>.

Wade, Robert. 1990. *Governing the Market*. Princeton: Princeton University Press.

Walton, John, and Charles Ragin. 1990. Global and National Sources of Political Protest. *American Sociological Review* 55:6 (December): 876–90.

Walton, John, and David Seddon. 1994. *Free Markets & Food Riots*. Oxford: Blackwell.

Waterbury, John. 1993. *Exposed to Innumerable Delusions*. Cambridge: Cambridge University Press.

———. 1989. The Political Management of Economic Adjustment and Reform. In Joan Nelson, ed. *Fragile Coalitions*, 39–56. New Brunswick: Transaction.

Weber, Max. 1976. *Wirtschaft und Gesellschaft*, 5th ed., by Johannes Winckelmann. Tübingen: J.C.B. Mohr.

Webb, Richard. 1999. *Una Economía Muy Peruana*. Lima: Ediciones del Congreso del Perú.

Welch, John. 1991. Monetary Policy, Hyperinflation, and Internal Debt Repudiation in Argentina and Brazil. Paper for 16th Latin American Studies Association Congress, Washington, DC, 2–4 April.

Werneck, Rogério. 1994. Wretched Statecraft. In Gustav Ranis, ed. *En Route to Modern Growth*, 127–44. Washington, DC: Inter-American Development Bank.

Weyland, Kurt. 2003. Was It the Economy, Stupid? Crisis and Charisma in the Election of Hugo Chávez. *Comparative Political Studies* 36:8 (October), forthcoming.

———. 2002. Limitations of Rational-Choice Institutionalism for the Study of Latin American Politics. *Studies in Comparative International Development*. 37:1 (Spring): 57–85.

———. 2001. Clarifying a Contested Concept: "Populism" in the Study of Latin American Politics. *Comparative Politics* 34:1 (October): 1–22.

———. 2000. A Paradox of Success? Determinants of Political Support for President Fujimori. *International Studies Quarterly* 44:3 (September): 481–502.

———. 1999. Neoliberal Populism in Latin America and Eastern Europe. *Comparative Politics* 31:4 (July): 379–401.

———. 1998a. Peasants or Bankers in Venezuela? *Political Research Quarterly* 51:2 (June 1998): 341–62.

———. 1998b. The Political Fate of Market Reform in Latin America, Africa, and Eastern Europe. *International Studies Quarterly* 42:4 (December): 645–73.

———. 1998c. Swallowing the Bitter Pill. *Comparative Political Studies* 31:5 (October): 539–68.

———. 1996a. *Democracy without Equity*. Pittsburgh: University of Pittsburgh Press.

———. 1996b. How Much Political Power Do Economic Forces Have? *Journal of Public Policy* 16:1 (April): 59–84.

———. 1996c. Neopopulism and Neoliberalism in Latin America: Unexpected Affinities. *Studies in Comparative International Development* 31:3 (Fall): 3–31.

———. 1996d. Risk-Taking in Latin American Economic Restructuring. *International Studies Quarterly* 40:2 (June): 185–207.

———. 1993. The Rise and Fall of President Collor. *Journal of Interamerican Studies and World Affairs* 35:1 (Spring): 3–37.

White, Stephen, Ian McAllister, and Olga Kryshtanovskaya. 1994. El'tsin and His Voters. *Europe-Asia Studies* 46:2: 285–303.

Whitefield, Stephen, and Geoffrey Evans. 1994. The Russian Election of 1993. *Post-Soviet Affairs* 10:1 (January–March): 38–60.

Williamson, John. 1990. What Washington Means by Policy Reform. In Williamson, ed. *Latin American Adjustment: How Much Has Happened?*, 7–20. Washington, DC: Institute for International Economics.

Wise, Carol. 1997. State Policy and Social Conflict in Peru. In Maxwell Cameron and Philip Mauceri, eds. *The Peruvian Labyrinth*, 70–103. University Park: Pennsylvania State University Press.

———. 1994. The Politics of Peruvian Economic Reform. *Journal of Interamerican Studies and World Affairs* 36:1 (Spring): 75–125.

Wittman, Donald. 1991. Contrasting Economic and Psychological Analyses of Political Choice. In Kirsten Monroe, ed. *The Economic Approach to Politics*, 405–32. New York: Harper Collins.

World Bank. 1999. *Czech Republic. Toward EU Accession. Main Report*. Washington, DC: World Bank.

———. 1997. *World Development Report*. New York: Oxford University Press.

———. 1994. *Peru: Public Expenditure Review*. Report no. 13190–PE. Washington, DC: World Bank.

———. 1990. *Argentina. Tax Policy for Stabilization and Economic Recovery*. Washington, DC: World Bank.

———. 1989. *Peru. Policies to Stop Hyperinflation and Initiate Economic Recovery*. Washington, DC: World Bank.

Xavier Filho, Sérgio, and Sylvio Costa. 1993. O Brasil quer Paulada. *Veja* 1251 (22 September): 25–28.

Yeltsin, Boris. 1995. *The Struggle for Russia*. New York: Times Books.

Zaller, John, and Stanley Feldman. 1992. A Simple Theory of the Survey Response. *American Journal of Political Science* 36:3 (August): 579–616.

Zambrano Sequín, Luis, and Matías Riutort Merino. 1990. *El Proceso Inflacionario en Venezuela*. Caracas: Academía Nacional de Ciencias Económicas.

INDEX

Acción Democrática (AD): Caldera, opposition to, 215, 237; Chávez reforms and, 247; electoral results, 214, 237; formal institutions, strength of, 156n20; Pérez and, 24, 48n16, 68, 98, 112, 139–40; public administration reform, resistance to, 232

Acción Popular, 102, 199n

Acuña, Carlos, 32, 35, 170

AD. *See* Acción Democrática

adjustment plans: Agenda Venezuela, 225–28, 231–33, 236–38; Bunge & Born plan (*see* Bunge & Born plan); Collor Plan (*see* Collor Plan); convertibility plan (*see* convertibility plan); initiation of, cross-regional experiences, 263–69; initiation of drastic, 103–10; of the 1980s, 71–72, 77–81; Plan Austral, 81–86, 90, 107; Plan Inti, 81–86, 89–90, 107; Plano Cruzado, 72, 81–86, 89, 107; Plano Real (*see* Plano Real); popular responses to late 1980s, 124–32; risks and expected value in the late 1980s, 118–19. *See also* market reform; stabilization plans; structural reform

Agenda Venezuela, 225–28, 231–33, 236–38

Alfaro Ucero, Luis, 237

Alfonsín, Raúl: heterodox programs of, 72, 81–82, 256n; Menem and, 101; Pacto de Olivos, 170–71; political establishment, ties to, 33; political position of, 85n, 86; pressure to leave office, 137; prior-option bias in the late 1980s, 88–90

Alianza Popular Revolucionaria Americana (APRA), 11n, 99, 198–99

Allende, Salvador, 266

Alliance for Labor, Justice, and Education, 194

Alsogaray, Alvaro, 27, 112, 120n37, 148

Álvarez, Carlos "Chacho," 201n, 202

Amato, Mário, 143, 146

Ames, Barry, 261

Andrade, Alberto, 186–87, 196, 199

Angeloz, Eduardo, 99, 101

APRA. *See* Alianza Popular Revolucionaria Americana

Argentina: adjustment plans, popular response to, 21–22, 35; adjustment plans of the late 1980s, 112–15, 120–21 (*see also* adjustment plans); characteristics of, 8; class sentiments in electoral politics, 180–82; constitutional reform, 169–71; convertibility plan of early 1991, 56; debt crisis and hyperinflation, 51–55; decline of neopopulist leadership (*see* neopopulist leaders, decline of); democracy, status as, 12–13; democracy and market reform in, 281–82; democracy and neoliberal stabilization, 25; democratic sustainability in, 250; government under de la Rúa, 201–4; institutional powers in, 23n8, 24; learning and zig-zags in policy, 49; market reform, 148–50, 157–63, 206–7 (*see also* market reform; structural reform); neopopulism in (*see* neopopulism); Pacto de Olivos, 170–71; recent turmoil in, 204–7; socioeconomic development compared to Peru, 200–201. *See also* Alfonsín, Raúl; Cavallo, Domingo; de la Rúa, Fernando; Duhalde, Eduardo; Frente del País Solidario; Menem, Carlos Saúl; Peronist Party/Peronism; Unión Cívica Radical

authoritarian regimes: inflation, difficulties in reducing, 282–83; popular support for establishing, 279–80; temporary progression toward in Peru, 12–13

Babangida, Ibrahim, 266, 272, 274

Balcerowicz, Leszek, 268, 271

Barco, Virgilio, 265n18, 266n20

Barrantes, Alfonso, 99

Bates, Robert, 261

behavioral economics, 4, 42, 262

Belaúnde, Fernando, 25n, 72, 77, 79, 84, 86

Biya, Paul, 265

neopopulist future of, 250; political parties, 24n9, 237–38; politics of market reform, 233, 236–38; social compensation measures, 22; stabilization measures of the 1990s, 220–21, 225–27. *See also* Acción Democrática; Caldera, Rafael; Chávez Frías, Hugo; Lusinchi, Jaime; Pérez, Carlos Andrés; Petkoff, Teodoro
Videla, Jorge, 72, 77

Wałęsa, Lech, 267, 277
Washington consensus, 20
Weber, Max, 189n
World Bank, 19–20, 105, 147, 175

Yeltsin, Boris, 67, 267
Yoshiyama, Jaime, 198

Zambia, 265
Zhirinovsky, Vladimir, 278n28

DATE DUE